ANABAPTIST CURRENTS

*History in Conversation
with the Present*

ANABAPTIST CURRENTS

History in Conversation with the Present

Edited by Carl F. Bowman
and Stephen L. Longenecker

Forum for Religious Studies
Bridgewater College
Bridgewater, Virginia

PENOBSCOT PRESS

Cover design and graphics by Carl F. Bowman

First printing September 1995

For information contact:
Forum for Religious Studies
Bridgewater College
Bridgewater, Virginia 22812

Manufactured in the United States of America
Printed on 60# acid-free paper

CONTENTS

Editors' Introduction

Take equal parts Mennonite Church and Church of the Brethren. Add a goodly portion of Brethren Church, General Conference Mennonite, Brethren in Christ, and Old German Baptist writers and thinkers. And what have you got? A sectarian ecumenical gathering—where you can be ecumenical in a sectarian way and sectarian in an ecumenical way without being accused of either. That's exactly what we had at Bridgewater College during the fall of 1993. About one hundred Brethren and Mennonites sat around a large table for three days to exchange ideas about "Anabaptism: A Heritage and its 21st Century Prospects." This book is the result of that conversation.

If the whole thing sounds dreadfully sectarian, we can assure you that the conference expanded ecumenical horizons. "You can't work with Mennonites," we were warned, "They'll dominate decision-making and grab all the glory." Whether this was true of Mennonites a generation ago we doubt, but it certainly did not describe our experience. From the beginning, the planning sessions with Mennonite colleagues were cooperative. Even though Bridgewater College formally hosted the conference, members of the Eastern Mennonite community (Albert Keim, Gerald Shenk, Steve Dintamin, and Calvin Redekop) joined Bridgewater's Forum for Religious Studies (Carl Bowman, Steve Longenecker, Emmert Bittinger, Robbie Miller, and David Metzler) in the conference's early conceptualization. The list of topics and presenters clearly reflects this inter-clan conversation. Not only did our Mennonite colleagues *not* grab the glory, they humbly faded into the shadows of Bridgewater's formal sponsorship after having invested heavily in the early planning.

If Brethren myths about Mennos were exposed as folly, the same can be said for their misgivings about Dunkers. Some Mennonite attenders had a hard time grasping the fact that Brethren were actually sponsoring such a meeting. Do *Brethren* care about Anabaptist issues? Do they see Mennonites as fellow travelers? Do they still struggle with issues of nonconformity and their position vis-à-vis the Protestant mainstream? Will Mennonites of note attend a Brethren-sponsored conference and take it seriously? Passing comments reflected a thinly-veiled amazement that the answer to each of these questions might be yes. Perhaps Brethren had not gone so far to the dogs after all.

Another ecumenical first: attendance was evenly split between Brethren and Mennonites. Several participants said they had previously attended meetings billed as "Anabaptist" that were in fact Mennonite with a handful of Brethren, or Brethren with a sprinkling of Mennonites, but never one that seemed genuinely—equally—Brethren and Mennonite. This parity was part of the conference design. We asked presenters to address both traditions, and the representation of presiders and presenters was about half and half. We didn't even require Brethren and Mennonites to enter through separate doors or sit on opposite sides of the room.

Now, before you write us into the record books as ecumenical pioneers, we must confess that the meeting was also hopelessly sectarian. None of us defined what *Gelassenheit* or feetwashing[1] were; we simply assumed that any Anabaptist scholar worth his or her salt already knew. GC, MC, OGBB, BIC, BRF, and other refreshing acronyms flew at an astonishing rate. Marpeck, Mack, Bender, Durnbaugh, Hostetler, Nead, and other names floated from the lectern without anyone whispering, "Bend what?" or "Durn who?" Again, scholars worth their salt knew, and those who had lost their salt did not attend in the first place. They had more important things to do on a weekend (like play golf). As near as we can recall, no Catholics, Episcopalians, or Unitarians attended, and we can't remember even a single Southern Baptist (an amazing oversight in the Shenandoah Valley, or an accomplishment, depending upon your viewpoint). So, while the conference may have broken ecumencial ground, it did so in a delightfully sectarian fashion. It was a conversation between Anabaptist second-cousins, who normally visit only rarely.

The logical structure of the book is as follows. It begins with theological issues of sin, salvation, and scriptural interpretation; followed by analyses of ritual, symbolism, and language; and concluding with discussions of discipleship, membership, ministry, and outreach. Each of the eleven topics is explored in two essays, one primarily historical and one more contemporary (thus the book's subtitle: *History in conversation with the present.*) Since we were flexible about the chronological breakpoint, so were our authors. Even so, the first essay in each pair tends to reflect back upon the heritage, while the second looks forward. We asked the contributors to be sweeping in their coverage of Anabaptist groups, and they achieved a remarkably balanced treatment of Brethren and Mennonite patterns. Comparative analyses are difficult because they require detailed familiarity with more than one faith tradition. Yet this volume represents a tentative first step in that direction.

Unfortunately, a number of the conference highlights could not make it into the book. Hymns, connected to session topics and sung between presentations, added to a sense of community and spirituality typically absent from profession-al conferences. Two worship services--a progressive experience at the Commu-nity Mennonite Church in Harrisornburg and a traditional Love Feast at the Montezuma Church of the Brethren--provided a real life conversation between tradition and modernism.

Among the many who contributed to this project, we will mention only a few. Wayne F. Geisert and Dale V. Ulrich, former President and Provost of Bridgewater College, not only offered college resources, but attended many of the sessions. Phillip C. Stone and Lee M. Yoder, current President and Dean for Academic Affairs, continue to provide strong support for our activities,

---

[1] "Footwashing," if you prefer the Mennonite usage.

including the production of this volume. Again, we express our gratitude toward our Eastern Mennonite associates. Since 1993, our informal cooperation has blossomed into a formal collaboration: a jointly sponsored conference on "The Holy Spirit and the Gathered Community" slated for the Fall of 1995. Finally, we are deeply indebted to our friend and colleague, Emmert Bittinger, who could have been listed as a third editor for this volume. His tireless efforts to push this project forward when we were both preoccupied with teaching and other activities were invaluable. In every sense of the word, he was our stealth collaborator, an effective behind-the-scenes presence.

Carl Bowman and Steve Longenecker
Bridgewater, Virginia
July, 1995

Conversation
ಐಐ I ಐಐ

Anabaptist
Understandings of Sin

"Sinners in the hands of an angry God," wrote Jonathan Edwards, to describe the relationship of early eighteenth-century Puritans with their Maker.   Edwards' catchy one-liner portrays humans, including believers, as predestined, distant from God, and, above all, as innate sinners.   In contrast to this ominous image, Dale Brown and Dawn Ottoni Wilhelm contend that Anabaptism presents a more hopeful theology.   Although Anabaptism acknowledges the human bent toward sin, it also teaches that God created humans with innate goodness.

Brown's essay, a historical study of Anabaptist theology, locates three uniquely Anabaptist understandings of sin: 1) original blessedness, 2) freedom of will and moral responsibility, and 3) redemption from sin through Christ.   From this, early Anabaptists concluded that some elements of the divine image survived the fall and that Christ, the "second Adam," can liberate all from the sin they inherited from the "first Adam."   Wilhelm, a parish pastor, suggests that these historical insights have contemporary applicability, especially for interfaith dialogue, baptism and conversion, Love Feast, and the role of children within the fellowship.   Instead of focusing on punishment for sin, she stresses the consequences of misunderstanding it.

Taken together, Brown and Wilhelm offer many lessons for modern Christians in the Anabaptist tradition.   Both rail against legalism.   While Brown cautions against ignoring sin, he also warns against making a God of lifestyle, and Wilhelm says that denominations should define themselves by belief (by "the Lord they love") rather than specific practices or rules.   Brown urges peace church pacifists to avoid a naive humanism that forgets that goodness is a gift of the work of grace, and Wilhelm regrets that guilt and a sense of personal imperfection often motivate disaster relief.   Both agree with the early Anabaptists that all individuals have a divine presence within them that enhances relationships between neighbors, believers, and between sinners and their God.   In short, we may remain sinners, but we are "blessed sinners in the hands of a merciful god."

1
Understandings of Sin:
Original Blessedness and the Second Adam

by Dale W. Brown

In preparation for this paper, I invited an alleged Anabaptist scholar to explain the essence of Anabaptist beliefs on sin. His retort was: "They are against it." I have discovered, however, if one were to write a systematic theology of pristine Anabaptism, the tome would not begin with doctrines about sin or the fall. For most sixteenth-century radicals, the starting point was that human beings are created in the image and likeness of God. Whereas Protestants have generally featured original sin in order to proclaim the need for redemption, Anabaptists have emphasized original blessedness in cherishing the doctrine of creation. Avoiding the propensity to descend into a Fall-Redemption typology, Anabaptism has generally embodied a Creation-Fall-Redemption soteriology. Salvation is believed to be the restoration of the divine nature to fallen persons. This corresponds with my conviction that Christians derive a notion of the fall only when a picture of the world as it should be accompanies the images of creation and prophetic visions of the nature of the peaceable kingdom. We discern how far we have missed the mark from our encounters with Jesus and His teachings.

Original Sin

"In Adam's Fall we sinned all." These words from a *New England Primer* express a familiar view of the solidarity of all persons in the sin inherited from our first parents. It was these presuppositions about original sin that led the classical Protestant Reformers to espouse themes such as the bondage of the will. The good news was that the sacrament of baptism eliminated the guilt of sin. This was accomplished through what has been named forensic justification, in which a person's status before God is changed through forgiveness without the sinful nature being eliminated. For Luther and other Protestant reformers, Christians remain *simul justus et peccator* (always justified and always sinners). This anthropology assumed the helplessness of humanity and was joined with faith in the sovereignty of God to proclaim that salvation is wholly of God.

Proof-texting selected Anabaptist texts proves their agreement with the classical Reformers. Melchior Hoffmann, Dirk Philips, Hans Denck, and

Menno Simons all held that the whole human race was corrupted, poisoned, and cursed through the transgressions of Adam, whose disobedience delivered all into the bondage of Satan.[2]

Modifications

But, as one reads more of their anthropological texts, one discerns many deviations from the doctrine of original sin. First, the radicals rejected deterministic notions of double predestination in order to preserve God's eternal goodness. They opposed Luther's espousal of the bondage of the will because of their strong belief in the freedom of the will and necessary moral responsibility of human beings. Second, with Balthasar Hubmaier more came to believe that some vestige of the divine image escaped the damning consequences of the fall. Hubmaier's analysis of the three states of humans became well known. Humans are created with body, spirit, and soul. Before the fall all were good. After the fall only the spirit remains free and without guilt.[3] Third, such views fit pervading Anabaptist proclamations that Christ was the second Adam. Their teachings incorporated literally the Pauline text that as in Adam all die, so in Christ all are made alive (1 Cor. 15:22). As Adam was the representative person to signify the fallen state of all humanity, so Christ, through his death, atoned for the sins of everyone. The emphasis on the universal work of atonement of the second Adam led to modifications from long held beliefs about sin inherited from the first Adam (Rom. 5:6; Matt. 19:13-14).

Alexander Mack, Jr., a later Anabaptist thinker, argued that we do not build a case against infant baptism by rejecting original sin, but in affirming the efficacy of Christ's death. His father had contested the rationale for infant baptism by writing that "children are in a state of grace because of the merit of Jesus Christ."[4] In this the Macks were a part of a radical legacy that accused the major reformers of works righteousness by requiring an act of baptism to nullify the guilt of sin. The counter charge has been that Anabaptists espouse a forensic atonement that changes the status of infants before God apart from ontological transformation (Jn. 1:29).

Dirk Philips granted that infants have innate inclinations toward evil. Unlike mature persons, however, children are not guilty because of the work of Christ. As Adam and Eve were in grace before their fall, so are children while in the age of innocence. This led in Anabaptist circles to a soteriological scheme which regards Adam and Eve's story to be every person's story.[5] We are born in innocence; we fall short and rebel against what we were meant to be in creation; and God's redeeming activity through Christ restores the divine image.

To rubrics of the first and second Adam, Anabaptists added motifs of first and second grace. Whereas Pilgram Marpeck had spoken of the grace of yesterday and the grace of today to distinguish between the old and new covenants, Hubmaier defined first grace as the original created goodness and second grace as Christ's work in restoring the divine image.[6] The first work of grace enables a person to repent, to make real decisions. Though the two works of grace are both ingredients in Anabaptist soteriology, we turn now to anthropological implications of first grace.

The text for a focus on original blessedness was the same as for later Quakers, namely, John 1:9: "The true light that enlightens everyone was coming into the world." Anabaptist leaders in South Germany and the Netherlands preached that Christ would not have set little children before us as an example to follow if he had not seen something innately good in them.[7]

The propensity to view human nature not from fallen, historical realities but from the original created nature point to perceived inconsistencies in early Anabaptist thought. These, however, can in part be attributed to the often unrecognized theological pluralism of the early leaders.

Influence of Mysticism

Alvin Beachy in his published dissertation, *The Concept of Grace in the Radical Reformation*, added an appendix in which he attempted to discern whether Anabaptism was a radicalization of Protestantism or a survived expression of medieval mysticism.[8] No doubt influenced by his professor, George Williams of Harvard, he concluded that Anabaptist leaders imbibed more from late medieval mystical streams. This was especially true of anthropological issues. One would need to make an exception of Hoffmann and others who were influenced more by Lutheran doctrine. It was Hans Denck and Hans Hut who drank more deeply in the waters of mysticism. Nevertheless many other Anabaptists appropriated mystical motifs from folk like Johannes Tauler and Brethren of the Common Life. They remained enamored with the popular mystical work, *Theologia Germanica,* after Luther had laid it aside. The background of Renaissance Humanism at Zurich and the Roman Catholic roots of many of the early leaders probably abetted these mystical tendencies.

It was the soteriologically endowed anthropology of the mystics that influenced them to believe that children not only inherit original sin but natural light (Jn 1:9). From the mystics they adopted notions of inner light, inner word, and the inner testimony of the Holy Spirit. Though most Anabaptists have remained insistent that the inner word must correspond to the outer word of Scriptures, the belief in the inner testimony opened doors to special visions, leadings, and natural theology. Mystical theology was compatible with strong Anabaptist emphases on the freedom of the will. It buttressed their belief that persons have the ability to resist sin because of the first gift of grace. Though the radicals differed from the magisterial reformers concerning the degree to which the divine image is destroyed by the fall, they also departed from many mystics in insisting on the necessity of the work of the Holy Spirit and the second work of grace in salvation.

Links With Traditional and Other Christian Views

Increasingly I discern striking similarities in the early Pietist and Anabaptist movements. One can find the pluralism between mystical and discipleship oriented biblicism in both early Anabaptism and the Pietist reform movements of the seventeenth and early eighteenth centuries. Both embrace tensions between the inner and outer word. Both histories narrate dramatic conversion experiences as well as testimonies about gradual growth in faith without sudden transitions and struggles. Spener exuded Anabaptist accents in preaching more sermons centered on the new life than on the new birth. Out of their Lutheran context Pietists may have imbibed a more pessimistic view of human nature than Anabaptists in general. However, one finds critiques of notions of original sin, bondage of the will, and predestination as among the Anabaptists. Both movements combine variations about the fallen state of human nature with an optimism about what God can do with and through persons. The response to an almost exclusive justification theology was the same. The God who is good enough to forgive us is powerful enough to change us. In viewing salvation as the restoration of the image of God, both movements stressed the original goodness or blessedness of human beings. For this reason early Pietists in colonial America spoke of awakenings more than conversions.

Now I will paint with a broad brush some Anabaptist versions of traditional views of sin. One common definition of sin in biblical studies is "missing the mark." Such a definition is compatible with teachings which define sin as failing to live so as to exemplify what it means to be created in God's image. Anabaptists agreed with Calvin in regarding sin as disobedience. Calvin's definition of sin as disobeying the will of God was translated by Anabaptists as disobeying the commandments of Jesus. Pride is another common definition of sin. Though often guilty of pride even about their humility, Anabaptists have insisted that we not boast. For any goodness we have comes from God's first grace in creation and is restored and empowered by the second grace of Christ. Anabaptists have often been accused of not perceiving the difference between sin and sins. But their relational theology is compatible with this distinction. To live in the Spirit is to be in proper relationship with God, others, and the rest of God's good creation. To walk in the flesh is to lack or refuse to be in proper relationships. Sin, then, results from a weakening of relationship with God, others, and the rest of God's good creation.

Now I share happenings from my own pilgrimage. A feminist member of one of my classes had recently given birth to her first child. She glowingly testified to the wonderful birth experience and added that only men theologians could conjure a doctrine such as original sin. Immediately, a Presbyterian sister injected that she had four sons and loved them dearly but still believed in the reality of original sin. In tears, another sister accused the others of assuming that if you have not borne a child, you are not capable of doing theology. This was one of the rare occasions when I was wise enough to earn my salary by allowing others to take over the class. This discussion connects with my own experience as a father. When our children were small and I returned after being away for several days, I often stood quietly by my sleeping progeny after they had been tucked into bed. I envisioned haloes gracing their angelic faces. If the next day I lived through some crisis situations and irritating quarrels with my spouse, the haloes slipped and were replaced with horns.

In this I resonate with Martin Luther King, Jr.'s essay that traced his "Pilgrimage to Nonviolence." King related how Reinhold Niebuhr had rejected the superficial optimism of human nature he had absorbed as a youth. At the same time, he was dissatisfied with a neo-orthodoxy that defined human nature in terms of its capacity for evil. He concludes, as did many Anabaptists, that the truth lies in some kind of synthesis of both. Humans are born both with inclinations for good and inclinations for evil.

Pitfalls of Anabaptist Anthropology

I want to conclude subjectively with some weaknesses and strengths of Anabaptist anthropology. First, legalism. From emphases on walking in newness of life in the light of the restored image of God, it is easy to make rules and lifestyle specifics more basic than the love of God. Anabaptist traditions have often been prone to make a god of goodness instead of living in response to the goodness of God. Second, a mind-flesh dualism. In posing distinctions between the spirit and the flesh, there have often been temptations to focus on sexual sins more than sins of disposition. Sexual aberrations have been punished more harshly than censorious spirits who manifest malice and gossip. Next, a church-world dualism. Anabaptists generally reject possibilities of complete perfection on the part of believers. But their propensity to locate all purity in a church without spot or wrinkle has often resulted in failure to discern sin within the church and to extend the activity of the Spirit beyond their communities of faith.

Strengths

My subjective listing of strengths will be perceived as liabilities by others. First, oft-acclaimed political contributions emerged from these anthropological assumptions. Separation of church and state and religious freedom have their basis in an Anabaptist view of human nature that stresses freedom of the will and the loving, nonviolent nature of God's activity.

Second, the discernment of the human condition from its created nature highlights the doctrine of creation along with doctrines of redemption.

Third, contrary to church-world dualism, an anthropology derived from the work of the second Adam extends the activity of God beyond the borders of the church.   The rejection of predestination resulted from the acceptance of a universal atonement by Anabaptists. They applied the forgiveness of the guilt of original sin by the second Adam to the mentally retarded and those who have never heard of the gospel of Christ.   Such universalist emphases by Christocentric and biblically-oriented Christians may be a helpful paradigm in our present era in which many view with suspicion dialogue with other world religions; peacemakers consider it essential.

Fourth, there may be a contribution in conceding the heretical synergistic tendencies of the Anabaptist heritage.   Gordon Kaufman in his presidential address to the American Academy of Religion was true to his heritage by articulating the need for a theology of moral responsibility. He spoke of the possibilities of a nuclear holocaust. His pleas are equally relevant to present ecological concerns and our greedy self-centered culture.

And finally, the belief that both innate goodness and the restored image are gifts of the work of grace should provide a corrective for the tendency of many peace church pacifists to imbibe a naive humanism. Remember before the "arrival" of new age folk and homosexuals when secular-humanists were the most dangerous personifications of evil? At that time it was difficult to agree that we should be against those who have deep concerns for and a passion to serve other humans. But I did come to the conclusion that theoretically, at least, our Christian tradition has a better foundation for humanist concerns.   I discerned the fallacy of a faith in humanity that ignores faith in God. If we love others because they are naturally lovely, and then they reveal unlovable manifestations of sin, we can quickly become disillusioned liberals. But if we love others because God loves them as God loved us when we were yet sinners, then we can keep on loving even when tempted to think they are unworthy of our love.

[2] See documentation by Alvin J. Beachy, *The Concept of Grace in the Radical Reformation* (Nieuwkoop, B. DeGraaf, 1977), 35-6.

[3] Balthasar Hubmaier, *Spiritual and Anabaptist Writers, The Library of Christian Classics, Vol. XXV* (Westminster Press, 1957), 117.

[4] Alexander Mack, "Rights and Ordinances," Donald F. Durnbaugh, *European Origins of the Brethren* (Elgin, Ill: Brethren Press, 1958), p. 352.

[5] Quoted by Dirk Philips in Beachy, 39.

[6] Ibid., 66.

[7] Alexander Mack, "Rights and Ordinances," in Durnbaugh, *European Origins*, 352.

[8] Ibid., 187ff.

2

Understandings of Sin: Contemporary Applications and Prospects

by Dawn Ottoni-Wilhelm

At an ecumenical conference for clergy, three of the delegates relaxed one evening after the arduous duties of the day. To put not too fine a point on it, Father O'Connell, Reverend Wilson, and Rabbi Cohen were indulging in a friendly game of poker.

Unfortunately, in their excitement they grew a little noisy and the hotel detective, in a burst of over zealousness, entered the room, confiscated the chips and cards, and held them for arrest under the strict anti-gambling statutes of the town in which the conference was being held.

The magistrate before whom they appeared was acutely embarrassed.

"Gentlemen," she said, "I would rather this had not happened, but there seems to be evidence of a misdemeanor, and since you have been arrested, I cannot dismiss the case without some investigation. Nevertheless, in view of your profession, I feel I can trust you to tell the truth. I will ask for no evidence other than your own words. If each of you can tell me that you were not gambling, that would be sufficient for me and I will release you. Father O'Connell . . ."

The worthy priest said at once, "Your Honor, surely it is important to be certain that we define what we mean by gambling. In a narrow, but entirely valid sense, what we describe as gambling is only truly so if there is a desire to win money, rather than merely to enjoy the suspense of the fall of cards. In addition we might confine gambling to situations where the loss of money would be harmful, as otherwise such loss might merely be viewed as a variable admission fee. . . ."

"I understand," the magistrate interrupted. "I will take it then, Father, that you were not gambling by your definition of the word. And you, Reverend Wilson?"

The good minister straightened his tie and said, "I entirely agree with my learned colleague, Your Honor. Further, I might point out that gambling is gambling only if there are stakes involved. Admittedly, there was money on the table, but it remains to be determined whether this money would eventually have found its way into the possession of an individual not its owner at the start of the game, or if, in fact, it was merely being used as a convenient marker that would indicate the progress and direction of successive plays. . . ."

"Yes, yes," the magistrate again interrupted. "I will accept that as satisfactory indication that you were not gambling, Reverend Wilson. And now you, Rabbi Cohen. Were you gambling?"

The pious rabbi's eyebrows shot upwards. "With whom, Your Honor?"

Although it is written, "All have sinned and fall short of the glory of God in Christ Jesus," each of us, like the card-playing clerics, has found ways of avoiding the uncomfortable reality of sin in our lives. For most mainline Protestant denominations over the past thirty years, the subject of sin has all but dropped from discussions at academic, worship, and informal settings. Sin may be alive and well among us in deed, but in word it is conspicuous by its absence. The age of tolerance and acceptance has so impacted the understanding and practice of theology that many have become uncomfortable with naming sin—our own or anyone else's. Furthermore, sin's close companion, guilt, has been identified by nearly all schools of modern psychology as a harmful deterrent in the realization of an individual's personal development.

In *Whatever Became of Sin?* Karl Menninger laments that we no longer speak of sin or guilt.[1] What our forebears called sin, we call behavioral problems. What they called guilt, we call emotional distress. In fact, the language of sin has been replaced by the language of symptom. For example, when we speak of the devastation of war-torn Sudan, we are usually speaking only of the surface of this tragedy; in the midst of war, sin works at much deeper levels of greed and pride than we are willing to recognize or perhaps claim as our own responsibility. More than sin, the war in Sudan is really sinful, rooted in a complex web of sinful desires and attitudes that may be closer to home than most of us care to recognize.

Thus, we struggle to identify sin. We struggle to name sin in our own lives and in the events around us, and we struggle to understand it. The pluralism of twentieth-century North America (including the ecumenical movement, dramatic changes in Catholic theology since the Second Vatican Council, and the persistent desire to recognize and tolerate, often without success, a diversity of religious beliefs and practices) has informed the Anabaptist understanding of sin. However, before examining the unique strengths and weaknesses of Anabaptist theology of sin and some potential applications of that theology, it will be helpful first to explore briefly the popular religious context in which their particular theology of sin resides.

Modern Context

The contemporary religious culture is dominated by at least two popular understandings of sin: namely, the idea of sin as good behavior practiced in excess and the idea of sin as goodness (or potentiality) that is not practiced (or realized) at all.

In the not-so-distant past, both Protestant and Catholic churches did not hesitate to identify the nature of sin and to delineate particular sinful behaviors, at times to legalistic extremes. For example, the concept of original sin and the description of the Seven Deadly Sins dominated most theological discussions for centuries. Recent popular theologies of sin, however, have shifted towards identifying sin less as specific evils to be eliminated and more as good instincts gone awry. In his book, *Cardinal Sins*, Catholic priest and sociologist Andrew Greeley captures this idea.

> The so-called cardinal (or "deadly" or "capital") sins are not sins at all but seven disorderly propensities in our personality that lead us to sinful behavior. Pride, covetousness, lust, anger, gluttony, envy, and sloth are sound and healthy human proclivities gone askew: self-respect, self-preservation, communion, personal freedom, self-expression, celebration, relaxation. The cardinal sins result not from fundamental evil but from fundamental goodness running out of control.[2]

No doubt Greeley's ideas strike a sympathetic chord with many North Americans who realize that sins of excess have come to dominate their materialistic and gluttonous culture, which has only begun to comprehend how its will to expand and accumulate has resulted in the exploitation, abuse, and diminution of many natural resources and people.

Equally powerful to understanding sin as good behavior practiced to excess is the idea of sin as unrealized goodness or potentiality. In the realm of popular psychology, there is no greater sin than not living up to one's potential; one has only to note the profitable proliferation of self-help books as well as the focus on self-realization within so many schools of psychology to recognize the current interest in developing the potentialities that lie dormant or buried within us.

Although significantly less popular than modern trends in psychology, feminist, black, and liberation theologies have also contributed to the understanding of sin as unrealized human potential. The systemic degradation of minorities and women has not only limited self-expression among individuals but has also denied the church the full expression of God's gifts, which may be found only when it recognizes the divine image in all of God's people. Such theologies have encouraged the church and the larger society to turn what may be a selfish preoccupation with self-realization into a healthy advocacy of the good gifts of God that need to be realized within and among persons if they are to faithfully serve God and their neighbors.

Of course, other interpretations of sin are gaining in popularity. Most notably, a growing number of Christians whose urgent desire to codify sinful behaviors and condemn those who violate a particular definition of sin or rules of living has drawn battle lines among Christians, particularly over abortion and human sexuality. In contrast to this movement towards identifying Christian faithfulness according to adherence to specific rules of living, *The Mennonite Encyclopedia*'s article on sin describes "modern-day evangelists" as persons who stand in contrast to Jesus, "who neither encouraged people to wallow in the guilt of their sin nor to resort to self-condemnation on the basis of their sin. He called them rather to repent of (turn from) their sin and follow him (discipleship, Mk. 1:14f)."[3]

Contributions of an Anabaptist Understanding of Sin

Given these particular approaches to sin in the larger culture, the present Anabaptist understanding of sin offers several unique contributions. Perhaps its greatest single contribution is its encouragement to relate all standards of living to the person and work of Jesus Christ. In contrast to the more popular ideas of sin as goodness realized in excess or goodness not realized at all, or sin as a specific list of behaviors to be condemned, Anabaptist theology reminds us that sin and righteousness are unrelated to a personal sense of self-realization or our own standards of what is good and bad. In traditional Anabaptist theology, sin and righteousness are only understood in relationship to Jesus Christ, who is the standard, the canon (our measure) for living. We are called to make disciples for Jesus Christ, and the characteristic dimension of Anabaptist faith is the ongoing commitment to live as disciples who follow the risen Lord Jesus.

As Dale Brown states in his work on the heritage of Anabaptist understandings of sin, traditional Anabaptist theology does not deny that all persons are corrupt, but it is unique in featuring three "modifications," as Brown calls them, to an otherwise strong adherence to the doctrine of original sin. Before exploring the ways in which these unique modifications may be applied to present religious practices, it will be helpful to examine how each of these features of the Anabaptist understanding of sin speaks to several questions and concerns of twentieth-century Christians.

According to Brown, "Whereas Protestants have generally featured original sin in order to proclaim the need for redemption, Anabaptists have emphasized original blessedness in cherishing the doctrine of creation." It is not surprising that from the starting point of a theology of original blessedness, Anabaptist understandings of sin have rejected the notion of double predestination and bondage of the human will. Emphasizing instead the inherent goodness of God's creation, early Anabaptists did not believe in God's having predestined some persons to eternal salvation and some persons to eternal damnation in order to preserve the goodness of God. Instead, as Brown points out, Anabaptists have adhered to a strong belief in the freedom of the will and the necessary moral responsibility of human beings.

Certainly this idea of the freedom of human will is essential to persons striving to live as disciples of Jesus Christ—persons who intentionally choose to follow the example of Christ rather than the urging of their culture, which is often at odds with His example. An emphasis on freedom of the will and moral responsibility is desperately needed as the growing awareness of global wars, hunger, and the vast array of unfulfilled basic human needs urges us to re-examine continually what it means to be a follower of Jesus Christ in our particular time and context. Although following the way of Christ may seem an impossible standard to attain, there is also great freedom (Gal. 5:1) and peace (Jn. 14:27) found in faithful service to Christ and our neighbors. The traditional and current emphasis upon moral responsibility and steadfast Anabaptist devotion to serving others as we struggle against sin is urgent because few people and institutions are yet willing to identify the connection between human suffering and moral negligence.

There are, however, two recurrent weaknesses in the understanding and practice of moral responsibility today. First, many good efforts towards hunger relief and responses to disasters of various kinds have been motivated not by a loving sense of thanksgiving or blessedness before the Creator but by guilt and a keen sense of our own imperfection. Modern psychology has indeed done us a favor in directing the church away from an unhealthy obsession with personal guilt while at the same time developing therapies (e.g., behavior modification and family systems therapy) that point persons toward recognizing and claiming personal responsibility for their attitudes and actions. As Anabaptists who believe in the original blessedness of God's creation, our reasons and motivations for responding lovingly to the needs of others run deeper than a sense of personal guilt or unworthiness can ever carry us. Our lives and labors need to be rooted not only in our experience of sin but also in our experience of God's healing grace (Isa.57:15-19). So that we do not become "weary in doing what is right" (Gal.6:9), service to one another needs to be a response to God's love for us in Jesus Christ, a response of love and thanksgiving.

The second danger in our interpretation of moral responsibility is the current tendency towards legalism in the desire to define moral responsibility. At a time when many denominations seek a sense of identity, it is especially appealing to try to establish laws of behavior that define identity by the laws they adhere to rather than the Lord they love. Far from the Anabaptist ideal of living in proper relationship with God, others, and the rest of God's good creation, moral responsibility has in recent years been defined more as right behavior or conduct than as right relationships. Anabaptists need not be legalistic in practicing of moral responsibility nor directionless in longing to be faithful disciples; the foundation of morality is God's love and direction may be found in following the example of Jesus Christ.

A second unique feature of the Anabaptist understanding of sin that Brown points to is the belief that some vestige of the divine image in all persons escaped the damning consequences of the fall. In other words, we may be corrupt, but we are not without hope for God's sacred presence resides within each of us. There are several significant consequences to this idea of the divine image abiding within every human being. First, in knowing that God is so intimately related to our very being, we cannot doubt our sense of personal value and self-worth. No matter how much guilt or sense of failure we may feel as we recognize our imperfection, we may remember that the sacred image of God abides within us and, therefore, a life of sin is not our inevitable fate (Ezek.18:20). Similarly, value of others is also heightened when we believe that in serving others we do indeed serve Christ (Mt.28). Not only the historic peace position but also the belief that children do not need to be baptized in order to find acceptance and salvation in Christ are founded upon the Anabaptist belief in the divine image or presence inherent in all persons.

As a pastor, I have little doubt that this idea of the divine presence abiding in each person and instilling a sense of value and blessedness is still foreign to most twentieth-century Americans. During a plane trip to my hometown of Detroit I found myself engaged in conversation with the man seated beside me. As the discussion inevitably moved towards our respective occupations, I waited for a few moments after disclosing that I am a pastor. (I have learned that most people need a moment or two to decide how they will respond to what is usually a new experience of meeting a woman pastor.) After a short while he said, "You're a pastor?" I nodded. "Oh. I'm sorry. I mean, you don't need to be sorry, but I'm sorry. There's so much I'm sorry for. . . ." And his confession ran on for over an hour. When I explained that I was not a priest and that I could not give him absolution, he looked puzzled for a moment and asked, "Then what exactly is your job, anyway?" It took me a long while before I could respond: "My 'job' is to listen for the voice of Jesus in everything that you are saying." I went on to try to clarify some of what he had shared with me regarding his sinful actions and attitudes, then I also pointed out some of God's gifts and grace evident in what he had described to me. In fact, as a pastor, I have found it much more fruitful to identify God's presence and gifts among my brothers and sisters (and within my church board) than to look for their sins and weaknesses alone. Many of us carry a tremendous burden of guilt and a personal sense of unworthiness that hinders our joyful service to Christ. We have learned well how to find fault with ourselves and one another but have yet to find the divine presence and love of God within us. It is true that what we seek we shall find—and Jesus Christ continually calls us to seek Him. In a society permeated with images of a judgmental and condemning God, the Anabaptist affirmation of the sacred presence within each person is good news indeed. When we recognize the sacred alive within each of us and loving us even when we sin (Rom. 5:6), we may open the way to experience God's grace in our lives.

The third unique feature of the Anabaptist understanding of sin that remains relevant is the assertion that Christ is indeed the second Adam. Drawing upon I Cor. 15:22, the early Anabaptists taught that as in Adam all die, so in Christ all are made alive. As Brown notes, this emphasis on the universal work of atone-ment of the second Adam led to significant deviations from the belief in inher-ited sin held by so many other Christian groups. Certainly, the concept of universal salvation has been greatly discussed and debated among various Ana-baptist groups. Although many Anabaptists today may not believe in universal salvation, this unique feature of the Anabaptist understanding of sin and atone-ment speaks to several concerns that are prevalent in society, including the un-derstanding of the place of children in the church, the need for religious conversion or transformation, and dialogue with other religious faiths. Whatev- er controversy persists regarding the understanding of Christ's universal atone- ment, this part of the Anabaptist understanding of sin as well as the emphasis on the freedom of the will, moral responsibility, and the divine image present a rich foundation for a variety of practical applications in expressing an understanding of sin and atonement.

Potential Applications

At least four areas of religious life are impacted by the Anabaptist under- standing of sin and atonement: 1) acceptance, treatment, and expectations of children in the life of the church; 2) understanding of conversion and practice of baptism; 3) practice of Communion and Love Feast; and 4) dialogue with other denominations and faith traditions. Each of these areas contains several potential applications of the Anabaptist understanding of sin.

First, the role of children in the faith community is profoundly influenced by the Anabaptist theology of sin and, in particular, our emphasis upon the original blessedness of creation. As the early Anabaptists maintained, children certainly have the inclination toward evil, but they are not guilty of sin because of the atoning work of Jesus Christ. Furthermore, Pietism has encouraged Anabaptists to believe that children not only inherit original sin but also inherit natural light (Jn. 1:9). As Brown points out, Anabaptists have also long believed that "Christ would not have set little children before us as an example to follow if he had not seen something innately good in them" (Mt. 19:13f). Therefore, the acceptance of children as members of God's family of faith is rooted in the belief that the divine image is indeed present in all persons from birth and that Christ's grace is efficacious for all (Jn.1:29).

There are several ways to express a commitment to children as persons who are blessed with God's image and grace. At least one Sunday morning worship each year may be devoted to children, including an extended children's message (in place of the traditional sermon and shared through some less formal medium such as puppetry or drama), children's hymns, and prayers appropriate to young persons. Even very young children may be entrusted to lead selected portions of worship services throughout the year; for example, children may offer very meaningful calls to worship or offertory prayers. The children in my congregation not only enjoy weekly story times during worship but also thrill to hear the entire congregation join in singing some of their favorite hymns, such as "Jesus Loves Me." At each stage of a child's development there are appropriate ways of recognizing a child's gifts in the life of the congregation. Newborns may be presented publicly and their parents supported as they and the congregation as a whole dedicate themselves to nurturing the children entrusted to them. At age four or five children may be dedicated as the pastor kneels with them before the congregation and offers a specific blessing and promise for each child. Developmentally, most eight-year-olds are ready to receive and recite from their own Bibles, presented to them as part of a whole service dedicated to Scripture and the importance of story telling in our faith tradition. By ten to twelve years of age, children may be encouraged to publicly share their own prepared faith statements or prayers in worship, and by age twelve to fourteen they may begin participation in voluntary membership classes for persons considering baptism and church membership. In public worship and Sunday School as well as in home worship and prayer time, all areas of religious life can be enhanced by the participation of children.

A second area of Anabaptist religious life strongly influenced by our understanding of sin and atonement is conversion and the practice of baptism. The traditional Anabaptist rejection of infant baptism was in no way a rejection of the reality of humanity's inclination toward sin. Rather, the unique Anabaptist emphasis on the freedom of will and the moral responsibility of all believers encouraged a sense of the continuing need for conversion among those who follow the way of Jesus Christ. Both dramatic and subtle experiences of conversion were honored among early Anabaptists who offered opportunities for public confession, testimony, and baptism.

There are several ways that the church today may encourage its members to express their on-going commitment to the process of conversion in the journey of faith. Just as children need age appropriate means of sharing their religious development, adults also need continually to give expression to their growth in faith and discipleship. Regular opportunities for corporate prayers of confession in worship as well as offertory responses or moments of silent or spoken dedications following Scripture readings and sermons may be meaningful to many. On occasion (e.g., at a special Thanksgiving service) lay persons can prepare public statements in worship testifying to God's presence in their lives over the past year. Deacons or other sponsors need to be aware of the particular gifts of each member of the body so that church nurture and service commissions may continually offer opportunities for persons to express their commitment of faith in concrete acts of service to the church and community at large. The rite of baptism may also be offered more regularly to adults not only as they explore church membership but also throughout their journey of faith. Certainly, youth are not the only ones who struggle to understand and make faith commitments. Adults also need to remember the enduring call of discipleship to walk in newness of life.

A third area of religious life affected by the understanding of sin is communion and/or Love Feast. Just as it may be meaningful for persons to confess regularly their sense of guilt and sin in prayers of confession during Sunday morning worship, so may more frequent celebrations of communion provide regular spiritual affirmation and experience of our acceptance by God. Great strength also may arise from intentionally developing Love Feast services that reflect forgiveness and a call to serve. For example, our congregation's practice of Love Feast contains not only the traditional elements of hymn singing, feetwashing, a simple meal, and communion, but also intentionally includes children; they are called to the center table and then sent off in search of the hidden communion bread, a sweet bread wrapped in linen, especially made for them to eat during communion. Our service also integrates some current service project that all members are asked to participate in, such as, most recently, bringing forward disaster relief kits to be sent to flood victims in the midwest. Far from being outdated, our practice of communion and Love Feast may be one of the best mediums for conveying an understanding of sin, God's sacred image alive in each person, and our call to moral responsibility and service.

Finally, a fourth area of religious life that is no doubt influenced by the understanding of sin is dialogue with other denominations and faith traditions. As the twentieth century draws to a close, awareness of other faiths and the terrible conflicts that arise between differing faith traditions is greater than ever. Belief in the divine image present in all persons as well as an understanding of Christ's work of atonement extended to everyone provide a strong foundation for entering into dialogue with others of differing religious perspectives. Because we believe that all persons sin and also carry the image of God within them, we may hold in tension the difficult task of both acknowledging the limitations and affirming the presence of God in other faith traditions.

As we turn towards the twenty-first century, the Anabaptist understanding of sin will undoubtedly address issues and needs which have not yet been considered. Still, Anabaptism has a heritage rich in meaning and in affirmation of the goodness of God's creation. May its traditional understanding of sin, its current interpretation of that understanding within the modern context, and the many potential applications of its understanding of sin all direct us to a deeper awareness of God's presence and grace.

[1] Karl Menninger, M.D., *Whatever Became of Sin?* (New York: Hawthorne Books, Inc., 1973). The story of the three gambling clerics is used with the permission of the publisher.

[2] Andrew M. Greeley, *The Cardinal Sins* (Rockefeller Plaza, New York: Warner Bros., 1981), introduction.

[3] Cornelius J. Dyck and Dennis D. Martin, eds., *The Mennonite Encyclopedia* (Scotsdale, Pa.: Herald Press, 1990), V, 821.

Conversation

ঙ৹ঙ৹ II ৪৹৪৹

Anabaptist Understandings
of Salvation

These essays by J. Denny Weaver and Virginia Wiles offer a vivid contrast in Anabaptist understandings of salvation. But despite their differences, both conclude that nonresistance is critical and that the modern church should sustain it.

Weaver brings a fresh approach to the old debate on the impact of Pietism, or revivalism, on traditional Anabaptist beliefs, especially nonresistance. His analysis of late nineteenth-century Amish and Mennonite writings leads him to conclude that ecclesiology (the understanding of the role of the faith community) is more influential than soteriology (the understanding of salvation) in preserving Anabaptist beliefs. When ecclesiology permits the inner spirituality of individuals to develop without guidance from the communion, then Pietism has the potential to undermine commitment to the faith community, a central feature of Anabaptism. When ecclesiology, on the other hand, maintains the "social dimensions of salvation," pietistic experience can actually strengthen dedication to the church and its tradition of nonresistance. Hence, Weaver reasons that the future of Anabaptist denominations as peace churches depends on maintaining a clear role for the community of believers rather than rediscovering Pietism.

Wiles concurs that nonresistance lies at the core of faith and proposes that only believers with strength can practice it. Relying on her own translation of Philippians 2:1-13, she argues that salvation through Christ brings strength rather than passivity or "mutual humility among humans." She agrees with Weaver that the faith community is intrinsic to the development of love of enemy but chastens it for failing to nurture the strength of its members. The emphasis on humble, passive nonresistance instead of powerful, active nonresistance neglects to teach believers to assert the strength that is theirs in Christ. When this power is realized, individuals learn that they cannot be victimized and are better equipped to "take their stand." According to Wiles, society in the twenty-first century will desperately need an Anabaptist witness of gentle strength.

1

Understandings of Salvation: The Church, Pietistic Experience, and Nonresistance

by J. Denny Weaver

This essay deals with the interaction of Pietism and Anabaptism.[1] Using broad brush strokes and painting on a large canvas, I want to sketch a way to interpret the impact of Pietism—whether thought to be positive or negative—on the Anabaptist churches. My suggestion serves to assess the history of Anabaptist churches as well as the potential future impact of Pietist forms on these communions as we look toward the twenty-first century. The heart of the article uses understandings of atonement and salvation from a cross section of Mennonite and Amish writers of the last half of the nineteenth century to illuminate both Anabaptist-Pietist relationships and to indicate what is unique about Anabaptist theology. I want to discuss these issues with a bit of the history of interpretation of Pietism and Anabaptism in mind. Thus, the first section deals briefly with that interpretation.

I

Pietism and Anabaptism have long had an intertwined history. Shared and parallel concerns about conversion or rebirth, an earnest and personal faith, commitment to the Bible, the conviction that true faith will manifest itself in a life modeled on Jesus and close fellowship of believers in small congregations and cell groups gave Anabaptists and Pietists a great deal in common. Mennonites imbibed a great deal from the springs of Pietism. At the same time, the spirituality of Pietists became something of a commentary on the state of existing Mennonite congregations. The Pietist element in the founding of the Church of the Brethren made the Pietist critique of Mennonites more explicit, particularly when Mennonites joined that movement in search of a more vibrant faith.[2]

The evaluation of Pietism's impact upon Anabaptism has varied. Writing as one converted to Anabaptism, Robert Friedmann gave a negative critique of Pietism. Friedmann acknowledged the shared and parallel concerns of Pietism and Anabaptism, even as he pointed out that terms such as "discipleship" and "cross" had different connotations when used by Pietists and Anabaptists. In

Friedmann's view, the negative impact of Pietism came at the point when Mennonites gradually lost their willingness to suffer and to work out their salvation through a radical following of Christ in the face of opposition. Pietism helped them to develop a faith that abandoned evangelization and emphasized inner joy and peace with the world as a substitute for the radical way of the cross of original Anabaptism. It meant "apparently, the gradual disappearance of that concrete Christianity which had been the goal of the original Anabaptists, and the substitution for it of an emotional Christianity which no longer caused the authorities of state or church any trouble." Pietism led Mennonites away from an aggressive faith and willingness to suffer and paved the way for them to become the "Stillen im Lande."[3] Ernst Crous seconded Friedmann's assessment of the differences between Pietism and Anabaptism.[4]

Not surprisingly, writers who speak for Anabaptist groups with a root in Pietism have seen fewer problems with it. Church of the Brethren theologian Dale Brown, in *Understanding Pietism*, investigates such charges as subjectivism, individualism, withdrawal, and other worldliness in the founders of Pietism, primarily Philipp Jakob Spener (1635-1705) and August Hermann Francke (1663-1727). Brown concludes that while the seeds of the problems are found in Spener and Francke, the founders themselves avoided the pitfalls. Thus modern Anabaptist groups can, with appropriate awareness of the negative potential, properly own the inherited, positive dimensions of Pietism. Whether a Christian today follows the traditional Pietist option of working for reform within the existing corporate structures or chooses the Radical Pietist and sectarian option of forming counter-structures, according to Brown, depends on the era in which one lives.[5]

Martin Schrag similarly rehabilitates Pietism from the perspective of the Brethren in Christ. He delineates three responses to Pietism by eastern Pennsylvania Mennonites during the eighteenth century: acceptance, rejection, and integration. Those who accepted Pietist forms joined the United Brethren in Christ of Philip W. Otterbein (1726-1813) and Martin Boehm (1725-1812). These Mennonites lost such Anabaptist emphases as a visible church and biblical pacifism and replaced discipleship with the conversion experience as the essence of salvation. Those who rejected Pietism did so in order to retain their Mennonite distinctives, such as nonresistance and a visible, corporate normativeness of the church. As an example of integration, Schrag identifies the River Brethren (later Brethren in Christ) as a group that blended Pietist and Anabaptist distinctives. His intent, like Brown's, is to show that outright acceptance or rejection of Pietism by Anabaptists were not the only options and that Pietism ought not be considered inherently dangerous to Anabaptism.[6] The rehabilitation efforts by both Brown and Schrag assumed what Carl Bowman calls a "balanced" view, namely that it is possible to find a "creative tension between Anabaptism and Radical Pietism with neither side getting the upper hand."[7]

The authors of the *Mennonite Experience in America* series undertake a rehabilitation of Pietism from the Mennonite side. Richard MacMaster describes a German Pietist subculture of colonial Pennsylvania in which the Mennonite churches "swam as fish in water." When Mennonites in colonial Pennsylvania no longer experienced the suffering that historically marked their church, Pietism offered a language of "humility" that helped to sustain their understandings of church distinction from the world. Furthermore, since the Mennonites and Brethren maintained nonresistance and accepted social ostracism during the Revolutionary War, it is evident that participation in Pennsylvania's Pietist subculture diluted neither their willingness to suffer nor their commitment to historic Anabaptist principles.[8] Similarly, Theron Schlabach demonstrates that Pietistic themes were thoroughly intermixed with Anabaptist emphases among nineteenth-century Mennonites and thus "helped to lay a groundwork for commitment to Mennonite tradition."[9]

Along with the rehabilitation efforts by Mennonite scholars, Bowman cites similar analysis by Brethren who assumed that the best alternative was a balanced blend of Pietism and Anabaptism.[10] Bowman's own approach to the relationship between Anabaptism and Pietism suggests an alternative, on the one hand, to the identification of one or the other of these currents as foundational and, on the other, to presuming that a balance must be sought between the two. Arguing that previous scholarship generally viewed Pietism and Anabaptism as religious "cross currents" (one of which usually prospered at the expense of the other with a few commendable instances of balance between the two), Bowman suggests that they may, in fact, be "mutually reinforcing currents." That is, "heightened (or lessened) spirituality may produce heightened (or lessened) obedience and church commitment; radical spirituality may yield radical or dissenting religious practices; and. . . such practices may reciprocally nurture such spirituality."[11] However one solves the Pietism-Anabaptism puzzle, Bowman suggests, the founders of the Brethren movement envisioned "a faith-works duality—an unyielding bond between belief and practice." In Bowman's words, "Obedience was faith's barometer."[12]

II

The remainder of this essay will continue to stir the issue of the impact of Pietism upon Anabaptist churches. In part, the argument builds upon—and is at least compatible with—Bowman's suggestion that Anabaptism and Pietism may be mutually reinforcing currents.

I suggest that Pietism has brought about both positive and negative impacts upon the Anabaptist churches. Going beyond Bowman, I want to suggest a way to decipher whether the "reinforcing currents" will result in more or less obedience and dissenting religious practices. The argument will demonstrate that Pietism's impact is not first of all a function of Pietism itself. It is rather a function of the ecclesiology practiced by those who adopt and use Pietist concepts and practices. This conclusion is based on an analysis of atonement and salvation in the writings of a cross section of Mennonite and Amish writers from the latter half of the nineteenth century. As a preparation for that analysis, the next section of the paper describes two understandings of the church as the framework in which to assess understandings of atonement and the interaction between Pietism and Anabaptism.

The believers' church tradition, which includes the several Brethren, Mennonite, and Amish denominations, is characterized by adult conversion, baptism, personal Christian commitment, and voluntary membership. However, these principles can cover two quite different images of ecclesiology, each of which fits under the rubric of believers' church. Is the church simply a voluntary assembly of saved persons, or is the church itself somehow intrinsic to the gospel? Stated another way, does God save primarily individuals or does God's grace also transform relationships among people? Stated yet another way, does the gospel deal primarily with individual guilt and salvation, or does the gospel have inherently social connotations? The first formulations focus more on the spiritual life of individual believers and their quest for God, viewing the church as a support group within which individuals can encourage each other in their spiritual quests and in their efforts to ethically live out their faith. The second formulations place more stress on the faith community, the expression of faith in the context of that community, and the conviction that an individual's Christian activity takes its meaning from the community. This distinction between the church as a voluntary assembly of the saved and the church as intrinsic to the gospel should be kept in mind in our analysis of the theological impact of Pietism on the Anabaptist churches.

III

I have analyzed the theological orientation of eight Amish and Mennonite writers, chosen to represent a spectrum of churchly options in the last half of the nineteenth century. Jacob Stauffer (1811-55) and David Beiler (1786-1871) represent Old Order Mennonites and Old Order Amish. Cornelius H. Wedel (1860-1910) and Gerhard Wiebe (1827-1900) embody progressive and conservative elements of the immigrant German-Russian Mennonites, who in 1874 began arriving from the Ukraine. Johannes Moser (1826-1908) reflects the early nineteenth-century Swiss immigrant tradition before it felt the full impact of various modernizing and Americanizing influences. John M. Brenneman (1816-1895) represents the majority Swiss-American Mennonite tradition, whose immigrant roots in North America reach back as far as the late seventeenth century. John Holdeman (1832-1900) abandoned that body in 1859 and formed the Pietistic and somewhat revivalist Church of God in Christ, Mennonite, commonly known as the Holdeman Mennonites. In 1865, south German immigrant Heinrich Egly (1824-1890) led a revivalist schism from the Amish to form what came to be called the Defenseless Mennonite Church.[13] These eight writers represent a cross section of latter nineteenth-century Mennonite and Amish groups.

The point of entry into the theology of these men is their doctrine of atonement. The research will then be extended to consider the wider theological context in which they talked about atonement. The results provide a number of conclusions that address the issue of the impact of Pietist currents upon Mennonites—and by extension—on other churches in the Anabaptist tradition.

All eight of these writers embraced some version of the satisfaction theory of atonement.[14] With one exception, they were self-taught, and their theology reflected their received tradition. Assuming the satisfaction theory of atonement, when they discussed the substitutionary death of Jesus, they addressed the foundation of salvation itself. Only the well-educated C. H. Wedel expressed awareness of the several theories of atonement and justified his use of substitutionary atonement. A knowledgeable conjecture is that the nineteenth-century Brethren as well as other Mennonite and Amish also adopted satisfaction atonement as part of the received tradition.[15]

Using the narrow question of atonement doctrine as the criterion, these eight men qualify as orthodox or evangelical.[16] That conclusion, however, does not accurately characterize their theology nor identify what is unique about their Anabaptist theological orientation. In other words, identifying these Mennonite and Amish writers in terms of their agreement with the received doctrines of Protestant orthodoxy says little about their religious outlook and identity. The broader context of atonement doctrine must be considered in order to identify the uniqueness of Mennonite and Amish soteriology.

One dimension of that larger context is the clear expectation that saved individuals must experience a conversion or rebirth. And beyond conversion, there is the expectation that its primary manifestation will be in terms of the obedient life of the saved individual. Stated another way, conversion is not a one-time event; it is rather a lifelong process of growth in grace. In this context, atonement constitutes a preparatory stage to conversion and the Christian life. That is, the atoning, substitutionary death of Jesus established the possibility of forgiveness of sins for those sinners who would make a personal decision to accept it. With sins forgiven, God's Spirit can then transform the sinner into a saved individual; he or she is converted. The life lived by the converted one following rebirth then provides the evidence that conversion has truly occurred and continues to occur. Atonement is thus the preliminary stage to the Christian life. These observations about atonement doctrine and the expectation of conversion being manifested in a righteous life exhibit the clear compatibility of all these writers with a general Pietistic framework.[17]

Among these Mennonite and Amish leaders some clear differences also existed around the questions of conversion and experiential faith. At one end of the spectrum, Heinrich Egly insisted on a revivalist-oriented, crisis conversion. In fact, such a conversion was required for membership in Egly's congregation in Allen County, Indiana. John Holdeman also insisted on a highly experiential conversion, although without revivalistic exuberance.

Among my eight subjects, Jacob Stauffer occupied the opposite end of the spectrum from Egly. Rejecting revivalism outright, and no doubt suspicious of too much stress on the experiential dimension of conversion, Stauffer understood the nonresistant life within the church as evidence of conversion. His primary emphasis fell on discipline as the way to maintain Christian life in the church. David Beiler's view resembled Stauffer's, except that Beiler had a larger place for the experiential dimension of conversion, and Gerhard Wiebe also fits in this grouping with Stauffer and Beiler.

Wedel, Moser, and Brenneman occupied mediating positions on the spectrum between outright rejection of revivalism and outright adoption of Pietist forms and revivalism. Using Bowman's terminology, these three might be said to have an even-handed "balance or blend" of Anabaptist and Pietist emphases. All three clearly made room for experiential dimensions of conversion and faith, while also stressing that it was the life following conversion that testified to the genuineness of conversion.

Within these broadly Pietist-compatible forms, Wedel and Moser were suspicious of revivalism, while Brenneman accepted it. Both Wedel and Moser opposed the requirement of a crisis conversion but allowed it for those who found it meaningful. They emphasized that conversion frequently happens gradually, as an ongoing growth process, and they stressed that feelings did not accurately validate the genuineness of an individual's conversion. In his discussion of this, Wedel noted the moderate view of Spener and cautioned against too much focus on Pietism's *Bußkampf* (efforts by Pietists to expiate their sins or do penance in order to gain salvation) with its great doubt and struggle to reach a great and sudden breakthrough. Certainty of salvation does not depend on inner feelings of repentance, Wedel wrote, "but on simple, childlike faith in the merit of Christ."[18]

Moser's opposition to a required experiential conversion stemmed in large part from encounters in Bluffton, Ohio, with the Reformed Mennonite Church, another small Mennonite splinter group with an experiential, Pietist-oriented conversion requirement, and with Heinrich Egly. Egly preached several revival meetings in Bluffton and attracted members from the supposedly unconverted Moser and his allegedly dead congregation. At one point in his "Autobiography," Egly wrote that "the old serpent" had opposed their work in Bluffton and that "John Moser was one of the instruments through which he worked against us."[19] Wedel's objection to revivalism was provoked, no doubt in part, by the impact of Mennonite Brethren revivalism on his congregation of Alexanderwohl, located ten miles north of Newton, Kansas. About 1880 Wedel's father and siblings all left Alexanderwohl to help found a new, more Pietist- and revivalist-oriented Mennonite Brethren congregation.[20] Thus both Moser and Wedel experienced revivalism as a force of outside agitation and division.

In contrast to Moser and Wedel, Brenneman accepted revivalism in modified form and even preached a few revivals, even as he acknowledged that feelings did not guarantee certainty of salvation. He saw that revivalism need not be limited to an event worked by an outside agent who was critical of the existing minister and congregation, the experience of both Moser and Wedel with revivalism. If understood properly, Brenneman contended, revivalism could also assist the local congregation. His efforts opened the door for revivalism to become the traditional way in which Mennonite young people were called to join the congregation. Brenneman's revivals thus called people to embrace Anabaptist beliefs rather than to seek an alternative to the experience of their Anabaptist congregation.

Their differences on revivalism and crisis conversion experiences notwithstanding, these eight Anabaptists agreed on the necessity of conversion and an existential faith. And they were agreed that it was not the conversion experience itself but the kind of life led by the supposedly saved person that certified rebirth as genuine and rendered testimony to the state of one's soul. However, as Dale Brown argues, these points of agreement are not unique to Anabaptism. Further, the intramural disagreements of these eight about revivalism and crisis conversion parallel arguments within other evangelical traditions. On these points, then, these Anabaptists can be made to agree with Pietist Protestantism.

The uniqueness of their theology appears, I believe, at another juncture. Within the Christian walk that validates conversion, one issue above all persuaded these Anabaptists of the authenticity of conversion: the capacity to be nonresistant and to love one's enemies. For example, Johannes Moser discussed atonement in order to say that Jesus died nonresistantly and that, when understood properly, "the entire context of Scripture teaches nonresistance."[21] To the end of his life his articles reflected the belief that nonresistance was intrinsic to the gospel and to the saved life. Moser's antagonist, Heinrich Egly, made the same point another way. Egly considered it impossible for the unredeemed person to obey Jesus' command to love one's enemies. "Can you love your enemy, and pray for him from the heart?" Egly asked. "If you can do that, then Christ's Spirit is within you." If not, "it is as clear as sunshine that your heart has not been recreated and renewed by God."[22] All eight individuals of this study considered nonresistance an intrinsic and ineradicable dimension of the gospel. For this essay, the quasi-adversarial Moser and Egly exemplify that point on which the eight agreed.

For these Mennonites and Amish, conversion, however vivid and whether instantaneous or developmental, was still only the beginning of the Christian life. It was not conversion per se, nor even the assumption that conversion would be manifested in life that distinguished these Anabaptists. Rather, it was the clear linking of the ongoing Christian life to nonresistance that most sharply distinguished these Anabaptists from other traditions of evangelical and Pietist Protestantism. Further, the theological link also ran in the other direction; for the most part, these writers included nonresistance as part of the doctrine of atonement. In some way, each believed that without nonresistance, there was no atoning death of Christ and no salvation. These observations mean that the uniqueness of Anabaptist theology is related to nonresistance. This integration of nonresistance into conversion and experiential faith as well as into atonement doctrine is one way to depict the uniqueness of nineteenth-century Anabaptist theology.

Pietist impulses underscore and strengthen experiential faith and the sense that a conversion has occurred or is occurring as an continuing process of growth. Clearly, therefore, Pietist impulses reinforced the Mennonite and Amish commitment to the Christian life and to nonresistance, even for those who refused to require a revivalist conversion and who argued that feelings were inadequate evidence of conversion. If Mennonites and Amish believed that conversion and the ongoing Christian life were linked and that nonresistance belonged intrinsically to that Christian life, then Pietist impulses that underscored personal conversion could clearly strengthen Mennonite and Amish beliefs and commitment to the church. Bowman is quite correct in suggesting that Pietism and Anabaptism can interact as mutually reinforcing currents.

This conclusion reached, other material from Heinrich Egly puts it in a different light. Egly's written legacy reveals a development of thought that is very illuminating when set over against the other nineteenth-century writers of my study. As previously noted, all writers across the spectrum of denominational options used nonresistance as specific evidence of genuine conversion and as a *sine qua non* of the Christian life. Egly's articles in *Herold der Wahrheit* and *Christlicher Bundesbote* made it quite explicit that loving one's enemies became possible only after conversion by the Holy Spirit. Acceptance of nonresistance and of loving one's enemies thus become the ultimate evidence that genuine conversion had occurred.

However, another perspective appeared in Egly's "Autobiography," concluded just a few months before his death on June 23, 1890. This unpublished work reflects the elderly churchman as he recounted numerous preaching tours and other events and reflected on the history of the denomination that he founded. In this writing, Egly's espousal of substitutionary atonement is clear. The necessity of a crisis or revivalist-oriented conversion for rebirth is also very evident. Another dimension is striking because of its absence. Nowhere in the "Autobiography" does Egly refer to nonresistance and love of enemies as the ultimate evidence that rebirth has occurred. In fact, he fails to mention nonresistance and love of enemies in the "Autobiography." Egly had retained his personal belief in nonresistance and his church had not yet abandoned the doctrine.[23] What he had done, in all likelihood without conscious awareness of the change, was to alter the validation criteria for conversion. No longer were nonresistance and love of enemies at issue. Instead, a vivid, crisis conversion experience became the testimony of conversion.[24] Although church practice had not yet caught up with the theological shift, the door was wide open to making nonresistance a matter of individual conscience, as happened in succeeding decades.[25]

Such shifts were not so much the fault of Pietism. While it is true that Pietism and revivalism offer existential experience as a substitute validation for salvation when the old discipleship confirmations are gone (thus greasing the skids under the slide in that direction), it is still the case that the substitution need not be made. One can be a Pietist and a revivalist without removing nonresistance and the church from the gospel. However, when that substitution does occur, for whatever reason, Pietism very much lends itself to supporting the result.

The doctrine of substitutionary atonement allows the same kind of substitution to occur in the area of theology. Defining salvation in terms of escape from guilt and deserved penalty—a legal transaction with God—provides a theological way to talk about salvation apart from considerations of discipleship, nonresistance, and love of enemies. It thus enables and reinforces an understanding of salvation that is separated from ethics.[26] That nineteenth-century Mennonites and Amish retained a strong belief in nonresistance in spite of their embrace of substitutionary atonement and Pietist forms is due, I believe, to their strong sense of the corporate church and their assumption that the life that demonstrates conversion is modeled on the teaching and example of Jesus. As long as they retained these convictions, Pietist and revivalist forms could reinforce them as well as add an ethical dimension to substitutionary atonement. When the assumptions shift and nonresistance is no longer considered intrinsic to the church and to salvation, Pietist forms and substitutionary atonement have the clear potential to exacerbate the shift.

This analysis demonstrates that whether Pietism serves to strengthen or to weaken the unique and historic emphases of the Anabaptist churches is not a function of the Pietist impulse per se. It is much more a function of the understanding of the church and the gospel that precedes the Pietist impulse. In terms of the two models of the believers' church depicted earlier, it seems evident that Heinrich Egly, probably unwittingly, evolved from a model of the church as intrinsic to the gospel to a model that understands the church as a voluntary assembly of the saved. When nonresistance and love of enemies are seen as intrinsic to the gospel, then social issues and relationship among people belong by definition to the nature of the church. In this instance, one could not belong to the church built on Christ without espousing the teaching of Christ "in all things." However, when focus shifts to the individual experience with emphasis on inner experience, then the social components of salvation recede to a secondary level of importance, and the church is no longer intrinsic to the gospel. Instead, the church comes to consist of those who unite together on the basis of their common experience of conversion, and the social component of the gospel is no longer foundational. Nonresistance and love of enemies, then, no longer provide evidence of genuine conversion and the church inadvertently becomes the voluntary assembly of the saved. Although *individuals* may retain a belief in pacifism or nonresistance, these no longer define the essence of the church as a believing community. While Pietism does not cause this evolution in understanding about the church, it certainly facilitates the shift.[27]

This discussion of the nature of the church and whether discipleship, nonresistance and love of enemies are intrinsic to the gospel seems a factor in many stories from the history of the Anabaptist churches. The two images of church appear involved in the story of Martin Boehm. He seemed to understand his silencing by the bishops as a matter of tolerance of his right to fellowship with English-speaking Christians, which implies that nonresistance and other Anabaptist distinctives lie outside the purview of salvation and the gospel. The bishops, in contrast, saw it as a matter of the church's and Boehm's acceptance of those who practiced war.[28] The two understandings of church appear implicit in the varying responses of the Brethren to the conundrum of M. G. Brumbaugh, a pacifist Brethren elected governor of Pennsylvania, who with great anguish called the state militia to arms in World War I as well as to quell labor riots.[29] The tension between the two understandings of church is evident in Steve Longenecker's study of Pietism and tolerance in colonial Pennsylvania. The Anabaptists taught an egalitarian salvation, open to all, in a converted community without hierarchy and with a leveling of social status. Even so, they still sought to maintain the supremacy of a private conscience that ruled an individual's relationship to God without intermediaries.[30] The two models of the church seem quite clear in the decisions of the Brethren in 1939 and 1948. While the official denominational position was restated that "all war is sin," it also agreed to accept whatever decision a member might make under the guidance of individual conscience.[31] The same is true for the recent request of a congregation from the Virginia Conference of the Mennonite Church to admit military personal as members without regard to their continuing military service. The two understandings of church and the gospel appear reflected in many anecdotes and in letters-to-the-editor of the denominational papers, which indicate a significant amount of grassroots support for the recent Gulf War and for the use of United States Marines in Somalia.

Conclusion

Carl Bowman suggests that Pietism and Anabaptism are mutually reinforcing currents, and my analysis supports this. Obedience is the barometer of faith, to borrow Bowman's phrase, when the gospel is assumed to have inherently social dimensions and the corporate church is intrinsic to the gospel. On the other hand, obedience does not serve as the barometer of faith if salvation is more felt than lived or if the church is not intrinsic to the gospel.

The historical argument about whether Pietism and revivalism have harmed or enhanced the Anabaptist churches is not, in the first order, a function of Pietism itself. It depends, rather, upon the ecclesiology into which the Pietist modes and methods are poured. If the ecclesiology, albeit implicitly, allows for the development of an inner spirituality essentially complete within the individual, then Pietism clearly has the potential to undercut the social components of the gospel and of lived Christian faith. On the other hand, if the Pietist idiom is introduced into an ecclesiology that maintains the social dimensions of salvation as intrinsic to the church, then Pietist forms can strengthen the commitment of individuals to that church.

This focus on the question of ecclesiology provides an additional, theological component to our understanding of past persons and events. It also has implications for the future. It suggests that the continuation of the Anabaptist churches as a distinctive peace church tradition depends quite heavily on maintaining an understanding of the church as the visible alternative community. If we assume that the gospel includes the practical teachings of Jesus—love of enemies, nonresistance, giving what one has—then focus on a sensate conversion and individual spirituality can reinforce commitment to that gospel. If the church is seen as the avenue through which to express the meaning of conversion and the gospel, then Pietism and the inner life have the potential to energize the church. However, if Pietism and revivalism assist an individual in finding ultimate meaning in his or her own inner experience apart from ethical, lived expressions of the gospel, then Pietist forms have the clear potential to weaken commitment to the social dimensions of the gospel. The difference depends, not on the Pietist experience, but on the ecclesiology into which it is introduced and practiced. The future of the Anabaptist churches as peace churches depends on maintaining a clear idea of the intrinsically social dimensions of the gospel more than it does on discovering or rediscovering Pietist roots. In considering the future of the Anabaptist churches, do Pietists and non-Pietists alike have the courage to say that the nonviolent teachings of Jesus are intrinsic to both the gospel and the church?

[1] In this paper, Pietism refers to the collection of practices and emphases, such as experiential conversion, experiential faith, growth in grace through regeneration and sanctification, devotional reading of the Bible, and close fellowship in cell groups, whose modern origin is the Pietist movement of Philipp Jakob Spener and August Hermann Francke. The term Anabaptist is used as a generic designation for all the modern groups with a root in sixteenth-century Anabaptism, including the several branches each of Amish, Brethren in Christ, Church of the Brethren, and Mennonites.

[2] Donald F. Durnbaugh has argued that the original Brethren "came out of radical Pietism and joined Anabaptism" (emphasis Durnbaugh's). See "The Genius of the Brethren," *Brethren Life and Thought* 4.1 (Winter 1959), 5; see also 9, 13, 18-27, 31. For the implied Pietist critique of Mennonites by the existence of Brethren, see comments by Alexander Mack, Sr., in Durnbaugh, 25, 26.

[3] Robert Friedmann, "Mennonite Piety through the Centuries: Its Genius and Its Literature," *Studies in Anabaptist and Mennonite History*, no. 7 (Goshen, Ind.: Mennonite Historical Society, 1949): 9-13, 72-88, 146.

[4] Ernst Crous, "Mennonitentum und Pietismus: Ein Versuch," *Theologische Zeitschrift* vol. 8, no. 4 (July/August 1952): 279-81; and "Anabaptism, Pietism, Rationalism and German Mennonites," in ed. Guy F. Hershberger, *Recovery of the Anabaptist Vision* (Scottdale, Pa.: Herald Press, 1957; 3rd printing, 1972), 237-41.

[5] See Brown's summary comments at the end of his chapters on ecclesiology, exegesis, ethics, experience, and eschatology, and his own perspective in the final chapter of *Understanding Pietism* (Grand Rapids, Mich.: Eerdmans, 1978). A similar argument appears in Dale Brown, "Anabaptism and Pietism: I. Points of Convergence and Divergence; II. Living the Anabaptist and Pietist Dialectic, Two Public Lectures Presented at the Young Center of the Study of Anabaptist and Pietist Groups" (Elizabethtown, Pa.: Elizabethtown College, 1990). A more implicit rehabilitation of Pietism for Anabaptists by a Church of the Brethren scholar is Donald F. Durnbaugh, *New Understandings of Anabaptism and Pietism* (Elizabethtown, Pa.: Elizabethtown College, 1987).

[6] Martin H. Schrag, "The Impact of Pietism upon the Mennonites in Early American Christianity," ed. F. Ernest Stoeffler, *Continental Pietism and Early American Christianity* (Grand Rapids, Mich.: Eerdmans, 1976), 74-122.

[7] Carl F. Bowman, *Brethren Society: The Cultural Transformation of a "Peculiar People"* (Baltimore: Johns Hopkins, 1995), 40.

[8] Richard K. MacMaster, *Land, Piety, Peoplehood: The Establishment of Mennonite Communities in America 1683-1790* (Scottdale, Pa.: Herald Press, 1985), chs. 5, 6, 10.

[9] Theron F. Schlabach, *Peace, Faith, Nation: Mennonites and Amish in Nineteenth-Century America* (Scottdale, Pa.: Herald Press, 1988), 88-95; see also Schlabach, "Mennonites and Pietism in America, 1740-1880: Some Thoughts on the Friedmann Thesis," *Mennonite Quarterly Review*, 57 (July 1983): 222-40.

[10] Bowman, *Brethren Society*, 40.

[11] Ibid., 39.

[12] Ibid., 42, 43.

[13] For biographical data on these eight individuals, consult *Mennonite Encyclopedia* (Scottdale, Pa.: Mennonite Publishing House, 1955-59), vols. 1-4 and (Scottdale, Pa.: Herald Press, 1990), vol. 5; Schlabach, *Peace, Faith, Nation*, (Scottdale, Pa.: Herald Press, 1988), James C. Juhnke, *Vision, Doctrine, War: Mennonite Identity and Organization in America 1890-1930*, (Scottdale, Pa.: Herald Press, 1989); Paton Yoder, "Tradition & Transition: Amish Mennonites and Old Order Amish 1800-1900," *Studies in Anabaptist and Mennonite History*, no. 31 (Scottdale, Pa.: Herald Press, 1991); and Adolf Ens, "Wiebe, Gerhard," *Dictionary of Canadian Biography*, vol. 12: 1891 to 1900.

[14] The analysis here summarizes results which I hope, eventually, to publish in a book-length manuscript on Mennonite and Amish understandings of atonement and salvation in the later half of the nineteenth century.

[15] *Rußland nach Amerika* (Winnipeg, Mb.: Druckerei des 'Nordwesten', [1900]); *Causes and History of the Emigration of the Mennonites from Russia to America* (Winnipeg, Mb.: Manitoba Mennonite Historical Society, 1981, trans. Helen Janzen).

[16] A longitudinal study of atonement in the Mennonite Church denomination supports that conjecture. See J. Denny Weaver, "The Quickening of Soteriology: Atonement from Christian Burkholder to Daniel Kauffman," *Mennonite Quarterly Review* 61 (January 1987): 5-45.

[17] In general terms, this observation is parallel to Pietism's acceptance of the inherited theology of orthodoxy. See Brown, *Understanding Pietism*, 27-47.

[18] Ibid., 36-8, 83-101.

[19] Wedel, "Glaubenslehre," *Heft* IV, 65-6.

[20] Egly, "Autobiography," 11.

[21] The influence and impact of Pietism on Mennonite Brethren is integral to their 1861 origins in Russia. Mennonite Brethren historian P. M. Friesen acknowledged Menno Simons and Eduard Wuest, a Lutheran pietist from Württemberg who had held revival meetings in Russia, as the two most important reformers on which the Mennonite Brethren church was founded. Peter M. Friesen, *The Mennonite Brotherhood in Russia (1789-1910)*, trans. and ed. J. B. Toews, Abraham Friesen, Peter J. Klassen, and Harry Loewen (Fresno, Ca.: General Conference of Mennonite Brethren Churches, 1978), 211-12.

[22] Johannes Moser, "Ueber die Wehrlosigkeit," *Herold der Wahrheit* 16 (January 1879): 2.

[23] "Unser Bestreben nach oben," *Herold der Wahrheit* 10 (December 1873): 195-6.

[24] Schlabach, *Peace, Faith, Nation*, 116.

[25] The fact that a shift occurred in Egly's outlook is apparent only when the "Autobiography" is looked at in the context of his articles in HdW and CBB. To date, no other published literature on Egly contains any analysis of the series of Egly's eighteen published articles. When examined in isolation, the items in the posthumously published *Friedensreich Christi* do not make clear the extent to which nonresistance as the proof of conversion permeated Egly's articles. Of the five reprinted, only three contain explicit references to nonresistance. When seen only in the context of that collection, nonresistance appears to be weak in Egly's thought. Other items in the collection, however, make a willingness to obey "all things" taught by Jesus as evidence of genuine conversion. When these articles are placed in their original chronological context, it is quite obvious that Egly included nonresistance in the "all things" and that nonresistance is thus more explicit in this collection than is at first apparent. One can speculate that the posthumous selection and editing of the articles reflected the evolution away from considering nonresistance as the crowning evidence of conversion and the Christian life.

[26] Stan Nussbaum, *Ye Must Be Born Again: A History of the Evangelical Mennonite Church* (n.p.: Evangelical Mennonite Church, 1980), 42.

[27] For several historical and theological dimensions of the discussion about atonement theories and ethics, see J. Denny Weaver, "Pacifism and Soteriology: A Mennonite Experience," *Christian Scholar's Review*, 15 (1985): 42-54; "Atonement for the NonConstantinian Church," *Modern Theology* 6 (July 1990): 307-23; "Christus Victor, Ecclesiology, and Christology," *Mennonite Quarterly Review*, forthcoming; and "Some Theological Implications of Christus Victor," *Mennonite Quarterly Review*, forthcoming.

[28] This tension between two models of church is apparent already within early Pietism. While Dale Brown does not use the two ecclesiological images per se, the tensions they depict are evident throughout *Understanding Pietism*, in particular, 35-63.

[29] Schlabach, *Peace, Faith, Nation*, 28-9.

[30] Carl Frederick Bowman, "Beyond Plainness: Cultural Transformation in the Church of the Brethren from 1850 to the Present," (Ph.D. diss.: University of Virginia, 1989), 440-9.

[31] Stephen L. Longenecker, *Piety and Tolerance: Pennsylvania German Religion, 1700-1850* (Metuchen, N.J.: Scarecrow Press, 1994).

2
Gentle Strength:
Contemporary Prospects for
an Understanding of Salvation

by Virginia Wiles

Let me introduce myself and my personal position in Anabaptist history. I am a New Testament scholar, specifically a Pauline theologian. Hence, my reflections, as always, will move out of a study of the faith of the early Christian churches as it is seen in the New Testament documents. I am a convert of sorts to Anabaptism, having been raised in a Southern Baptist home and joined the Church of the Brethren in adulthood. Although my father had always inter-preted the Baptist heritage for me as an Anabaptist heritage (he was something of a heretic among the Southern Baptists), my view of Anabaptism is particular-ly colored by my experience within the Church of the Brethren.

J. Denny Weaver helpfully outlines important tensions and perceptions regarding the understandings and experience of salvation. I want to pull forward two specific contributions: his emphasis on nonresistance and love of enemy and his insistence that the church is intrinsic to the gospel.

Looking toward the future demands a certain amount of imagination; it also requires some perception about both the past and the present. Weaver does an admirable job in setting forth some important insights from the past. I will, necessarily, give some readings of the present. But I want to imagine with you a future. Weaver argues that the uniqueness of Anabaptist theology appears in "the Christian walk that validates conversion". Specifically, salvation is confirmed by "the capacity to be nonresistant and to love one's enemies." It is this aspect of the Anabaptist understanding of salvation that I want to imagine into the future. Here, it seems to me, is precisely where the Anabaptist identity lies. This is its strength; it is the gift that Anabaptists are privileged to claim.

The Strength of Nonresistance

It is perhaps a commonplace among Anabaptists that nonresistance is not weakness; it is not passivity. But the life of nonresistance, despite protests to the contrary, is often expressed in passivity, in a denial of strength, in a failure to claim what God has entrusted to us. Anabaptists have nurtured in themselves and in their children a "humble spirit." And it is especially this notion of a "humble spirit" that I want to address in the first part of my essay.

From the fourth century until today humility has been understood to be "the supreme Christian virtue." This, according to John Chrysostom, is what it means to be Christian—to be humble.[1] And yet, it is odd that this very notion of humility is barely present within the Scriptures themselves. Indeed, it could be argued that the notion of humility as a virtue is a creation of the post-Constantinian church.[2]

In the New Testament, the word humility occurs in a limited number of places. These occurrences may be categorized into two groups. First, we find the sayings like "whoever among you would humble yourself will be exalted" (Matt. 23:12; par. Lk. 14:11; 18:14). These sayings (as well as the ones in 1 Peter and James)[3] are dependent upon the notion of humility before God as found in the Hebrew Scriptures and in the LXX.[4] They refer specifically to humility before God, that is, a recognition of our humanness, our creatureliness. This is not, however, an "I am a worm" mentality; for the Hebrew Scriptures are clear that humanity has immeasurable worth, created in the image of God (Gen. 1:27), crowned with glory and honor (Ps. 8). And to some extent, humility before God entails a claiming of that rightful place in God's creation. What is not in evidence in the Hebrew Scriptures—or in the New Testament—is the expression of this humility as a mutual humility among humans.[5]

The second group of references to "humility" in the New Testament (and in the Hebrew Bible) would be better translated "humiliation," for they refer to social humiliation, to a social abasement, to some kind of negative social circumstances.[6] Indeed, all of Paul's uses of the word ταπεινός (and cognates) are descriptions of such social humiliation.[7] Paul finds no use for a virtue of (mutual) humility within the community. His vision of Christ and the salvation that comes through Christ was one of strength, not humility. One text will suffice for illustration.

Paul's exhortation to the Philippians in Philippians 2:1-13 has generally been read as a "call to humility." The Philippians were, so the scholars and preachers have said, a proud and divisive church, and Paul writes to instruct them to be humble, for only in humility can church unity be maintained.[8] But I offer another interpretation of this important text. I will not be able to do this fully but only in brief form.[9] First, I will present my own translation of the text, one that is at some crucial points considerably different from those in English Bibles.

[1]Therefore, if there is any consolation in Christ, if there is any comfort of love, if any fellowship of spirit, if any affection and tenderness, [2]fulfill my joy, in that you perceive the same, having the same love, united in soul, perceiving the whole. [3]Do nothing on the basis of competitive self-promotion or the assumption of a false glory, but, mindful of your present humiliation, regard one another as your own leaders, [4]each of you looking out not only for your own interests, but each and every one of you looking out [also] for the interests of the others. [5]Perceive this among yourselves, which indeed you are in Christ Jesus, [6]who, though he was in the form

of God, did not regard equality with God as something to be exploited [7]but emptied himself, taking the form of [human] slavery, being born in human likeness. And being found in human form, [8]he submitted himself to humiliation and became obedient to the point of death—even death on a cross. [9]Therefore God has highly exalted him and has given him the name that is above every name, [10]so that at the name of Jesus every knee should bend· in heaven and on earth and under the earth, [11]and every tongue should confess that Jesus Christ is Lord, to the glory of God the Father. [12]Therefore, my dear friends, just as you have always obeyed, not only as in my presence with you but now much more in my absence, with fear and trembling work out your own salvation. [13]For God is the one who is at work among you, both to will and to work for the sake of God's good pleasure.

Paul writes to the Philippians to encourage them. His letter is one of joy and confidence, certainly not one that rebukes or rebuffs the Philippians. They are his dear and trusted friends. But now Paul is in prison, facing the possibility of death (Phil. 1:19-26; 2:17-18). And the Philippians can no longer depend upon Paul to guide them, so he encourages them in Philippians 1:27 to learn to "govern their own community according to the standard of the gospel."[10] His instructions to the Philippian congregation about how they are to govern their community sound familiar to our "Free Church" ears: Everyone is responsible for the welfare of the church; all are leaders in some respect in the new community and no hierarchy is to exist, but rather each and every member of the community is a minister within the church.[11]

Now this may sound exciting; it certainly sounds right. But it may very well be that it was a bit unnerving for the Philippians. They had always been able to depend on Paul. He was their "father" in the faith; he had brought the good news of salvation to them; he knew what this life in Christ was all about. But now their guide was not going to be with them anymore. They were on their own. How on earth could they do it? Wouldn't it really be better simply to pick one or two of Paul's closest associates—say, Euodia and Syntyche (Phil. 4:2)—and trust those appointed leaders to tell them what Paul would say if Paul were still present with them? Things would be so much easier that way. They could do the thinking; they could guide and make decisions for them.

But no. Paul insists that every member of the congregation must learn to think like a leader.[12] Think this way, Paul says in Philippians 2:5. That is, every member of the congregation, in the context of the community of faith, is to learn to interpret their concrete situation as God's people in this way.[13] Their paradigm for interpretation was to be found in the story of Jesus Christ, who, though He was in the form of God, became fully human and suffered the conditions of frustration, slavery, oppression, and humiliation that all humans experience. Indeed, His obedience to His fate as human was so complete that He even suffered death, and a humiliating death at that—death on a cross.

But wait, the story is not over! For God has acted! This one who has suffered our fate is not a victim! God has exalted Him and given Him the highest name, the highest authority. He is Lord—Lord of the entire cosmos!

Where do the Philippians stand in relation to this Lord? Paul is unequivocal. The Philippians are in Christ. They are not "under" Christ, as are the principalities and the powers.[14] Rather, the Philippians—and all those who acknowledge the reality of the eschatological revelation of God in Christ—stand in this one who is Lord of the universe. Those who acknowledge His present Lordship are no longer "enslaved under the elemental spirits" or "under the law;"[15] they have been transferred to a new Lord and thus claim to live and act in His authority and power.

The hymn that Paul quotes in Philippians, then, is not a call for humility. Our response to the hymn—that is, to the story of Christ—is not to be one of stooped shoulders and shuffling feet. Rather, the call is a call to strength, to a recognition of our true identity in Christ, the Lord of the universe. Our stance is one of shoulders thrown back and heads held high. We are not victims but are, rather, "more than conquerors" through Jesus Christ (Rom. 8:37). As Jesse Jackson would say, "We are somebody!"

And so, Paul says, do not fear that I am absent from you. You are fully competent in Christ Jesus to "work out your own salvation . . . For God is at work among you" (Phil. 1:12-13). The Philippians need not depend upon Paul nor need they "replace" him by establishing a church hierarchy of bishops and deacons (Phil. 1:1). For inasmuch as they are in Christ, they can (and, Paul believes, will) work out their experience of salvation in their own unique historical context. Indeed, they will "shine as stars in the world" (Phil. 2:15). They need not be perplexed about the persecution they are experiencing (Phil. 1:28-30), for this "present humiliation" (see Phil. 3:21) is nothing more than a sign to their opponents that God is, indeed, among them (Phil. 1:28-30). The world may misperceive them as victims, but the Philippians—if they perceive the reality of the gospel in their midst—will know better. They are not determined by anything that this world wreaks upon them but rather find their strength in that eschatological scene where Jesus Christ is Mighty Lord (Phil. 2:9-11). And thus, even in the midst of humiliation they know that they are not victims, that they are more than survivors. They are the sons and daughters of God, joint heirs of Christ (Rom. 8:23, 29-30; Gal. 4:4-7).

This is the kind of strength that Anabaptist foremothers and fathers have known. The early Anabaptists were, certainly by necessity, strong people. But I suspect that it was more than simply social necessity. Their strength was the strength of salvation, the strength that comes through the confession that Jesus Christ is Lord. It is the strength that was declared in those baptismal waters as they acknowledged the reality of Christ's Lordship. Indeed, their commitment to and their practice of nonresistance was a strength, not passivity. And it is this strength that Anabaptists must reclaim as they enter the twenty-first century.

Anabaptists have, I believe, much to be concerned about in their midst—indeed some things to be ashamed of. There is today much discussion in church groups about abuse of power. It is a discussion that is informed by the clinical practice and experience of psychotherapists with those who have been "victims of the abuse of power." The church needs to listen to the experience of the psychotherapeutic profession, listening with ears attuned to hearing what the gospel has to offer in light of that experience. But it needs to be clear that neither psychology, sociology, political science, nor any other field of human research can be adopted as "church theology" without evaluating the insights of that research by the measuring rod of the Gospel. And I believe it is time that the church apply this measuring rod to the discussions swirling within it about abuse of power.

Any reading of the Gospel makes it clear that abuse of power is wrong, and it ought not to be found among those who claim to order their lives according to that Gospel. That adults would use their power against children and youth in abusive ways is abhorrent. But that there are adults who claim that as adults they have been the "victims" of the abuse of power ought to shame us. For this means that Anabaptists have raised children in their midst without teaching them to claim and assert the strength that is theirs in Christ. These "adults" evidently did not learn from their Anabaptist parents and congregations how to claim the strength that is in Christ, how to take their stand, to say "no" when no is needed, to perceive in themselves that ultimately no one can "victimize" them—for their identity and their power is secure in the eschatological glory of God. These adults need care, to be sure, but they are symptoms of a more serious problem. The church needs to ask whether its emphasis on a humble, passive nonresistance rather than a powerful, active nonresistance has led it to fail its children and, thus, itself.[16]

It is simply inconceivable that Jesus or Paul or the early Anabaptist mothers and fathers would have ever claimed that they were victims of the abuse of power. In some sense, of course, they were—as are all humans, and perhaps particularly those humans who are faithful believers in Christ. But none of the "heroes" of the faith would have perceived themselves as victims. By God, they were not victims. By God, they were strong. By God! God's response to the Cross of Christ denies the "luxury" of perceiving ourselves as "victims." We must—each and every one of us—claim our strength in Christ. For, in Christ we have been crowned with glory, honor, and power, and it is to the shame of Anabaptists if they have not imparted this perception of strength to their members.

Love of the Enemy

But it must be said that the strength that comes through salvation is a particular kind of strength. And it is here in the definition of strength that Anabaptists have much to contribute to their world—both the secular and ecclesiastical worlds. Believers bear witness to the strength of nonresistance that they see in Jesus' life and teachings, to a strength that empowers them to love the enemy. This is not a strength that the world knows. It is not the power of the sword or the power of might or the power of "right." This strength is not even to be found in the "fight for justice" that is so popular in church circles today.

Weaver helpfully articulates—yet again—that for Anabaptists the gathered community is intrinsic to the gospel. For it is in the gathered community above all else that believers learn love for the enemy. The central ritual is an enacted parable of this love for the enemy. For, when Jesus knelt to wash the feet of the disciples, He was washing not only the feet of his friends, but also the feet of those who would shortly desert Him, deny Him, and even betray Him. This one who, in the record of Matthew, called His followers to love the enemy, acted out for them a parable of love for His "enemies."

And so the theme plays. It is not the blare of the trumpet calling us to stand and execute justice upon the head of our oppressor. No, the tune is a gentler tune—the whispering ripple of the laving of water upon the feet of our enemies. This moment, the moment of active love for the enemy, is, in the language of the apostle Paul, grace. "For while we were yet enemies, Christ loved us and gave himself for us" (Rom. 5:8-10; Gal. 2:20). Here is where salvation lies. Love for enemy describes both the conditions and the consequences of salvation. We are saved because one who we thought was our enemy has loved us. And it is precisely that love that transforms us into "lovers of our enemies."

Such is the logic of "salvation by grace." And although the language of Paul, the language of grace, has perhaps not been the conscious language of faith, the practice of nonresistance and love for one's enemies is inexplicable without the prior presence of what Paul called "Grace": that God loved us while we were yet enemies.

If scholars and ministers are to understand Salvation for the twenty-first century, then they will need to attend to the "simple graces" that are already alive in their local communities. They will need to retrain their eyes to see the many and manifold graces that empower the daily lives of their people. For Anabaptists do experience grace—when they take off their shoes and socks and kneel to wash their sisters' feet. And they know grace when, on those all too rare occasions, someone they thought was an enemy expresses love toward them. For modern Anabaptists to be a people who can and will "love the enemy," they will need to learn and to teach a sense of gratitude rather than stir the pots of anger. They will need to nurture an awareness that is already among them in their "little communities" throughout this country and that the fruit of salvation is indeed "love, joy, peace, patience, kindness, generosity, faithfulness, gentleness, and self-control" (Gal. 5:22).[17]

It is only a strong people who can live such gentle lives. And such strength can only be a reality among those who have experienced the grace of God that is in Christ Jesus our Lord. I am convinced that the world, as it enters the twenty-first century, desperately needs this witness of gentle strength. And I am equally convinced that the people who are called Anabaptist are richly gifted by God to bear just such a witness of gentle strength—among themselves and for our world.

[1] See, for example, Chrysostom's fifth homily on Philippians, where he says, "Oh how full of true wisdom, how universal a gathering-word of our salvation is the lesson [Paul] has put forth. . . . For humanity [sic: read, humility] is the cause of all good. . . . Not simply humility, but intense humility" (translation in *Ante-Nicene Fathers*).

[2] Humility (ταπεινοφροσύνη) was a favorite word of Chrysostom and his eastern associates. Of the 967 occurrences of this word in all of extant Greek literature, over 700 uses are found in the combined writings of Chyrsostom, Basil, and Gregory of Nazianzus.

[3] See James 4:6, 10; Lk. 3:5; 1 Pet. 5:6; and Acts 8:33.

[4] See, for example, Ps. 55:19; 119:75; 1 Sam. 2:7; 2 Sam. 22:28; Hos. 14:9. The Hebrew word 'ânâh is used in a variety of ways in the Hebrew Bible. The most frequent use is as a description of physical and social oppression; it is particularly used to describe rapes. See, for example, Gen. 15:13; 34:2; Ex. 1:12; Jud. 19:24; 20:5; 2 Sam. 13:12, 14, 22, 32; Ez. 22:10, 11. It is also used, however, of humility before God. See, for example, 2 Chr. 33:12, 23; 34:26, 27; Isa. 58:3; Dan. 10:12; and Sir. 7:17. In the LXX, the Greek word ταπεινός is consistently used to translate those instances where the reference is clearly to oppression. On the rare occasions where 'ânâh is used to refer to a "virtue" the Septuagintal translators consistently used the Greek word πραυτης in translation. This indicates that the Greek word ταπεινός (and cognates) carried a negative meaning for those who used the Greek language. It was only later Christian tradition that began to use this word in something of a positive sense.

[5] See Ragnar Leivestad for a similar assessment of the understanding of "humility" in the *Hebrew Bible*. R. Leivestad, "ΤΑΠΕΙΝΟΣ - ΤΑΠΕΙΝΟΦΡΟΝ," *Novum Testamentum* 8 (1966), 36-47.

[6] See especially Acts 20:19 where, although ταπεινοφροσύνη is often translated as "humility," the sense is better conveyed by "humiliation," given that ταπεινοφροσύνη is coupled and paralleled with δακρύων καὶ πειρασῶν (tears and trials).

[7] For Paul's uses of ταπεινός and cognates, see Rom. 12:16; 2 Cor. 7:6; 10:1; 11:7; 12:21; Phil. 2:3, 8; 3:21; 4:12.

[8] See the relevant commentaries. For example, G. Hawthorne, *Philippians* (Waco, Tex.: Word Books, 1987); J. B. Lightfoot, *St. Paul's Epistle to the Philippians* (London: Macmillan, 1903, 4th ed.); Karl Barth, *The Epistle to the Philippians*, trans. J. W. Leitch (London: SCM Press, 1962); and J. F. Collange, *The Epistle of Saint Paul to the Philippians*, trans. H. W. Heathcote (London: Epworth Press, 1979). There is scarcely a commentary that does not adopt some form of this view of the problem at Philippi. Ernst Lohmeyer's commentary is an exception, but even he emphasizes the necessity of "humility" in his comments on Philippians 1:27-2:18. See E. Lohmeyer, "Der Brief an die Philipper," ed. W. Schmauch, *Kritisch-exegetischer Kommentar über das Neue Testament* (Göttingen: Vandenhoeck & Ruprecht, 1953).

[9] For a fuller exposition, see my dissertation, "From Apostolic Presence to Self-Government in Christ: Paul's Preparing of the Philippian Church for Life in His Absence" (University of Chicago, 1993).

[10] Μόνον ἀξίως τοῦ εὐαγγελίου τοῦ Χριστοῦ πολιτεύεσθε. . . .In contrast to most English translations, I have translated the Greek word πολιτεύεσθε in such a way as to retain its essentially political connotation. The word, both in classical and hellenistic Greek, indicates "participation in the government." For early Christian usages of the word in this sense, see, e.g., Polycarp, *Letter to the Philippians* 5:2 (borrowing from Phil. 1:27, but in the context related to church leadership); and Origen, Contra Celsum 3.30.

[11] Note especially Phil. 2:3-4. My translation given above is significantly different from the usual English translations. For support of this translation see the use of ὑπερέχοντασ (either "superior to" or "leaders") in Rom. 13:1 and 1 Peter 2:13. Note especially the textual variant in P[46] and Vaticanus, where these manuscripts have the article in front the participle, indicating that they understood Paul to be speaking of "the leaders." See also the suggestions for this reading given by Bernhard Weiss, *Der Philipperbrief ausgelegt und die Geschichte seiner Auslegung* (Berlin: Hertz, 1859), 139; and K. Thieme, "Die ΤΑΠΕΙΝΟΦΡΟΣΥΝΗ Philipper 2 und Rmer 12" *ZNW* 8 (1907), 18-20.

[12] Note that Aristotle indicates that φρόνεσις is a virtue that is particular to rulers. It is the ruler's task to "think" for his people: to interpret their concrete situation in light of their constitution and then to act accordingly. See Aristotle, *Politics* 3.2.11. The LXX also uses the verb φρονέω in this way. See 1 Ki. 3:11ff; Ps. 78:72; Wis. 6:24; Isa. 44:28.

[13] See Wiles, "From Apostolic Presence," 92-9, where I conclude that Paul's use of φρονεῖν (see Phil. 2:5) has to do with "perceiving according to a paradigm."

[14] The notion of being "in Christ" is related to the Pauline image of the church as the "body of Christ." The difference between being "under Christ" and being "in Christ" is analogous to

the contrast between the deutero-Pauline image of Christ as the "head" of the body (see Eph. 5:23) and the image in the genuine Pauline writings of the community being the "whole" body of Christ (see 1 Cor. 12:12-27). In the deutero-Pauline image submission is the relevant expression of the church's relation to Christ; in Paul's own conception, the church is rather the concrete expression of Christ himself in the world. This also has implications for notions of the "imitation of Christ." Imitation of Christ, given Paul's conception of the church as the body of Christ, is necessarily a corporate responsibility, rather than an individual one. No individual can "imitate Christ" by him or herself; it takes the whole body acting in concert to "imitate Christ." Scholars generally fail to recognize this crucial element in Paul's theology.

[15] See especially Gal. 4.

[16] I am tempted to bring Nietzsche to testify against us at this point. In his *Genealogy of Morals*, Nietzsche poses a dialogue with a certain "Mr. Foolhardy": "Would anyone care to learn something about the way in which ideals are manufactured? [T]hey are transmuting weakness into merit. . . . Impotence, which cannot retaliate, into kindness; pusillanimity into humility; submission before those one hates into obedience to One of whom they say that he has commanded this submission—they call him god. The inoffensiveness of the weak, his cowardice, his ineluctable standing and waiting at doors, are being given honorific titles such as patience; to be unable to avenge oneself is called to be unwilling to avenge oneself—even forgiveness ("for they know not what they do—we alone know what they do.") Also, there's some talk of loving one's enemy—accompanied by much sweat." Friedrich Nietzsche, *The Birth of Tragedy and The Genealogy of Morals*, trans. Francis Golffing (Garden City, N.Y.: Doubleday, 1956), 180-1. To what extent would Nietzsche's criticism of Christianity describe the failures of Anabaptists to claim and teach a strong Christianity?

[17] See R. Scroggs' interpretation of this "virtue list" as a description (rather than a prescription) of "redeemed humanity." Robin Scroggs, "The Next Step: A Common Humanity," *The Text and the Times* (Minneapolis: Fortress Press, 1993), 96-108.

Conversation
ಖಖ III ೞೞ

Biblical Interpretation

Drawing on recent social history of early Anabaptism, John Roth's examination of Anabaptist hermeneutics finds variation. While early Anabaptists may have agreed on the importance of literalism and congregational discernment as approaches to Scripture, they found no consensus on specific interpretations. Rather, they used the ban as a "partisan weapon" against each other and argued over a variety of issues, including community of goods, war taxes, and ecclesiology. But if early Anabaptists were not of common mind, they nonetheless remained in conversation. Roth points out the dangers of generalizing from a limited number of primary sources to the whole Anabaptist fabric; better, he suggests, to cast a wider net over the entire movement to create a fuzzier but more accurate image.

Willard Swartley finds greater unity in the tradition and identifies several common hermeneutic themes. First, early Anabaptists formed their identity by immersing themselves in Scripture. Second, persecution required them to reflect especially upon the practical and ethical meaning of Scripture. Their emphasis upon community discernment, discipleship, and the Spirit arose against this socio-historical backdrop. According to Swartley, these motifs have much to offer to contemporary discussions about hermeneutics. Community discernment, in particular, offers a corrective to religious individualism and autocratic leadership.

1

Community as Conversation: A New Model of Anabaptist Hermeneutics

by John D. Roth

In an essay published in 1955, noted historian and theologian Harold S. Bender summarized the hermeneutical assumptions which informed the Anabaptist interpretation of Scripture. The Anabaptists, he suggested, endorsed the Reformation slogan of *sola Scriptura*, but unlike the reformers—who were "led at times by theological and practical considerations to depart from the strict teaching of Scripture"—the Anabaptists were "more radical and consistent in their application of the principle." In addition, the Anabaptists assumed the "supremacy of the New Testament" over the Old Testament, sought to find a healthy balance between the Inner and the Outer Word, and "tried to obey the commands of Christ and teachings of the New Testament literally."[1]

In the decades that have followed Bender's article, Anabaptist scholarship has undergone a significant transformation. If Bender and his generation focused primarily on Zurich and the Grebel circle as the birthplace of the movement, more recent studies have demonstrated that legitimate claims for Anabaptist origins might also be made for the followers of Melchior Hoffman in the Low Countries or the converts of Hans Hut in Central Germany.[2] A field formerly dominated by theologians has since made room for social historians who have inquired into the economic and political context within which the Anabaptist movement took its distinctive shape. And the once comfortable notion of "evangelical Anabaptism" as a clearly-defined, normative standard against which other sixteenth- as well as twentieth-century expressions of faith might be judged, has given way to a view of Anabaptism whose boundaries were much more fluid and dynamic than earlier scholars were willing to concede. But despite the fact that these new emphases and approaches have encouraged a reappraisal of virtually every assumption in the older historiography, it would appear as if the study of Anabaptist hermeneutics has remained relatively immune to these revisionist impulses. While scholarship on Anabaptist hermeneutics since Bender has refined his summary and broadened the scope of inquiry, it has not challenged the premises or the essential content of his conclusions.[3]

This essay will not attempt to overturn the established scholarly consensus regarding the Anabaptist understanding of Scripture. It will, however, suggest that recent trends in scholarship, particularly those prompted by social historians, raise a set of questions for the study of Anabaptist hermeneutics that have not yet been fully explored. One consequence of these questions may be a new understanding of the Anabaptist approach to Scripture that is more sensitive to the diversity within the Anabaptist movement, more careful to distinguish between stated principles and actual practice, and more attuned to the broader social, political, and economic context within which discussions about Biblical interpretation occurred.

Anabaptist Hermeneutics: The Traditional Interpretation

Anabaptism took shape within the broader contours of the Protestant Reformation, a movement of religious and social reform deeply committed to the careful study of Scripture by laity and clergy alike and utterly convinced of the Scripture's authority and relevance in all matters of faith and daily life. Thus, in their insistence that the Bible was the final arbiter of religious debate, the Anabaptists did not differ markedly from other Protestant reformers, even those who quickly denounced them as schismatics and heretics. Rather, Anabaptists parted company with the magisterial reformers on the question of how the truths of Scripture were to be interpreted and applied; the issue, in other words, was one of hermeneutics.

Determining exactly what those distinctly Anabaptist hermeneutical principles were, however, has been made more difficult by the fact that few Anabaptist leaders wrote explicitly on the issue.[4] Indeed, the evidence upon which the traditional interpretation of Anabaptist hermeneutics rests is gleaned from an eclectic set of sources: theological treatises, court interrogations, martyrologies, hymns, transcriptions of disputations, and confessions of faith. But from these various sources a composite picture of hermeneutical principles has emerged.[5] According to the standard scholarly consensus, now almost forty years old, the essential elements of that hermeneutic included the following:

- The meaning of Scripture was clear, even to the unlearned. All points of confusion or apparent contradiction in Scripture could be clarified by Scripture itself, that is, by reference to other biblical passages rather than to private revelation or tradition.

- The life and teachings of Jesus offered an important key to unlocking the mysteries of the written word. All of Scripture, both the Old and New Testaments, needed to be interpreted in a way that was consistent with the revelation of God in Jesus Christ.

- A simple and literal obedience to the clear commands of Scripture, particularly the teachings of Jesus, was inextricably linked to a life of faithful obedience.

- A distinction was to be made between the Old Testament (covenant, promise, warfare) and the New Testament (grace, fulfillment, suffering love). Particularly in their teaching on the oath and the sword, the

Anabaptists granted to the latter an authority superior to that of the Old Testament.

- God speaks both in the Outer (or written) word of Scripture as well as in the Inner (or spiritual) word of revelation. Both are necessary for a proper understanding of God's will, but either one could easily be stressed to the detriment of the other. The Anabaptists sought to balance the Outer word and the Inner word.

- Scripture is best interpreted as a communal process, in the context of a body of believers who, with the help of the Holy Spirit, gather to study God's Word and to discern God's will.

Over the past forty years these basic principles have been restated and amplified in numerous articles and monographs. One particular line of research has focused on the hermeneutics of specific Anabaptist leaders. Overwhelmingly theological in orientation, these studies of such leaders as Menno Simons, Pilgram Marpeck, Peter Riedemann, and Dirk Philips have indeed sharpened the understanding of the hermeneutical nuances within the Anabaptist movement, and they have provided a rich source of illustrations to buttress the general principles noted above.[6]

Other scholars working in a slightly different vein have attempted to refine or reconceptualize the overarching principles of Anabaptist hermeneutics by giving particular emphasis to a specific theme. Thus, for example, John Howard Yoder has helped to popularize the concept of the "hermeneutical community" as a distinctively Anabaptist approach to Scripture. In contrast to both medieval Catholicism and the magisterial reformers, the Anabaptists interpreted Scripture as a communal exercise, thereby denying a prior authority to tradition, formal creedal statements, or the political interests of the state.[7] Taking a slightly different tact, C. J. Dyck and others have written eloquently of an Anabaptist "hermeneutics of obedience," arguing that early Anabaptists refused to separate proper Biblical interpretation from a life of obedience to God's will as revealed in Scripture.[8] Other scholars have highlighted the Christocentric nature of Anabaptist hermeneutics, suggesting that the Anabaptists interpreted Scripture primarily through the lens of Christ's example and His teachings.[9] And one historian has even proposed, not altogether convincingly, that the Anabaptists had a distinctive "hermeneutics of grace."[10]

These various efforts to capture the essence of Anabaptist hermeneutics have much to commend them. As "ideal type" summaries they provide useful analytical categories, particularly for large-scale comparison with other Reformation traditions. Moreover, within contemporary church contexts the principles delineated in these studies may well have a legitimate pedagogical function. But from the perspective of a social historian, such summaries tend to conceal as much as they reveal. In what follows below, I would like to offer a short critique of the traditional scholarly interpretation and sketch briefly by way of conclusion, the outline of a new model for understanding Anabaptist hermeneutics.

The Reality of Anabaptist Diversity

As noted above, much of the traditional scholarship on Anabaptist hermeneutics has approached the topic deductively, compiling numerous quotes from a variety of sources into a composite summary of distinctive principles. But though this deductive approach may be useful in defining a normative Anabaptist ideal, it also creates the impression that the Anabaptists spoke clearly, coherently, and consistently on theological and ethical matters. Such was emphatically not the case. While sixteenth-century opponents of the Anabaptists clearly exaggerated the schismatic nature of the movement, recent studies have made it clear that Anabaptism was a diverse, even fragmented movement, characterized by deep hostility and divisions within and among various groups.[11]

From the perspective of hermeneutics, this diversity becomes interesting from several angles. To what degree, for example, did the distinctive traditions that coalesced during the course of the sixteenth century reflect genuinely different approaches to Biblical interpretation? The history of Swiss Brethren and Hutterites relations illustrates the complexity of the question. According to most accounts, the Swiss Brethren and the Hutterites shared very similar hermeneutical principles. Both were inclined toward literalist interpretations of the New Testament, giving a strong ethical component to their biblical study. Both emphasized the centrality of the visible church, the importance—at least in principle—of communal discernment of Scripture, and the willingness to submit to church discipline. In their theology both stressed a two-kingdom dualism and tended to read Scripture in terms of a cosmic battle between the forces of good and evil. Compared with many other Anabaptist groups, the hermeneutical emphases of the Swiss Brethren and Hutterites were remarkably similar.

Yet ironically enough, these shared hermeneutical principles did little to unify the two groups, either internally or in their relations with other Anabaptist groups. The early history of the Hutterites was dominated by a fiercely-contested struggle for leadership among the Gabrielites, the Philipites, and supporters of Jakob Hutter in which the ban became a partisan weapon, freely employed by all involved in the dispute.[12] Even after internal order was restored among the Hutterites, new sources of antagonism presented themselves, particularly in regards to the Swiss Brethren. Throughout the last half of the sixteenth century relations between the Hutterites and the Swiss Brethren steadily deteriorated as explicit differences over such theological principles as community of goods, war taxes, marital separation, and the practice of church discipline hardened in a series of sharply-worded letters and polemics.[13] To make matters worse, Hutterian missionaries were also gaining numerous converts among the Swiss Brethren. After a large number of Swiss Brethren near Kreuznach left the congregation in 1557 to join the Hutterites in Moravia, the leader of the group—a man named Farwendel—called the Hutterites "a cursed people" and excommunicated himself for not having guarded his flock sufficiently against them.[14] A decade later, Hutterian leaders explicitly charged the Swiss Brethren with apostasy and in the *Chronicle* entry for 1567 suggested that the willful ignorance of the Swiss "will be a judgment on them on the last day."[15]

Clearly in the case of the Swiss Brethren and the Hutterites a shared set of hermeneutical principles did not yield a common mind on a whole set of theological questions, including such crucial matters as ecclesiology, child nurture, mutual aid, and missions. Yet these important differences between the Swiss Brethren and Hutterites, and the hostility which characterized their relations in the sixteenth century, tend to be glossed over or lost altogether in the traditional approach to Anabaptist hermeneutics.[16]

Granted, in one specific area—the question of the Inner/Outer Word—students of Anabaptist hermeneutics have acknowledged a measure of diversity among Anabaptist leaders and have charted a variety of Anabaptist positions, usually along a continuum between a "literalist" and a "spiritualist" approach to Scripture."[17] Here, however, a different kind of conceptual problem arises. For even though the distinction between a literalist and a spiritualist approach to hermeneutics may be helpful in the most general sense, the actual principles of interpretation employed by specific Anabaptist leaders cannot be made to fit neatly along this continuum. Thus, men such as Thomas Müntzer, Melchior Hoffmann, Hans Denck, Caspar Schwenckfeld, and even Hans Hut are all often gathered together under the "Spiritualist" rubric. And indeed, each of them did appeal to the active role of the Spirit in the interpretation of Scripture. But in terms of theological presuppositions and concrete applications, fundamental distinctions must be made, for example, between the revolutionary mysticism of Thomas Müntzer and quietist individualism of Caspar Schwenckfeld, or between the latent apocalypticism in Melchior Hoffman, the irenic ecumenism of Hans Denck, and the eschatological zeal of Hans Hut. While it may indeed be possible to isolate quotations from these leaders to support one or more of the general hermeneutical principles ascribed to the Anabaptist movement, it is clear that the differences among those who favored the "Inner Word" as a hermeneutical principle are at least as striking as their similarities.

Similar examples of intramural hostility and hermeneutical variety abounded in the sixteenth century, yet the general literature on Anabaptist hermeneutics has tended to blur this diversity in the interest of unity and coherence.

Application of Hermeneutical Principles

Even assuming that an Anabaptist consensus on hermeneutical principles persisted despite this diversity in theological orientation, a second closely-related question remains: namely, how—or if—these principles were ever actually implemented in the life of the congregations and communities they served.

Obviously, ideas and convictions can have merit and deserve study quite apart from their embodiment in concrete situations, but from the perspective of a social historian, questions regarding reception and application become particularly relevant. Moreover, it is precisely this point—the congruence between precept and practice—that the traditional historiography has argued distinguished the Anabaptists from mainline reformers. To pose the question of application, after all, is only to apply the same standard to the Anabaptists that students of the Anabaptist movement have applied critically to Zwingli and the other reformers. A few examples serve to illustrate the broader point.

First, how consistently did the Swiss Brethren—or any other Anabaptist group—actually implement the ideal of a "hermeneutical community"? Much has been made of the fact that the Brotherly Union composed in 1527 at Schleitheim appears to have emerged out of intense communal discussion, and a similar process may well have governed proceedings at Augsburg in the same year and in 1527 at Teufern.[18] But what is the evidence that after 1530 this mode of interpretation actually became an established principle in the life of Swiss Brethren congregations, or that it was ever a common practice in the various other Anabaptist traditions? Menno himself certainly does not seem to have practiced this principle very consistently, despite several passages in his writings that point to the communal discernment of Scripture as an ideal. And in the most communal of all the Anabaptist groups—the Hutterites—the principle of the "hermeneutical community" was almost immediately qualified by the emergence of a powerful hierarchy of communal leadership and a very high regard for the authority of tradition in Biblical exegesis. The point here is not to deny that the principle of the "hermeneutical community" found expression among the Anabaptists but rather to ask how this ideal actually worked itself out in practice. Clearly, this is an area calling for more research.

Secondly, the life and thought of Balthasar Hubmaier poses a related question regarding the connection between precept and practice. Hubmaier was a well-educated man, probably the most accomplished theologian of Anabaptism in the first generation. Moreover, on the question of hermeneutics, Hubmaier offers a gold-mine of quotations to support the traditional consensus view on Anabaptist hermeneutics. It was Hubmaier who argued most vigorously for the principle of the hermeneutic community, insisting that the honest, spirit-inspired reading of Scripture by simple lay folk offered a better understanding of the will of God than the scholarly treatises of the learned.[19] Until recently, however, Hubmaier himself was virtually written out of the canon of acceptable Anabaptist leaders, in part because he defended the use of violence by Christian magistrates, an anathema to the "evangelical Anabaptist" position. How can it be that someone who espouses the "correct" Anabaptist hermeneutical principles be led to conclusions that were only "marginally" Anabaptist? Without addressing the question of Hubmaier's proper place within the Anabaptist pantheon, the apparent gap between Hubmaier's hermeneutical premises and his theological conclusions seem to merit more reflection.

Thirdly, what are we to make of the claim that the Anabaptists, in contrast to their Protestant counterparts, followed the commands of Scripture "literally"? In the sixteenth century, the claim was put in its most explicit form by the Swiss Brethren in Zurich, who refuted Zwingli's defense of infant baptism with the claim that the true Christian did only those things explicitly commanded in Scripture.[20] The principle found its most extreme—and presumably consistent—expression in the 1520s when a group of Swiss Anabaptists in Appenzell allegedly played childrens' games in the streets in obedience to Christ's injunction that "unless you become as children you cannot inherit the Kingdom of God."[21]

But a milder and more common version of Anabaptist literalism has focused on the question of ethics and obedience to Jesus' teachings: in Hans Denck's famous phrase, the only way one could truly know Christ was to follow Him in life. And, according to the traditional consensus, the Anabaptists did exactly that.

This notion of a literalist understanding of Scripture, however, is problematic at several different levels. In the first place, by suggesting that the Anabaptists moved directly from scriptural imperative to ethical action—without any intermediate cognitive reflection—the claim represents a virtual denial of hermeneutics. If it were indeed true, then the Anabaptist hermeneutic should consist of this point alone, since all other reflection on the matter would be superfluous. Moreover, notwithstanding the heroic witness of the martyrs, the claim to literalism is simply not historically correct. In the course of their daily lives, the Swiss Brethren engaged in numerous activities that were not "directly commanded" by Scripture. Zwingli's exasperation with the Brethren on this point is fully understandable.

But the most important problem with the claim to a literal obedience to Scripture is that it masks the creative way that various Anabaptists groups did indeed interpret difficult passages of Scripture and the means by which particular interpretations were defended and reinforced. Almost simultaneous with the beginnings of the movement, a whole range of extra-Biblical resources appeared among the various Anabaptist groups which served to orient Anabaptists engaged in Biblical study as a kind of "canon within the canon." In addition to oral traditions—which are the hardest for the historian to identify—these resources included letters, confessions of faith, accounts of disputations, concordances, martyr stories, apologetical writings, and a rich tradition of hymnody, all of which had a decisive effect on the shaping and reinforcing of distinctive hermeneutical traditions within the Anabaptist movement. An insistence on Anabaptist literalism as a principle separating them from Catholics and Protestants overshadows the ways in which elements of tradition, creed, charisma, and the authority of office also shaped the Anabaptist reading of Scripture in decisive ways.

Social-Historical Context of Anabaptist Hermeneutics

Finally, in a closely-related vein, a strong emphasis in the traditional interpretation of Anabaptist hermeneutics on theological concerns has minimized—if not altogether ignored—considerations of how an Anabaptist reading of Scripture might have been shaped by the particular social, political, or economic context of its readers. The point here is not to rehearse the complex philosophical discussion of historical causation (idealism vs. materialism) or to suggest that the interpretation of Scripture is solely a function of one's cultural-social setting (*der Sitz im Leben*). But our understanding of Anabaptist hermeneutics would be enriched if greater consideration were given to the various contexts within which the Anabaptists read the Bible.

At a rather mundane level, one might begin by asking a textual question: what versions of the Bible were available to the Anabaptists? Which did they prefer and why? Historian Werner Packull has recently suggested that the Swiss Brethren emphasis on the New Testament in their formative years in Zurich might be explained by the simple fact that until 1529 the entire Old Testament was not widely available in the vernacular for lay bible study. Since for five crucial years the New Testament was the only Scripture easily accessible to the fledgling Swiss Anabaptist group, it should come as no surprise, claims Packull, that they gave it pride of place in the formation of their theology.[22] Packull's suggestion that the New Testament orientation of the Anabaptists was a kind of historical accident, determined more by the history of print than by theological conviction, is not entirely convincing. But his argument does raise important questions for the study of Anabaptist understanding of the Bible. In a similar way, Arnold Snyder has insightfully reminded us that early modern Europe was an oral—and, one could add, a visual—culture much more than a print culture. Thus, many Anabaptists first encountered Scripture through the spoken word—sermons, disputations, discussions—rather than the written word, and in a communal context of conversation and debate rather than as individuals engaged in silent reading and study.[23] How did the predominantly oral setting of sixteenth-century Bible study shape Anabaptist understandings of Scripture?

At another level, the study of Anabaptist hermeneutics must take more seriously the interplay between theological principles and the specific social, economic and political realities within which these principles found expression. More than two decades ago, J. F. Goeters called attention to the importance of the tithe in the countryside around Zurich and the economic frustration that lay behind the Anabaptist rejection of the tithe as unbiblical.[24] Martin Haas and others have argued that the Swiss Brethren understanding of separatist church as expressed in the Schleitheim Confession of 1527 emerged more as a practical response to the failure of the Peasants War than as a faithful application of Scriptural studies.[25] Hans-Jürgen Goertz has recast the entire Anabaptist movement—including the principle of the "priesthood of all believers"—within the context of late medieval anti-clericalism.[26] James Stayer has written insightfully on the various settings within which different Anabaptist understandings of mutual aid and the community of goods emerged.[27] And Werner Packull has noted striking similarities between the reform program and leadership of the early Anabaptist movement in Switzerland and the abortive Peasants' War of 1525.[28]

Again, the point here is not to suggest that Anabaptist hermeneutics were merely a reflection of material forces or pragmatic considerations, but it is also clear that Anabaptist theology did not emerge directly from Scripture. While the importance of context has long been acknowledged in broader Anabaptist historiography, its implications for Anabaptist hermeneutics largely remain to be drawn. A deeper appreciation for context would go a long way to explain the consolidation of different traditions within Anabaptism and the particular means by which these traditions were legitimated.

Conclusion

Is there a "distinctively Anabaptist" hermeneutic?

I have suggested here that many of the traditional assumptions regarding an Anabaptist hermeneutic may need to be reconsidered in light of recent scholarship on the Radical Reformation. The Anabaptist movement was clearly more diverse than the composite summary of hermeneutical principles would imply; it is not at all clear that the principles articulated by various leaders were actually implemented in particular congregational settings, and more attention needs to be given to the dynamic interaction between theological principles and the social, political, and economic contexts within which particular traditions emerged.

In light of this critique, what then can be said of an Anabaptist hermeneutic? What, if anything, was distinctively "Anabaptist" about their interpretation of Scripture? Is there any hope of defining Anabaptism in terms of a specific set of theological doctrines or ethical practices? An appropriate response to such questions will not be found, I think, in the distillation of yet another set of principles, now even more general and abstract to accommodate the reality of diversity within the movement. But neither would it be appropriate to reject out of hand the "ideal type" summary established by the traditional scholarship. Instead, drawing on the basic themes of the traditionalist summary I would like to suggest a new model for understanding Anabaptism—particularly as it coalesced during the last half of the sixteenth-century—and the place of hermeneutical principles within the movement.

I begin with an insight taken from historian David Sabean's work on village culture in early modern Germany. Sabean challenges the traditional scholarship on rural communities that—like Anabaptist scholarship—has tended to define community in structural, functional, or normative terms.[29] While not denying the relevance of these approaches, Sabean argues that in the end, rural communities in early modern Germany were not united by a specific set of shared values, the familial bonds of love, or even a clear sense of corporate purpose. Rather, communal boundaries were defined by the fact that "members of the community [were] engaged in the same argument, the same *raisonnement*, the same *Rede*, the same discourse, in which alternative strategies, misunderstandings, conflicting goals, and values are threshed out."[30]

What Sabean envisioned for studies of village life in early modern Germany may also be instructive for a clearer understanding of the Anabaptist movement and the various expressions it took in the late sixteenth and seventeenth centuries. If he is correct, the Anabaptist use of Scripture can be described best not as a set of fixed, normative hermeneutical principles, but rather as a series of arguments or debates into which participants were drawn precisely because they agreed on the importance of the issue being debated. The summary of Anabaptist hermeneutics compiled by the traditional historiography is helpful, therefore, in that it points toward a frame of reference within which discussions and disagreements regarding proper Biblical exegesis took place.

But these principles were salient not because they resolved all exegetical questions. To the contrary, embedded within each of the basic hermeneutical principles were fundamental tensions—in some cases outright contradictions—that led almost inevitably to disagreement and debate and to varying understandings as to how these tensions might be resolved.

The ideal of the "hermeneutical community" serves as a useful illustration. The notion that Scripture should be interpreted by a gathered body of earnest Christians was a powerful concept, but it was (and is) also inherently problematic. In actual practice, it inevitably raised a host of unanticipated questions. What, for example, was the role of the trained expert within the congregation who brought knowledge of the Biblical languages and historical or contextual insights into the discussion? What prevented the hermeneutical community from degenerating into a "least common denominator" approach to Scripture in which lay people simply pooled their ignorance? How was authority to be legitimized within the hermeneutical community? What was the place of charismatic leadership? How was tradition integrated into the active process of discernment? Who decided when consensus had been reached? All of these questions, and many more, quickly belied the notion that communal interpretation was merely a question of discussion and agreement. And the fact that these questions could be answered in a variety of ways accounts, at least in part, for the diversity that characterized the Anabaptist movement from the very beginning.

Nevertheless, even though by the end of the sixteenth century the principle of the "hermeneutical community" was not an explicit theological theme among any of the various Anabaptist groups and even though routine Bible study along this model does not seem to have been fully integrated into local congregation life, the ideal of congregational involvement in the process of spiritual discernment persisted, and it continued to echo among the varied descendants of the Anabaptists throughout the seventeenth century and beyond as a focus of debate, renewal, and even as a principle of unity.

Frequently the debate over the role of the local congregation in scriptural interpretation found expression in questions related to church discipline. Most Anabaptist-related groups agreed that the authority to "bind and loosen" implied some sort of congregational process of discernment regarding acceptable doctrine and practice. Yet practical considerations of *what* constituted disciplinary offenses, *where* the authority to excommunicate actually rested, and *how* church discipline should be implemented became the focus of a long series of acrimonious divisions. In 1557, for example, representatives from various German and Dutch Anabaptist groups gathered at a conference in Strasbourg to debate the issue. But when the group refused to adopt Menno's hard-line position on spousal shunning and called for greater congregational involvement in matters of church discipline, Menno and his followers responded by excommunicating the entire German fellowship.[31] Soon thereafter, echoes of the same disagreement found local expression in the Netherlands when the so-called Waterlanders broke with Menno and other more conservative leaders over the issue of the ban and the corporate role of congregation in church discipline. Part of the Waterlander dissent was a concern to preserve greater latitude for individual differences and a plurality of theological viewpoints within the congregation.

And the debate over the authority of the congregation refused to die. In the middle of the seventeenth century, congregations in Hamburg-Altona were deeply divided by a renewal movement—known as the Dompelaars—that insisted on baptism by immersion, footwashing, and evening communion with unleavened bread in faithful fulfillment of the literal commands of Scripture. Only a few years later, in 1657, a new and even deeper division wracked the Dutch church when David Spruyt and Galenus Abrahams de Haan at Amsterdam published a series of articles that, among other things, gave lay persons the freedom to preach, teach, baptize, and administer communion. The local debate in the Amsterdam congregation quickly escalated into a vituperative polemical exchange—known to historians as the "War of the Lambs"—that focused on questions related to church membership and the exercise of church discipline. Eventually the Waterlanders themselves split into two opposing groups—the Sonnists and Lamists—a division that persisted for a full century and a half.[32] Nor was the debate confined to the Low Countries. Among the many issues that separated the Swiss Anabaptists from the followers of Jakob Ammann in the so-called Amish Division of 1693 was the question of congregational authority in matters of church discipline.[33]

Clearly, more was at stake in each of these divisions than merely the issue of the hermeneutical community. But the notion of active congregational involvement in biblical exegesis seems to have been a persistent ideal within the groups that descended from the Anabaptists and that ideal continued to provide a source of ferment and renewal in a wide variety of contexts and circumstances.

In a similar fashion, one could look at the latent tensions with the ideals of Biblical literalism, or the Christocentric approach to Scripture, or the "supremacy" of the New Testament over the Old Testament. To the extent that various groups continued to take these principles seriously by debating and discussing them, they were part of a shared conversation that can legitimately be described as Anabaptist. But insofar as each group resolved the apparent tensions or contradictions in different contexts, finding a variety of theological resolutions to the practical conundrums thrown up by the principles, it came to embody a genuinely distinctive tradition whose richness and integrity is often lost by a single-minded focus on normative principles.

To define the Anabaptist use of Scripture in terms of tensions, argument, and debate does not negate the importance or the relevance of the ideal. But it does suggest a more dynamic model for understanding Biblical interpretation that drew the spiritual ancestors of the Mennonites and Brethren into a common conversation, though not always a common mind.

[1] Harold S. Bender, "Bible," *The Mennonite Encyclopedia: A Comprehensive Reference Work on the Anabaptist-Mennonite Movement* 4 vols. (Hillsboro, Ks.: Mennonite Brethren Publishing House, 1955-1959), I, 323.

[2] The classic article on this point is James M. Stayer, Werner O. Packull, and Klaus Deppermann, "From Monogenesis to Polygenesis: The Historical Discussion of Anabaptist Origins," *Mennonite Quarterly Review* 49 (April 1975): 83-121.

[3] See, for example, the articles collected in Willard Swartley, ed., *Essays on Biblical Interpretation: Anabaptist-Mennonite Perspectives* (Elkhart, Ind.: Institute of Mennonite Studies, 1984).

[4] The main exceptions are Pilgram Marpeck, whose "Testamenterläutterung," an 800-page manuscript, focused extensively on the relationship between the Old Testament and the New Testament. See also J. C. Wenger, "An Early Anabaptist Tract on Hermeneutics," *Mennonite Quarterly Review* 42 (January 1968): 26-7; and Stuart Wood Murray, "Spirit, Discipleship, Community: The Contemporary Significance of Anabaptist Hermeneutics" (Ph.D. diss.: Oxford, The Whitefield Institute, 1992), 27-30, which speaks to the problem of sources for the study of Anabaptist hermeneutics.

[5] For some of the standard summaries in addition to Bender, see J. C. Wenger, "The Biblicism of the Anabaptists," ed. Guy F. Hersberger, *The Recovery of the Anabaptist Vision* (Scottdale, Pa.: Herald Press, 1957), 167-79; Walter Klaassen, "Anabaptist Hermeneutics: Presuppositions, Principles and Practice," in Swartley, *Essays*, 5-10; John H. Yoder, "The Hermeneutics of the Anabaptists," *Mennonite Quarterly Review* 41 (October 1967): 291-308; Bruno Penner, "The Anabaptist View of the Scripture," (Th. M. Thesis: Bethany and Mennonite Biblical Seminaries, 1955); and Henry Poettcker, "Anabaptist Mennonite Hermeneutics in the 16th century," ed. C. J. Dyck, *The Witness of the Holy Spirit: Proceedings of the 8th Mennonite World Conference* (Elkhart, Ind.: Mennonite World Conference, 1967), 363-71. Murray, *Spirit, Discipleship, Community* provides the most recent and most exhaustive survey of this general position.

[6] See, for example, Henry A. Poettcker, "The Hermeneutics of Menno Simons: An Investigation of the Principles of Interpretation Which Menno Brought to His Study of Scripture" (Th.D. Diss.: Princeton Theological Seminary, 1961); William Klassen, *Covenant and Community: The Life, Writings and Hermeneutics of Pilgram Marpeck* (Grand Rapids, Mich.: Eerdmans, 1968); Robert C. Holland, *The Hermeneutics of Peter Riedemann, 1506-1556* (Basel: Friedrich Reinhart Kommissionsverlag, 1970); Douglas H. Schantz, "The Ecclesiological Focus of Dirk Philips' Hermeneutical Thought in 1559: A Contextual Study," *Mennonite Quarterly Review* 60 (April 1986): 115-27.

[7] Yoder, "Hermeneutics," 21, claims that it is "a basic novelty in the discussion of hermeneutics to say that a text is best understood in a congregation." This is also a central theme in much of Yoder's other work. See especially, "The Hermeneutics of Peoplehood," *The Priestly Kingdom* (South Bend: Notre Dame University Press, 1984), 15-45.

[8] C. J. Dyck, "Hermeneutics and Discipleship," Swartley, *Essays*, pp. 29-44; see also the insightful reflections on this same theme by Ben Ollenburger, "The Hermeneutics of Obedience: Reflections on Anabaptist Hermeneutics," Swartley, *Essays*, 45-61.

[9] See, for example, Walter Klaassen, "The Bern Debate: Christ the Center of Scripture," *Mennonite Quarterly Review* 40 (April 1966), 148-56; and Murray, *Spirit, Discipleship, Community*, 104-47. The Christocentric theme is especially strong in the writings of Menno as, for example, "All the Scriptures . . . point us to Jesus Christ that we are to follow him," *Complete Works*, 749.

[10] Alvin J. Beachy, *The Concept of Grace in the Radical Reformation* (Nieuwkoop: DeGraaf, 1977), 129; for a critique of Beachy's work on this point, see Murray, *Spirit, Discipleship, Community*, 278-80.

[11] Even by the end of the sixteenth century, when many of the fringe or splinter groups had withered away, there were still at least five distinctive groupings within Anabaptism, each shaped by its own history of origin, leadership, socio-political context and emerging traditions. These groups would include the Swiss Brethren, the Hutterites, the Waterlanders, North Germans, and Flemish (followers of Menno).

[12] Werner O. Packull, *Rereading Anabaptist Beginnings* (Winnipeg, Manitoba: CMBC, 1991), 59-78.

[13] Leonard Gross, *The Golden Years of the Hutterites* (Scottdale, Pa.: Herald Press, 1980), 164-93.

[14] The story comes from Claus-Peter Clasen, *Anabaptism: A Social History, 1525-1648* (Ithaca, N.Y.: Cornell University Press, 1972), 40; this apparently is not the complete story since Farwendel ended up joining the Hutterites; *see Golden Years*, 166, and "Farwendel," The *Mennonite Encyclopedia:* II, 313.

[15] *The Chronicle of the Hutterian Brethren* (Rifton, N.Y.: Plough Publishing House, 1987), 394.

[16] And the acrimony was not only bilateral. In the 1540s, Pilgram Marpeck—often regarded in the popular historiography as a model of moderation—had an angry exchange with the Swiss Brethren at Appenzell during his tenure as pastor in Graubünden after which the two groups refused to recognize each other as congregations of God. According to Clasen, *Anabaptism*, 38-9, Marpeck later went on to denounce the Swiss Brethren and Hutterites as "two harmful and destructive sects," and his followers in Moravia—the so-called Pilgramites—formally excommunicated the Hutterites.

[17] But they have tended quickly to dismiss the extremists, particularly the spiritualist "fringe" in favor of particular efforts to mediate between the two extremes, especially that of Pilgram Marpeck.

[18] In the last case, a group of some forty Anabaptist leaders rejected the claims of Augustine Bader to have been called to a special position in the kingdom of God.

[19] See especially Hubmaier's "Theses Against Eck," eds. H. Wayne Pipkin and John H. Yoder, *Balthasar Hubmaier: Theologian of Anabaptism* (Scottdale, Pa.: Herald Press, 1989), 49-57.

[20] Leland Harder, ed., *The Sources of Swiss Anabaptism* (Scottdale, Pa.: Herald Press, 1985), 314, and especially Zwingli's exasperated response on 318-9.

[21] The story, perhaps apocryphal, is told in Johann Kessler's *Sabbata*, a contemporary chronicle of the Reformation in St. Gallen and the surrounding countryside.

[22] Werner O. Packull, "Swiss Anabaptist Biblicism Revisited or The Forgotten Factor in Swiss Anabaptist Biblicism: The Availability of Scripture" (unpublished paper read at the SCSC conference, Atlanta, Ga., October, 1992). The first Zurich edition of the New Testament in the vernacular appeared in 1524.

[23] Arnold Snyder, "Word and Power in Reformation Zurich," *Archiv für Reformationsgeschichte* 81 (1990): 263-85; see also Snyder's "Biblical Text and Social Context: Anabaptist Anti-clericalism in Reformation Zurich," *Mennonite Quarterly Review* 65 (April 1991): 169-91.

[24] J. F. Gerhard Goeters, "Die Vorgeschichte der Täufertum in Zürich," eds. Luise Abramowski and J.F. Goeters, *Studien zur Geschichte und Theologie der Reformation* (Neukirchen: 1969), 239-81.

[25] Martin Haas, "Der Weg der Täufer in die Absonderung," ed. Hans-Jürgen Goertz, *Umstrittenes Täufertum* (Göttingen: Vandenhoeck & Ruprecht, 1975), 50-78.

[26] Hans-Jürgen Goertz, *Die Täufer: Geschichte und Deutung* (München: Beck, 1980).

[27] James Stayer, *The German Peasants' War and Anabaptist Community of Goods* (Montreal: McGill-Queens University Press, 1991).

[28] Werner O. Packull, "The Origins of Swiss Anabaptism in the Context of the Reformation of the Common Man," *Journal of Mennonite Studies* (1988): 36-59.

[29] David Sabean, *Power in the Blood: Popular Culture and Village Discourse in Early Modern Germany* (London: Cambridge University Press, 1984). Structural approaches to community studies usually focus on formal group organization, emphasizing legal and sociological definitions; functional approaches tend to highlight the exercise of authority, particularly in the distribution of power and resources; normative approaches emphasize theological or ideological principles as an organizing theme.

[30] Sabean, *Power*, 13-36.

[31] It is interesting to note that the South Germans, who were excommunicated by Menno and never personally under his influence, preferred to use his name as their group identification, while the Dutch, who were Menno's immediate followers, finally rejected it in favor of Doopsgezinden.

[32] The best account of these events is still B. C. Roosen, *Geschichte der Mennoniten-Gemeinde zu Hamburg und Altona* (Hamburg: 1886), 39-55.

[33] This theme could also be traced in the question of lay pastorate and debate over seminary training.

2

The Anabaptist Use of Scripture: Contemporary Applications and Prospects

by Willard Swartley

*From the Anabaptists we learn little of value
for the contemporary use and interpretation of Scripture.*

*From the Anabaptists we learn almost all we need to know
about the contemporary use and interpretation of Scripture.*

Are both these statements true? I think they are, but each is true in respect to different dimensions of the use of Scripture. If the topic is technique and method, then the Anabaptist contribution has limited value. If, on the other hand, the focus is on understanding the nature and function of Scripture and the church's use of it, then the second statement is true. To test these dual claims—and I have heard both in different settings and from different people—I assessed the twenty-two learnings resulting from my hermeneutical case study, *Slavery, Sabbath, War and Women*. The score runs twelve to the Anabaptist credit, and eight learnings deriving from other sources to which Anabaptism does not directly contribute. We shall return to this matter later.

John Roth reminds us of the necessity to distinguish between a selective use of Anabaptist sources that serves our theological or churchly edification and the more precise historical analysis of the sources for the purpose of scholarly investigation and description. In the former approach, the goodies in Anabaptist thought are creamed from the vast array of perspectives, homogenized, and then set forth as inspirational, even authoritative, for the thought and action of contemporary churches which by confession stand in the Anabaptist tradition. In the latter approach, careful attention is given to the polygenesis of Anabaptism and the resultant polyvalent meaning of the movement.[1]

Foundational Convictions

One might question whether the six distinctive features of Anabaptist hermeneutics that Stuart Wood Murray sets forth meet the strictures of this historical, descriptive approach. But it appears that Murray has utilized a wide range of primary sources; he has certainly not confined himself to Swiss Anabaptism, nor to Dutch. Further, Roth himself says that these categories offer a helpful framework to structure discussion and that the new historiography has virtually left untouched the topic of hermeneutics, i.e., the Anabaptist use of Scripture. Even with Murray's work and Lydia Harder's recent Masters thesis on "Hermeneutic Community: A Study of the Contemporary Relevance of an Anabaptist Approach to Biblical Interpretation,"[2] I suspect that there are lacunae in the research to be done.

Several pages of reflection on Menno's use of Scripture in an article by Ben C. Ollenburger on another, but related, subject have tipped me off in this hunch. Ollenburger compares how Scripture functions for several contemporary theologians—Kaufman, Tracy, Farley—and then points out striking correlation between George Lindbeck's "intratextual" proposal and Menno's use of Scripture. In Menno's "Meditation on the Twenty-Fifth Psalm" or "The Cross of the Saints,"[3] it is clear that Menno understood himself and his experience through or by means of the Scripture. Menno does not seek to understand the text on the basis of his experience, but he locates and situates himself in the story and the claims of those texts in order to understand himself. He uses "biblical concepts as explanatory instruments."[4] Thus Menno's use of Scripture is "intratextual," i.e., he knows Scripture so well that he can move from his experience to the appropriate text that illumines his experience. Lindbeck, and others today, call for a defining, shaping function of Scripture; by telling its story, we know ourselves through its story and word. Its function is identity-formation. We become intratextual in our self-understanding. This view of Scripture is advocated also by numerous current emphases on narrative study and story-telling, connected with well-known names in diverse fields, including Tom Boomershine, Thomas Groome, Stanley Hauerwas, Hans Frei, George Lindbeck, and David Kelsey.[5]

The extent to which the Anabaptist writers steeped themselves in Scripture is overwhelming. In this sense John C. Wenger correctly speaks of the biblicism of the Anabaptists. As he puts it, "Amazing is not too strong a word, for the fact is that untrained lay brethren often proved more than a match for the Roman Catholic doctors of theology who interrogated them."[6] Clearly, they read and studied Scripture assiduously, with one stating the goal to memorize one hundred chapters of the New Testament. Frits Kuiper contends that "the key for understanding the Anabaptist movement is found in its special form of biblicism."[7] The extent to which Anabaptists formed their thought and speech by means of Scripture is evident throughout their writings but especially in Marpeck's first letter to the Swiss Anabaptists, "Judgment and Decision."[8] Generally, the Anabaptists held that the meaning of Scripture was plain and simple, and scholarly learning only made one clever to avoid its obvious meaning. So Hubmaier says as he begins his defense on "The Christian Baptism of Believers":

Although I do not reject tongues or languages for the exposition of dark passages, still for sun-clear words one needs neither tongues nor lungs. Herewith I beseech and admonish you that you lay hold on the Scripture for that. Judge in your minds and consciences according to the simple Word of God. Let the Word of God alone be peacemaker and judge. Then you will not err.[9]

To aid this phenomenal mastery of Scripture among Anabaptists, several Bible Schools were developed early on (in Zurich and St. Gall). As Ross Bender observes, their reason for learning Scripture was not only to gain knowledge but to be enabled to make decisions correctly in order to do God's will. Thus, numerous practical questions drove them to the Scriptures, which they held to be fully authoritative and a sufficient guide for life's questions.[10]

Further, as Murray puts it, the focus of biblical interpretation was ecclesiocentric and oriented to discipleship and mission. Scripture was read in order to understand how the congregation should worship, witness, and act toward each other and "the world."[11]

Because Anabaptists steeped themselves in Scripture in order to derive self-understanding, guidance, and empowerment, they naturally used Scripture for those functions that the text itself suggests. Indeed Anabaptism demonstrates an uncanny ability to blend the first and sixteenth-century horizons. The text lives in them; they live in the text.

I propose two fundamental convictions about Scripture that characterize Anabaptist use, despite their polygenetic origins and character. First, Scripture is true and powerful—able to demolish strongholds and perform the work of regeneration in the believer's life. Any cursory reading in primary sources leaves this overwhelming impression. For example, Felix Mantz' "Petition of Defense" (Zurich) asserted that

the eternally true word of God will sing in the heart of each one that this is the truth, whether he be against it or not. [I] do, however, know for sure that if the only Word be allowed to speak for itself freely and simply, no one will be able to withstand it, and that God will bring to naught the devices of the ungodly.[12]

Menno is equally clear that Scripture is true and powerful, able to perform the work of regeneration within the believer's life.[13]

This confidence in Scripture confronts our contemporary disposition to relativity, the denial of ruling truth.[14] I do not use the word "objective" because that is a post-sixteenth century odyssey in intellectual thought. Rather, the Anabaptists' view of truth, which they shared to a considerable extent with the other Reformers, was that Scriptural truth was power that could effect change and calls humans to submission, obedience, and discipleship. From this perspective, *Gelassenheit* is empowerment. And even though Anabaptists disagreed among themselves (see note 1), they did not question the authority or adequacy of Scripture. Underneath differences in understanding was the conviction held by all that God's Word is true, powerful, and empowering. Second, this primary conviction sustained the Anabaptists amid persecution and suffering, especially for the sake of practicing true baptism and, for most, eschewing the use of the sword, the weapon of worldly power.

Searching for a Hermeneutical Grid in the Anabaptist Use of Scripture

The first part of this paper makes observations about "first order" use of Scripture, i.e., how it functions at the reflexive life-giving level. Most work done on the Anabaptist use of Scripture, however, describes "second order" use, the reflective, conceptual level, which for Anabaptism grew out of debates and efforts to explain their self-assured identity via Scripture.

In reflecting on the hermeneutical principles that Murray contends are distinctive in Anabaptism, I am astounded at the degree to which contemporary hermeneutical discussion is discovering, as if anew, these cardinal marks of Anabaptist hermeneutics. But there is a problem in projecting these "distinctives" as normative of Anabaptism in light of current analyses (e.g. John Roth's essay) regarding the diverse, polygenetic nature of Anabaptism. On this point, however, New Testament scholarship can give fruitful models for analysis, since it is commonplace to acknowledge wide diversity in New Testament thought. In his forthcoming book, *Use of the New Testament for Contemporary Ethics*, Richard Hays proposes that four interacting routes—rules (moral law); principles or ideals; analogies in thought or situation; or symbolic world analyses—traverse the bridge. While modern Anabaptists could use this model to guide them in utilizing Anabaptist writings, it is more appropriate to examine sixteenth-century Anabaptist writings to see if they reflect this model at work.

At another level, Hays' proposals are more immediately useful. He proposes that contemporary ethical use of Scripture must engage in a fourfold type of study of the documents—descriptive, synthetic, hermeneutical, and pragmatic—and in that order, though first and second stage work and perception may be altered by latter stage work and action. This approach provides a way to do scholarly descriptive work, provided we follow through to the pragmatic, i.e., how it is lived out in life, without sabotaging a fundamental Anabaptist commitment that forbids scholarly analysis for its own sake, detached from ecclesial accountability.

Further, Hays' work at the synthetic level is instructive for our appropriation of the Anabaptist phenomena as well. He argues that the New Testament, even amid its diversity, gives three focal images that function as a valuing grid for the diversity. These images are community, cross, and new creation. Those emphases that accord with these images derived from a synthetic analysis of the descriptive material are to be regarded normative and the basis for the hermeneutical task. Once this is done, then the tradition functions in normative ways for the life of the community.

It is striking that the main title of Stuart Murray's dissertation is "Spirit, Discipleship, Community," a triad of concepts parallel to Hays' synthetic priority grid for New Testament ethics, as follows:

Hays' Synthetic Grid for New Testament Ethics	Murray's Anabaptist Hermeneutic Grid
Community	Community
Cross	Discipleship
New Creation	Spirit

I propose that we look along the lines of this conceptual synthetic grid for the contemporary authoritative function of Scripture in those churches that claim Anabaptist connection.[15]

Perhaps H. S. Bender was almost right after all; intuitively he selected a similar synthetic grid.[16] Discipleship is in all three, though Hays' "Cross" comprises a broader dimension than *Nachfolge*. Community overlaps with what Bender called "a new conception of the church as brotherhood"; perhaps he would now use the term "community" instead of brotherhood. Bender's focus on "a new ethic of love and nonresistance" also overlaps with new creation and Spirit, in that all three designations focus on eschatological newness. Spirit designates the empowerment; new creation, the ontology, which includes the resurrection life, indispensable to Anabaptism; and love and nonresistance, the ethic of new peoplehood. If Murray's work is accepted, it lends credence to Bender's conviction that Anabaptists were biblicists, and that in an astute sense. They were biblicist not in the sense of being simple-minded literalists, but in the sense that they had perceived the indispensable core of New Testament salvational and ethical claims.[17]

A Model for a Contemporary Hermeneutic: Scripture as Truth in Service of Communal, Cross-Formed, New Creation

If the foundation is Scripture, the vision is a "Baptizers' Peace Church" marked by just those components here identified as core for valuing New Testament ethics. Here I develop briefly these three key elements of the New Testament/Anabaptist synthetic model. Then I will suggest what they might mean for modern Anabaptists.

Community: Formation and Maintenance

First, it is important to note that the Anabaptist community was formed by reading the Bible from the perspective of a persecuted, suffering people. Given our contemporary "sociology of knowledge" understandings, we are now able to see that Anabaptists read the Bible through a different lens than did the Catholic or established Protestant churches. Since almost all the New Testament literature was preserved during the first three centuries by a persecuted, suffering church that kept only those writings that were worth dying for, i.e., those that empowered them in their suffering,[18] it is no wonder that the suffering Anabaptists found Scripture to be so powerful in sustaining them in their experience.

The study of the hermeneutics of the poor and oppressed today, reflected by peasants studying Scripture in base communities,[19] provides an analogy to this fundamental characteristic of Anabaptist hermeneutics, though there are essential differences between these movements as well. While the importance of these differences relating to ecclesiology, eschatology, and use of violence cannot be minimized, the common feature of reading Scripture eagerly and intensely for direct guidance on how to sustain oneself and one's community, to act and counter-act, and to envision the future in a situation of oppression and persecution are foundational similarities.

A second aspect of communal identity arises from the Anabaptists' view of the relation between knowledge and obedience. As Denck put it, no one "can truly know except he follow him with his life. And no one can follow him except insofar as one previously knows him."[20] Hence, only the person "who is committed to the direction of obedience can read the truth so as to interpret it in line with the direction of God's purposes."[21] Anabaptists held that obedience and discipleship are necessary to understand Scripture as the Word of God. Irvin B. Horst has described this as an epistemological principle and a distinctive emphasis within the sixteenth century on the nature and method of knowing.[22] An important dimension of this conviction was that obedience to biblical truth applies to all dimensions of life.[23] Their understanding of Scripture requires obedience in the public as well as the private spheres of life. This means refusing to participate in vocations that jeopardize obedient discipleship. Granted, Anabaptists differed in their judgments regarding which public functions were permissible, but the hermeneutical principle was the same.

In a third related area, we have some indication that the Anabaptists maintained their identity through the practice of community discernment in the testing phase of hermeneutical insight. Admittedly, leaders played a key role in perceiving and expositing Scripture; they held that Scripture was plain and that the gathered believers could understand the Scripture. In response to John Eck, Balthasar Hubmaier called for the gathered believers to decide who speaks more clearly the truth of the Scripture. Here, as in other settings, the Anabaptists applied the Rule of Paul (1 Cor. 14:29) which envisioned that all members have something to contribute to the discernment process.[24] John H. Yoder claims, "It is a basic novelty in the discussion of hermeneutics to say that a text is best understood in a congregation."[25] This insight has much in common with current hermeneutical developments in liberation theology and interpretation theory more broadly.[26]

Cross and Discipleship: Core Tests of Faithful Commitment

The Anabaptists believed that all Scripture culminates in the Gospels' story that witnesses to Jesus' life, death, and resurrection power and also calls people to costly discipleship (following the way of Jesus even into suffering). Stuart Murray proposes that while the Reformers used a Christological hermeneutic, Anabaptists practiced a Christocentric interpretation (104-42). The former is oriented to theological doctrine; the latter focuses on orthopraxis, faithfully following the way of Jesus Christ. From this central commitment other distinctive beliefs and practices emerged, particularly the baptism of adult believers and church discipline—"binding and loosing" (Matt. 18:15-18)—in which members were mutually accountable for following the way of Jesus and the teachings of Scripture.

A "Syllabus Locorum" in the front of a Greek New Testament, printed in 1619 in Geneva by Petrus de la Rouiere, indicates that someone or some group, likely of Calvinist Orthodoxy, was able to identify set Scriptures in each of the New Testament books in which Anabaptist interpretation disagreed with both Protestant and Catholic interpretations, which the compiler labeled as "Orthodox." Many of these cited texts are related to topics of kingship and kingdom, the old covenant, and the "hard sayings" of Jesus. This early piece of evidence indicates that the issues of discipleship and the relation between the Testaments lay at the heart of the Anabaptist hermeneutic.

Alongside a Christocentric orientation focusing on faithful discipleship, combined with the other features above, the Anabaptists came to regard the two Testaments differently in respect to their authority for giving direct guidance for life's ethical decisions. Most Anabaptists refused participation in war because of Jesus' teaching of nonresistance and "love of enemy."[27] Due to differences between the testaments in regard to believers' participation in war, Anabaptists regarded the Old Testament, with its pre-Christian practices, as preparatory to the New. The fullness and completeness of revelation in and through Jesus Christ means a new time, a new reality, and a new possibility for living according to God's way. To describe the real differences in time and revelation, Pilgram Marpeck used the images of "summer and winter," "figure and essence." The extent of divine knowledge and saving faith in one time cannot be confused with that of another time. In the Old Testament Christ had not yet come, had not yet died for human sin, and had not yet brought the reality of the kingdom of God. In an 800-page treatise, *Testamentserleuterung*, Marpeck explained and illustrated how the two testaments are to be understood in relation to each other.

Spirit and New Creation

In at least three areas the role of the Holy Spirit was crucial for Anabaptist use of Scripture. First, regeneration was by the Spirit. Anabaptists used new birth language more than justification by faith. Alan Kreider has shown from a study of salvation language in the *Martyrs' Mirror* how central Spirit birth, conversion, and new creature language are to Anabaptist thought.[28] The neglect of this emphasis in the post-Bender Anabaptist scholarship explains the recent effort to redress the balance.[29] Stuart Murray argues also that this aspect, including charismatic phenomena, has been neglected in the research. Prophetic dreams and visions, miracles, and prophetic utterances occur in more than just fringe groups; they are present in some of the main congregations. Marpeck's recounting of martyrdoms also mentions some raised from the dead after they were hanged, drowned, or otherwise killed.[30]

Second, from this foundation of Spirit-empowerment Anabaptist interpretation of Scripture frequently appeals to the Holy Spirit as the source of insight and illumination in understanding Scripture.[31] Marpeck, Menno, Hutter, Denck, and others appeal to the Holy Spirit, who instructs, illumines, and arms with the mind of Christ.[32] Marpeck warns against forcing the Holy Spirit and confusing or masquerading personal desires as the Spirit's leading. Further, instruction by the Holy Spirit far excels learning from books—and this is the root of the Anabaptist suspicion of scholarship.

Third, as in most strong Spirit movements, the issue of the relative place of Spirit and Word, or the way they are related, emerges. Hans Denck, more than most Anabaptists, stressed the primacy of "the inner word," referring to the testimony of the Spirit in illuminating the text and revealing the truth. Thus Denck says, "Holy Scripture I hold above all human treasures but not as high as the Word of God that is living, powerful, and eternal—unattached and free of all the elements of this world."[33] But W. Wiswedel rightly argues that Anabaptists generally regarded the "Outer Word," i.e., Scripture, as authoritative over the "inner Word" of the Spirit.[34] In argument against Spiritualists, Marpeck upholds the primacy of Word over Spirit, the Outer Word over the Inner,[35] but in argument against what he considered legalism among Swiss Anabaptists, Marpeck, as well as other writers, appeals to the Spirit over the letter.[36] On this particular point it is important to recognize significant diversity among the Anabaptist leaders, occasioned often by the context of the argument and the issues put forth by their opponents. G. G. Gerner resolves this tension between these tendencies to both biblicism and spiritualism by proposing that the distinctive feature encompassing both emphases was the Anabaptist "Hermeneutik des Apostolischen, des Gesandt-Seins, des Missionarischen."[37]

In his thorough study of south German Anabaptist hermeneutics, Gerner examines the crucial role that numerous Scriptures carried in relation to key topics: *der Befehl Christi, die Regel Christi* (on this see also E. Schlabach's work), *die Pflanzung Christi und der Brauch der Apostel, und das Gesetz Christi*. In these topics some common strands of emphases recur: *das Wort Christi, der Geist Christi, der Apostel Christi, und der Leib Christi*. The reality of the Spirit and the self-perception of the community as bearers of God's new age are the muscles that make Anabaptism missional.

Meaning for Today

Here again Murray is helpful in that he utilizes his Anabaptist study to address current ecclesial experience and concerns. What does it mean for us to be interpreting communities with identity and boundaries? In the contemporary world when we are witnessing anew the breakdown of church-state alliances, what does it mean to be an unprotected people who through radical discipleship become vulnerable to persecution and suffering? In a missional context in which charismatic churches—the churches of the Spirit—flourish, what does it mean to be a new creation/Spirit empowered people? Here, certainly, links must be made with new emphases on Christian spirituality.

1. It is striking how much the distinctive features of Anabaptist hermeneutic are currently "hot" topics in the broader hermeneutical discussions of today. The Anabaptist emphasis on congregational or community discernment as an essential part of interpretation has many resounding echoes in the current role of community in understanding and living the faith story. Lydia Harder's "Hermeneutic Community"[38] documents well the relevance of this Anabaptist emphasis to broad currents of present-day hermeneutic discussion.[39] Stanley Hauerwas' multifaceted emphases make community an important component of the narrative shaping/character formation complex. Or, consider the emphases of Old Testament scholar James Barr regarding the primary function of community in interpretation, both in recognizing the nature of Scripture's formation and the interpretive task.[40] The Anabaptist emphasis has a potent contribution to make in three contemporary arenas: against the reign of individualism, bolstered by the dominant culture and fortified by currently regnant psychologies; as correction to the chasm that has emerged between scholars and lay people; and as antidote to postmodern emphasis on deconstruction. On the first point, two obstacles listed in the 1977 Mennonite Church statement on biblical interpretation summarize obstacles to faithful interpretation as 1) "Culture and thought so heavily influenced by western individualism that 'private interpretations' become the norm, thus making testing by the community difficult, and 2) final appeal to individual human reason or personal private experience as the judge of truth, hence resisting the role of the community in interpreting the Bible.[41]

The rift between scholars and lay people is a foremost illness of present-day reality, and the Church of the Brethren and Mennonite groups are not immune. Where is the place for testing in the congregation? How does it happen? We do well to look more carefully at the Anabaptist legacy in this regard. As Murray points out, we need to value the scholars, but scholars must see themselves and their work as part of the congregation. Further, we must extend the discerning group into the past, across diverse cultures, and across economic and political barriers.[42] On the point of deconstruction, one need only point out that while we may deconstruct a text to deprive it of "stable meaning," we cannot deconstruct a community shaped by the text. The community is flesh and blood witness. It shows meaning, even if it is not always faithful in its witness to the gospel. It never is nothing.

2. As Murray explicated, the Anabaptist use of Scripture has relevance to both current liberation and radical discipleship movements. Points of overlap and critique exist between Anabaptism and liberation theology.[43] Murray describes what he called a growing worldwide network of radical discipleship which lives out of the Anabaptist vision.

3. The Anabaptist use of Scripture can contribute fruitfully to contemporary charismatic churches. Many have not developed a hermeneutic; some are also vulnerable to autocratic leadership, individualism, or erratic spirit-enthusiasm. The Anabaptist experience of appealing to the Spirit, testing of the prophet, and validating by the community provide much needed perspectives for today's fastest growing churches.

I end this analysis with the problem of a one or two-legged stool. The three components of the Anabaptist hermeneutical grid are also essential to the use of Scripture by modern believers if they are to be a faithful church in the Anabaptist tradition. Perhaps some churches do well on new creation emphasis but neglect cross or community. Or, we might look to Scripture with the cross/discipleship perspective but neglect new creation and Spirit. The challenge for Anabaptists is to keep all three approaches to Scripture before them so that the stool on which they sit is strong. Then, with Menno they can speak of the sure foundation that nothing else can replace. For each of these perspectives provides a complementary dimension of the fullness of Christ, on whom the true church is built.

Conclusion

Having given Anabaptism high marks for its potential contribution to biblical hermeneutics in the twenty-first century, I return to my opening paragraph, which distinguishes between areas in which Anabaptist hermeneutics do and do not contribute. The Enlightenment and today's liberationist and feminist agenda present issues for which there is no straight line from the sixteenth century into our modern era.[44] The numerous qualifiers in my list of eight points to which Anabaptism does *not* contribute shows how precarious this task is. The purpose of this analysis is to be suggestive and not definitive. On the one hand, we must beware that we do not claim too much from a movement that had its own internal differences and for whom biblical study was defined by specific issues in the sixteenth-century socio-political environment. On the other hand, we must not discount their insight and contribution on the basis of these particularities, for analogically we can gain insight from them on contemporary use of Scripture for a particular array of questions, needs, and issues.

Further, there are some hermeneutical fallacies into which Anabaptists and modern interpreters at times blunder, especially over arguing a point on the basis of the evidence. For the humor of the day, I call attention to such in Hubmaier, who to argue against the baptism of children constructs an argument from silence. He says that the people and the soldiers came to John the Baptist and asked what they should do to be baptized, but there is no mention of children coming and asking what they should do. Jesus told the people, "Whoever has two shirts, give to one who has none." If children were also included then we should also read in the text, "The child who has two diapers should give to the one who has none!" [45] How many times in the use of Scripture has the fallacious argument from silence been used, and so often less humorously!

Granted certain limitations of the Anabaptist use of Scripture to our time, this paper nonetheless makes bold claims and broad leaps, intentionally so. As a New Testament scholar with hermeneutic interest in and confessional identity with Anabaptism, I have tried to identify lines of continuity between wider New Testament and theological-ethical discussions and Anabaptist uses of Scripture. I hope it is not an overstatement to say, paraphasing what was said of Queen Esther, you—the Anabaptist use of Scripture—have come to such a time as this—our twenty-first century. You are making a place for our future!

Attachment: Correlation of Anabaptist Use of Scripture With "Summary of Learnings" From My Book, *Slavery, Sabbath, War and Women* (pp. 229-234)

*For each point, the number in parenthesis indicates
the "learning" number from Slavery, Sabbath, War and Women*

I. Points where Anabaptist use of Scripture informs contemporary "learnings."

1. (1-2) Avoid selective use of evidence; seek to take the entire biblical witness seriously. Value plain, "literal" meaning.
2. (6) Factor of social location: learn from the poor, the slave, the disenfranchised, the persecuted, and the oppressed.
3. (7) Consider the influence of church tradition. Here the Anabaptists tended to tilt negatively, whereas the learning also calls for positive evaluation.
4. (8) Sustained reading and study of the biblical text to overcome personal and social resistance to its message.
5. (11) Relationship between the Old and New Testaments is important for biblical interpretation.
6. (13) While Anabaptists said little about contextualizing Scripture to contemporary environment, it emphasized more the second part of this learning, the contextualizing of the culture and the world to the norm of the Gospel.
7. (13-15) Strong missionary orientation heightens authority of the Bible, and utilizes diversity positively.
8. (16) The divine and human dimensions of biblical revelation are not such that they can be materially distinguished as though some parts are divine and others human. Rather, the Bible consists of divine revelation in history.
9. (18) The Bible should be used to address social and political issues in both the church's life and witness. Analysis of one's society should be made from the criteria of Christian values informed essentially by the Bible.
10. (19) The purpose of biblical interpretation is discovery of God's purpose and will for humanity and the edification of God's people. Interpretation stands in the service of obedience and worship.
11. (20) Biblical interpretation is not a private enterprise, but should be tested and validated by the community of faith.
12. (21) The interpreter should regard the community of faith, rather than the society as a whole, to be accountable to the biblical teachings.

II. Points where Anabaptist use of Scripture does not inform "learnings"

1. (4) The interpreter should give priority to theological principles and basic moral imperatives rather than to specific counsel and particular topics when these two contradict. (This could be disputed, because Anabaptist use of Scripture shows some keenness in this regard, but appears not to consistently follow it through as a hermeneutical principle.)

2. (5) Carefully reflect upon factors that influence one's use of Scripture: religious, social, political, economical, and psychological. (There seems to be little evidence that Anabaptists spent time thinking about these issues.)

3. (7) The positive contribution of church tradition (Anabaptists gave little attention to the positive function of tradition as an element of passing on the faith from one generation to another.)

4. (9) The biblical interpreter should recognize the temporal and cultural distance that exists between the world of the Bible and the world of the believer when addressing social issues (however, the Anabaptists did not allow the distance between the text and the interpreter to excuse us from Christian discipleship—a point I make in regard to the significance of this distance).

5. (10) A historical critical method is useful in biblical studies to enable us to respect the distance between the interpreter and the text, allowing the text to speak its distinctive message from the context of its historical and cultural setting.

6. (12) Both diversity and unity of thought are present in the Bible. This point might fit in group I above, because the Anabaptists did recognize considerable diversity between the Old and New Testaments. However, it seems to have not recognized or emphasized diversity within the New Testament, a point recognized in contemporary scholarly work.

7. (17) The more occasional nature of some biblical teaching needs to be taken into account. Specific instruction occasioned by specific problems and needs should not be regarded as timeless prescriptions.

8. (22) Biblical interpretation as co-creation with God (Anabaptists appear to have not reflected upon the awesome role that the interpreter plays, even though they engaged with most vigorous debates with people of other hermeneutical persuasion).

1   In his recent dissertation, "Spirit, Discipleship, Community: The Contemporary Significance of Anabaptist Hermeneutics" (Oxford: The Whitefield Institute, 1992), Stuart Wood Murray develops his description of Anabaptist uses of Scripture in six chapter topics: The Bible as Self-Interpreting, Christocentrism, the Two Testaments, Spirit and Word, Congregational Hermeneutics, and Hermeneutics of Obedience. None of these notions is new; only the extent of analysis and synthesis of primary and secondary material breaks new ground. The part of Murray's dissertation that is substantively new is his last sprawling chapter of 145 pages, "The Contemporary Significance of Anabaptist Hermeneutics." I shall return to his contribution later. I am indebted especially to both his main title and last chapter for my work here.

2   Newman Theological College; Edmonton, 1984.

3   *The Complete Writings of Menno Simons, c. 1496-1561* (Scottdale, Pa.: Herald Press, 1956), 63-86, 579-622.

4   Ben C. Ollenburger, "The Concept of a 'Warrior God' in Peace Theology," ed. Willard Swartley, *Essays on Peace Theology and Witness* Occassional Paper 12 (Elkhart, Ind.: Institute of Mennonite Studies, 1988), 123.

5   See Tom Boomershine, Thomas Groome, Stanley Hauerwas, Hans Frei, George Lindbeck, and David Kelsey.

6   John C. Wenger, "The Biblicism of the Anabaptists," ed. Guy Hershberger, *Recovery of the Anabaptist Vision* (Scottdale, Pa.: Herald Press, 1957), 167.

7   See Willard Swartley, ed., Essays on Biblical Interpretation: Anabaptist-Mennonite Perspectives (Elkhart, Ind.: Institute of Mennonite Studies), 115-6.

8   William Klassen and Walter Klaassen, trans. and eds., *The Writings of Pilgram Marpeck* (Scottdale, Pa.: Herald Press, 1978), 311-61. For Dirk Philip's writings see the thirty-four page "Scripture Index" eds. Cornelius J. Dyck, William E. Keeney, and Alvin J. Beachy, eds., *The Writings of Dirk Philips 1504-1568* (Scottdale, Pa.: Herald Press, 1992), 653-87).

9   See *Hubmaier*, trans. by Pipkin and Yoder, p. 99.

10 Ross T. Bender, "Teaching the Bible in the Congregation," Swartly, ed., *Essays,* 294.

11 See Murray, "Spirit, Discipleship, Community," 359.

12 Felix Mantz, "Petition of Defense," Leland Harder, ed., *The Sources of Swiss Anabaptism: The Grebel Letters and Related Documents* (Scottdale, Pa.: Herald Press, 1985), 314.

13 See Henry Poettcker, "The Hermaneutics of Menno Simons: An Investigation of the Principles of Interpretation which Menno Brought to his Study of Scripture (Th.D. diss.: Princeton Theological Seminary, 1961); and Poettcker, "Menno Simon's Encounter with the Bible," Swartley, ed., *Essays,* 68-9.

14 Rodney Sawatsky's recent article, "The Quest for a Normative Hermeneutic," *Conrad Grebel Review* 11 (1993): 9-12, takes up the matter of relativity as a methodological issue for how the sixteenth-century phenomenon functions for us today. He quotes J. Larwence Burkholder's statement on discipleship: "The Anabaptist conception of discipleship stands for the rejection of all historical relativities" (in G. F. Hershberger, ed., *Recovery,* 137). Both Burkholder and Sawatsky are addressing slightly different issues than the one discussed here. For Sawatsky the issue is a theological hermeneutic of sixteenth-century sources and for Burkholder it is a question of purist ethic. So the issue of relativity has different nuances in different settings of discussion. In this paper, the point is the normativity and authority of Scripture. Because the Anabaptists were settled on that issue and had a clear view of those places where Scripture called them to cross-cut against their social world, they could live out a discipleship that appears to us now to be free of all relativity. But, in actual fact, there were differences among Anabaptists in the living out of the vision, and thus ethical relativity does emerge (see, e.g., "Marpeck's letters to the Swiss Anabaptists," eds. Klassen and Klaassen, 309-68).

15 My hunch is that some congregations of faith and, especially, individuals outside the so-called believers church tradition may actually pick up more on these emphases than those who formally claim to be heirs to the tradition.

16 See "Vision," ed. Hershberger, *Recovery,* 42.

17 I am aware that this appears like a "canon within the canon" approach to scriptural authority. Perhaps it is. I doubt that such can be avoided when one acknowledges that the hermeneutical task is intertwined with theological discernment.

18 See here the theses of William R. Farmer in *The Formation of the New Testament Canon,* co-authored with Denis M. Farkasfalvy (New York: Paulist Press, 1983), 31-41.

19 See the essays by H. Zorrilla, R. Padilla, L. Rutschman, W. Swartley, R. Sider, and J. Driver in D. Schipani, ed., *Freedom and Discipleship: Liberation Theology in an Anabaptist Perspective* (Maryknoll, N.Y.: Orbis Books, 1989), 17-75, 85-111.

[20] Clarence Bauman, *The Spiritual Legacy of Hans Denck: Interpretation and Translation of Key Texts* (Leiden: E. J. Brill, 1991), 113, lines 7-8.

[21] John Howard Yoder, "The Hermeneutics of the Anabaptists, ed. Swartley, *Essays*, 27.

[22] See Irwin B. Horst, Proposition V of Theses, appended to his doctoral dissertation for its defense.

[23] Ollenburger, "The Concept of a 'Warrior God' in Peace Theology, Swartley, ed., *Essays*, 48.

[24] See Ervin Schlabach, "The Rule of Christ Among the Early Swiss Anabaptists (Th.D. diss.: Chicago Theological Seminary, 1977).

[25] Swartley, ed., *Essays*, 20-1.

[26] See Lydia Harder, "Hermeneutic Community: A Study of the Contemporary Relevance of an Anabaptist-Mennonite Approach to Biblical Interpretation" (Th.M. Thesis: Newman Theological College, 1984),

[27] Diversity within Anabaptist hermeneutics must also be recognized on many of the above points. In a few cases the diversity trespasses the limits of basic Anabaptist convictions. Especially in the shift from a nonresistant, peacemaking stance to a dominating, violent position in the city of Münster (1530-36), a deviant hermeneutical strand emerged. Not unlike Marpeck's view that the conduct of God's people must accord with the distinctive time and content of divine revelation, the theological and political perception of the Münsterite leaders (Melchior Hofmann's eschatology and Jan van Leyden's political ideology) shifted from nonresistance to violence because they regarded their time as the endtime, the time of God's wrath to be meted out upon the wicked—and through them as God's agents. Hence this eschatological perception introduced a new hermeneutic, calling for Davidic type kingship, a rule by twelve elders, holy war, the death penalty, and even polygamy. For an analysis of the similarities and differences between the Münsterite hermeneutic and more normative Anabaptism, as well as that of contemporary liberation theology, see Swartley in Schipani, *Freedom and Discipleship*, 68-73.

[28] "The Servant," 12.

[29] See especially Stephen Dintaman, "The Spiritual Poverty of the Anabaptist Vision," *Conrad Grebel Review* 10 (1992): 205-8.

[30] Murray, *Spirit, Discipleship, Community*, 198-200.

[31] See Cornelius J. Dyck, "Hermaneutics and Discipleship," ed. Swartley, *Essays*, 35-8; and Poettcker, "Hermeneutics of Menno Simons," 71-3.

[32] Murray, "Spirit, Discipleship, Community," 206-8.

[33] Clarence Bauman, *The Spiritual Legacy of Hans Denck: Interpretation and Translation of Key Texts* (Leiden: E. J. Brill, 1991), 251; cf. E. J. Furcha, *Selected Writings of Hans Denck: 1500-1527* (Lewiston, N.Y.: The Edwin Mellen Press, 1989), 287; and Walter Klaassen, *Conrad Grebel Review* 3 (n.d.): 142.

[34] W. Wiswedel, "The Inner and Outer Word: A Study in Anabaptist Doctrine of Scripture," *Mennonite Quarterly Review* 42 (1968): 171-91.

[35] *The Mennonite Encyclopedia: A Comprehensive Reference Work on the Anabaptist-Mennonite Movement*, 4 vols. (Hillsboro, Kan.: Mennonite Brethren Publishing House, 1955-59), I, 324-8.

[36] See William Klassen, "Anabaptist Hermaneutics: The Letter and the Spirit," ed. Swartley, *Essays*, 81-7.

[37] Georg Gottfried Gerner, "Der Gebrauch der Heilgen Schrift in der oberdeutschen Täuferbewegung," (Inaugural diss.: Heidelberg, 1973), 138.

[38] See especially 59-161.

[39] Community is also an important criterion of assessment of contemporary "Christian Feminist Biblical Interpret[ers]" (Phyllis Trible, Letty Russell, Elisabeth Schüssler Fiorenza) by Nadine Pence Frantz in her recent doctoral dissertation: "Theological Hermeneutics: Christian Feminist Biblical Interpretation and the Believers' Church Tradition" (Ph.D. diss.: University of Chicago, 1992).

[40] See Swartley, *Slavery, Sabbath, War and Women: Case Issues in Biblical Interpretation* (Scottdale, Pa.: Herald Press, 1983), 216-7; and Swartley, *Essays*, 252.

[41] Swartley, *Slavery, Sabbath, Women and War*, 243.

[42] Murray, "Spirit, Discipleship, Community," 425-30.

[43] See Swartley in Schipani, ed., *Freedom and Discipleship*, 65-9.

[44] See here the articles in *Conrad Grebel Review* 10, (1992), especially Lydia Harder's essay.

[45] In Pipkin and Yoder, 108.

Conversation
೫೫ IV ೫೫

Anabaptist Worship

In a wide-ranging essay that surveys the history of Anabaptist worship, John L. Ruth draws upon sources from Old Order hymns to Harvard Yard to tourists in a Swiss cave. He identifies the main themes of Anabaptist worship as "gathering, preaching the Word, and nurturing church order characterized by obedience, mutuality, and fellowship." Moreover, worship includes an experience of love that participants feel. He urges modern Anabaptists, with their emphasis on comfort, amenities, and worship committees, to compare their worship with the tradition, "when theme was everything," and allow "wiggle room for the Holy Spirit."

Robert R. Miller suggests practical ways to infuse the Holy Spirit and the Anabaptist tradition into corporate worship. He gently suggests that contemporary worship often resembles "a tired old nag pulling a cart" and advocates reinvigoration. Unlike Ruth, he favors worship committees as a fuller expression of the gathered community and suggests greater use of multi-media, the arts, lay preaching and participation, new rituals, and silence in the worship of God.

1
Glimpses of "Swiss" Anabaptist-Mennonite Worship

by John L. Ruth

Growing up worshipping in a rural Mennonite mission congregation in eastern Pennsylvania, I experienced an imitation of the routines of the larger, traditional "Franconia Conference" congregations that had spawned ours. In 1949, at the age of nineteen, I went to a city mission, was ordained a minister there at twenty, and stayed for seven years. We worshipped there with children learning choruses and sang from the *Triumphant Service Songs* of nondenominational derivation. Up to this point I had heard little about an "Anabaptist heritage," although we were certainly living with remnants of it.

Then for several years I attended the Memorial Church in Harvard Yard. It was an intense encounter: hearing the famed George Buttrick preach, trying to bring this all-round eloquence into meaningful relation with the resonance of the store-front mission hall, and looking for some interface between them. We actually heard a whole roster of star preachers at Harvard: Martin Luther King, Jr., James McCracken, Reinhold Niebuhr, Ralph Sockman, Paul Tillich, and so forth. It added weight to the morning to hear President Nathan Pusey, whose portrait had recently graced the cover of *Time*, read the Old Testament lesson. Anticipation rose as the choir sang exquisitely, the New Testament lesson was read, and the preacher stepped into the lectern. People shifted expectantly in their seats, knowing that what followed would be good. And it always was: stimulating, wide-ranging, penetrating, sensitive, *au courant*. I remember some of the sermons over thirty years later. Everything would come off on time and good.

After the benediction, the congregation (usually a full one) disappeared with a rapidity disorienting to someone from a Mennonite background. At an Old Order Mennonite or Amish or Brethren meeting nobody makes a fast move after the dismissal; children sort of drift away, but it takes awhile to get to the end of your bench, and you move out slowly, talking as you go, in clumps. But this Harvard congregation had a habit of evanescing into thin air. As my wife and I didn't move quite that fast, we came back down the aisle last. One of those mornings I heard a yakkity-yak-yak coming from somewhere, sounding as though there was still something going on. Looking into the anteroom I recognized a familiar phenomenon—Mennonites (from the Boston area) "visiting." For them the "service" was not quite over until they had re-established their fellowship, completing the "gathering." It was a pattern that doubtless stemmed back to Anabaptist times and values.

Another unusual moment of worship that I tend to recall occurred among a collection of tourists visiting the "Anabaptist Cave" in eastern Zurich, Switzerland. It's always impressive, to say the least, to stand there and sing "Faith of our Fathers" with sharers of the Anabaptist tradition. So impressive, that my fellow tour-leaders felt we ought to observe "communion" while we were so close to something sacred in our spiritual identity. Not liking the idea of communion as atmosphere, as sort of an added blessing, I at first demurred at some length. I once lived in a New England village where they would throw in communion at the Men's Pancake Breakfast because that was the only time, outside of Christmas and Easter, that the men were in church. By having communion at the Breakfast you could make sure they had the experience without the disturbing intrusion of thoughts on commitment or unity.

With my spiritual training, communion-in-the-cave seemed too cute. It took for granted what Bishop Benjamin Eby of Canada had said in 1840 "must never be omitted": a pre-communion inquiry into the genuine mutual covenant of a congregation. But I finally went along with the idea, as I have with many other things in modern church life, often with some sadness. (The one couple I have married who insisted on having "communion" in their wedding, in a magnificent Gothic church, was the quickest of all to divorce thereafter.) So we had the cave-communion, which was "impressive" and even tear-drawing. So much so, that we were sad to have needed to leave one or two of our elderly group, unable to make the arduous climb to the cave, in the bus. They shouldn't have been left out, someone said, as we reboarded, with the leftover bread and wine, and we paused to "serve" the several elderly participants as well.

As my co-leader took the "elements" up the long aisle to the back of the bus, most of us could not see what was going on. However, amid forty or fifty chattering people a silence descended. All that was audible was maybe the tinkling of bells on the Brown Swiss cows in the adjacent meadow. It got even quieter, and stayed that way, seeming to take a surprisingly long time for them to do whatever they were doing back there. The intensity and duration of the quiet spoke: This is one time when there is no concern about time. This is one time when we won't joke. We can joke about practically anything, even burning martyrs, but we will not joke now, in the presence of the symbols of the Center of our faith. We are including these members because they are just as important as the more athletic youngsters who had the glamour of the climb and the cave.

I think of that studied and profoundly speaking silence as paradigmatic. In comparison with the main ecclesiastical tradition, it was often what the Mennonites didn't have that said something about who they were, or about which they might be inarticulate. The very absence forced one, if one responded honestly, to work at imagining the body and blood of Christ. One participated even when one had no visual evidence; the silence itself told one what was going on. Though one was not the subject of an orchestrated "service," one was intensely present. Of course, the absence was not as extreme as that of the Quakers. We weren't mystical enough for that.

In what way do Anabaptists/Mennonites feel the intensity of a *hoc est corpus meum*? Where for them does the intersection of time and eternity become a sensation? At what holy point in their "liturgy," however informal, does the bell ring? Traditionally, not in overt cascading enthusiasm nor in miraculous breakthrough of expression, whether eloquence or glossolalia. Rather, in the becoming conscious of and the shared sense of the presence and word of Christ in a reconciled and reconciling community.

I'll frame my remarks with two hymns that have been accepted by Mennonites (the second one by Brethren as well)—one from early experience and the other just recently—as crisp expressions of what Christian worship is. Both songs are from the Netherlands. The first is by a Mennonite minister of German origin, writing around 1600, and the other one by a Catholic priest in 1968. In referring to the experience of worship, the first hymn speaks of "this hour," and the second of "this place."

First, Leenaerdt Clock's *Lobsang*, which is still sung across North America today as the second song in every Sunday morning gathering of the Old Order Amish:

German[1]   English[2]

O Gott Vater, wir loben dich   Oh God, Father, we worship you,
Und deine Güte preisen: And celebrate your goodness.

Why?

Dasz du O Herr so gnädiglich,   Which you, O Lord so graciously
An uns neun hast bewiesen.   Anew have shown unto us.

Anew, that is, on three levels: new in Christ, new in the historical renewal of the Christian Church, and new every time we are privileged to gather in Christ's name.

Und hast uns Herr zusammen gführt,   And have together led us here,
Uns zu ermahnen durch dein Wort,   To be admonished by your Word;
Gib uns Genad zu diesem.   Give us grace to receive it.

This is what we have come expecting, in our worship: to be admonished, even warned, according to the Word. It is the encounter with the Word in the gathering that is the keynote.

Öffne den Mund, Herr, deiner Knecht,	Open your servants' mouths, O Lord,
Gib ihn Weiszheit darneben,	And thereto give them wisdom,
sie dein Wort mög sprechen recht,	That they may rightly speak your Word,
Was dient zum frommen Leben,	That leads to righteous living,
Und nützlich ist zu deinem Preisz,	And fitting is to give you praise
Gib uns Hunger nach solcher Speisz,	Give us the hunger for such food,
Dasz ist unser Begehren.	This is our true desire.

What is about to be heard is not going to be academic, theological, or sacerdo-tal; it's about what it means to live right. The very thought that we shall re-ceive such instruction is the joy of the encounter with the Word.

Ob unserm Hertzen auch Verstand,	Give understanding to our hearts,
Erleuchtung hie auf Erden,	Light for our earthly journey,
Dasz dein Wort in uns werd bekandt,	That your Word might be known in us,
Dasz wir fromm mögen werden,	Leading to pious living
Und leben in Gerechtigkeit,	And living in true righteousness,
Achten auf dein Wort allezeit,	Always attentive to your Word —
So bleibt man unbetrogen.	Thus undeceived remaining.

Give us your word so that we may live righteously. I don't know if this sounds more like law to you than grace, but in terms of the author's thought, it is a matter of joy. Joy in the Word, as shared by the congregation. As I shall note later, joy is a recurring theme in the songs of the *Ausbund*.

Dein O Herr ist das Reich allein,	Yours only is the Kingdom, Lord,
Und auch die Macht zusammen,	And also yours the power;
Wir loben dich in der Gemein	We praise you in the fellowship
Und dancken deinen Namen,	And thank your Name together,
Und bitten dich aus Hertzen Grund,	And pray to you from depth of heart,
Wollst bey uns seyn zu dieser Stund,	Abide with us here in this hour,
Durch Jesum Christum, Amen.	Through our Christ Jesus, Amen.

An ex-Amishman tells me that whenever he hears that song sung in the Amish way, he cries. Even though he prefers to be Mennonite rather than Amish, he has the song powerfully recorded on his sensorium. When we listen to such singing, we go through a time-warp. It takes more than a few minutes to decode what is going on there.

The other day I was with a group of Old German Baptist Brethren, often called Dunkers. They always sing before they leave a meeting, and they sing the slow way, though entirely in English. I've gotten to know some of these people through their annual visits to our community, where they revisit American Dunker roots, and I am asked to show them around. As I listened this last time, they sang the old hymn, "Oh God, our help in ages past." When the rhythm seems to call the singers to march forward briskly, they resist until this urge has lost its power to control. Only then, after they have defined the rhythm as one of patience instead of insistence, do they move on in the melody. Similarly, they adapt the tune itself to their own principle. At the end of the clause, "From everlasting thou art God," the original tune pauses on an upward-moving tone (ti) that implies a forthcoming resolution. Instead, these Dunkers bring the tune down to the fifth (sol), where it can rest as an assertion or recognition by itself—"Thou art God"—not needing completion. It doesn't challenge, or leave open, an idea. The melody just comes back down and rests. The effect is one of resignation instead of questioning.

I am not endorsing this tendency to bend tunes and meters to one mood, but I am saying that these Dunkers' doing so makes a palpable statement. One could decode from it residual Pietist and Anabaptist values that, against all chronological and cultural probability, are alive among "Old Order" groups today.

Until recently, little or nothing under the heading of "worship" was listed in the indexes to most books on Mennonite history. Now there's a plethora. For centuries, manner and content of worship were taken for granted by Mennonites, rather than discussed and analyzed. Thus, when as a young minister thirty years ago I was questioned by an Anglican pastor about our way of celebrating the Eucharist, I responded that the form was not an especially interesting topic to us. What we were interested in was whether or not we were seriously prepared to receive communion. I remember his visible disappointment with this answer. While he had come to talk because he was "interested" in the Mennonites, my comment seemed to make him feel that we were not serious about something basic. Perhaps I should have begun by trying to describe what have been termed the "implicit ritualized sacraments and liturgies"[3] of Mennonite behavior in worship.

Significant to this topic are the names American Mennonites have given to their church buildings. Around 1720 those at Skippack, just north of Philadelphia, built what at one point they called a *Vorgader Hausz*. Whatever the correct spelling might have been, there is clearly something of the Dutch language in it. In the Pennsylvania German language that predominated for two centuries, the same idea is clear: *Versammlinghaus*. The central idea is nothing more specific than meeting. It is not even a *Bethaus* (prayer house)—a term sometimes used by later pietistic German Mennonites.

It is certainly not a *Kirche*, a "church." Worldly people go to church. "Church" is where the name of God is used without the covenant of required, cross-bearing discipleship. "Church" is where the government and the faith of Christ are hopelessly hybrided. From "church" comes persecution and trouble. "I haven't been to church for forty years," said one old Swiss Anabaptist woman, "and I don't want to start now." "What would I want in that pile of stones?" asked another. Even today the Amish don't go to a church. But they worship.

On a sign at the little Mennonite "hidden church" at Pingium, Friesland, where Menno Simons first served in the priesthood, are the words "*Mennos*

Vermaning" (Menno's place of admonition). Here again, the meaning is not sacerdotal but functional. People came to this building that wasn't even allowed to look like a church, not to "have a good worship experience," but to be admonished or taught "what leads to righteous living."

In Lancaster County, Pennsylvania, the term long used by Mennonites was "*G'mayhouse*"—Pennsylvania Dutch for the High German *Gemeinde Haus*. This simply means, "Community House," or house belonging to the *G'may*—the congregation or faith community. And, indeed, the Lancaster meetinghouse was primarily a large house, complete with fireplace, table, and even *Küch* (literally, kitchen, but here referring to something like an anteroom). Anything more than this, architecturally, such as a pulpit, raised or not, or steps rising from ground-level to the entrance, was seen as a mark of the "higher churches."

Today's American Brethren and Mennonite church architecture gives a mixed statement—including everything from the Quaker-type meetinghouse to the battlement-towered edifice declaring that Mennonites are now respectably middle-class American Christians along with Methodists and Presbyterians. Words like "sanctuary," "narthex," or "sacred desk" are frequently heard.

The process by which a Mennonite congregation places a cross on the wall behind the pulpit is usually characterized less by a response to Anabaptist emphases than by the initiative of individuals feeling that it is time to look more like a church. The explanation for this change given in one congregation was that the cross had been offered by a man in memory of his recently deceased wife, and no one in the congregation had wished to hurt his feelings by turning down the offer. Much the same explanation was given for the introduction of a steeple on the new "church" of a previously traditional congregation. The head of the building committee had wanted one, and since he had terminal cancer, other members, against their own preference, accepted his plans to place an order with a church architecture firm.

Some Early Statements Relating to Worship

Conrad Grebel's well-known September, 1524, letter to Thomas Müntzer, written in the ecstasy of finding a separate and pure ecclesiology, reacts sharply against institutionalized, formulaic ritual in worship. Grebel sees in the conventional liturgy of his time many "human, unprofitable, and unchristian rites and ceremonies" that are mistakenly felt to be means of obtaining salvation. In the flush of his reaction, he argues that singing should be omitted in public worship: "We find no teaching in the New Testament about singing, and no example of singing." (!) With twisted interpretation, Grebel argues that Paul admonishes Christians to sing (only) "in their hearts." Whatever isn't specifically commanded should be regarded as forbidden, as clearly as if the Scripture said, "Do not sing." Doubtless influenced by some of Ulrich

Zwingli's reformist ideas, Grebel's are an interesting gloss on the radicalness of the Anabaptists' reactions.[4]

At Communion, Grebel goes on, "Only the words of Matthew 26, Mark 14, Luke 22 and 1 Corinthians 11 shall be used: no more and no less. The minister of the congregation (*"der diener uss der gmein"*) shall pronounce them, reading from one of the Gospels or Paul." "Common bread" and "a common drinking vessel" shall be used. "This will eliminate the adoration, and guarantee a true knowledge and understanding of the Supper." "One must eat and drink in the Spirit and in love" and "with joy." "It shall signify to us that we are truly one loaf and one body, and that we intend to be true brothers one with another. But if one should be found who is not minded to live the brotherly life, he eats to his condemnation. He brings shame on the inward bond, which is love, and on the bread, which is the outward bond."[5]

For Grebel, "the supper" is "not a sacrament." Since it is, importantly, an "exhibition of unity," "no one shall receive it alone, neither on a deathbed nor otherwise." It "should be observed often and much, but not "in temples for that creates a false adoration." Interestingly, Michael Sattler also urges that the Supper should be held "as often as the brothers are together."[6]

In all matters regarding church life the controlling principle is to "operate only according to the Word, and draw and establish from the Word the rites of the apostles." These strictures point to a fundamental valuing of the Scriptures as the point of departure for worship: "Use the Word to form the Church of Christ." We are to gather around the Word, which is made flesh. The first baptism of 1525 took place in a Bible study group that was preoccupied with a redefinition of church authority. Soon thereafter, when members of the Blaurock circle in Zurich had been arrested and released, they came together and "spoke so much of God" that they finally "desired the table of God."[7]

The 1527 "Schleitheim Confession" likewise concerns itself not with ritual form but with who may properly participate. Baptism may be given to

all those who have been taught repentance and the amendment of life and believe truly that their sins are taken away through Christ, and to those who desire to walk in the resurrection of Jesus Christ and be ouried with Him in death, so that they might rise with Him; to all those who with such an understanding themselves desire and request it from us.[8]

As for communion, those wishing to participate are not told how it is done, but that they "must beforehand be united in the one body of Christ, that is the congregation of God, whose head is Christ, and that by baptism."[9]

The Confession's author, Michael Sattler, wrote that the congregation "should meet at least three or four times a week, to exercise themselves in the teaching of Christ and his apostles and heartily to exhort one another to remain faithful to the Lord as they have pledged." When gathered, the brothers and sisters should "take up something to read together. The one to whom God has given the best understanding shall explain it; the others should be still and listen, so that there are not two or three carrying on a private conversation, bothering the others. The Psalter shall be read daily at home."

Frivolity, said Sattler, was to be absent from church life.[10] And the effect of gathering/worship would help to clear the air regarding those attending with false motives.

> "I pray God," wrote the milder Pilgram Marpeck, "that he will not allow me to be separated from such a gathering and fellowship of the Holy Spirit, it makes no difference who they are or where they gather in the whole world. I hope to be in their fellowship and to submit myself to the rule of the Holy Spirit of Christ in the obedience of faith.[11]

Still another sober voice from early Anabaptist leaders was Peter Rideman, who wrote: "We have a day of quiet in which to *read the Lord's Word and listen to it*, and thereby revive our heart to continue in the grace of God. We keep the day to *exercise ourselves in the Word of God*."[12]

What we have so far are:
1. Gathering, which itself is a sacrament.
2. Sharing the reading the Word.
3. Explaining and admonishing.
4. Listening and understanding.
5. Accepting the Rule of Christ, which has serious implications for the practice of communion.

A Striking Glimpse of Early Anabaptist Worship

Two governmental reports of a substantial meeting by Strasbourg Anabaptists on July 25, 1545, provide revealing insights into the early Anabaptist mentality. The secret gathering took place outside the city, at night in a woods by the Bruche River at Eckbolsheim.[13]

The first report is rather simple. At the sound of a staff striking a tree, 300 persons emerged from the woods to gather at one spot. After ten p.m. a man rose to preach until one o'clock in the morning. Someone held a light up to the Bible and another went around with a staff keeping people awake. At one point two men were "installed" (*uffgestellt*), one of them, named Barthel, as a *Vorsteher*. After the preaching, the gathering shared a meal.

The second report, by two boys, is more detailed.[14] The boys understood the sermon, "about the Children of Israel both in and outside of Egypt," as an assuring of the gathered flock "that God would do the same with them, the Baptists, as the eternal people [*Volck*], and would root out and destroy all other peoples that were not of their religion (since they alone had the right religion) such as popish, Lutheran, Zwinglian, Philippian." Another theme of the sermon was "the Temple of God from Revelation 11, how that it [extended] *weit und breit* under the whole heavens." What Christ said would be erected on Peter was not "the *Münster* or other stone churches." This was an admonition to the listeners to come away from their regular *gemeinen* into their special *gemein*.

The preacher went so far as to claim "that one could not find God anywhere except in the wilderness and darkness."

A second preacher asked for a light and read the 11th Chapter of Hebrews without much commentary, then rehearsed the story of Zacchaeus as an example of true rather than incomplete repentance.

A third speaker said that Lutheran preaching that Christ died for our sins was deceptive, in effect, since we must "expiate our own sins [*unser selbs eigen sünde büssen*]." In conclusion the preacher warned the flock, "Let no one mis-advise you that we earn nothing with our good deeds."

Although five or six sisters present "wished to be baptized," it was decided not to have this ceremony, since the flock was not entirely present [*nit gar beyeinander gewehsen*]. In this version of what happened,

> They removed one named brother [Barthel] from the deacon's office [*Helfferambt*] and ordained in his place a brother Peter, who shall remain here in the city. . . . There was also one present, named Brother Claus, who desired to return to their *Gemeind*. Him, for a long time, they did not wish to receive again, because he had gone back again to the Lutherans.

Finally they

> began to pray for all their sisters and brothers. And especially for the brotherhoods such as those in Upper Alsace, those in Baden, at Breisach in the Breisgau, and the brotherhood at Metz. . . . Their prayer proceeded with great earnestness, with cries and weeping.

As morning dawned, "a cloth was spread, and beer and bread were laid on it. Some ate, others did not." Interestingly, those attending had brought along the tools of their trade, such as hammers, saws, and hay-forks but no swords or knives. From another source we learn that this helped to allay suspicion as they traveled toward the hidden meeting. Further, if someone complained at the end of the meeting that he had no tools for his trade, a tool or tools would be found for him from among the brotherhood.

While these reports are naive and skewed, they register the main motifs of Anabaptist worship, even from an outsider's point of view. Once again we have gathering, preaching the Word, and nurturing a church order characterized by obedience, mutuality, and fellowship.

A statement of church order drawn up by Alsatian Anabaptists forty years later than the meeting we have just observed continues the original attitudes on worship.[15] While at the Lord's Supper "no fixed rule" need be "observed as to whether the minister shall break and give or each one break"; "no one shall be forced to accept [a particular] usage," or form of the rite. What is important is the preparation of each heart and of the congregation itself. There must be admonition, prior to the observance, so that there will actually be "one bread and one manner of breaking."

The gathering and the conscious observance of "the Rule of Christ" in binding and loosing are a part of the corporate worship. Without that continuing sense of Christ's reconciling us to himself and each other, the worship is incomplete. Therefore, the "rites" include a making visible of church discipline. Although "the kneeling and self-humbling of those who have sinned and return with penitent hearts shall take place in the heart before God," the congregation as a community must experience what is happening. "The actual kneeling in posture shall not be done away with" by the claim that there has already been a subjective, individualistic "experience." It is part of worship to share this visualization. One might observe that at the point when such a visible sharing of deep repentance is considered morbid or punitive, the congregation has shifted from the original Anabaptist emphasis.

The soteriology is acknowledged in placing the reconciliation of the Cross at the center of human experience. Thus in worship, as in other spheres, there must always be a recognition of the difference between covenantal fellowship and neighborly respect. Whereas "brothers and sisters" are to greet each other with a "Lord's Kiss" (*Küss des Herrn*), those who have not been received into fellowship "shall . . . be greeted with . . . the words, 'The Lord help you.'"

Amidst such Anabaptist seriousness, a recurring note that should not be overlooked is that of joy. "My soul rejoices in God" (*Mein Seel freut sich in Gott*) writes Felix Manz before his drowning in 1527. Or, prisoners at Passau in the 1560s begin a corporately written hymn by announcing

Mit Freuden wolln wir singen,	With joy we would be singing
Wie wirs beschlossen hon . . .	As we've concluded here. . . .
Frölich wolln wirs anfangen	Gladly we will begin it
In Fried und Einigkeit. . . .	In peace and unity. . . .

Song #14 in the *Ausbund*:

Die beste Freud aus Gottes Wort	The best joy comes from God's own word
herkomt, und füllet alle Ort,	And fills all lands and places
Hochteutsch und Niederlanden.	High German or Low Countries.
Wer sich dem recht ergeben hat	Who rightly has accepted this
Der wird erfreut in Banden.	Will know true joy in prison.

Song #64 dwells on the joy of "future glory."

Hertzlich thut mich erfreuen	What hearty joy it brings me —
Die Liebe Sommer-Zeit,	The lovely summer-time,
Wenn Gott wird schön verneuen	When God shall be renewing
Alles zur Ewigkeit,	All things eternally.
Den Himmel und die Erden	The earthly and the heavens
Wird Gott neu schaffen gar.	God will make wholly new,
All Creatur soll werden	Creation shall be rendered
Gantz herrlich hübsch und klar.	All glorious and fair.

Also wird Gott neu machen	God will make all things over
Alles so wonniglich,	With such delightfulness
Vor Schönheit wirds gar lachen,	That they will laugh with beauty,
Und alles freuen sich.	And everything rejoice.
Von Gold und Edelsteine	With gold and precious jewels
All Ding wird seyn geschmückt. . . .	All things will be adorned. . . .
Die ewig Zierheit grosz,	The great eternal charm
Man kans mit nichts vergleichen,	Is far beyond comparing
Die Wort sind viel zu blosz.	Mere words are much too plain.
Darum wollen wirs sparen	Therefore we'll not attempt it
Biß an den Jüngsten Tag:	Until the Final Day:
Dann werden wir erfahren	Then we will have experience
Was Gott ist und vermag.	What God is, and can do.
Er wird uns unser Leben,	Then he, our very living,
Den Leib mit Haut und Haar	The body, skin and hair,
Gantz völlig wieder geben,	Will fully restore to us,
Das ist gewiszlich wahr.	This certainly is true.
Uns Leib und Seel verklären	Transfigure soul and body
Schön hell gleich wie die Sonn,	As bright as is the sun,
Nach Lust wie wirs begehren,	According to our longing,
Uns geben Freud und Wonn.	And give us joy and bliss.
Da wird man hören klingen	There one will hear resounding
Die rechten Säyten-Spiel,	The bowing of right strings,
Die Music Kunst wird bringen	The art of music bringing
In Gott der Freuden viel.	God's manifold delight.

Before leaving the quiet, hiding conventicles of the seventeenth century, we may further establish the persistence of several motifs now familiar. After the arrest of several *Täufer*, who were meeting in a home on a hill called the *Dürsrütti*, just above the town of Langnau in the Emme River Valley of Bern, a local poet enshrined the event:

> In Matthew 5 we find it so
> How Christ upon the Mount did go,
> And there taught with decisiveness
> Examples eight of blessedness.
>
> Now in the nine and fiftieth year
> A small flock was assembled here
> And there they had the selfsame Word
> As on the Mountain by the Lord.

It could not be clearer: the purpose of gathering is to share the Word of Christ. In so doing, we identify with and become part of the biblical story, most specifically, the Gospels.

Two years later there was another arrest of Anabaptists likewise meeting in a home, this time in High Germany, just east of the Rhine and south of Heidelberg. They had all recently come, found the authorities, as "pure Swiss" from the Canton of Zurich. They had been living on eight neighboring "hofs" where they had been allowed to rent lands. Caught just as they began to sing a hymn, they confessed that they had been meeting like this in several buildings, or in the nearby forest, for two years but without bothering any one or doing any proselyting. In fact, they had held their meetings in complete quietness. When they were slapped with a weighty fine, they protested that it was more than they could afford. Simple as this kind of gathering was, they could not do without it, and if they were legally forced to give it up, they would once again have to search for a new place to live.[16]

Such glimpses as we can gain of eighteenth-century Mennonite worship in Pennsylvania make understandable a European observer's comment that the services were "often very sleepy affairs."[17] Not so those of the Dunkers, which were characterized as much more expressive, if not frenetic. Having grown up myself in a community whose oldest ministers were still using a sing-song, rote-like, scripture-quoting pulpit manner, I had to wonder on occasion what held the gathering together. It certainly wasn't the quality of the sad or monitory-sounding preaching. At the same time, I could feel the power of the gathering. It was a shared touching of our faith's home base, a weekly returning to the center of our lives, communally acknowledging the invisible sphere of spiritual reality that brooded over our life.

Our willingness to assemble thus, without benefit of aesthetics, may have seemed to us, in part, a confession of the depth of our faith. But historically, the rote-like, non-demonstrative quality of our worship, with its untrained preachers stringing together one scripture quotation after another, was an open invitation to more evangelistic and expressive church-groups such as the Dunkers, Moravians, or United Brethren. In the 1760s, persons starved for emotional involvement in worship reacted enthusiastically to the impassioned preaching of Martin Boehm, who had been ordained both minister and bishop by the Mennonites of southern Lancaster County around the time of the French and Indian War. Breaking out of the old droning pattern, Boehm found himself standing amidst the congregation, who were shedding unusual tears, and finding this appropriate. Though he himself described the raised emotions as "all new," they had been evident around Lancaster County in English since the visits of George Whitfield two decades earlier. The scenes of revivals in Boehm's house were actually part of a Methodist beginning in the County.

A ritualized form—"Experience Meetings"—emerged from the ministry of Boehm and other "United Brethren" preachers. It became a standard part of worship for individuals to narrate their conversion-stories. Anyone who has heard the survivals of this phenomenon in the twentieth century can readily recognize the genre. It was resisted by traditional Mennonite leaders, such as Bishop Christian Burkholder in 1792, and as late as 1880 we can hear the

Moderator of the Lancaster Mennonite Conference admonishing his fellow ministers to preach "the gospel of truth and not our experience."[18] A century later than that, however, I heard a fellow minister imploring God to give our congregation "a good worship experience," and the frequent emerging of "worship centers" with non-geographic names after 1970 seems to indicate an irrepressible yearning for an overt expression of emotion "in church."

At the same time, vestiges of Anabaptist scruples of the quietist type remain surprisingly strong in "Old Order" worship from Ontario to Indiana. There is still, in the most conservative groups, the preference or even rule of always taking a text from the Gospels, with the rest of the Scriptures used in a supporting role. Some commentary by a "Stauffer" Mennonite in 1990 helps to clarify this picture. His conservative fellowship, he recalls, traditionally

> did not like it when a minister based his sermon too much on the Old Testament. Even the Apostles' writings were something to be careful with. All regular church service texts were taken out of the four Gospels. They apparently held the Sermon-on-the-Mount foremost, followed closely by the rest of the Gospels. Next came the Epistles, then the Old Testament and the Apocrypha.[19]

A list of hymns appropriate to certain texts for preaching, in an appendix to the 1821 edition of the Lancaster Mennonite *Unpartheyisches Gesangbuch* (1st edition in 1804), confirms this rule.

A fine résumé of older worship values among Lancaster Mennonites was drawn up around 1940 by a Mennonite born in 1884, recalling the worship of his youth in the Weaverland Congregation.[20] "No exact time," he recalled,

> was set for the beginning of the service. When the song leaders thought enough people were present, one of them would announce a hymn and start singing. Both the chorister and the congregation remained seated. After a few hymns had been sung, the preachers and deacons would enter the auditorium and take their place on the preachers' bench. When the singing had ceased, the ministers took charge of the service.

Next came "opening remarks by a preacher." (In earlier years there had been actually been a short introductory sermon, without a text). Silent prayer followed, with the congregation on its knees. Next a deacon read a scripture lesson selected by the minister about to preach the main sermon. This minister was said to have "had the text." When he was finished he gave "further liberty," an invitation for other deacons and ministers present to bear witness as to the authenticity of his discourse. All the ministers and deacons, while remaining seated, then gave "testimony," expressing their approval of the sermon and frequently adding a few remarks of their own. The main preacher then responded with appreciation for the testimonies, sometimes made a few additional remarks, and called the congregation again to kneel. Sometimes he called on another minister to lead this audible prayer. After this the preacher either called for a hymn he had chosen as appropriate or allowed the song-leader to choose one.

If the main preacher was a visitor, one of the home ministers then arose and "introduced" him after the fact, as well as any other visiting ministers or deacons and made any other necessary announcements. The one who had preached then arose, asked the congregation to arise, and pronounced the benediction. "In earlier years the congregation had risen after the closing prayer and remained standing with their backs to the preachers while the benediction was pronounced. Then all were seated for the closing hymn. Thus there was no singing from the time the ministry took charge until after the benediction had been pronounced."

The question of unity and yielding to what is being proclaimed from the Word permeates the entire service. Amos B. Hoover, an Old Order Mennonite historian, records that during a time of disagreement in the Weaverland Mennonite congregation, when part of the congregation did not agree with the stand of their bishop, "at times half of the congregation would not kneel for prayer during worship services." Hoover goes on to observe that

> It was the early Swiss Mennonite custom, and perhaps a tenet of faith, that children did not kneel for prayer, nor non-members, nor persons who felt the minister was not sound. Mennonites in general have dropped this practice, except the Old Order Mennonites of Virginia. The original method of inviting the church to prayer, however, is still very apparent among Old Orders when the minister usually says, "Wonn dir mit ihr ehns und ehnig sin, so kommt laset uns bete" (If you are at one in harmony with me, let us pray).[21]

Quaker Sandra Cronk has made a sympathetic analysis of "Ritual and Myth-Interpretation" among Old Order Amish and Mennonites. She finds the controlling motif to be *Gelassenheit*, which I feel she has accurately placed as central to the understanding of quietistic descendants of the original Anabaptists. In fact, "the Old Order movement arose in both Amish and Mennonite churches to protect what had become the traditional ritual system based on *Gelassenheit*." When looked at in a positive light, the strict simplicity of worship reveals many related spiritual values. By using a home or meetinghouse, believers locate the holy in the community life rather than in a building where it convenes. Though considered non-liturgical, Cronk sees the very specific ways in which Scripture reading, preaching, and singing are performed as "religious rituals in the deepest sense of that word."[22]

The antiquity of *Ausbund* songs, and the slowness of singing, also preserved from a pre-modern era, are related to *Gelassenheit*. One certainly has to yield one's sense of haste, or individual impulses, to this shared, patient experience. Cronk might have mentioned that by using the *Ausbund* the Amish take as their own expression the very idioms of the first leaders of their fellowship.

The use of two sermons emphasizes the centrality of encountering the Word in joint worship. Since the sermons repeat the Biblical stories, people are learning while worshipping. Actually, learning can be a form of worship: the service is "the primary means of educating members about how to live in conformity with God's laws undergirding creation."[23] The insights presented come from the "interpretation of the life, teaching and death of Christ." Though the worshipers do not ritually re-enact or re-create the details of Jesus life, they do "try to incarnate the underlying pattern of Jesus' life of surrender for their participants."[24]

Whatever special church ceremonies there are—the "highest drama" being ordination—are "intimately connected with the proper functioning of the social order." "Even the seating at worship recognize[s] the paramount importance of the worshippers' roles in this order."[25] And "the elevation of [the rite of] visiting to the level of worship by holding each on alternate Sundays [helps] to recognize the significance of the network of social relationships in the brotherhood as the incarnation of powerlessness and love."

Finally, Cronk meditates on the fact that the Amish still have a meal after a service, which we might see as a continuation of a pattern we observed near Strasbourg in 1545. Though not incorporated into the service in the manner of a Brethren love feast, the meal nevertheless has some of the same meaning. "It [is] a corporate expression of communion, a concrete, yet highly stylized representation of the love and fellowship in the body of Christ." The menu of the full (not token) meal is standardized, thus rather ritualistic.

Indeed a modern visitor experiences wrap-around "thought felt" in the ambiance of a present-day Old Order Amish service. The incantatory preaching; the occasional breathtakingly homely example, as when a preacher says it just occurred to him yesterday that the breath God breathed into Adam's nostrils was the very breath he felt in his own lungs; the languorous, reverential songs; the startling genuflection running like a shock through the standing worshipers, at the end of the last prayer.

In Hutterite worship, too, one is impacted by the simplest of modes. The piercingly loud women's voices in the singing (a Hutterite may claim that this is a continuation of Anabaptist martyrs singing loudly enough in prison to be heard by their fellows); the ritualistic written sermons, laced from end to end with Scripture, read from old manuscripts; the rigid kneeling, without leaning or support.

In my Mennonite community the last thirty-five years have brought a thorough change in worship modes. I'll illustrate this with an experience I had on a Good Friday in 1967 at the Franconia Mennonite Meetinghouse. I had been asked to preach, but when the deacons, ministers, and bishops gathered in a circle in a little room beside the auditorium, fifteen minutes before the beginning, no one had yet been selected to "have the devotions." Each brother passed the assignment around the circle until finally someone took it. Then the thought of having a German hymn came up, since this was a key traditional meeting, and the congregation had never quite stopped singing an occasional German hymn. Unfortunately, the one song-leader still capable of leading in German was absent, so they asked if I could lead it. When I said I didn't know the tune, they sent for an old deacon, and he came into the little room and sang it for me. After I thought I had it, he went back to his seat. Unfortunately, by the time we were ready to sing, I had lost the tune. Yet I hated to disappoint the people. So I opened my mouth on a moderately high note, and sang the first syllable. Just as I had hoped, the congregation sailed away with the song, and I, who looked as though I was leading it, dutifully followed.

Today, though we like more surprises, we are protected from emergencies by the prevenient work of "worship committees." Whereas Ulrich Zwingli began his reform by departing from canonical readings, we now have orchestration, even designer worship.[26] It won't hurt us to compare our procedures with those of a time when there were no amenities, when the dimension of prophetic course-correction was not ruled out by politeness and "good feeling," when corporate worship was seldom enough possible that it was deeply longed for, and when theme was everything. I have been in communion services in Pennsylvania and Indiana where the ministers repeatedly urged the congregation to "relax and be comfortable." Having been nurtured in pre-worship committee days, I have occasionally asked worship committees if they have left any wiggle-room for the Holy Spirit.

A key element in passing on a worship value, especially if the rite is austere, is including the experience of love that the participant can feel. On this topic, I recall an anecdote shared with me years ago by Brethren leader Earl Fike. At his first love feast—perhaps at the age of about ten—his grandfather took him through the experience of killing a lamb, coming to the table, listening to the sermon, etc. Then the two paired up for the footwashing rite. In the midst of the solemn and novel (for the boy) experience, when the grandfather had dried the boy's foot with a towel, he reached under the boy's foot and tickled it, without smiling. The love of the feast, of the Christ of the feast, and of a grandfather fused in the boy's experience and memory.

Now, in closing, for the second of the two hymns I promised. This is the opening one in the new joint Brethren-Mennonite hymnal. Text editor Kenneth Nafziger says that his initial reaction to hearing it sung was emotional to the point that he could not help sing: it hit the mark of articulation so squarely. The very irony of its coming from a Catholic writer (1968) makes it richer in resonance. It is appropriate to the simplest of settings—"only a house. . .yet. . . ."
Here is all an Anabaptist had ever wanted: God's presence, God's Word, God's justice, and God's peace. When we have this we have all. Here is no poverty of vision. No busy reminders to include "spirituality" in the "experience." We can praise, while we wonder, with full thanks and full imagination.

What is this place where we are meeting?
Only a house, the earth its floor.
Walls and a roof, sheltering people,
Windows for light, an open door.
Yet it becomes a body that lives
     when we are gathered here
And know our God is near.

Words from afar, stars that are falling,
Sparks that are sown in us like seed.
Names for our God, dreams signs and wonders
Sent from the past are what we need.
We in this place remember and speak
     again what we have heard:
God's free, redeeming Word.

And we accept bread at His Table,
Broken and shared, a living sign.
Here in this world, dying and living,
We are each other's bread and wine.
This is the place where we can receive
     what we need to increase:
God's justice and God's peace.[27]

What do Anabaptists want in worship? To feel the Word working:
reconciling, melting, and renewing—creating a new order: correcting, promising
a new hope, and leading us to forgive. When that happens we can sing with
Isaac Watts, in his simple Dissenting chapel:

Oft have I seen thy glory there,
And felt the power of sovereign grace.

100 / John L. Ruth

Ausbund, Das ist: Etliche schöne Christliche Lieder (Germantown, Pa.: Christoph Saur, 1742), hymn #131, 770-1.

2 "O Gott Vater," *Hymnal Selections* (Elgin, Ill.: Brethren Press, 1992), I, 11 (jointly issued audiocassette series accompanying *Hymnal: A Worship Book*).

3 Dennis D. Martin, "Catholic Spirituality and Anabaptist and Mennonite Discipleship," *Mennonite Quarterly Review* 62 (January 1988): 8.

4 J. C. Wenger, trans., *Conrad Grebel's Programmatic Letters of 1524* (Scottdale, Pa.: Herald Press, 1970), 15, 19.

5 Ibid., 21.

6 Ibid., 23.

7 Ibid., 11, 23.

8 "Brotherly Union of a Number of Children of God Concerning Seven Articles," ed. and trans. John H. Yoder, *The Legacy of Michael Sattler* (Scottdale, Pa.: Herald Press, 1973), 36.

9 Ibid.

10 Ibid., 44-5.

11 Quoted in John R. Martin, "Anabaptist Spirituality" (paper presented at a Mennonite Consultation on Spirituality at Ashland College, Ashland, Oh., August 14-16, 1986), 7.

12 Quoted from Peter Rideman by Paul M. Miller, "Worship Among the Early Anabaptists," *Mennonite Quarterly Review* 30 (October 1956): 246.

13 "Zeugenverhör über eine Wiedertäuferversammlung in Strassburg," copy of transcription supplied by Jean Roth of Strasbourg with the following indication of source: "Auszug Wenckers aus den nicht mehr vorhanden Protokollen der Strassburger (Wiedertäuferherren): Str. Th. A. 176 (Var. eccl. XI), f° 379 r° - v°."

14 Transcription of "Aussagen zweier Zeugen über die Täufer Versammlung vom 24/25. Juli," supplied by Jean Roth, Strasbourg, with the source indicated as "Verhör widertäuffer betreffend den letzten Julij anno 1545. Productum vor rhät und XXI den 1 augusti anno 1545. Str. Th. A. 176 (Var. eccl. XI) fol. 379 v° - 380 v°."

15 H. S. Bender, "The Discipline Adopted by the Strasburg Conference of 1568," *Mennonite Qarterly Review* 1 (January 1927): 64-5.

16 Ernst H. Correll, *Das Schweizerische Täufermennonitentum* (Tübingen: J. C. B. Mohr, 1925), 81.

17 *Der durch Europa und America aufmerksame Reisende* (Altona: Johann L. F. Richter, 1777), ed. Donald F. Durnbaugh, ed., *The Brethren in Colonial America* (Elgin, Ill.: Brethren Press, 1967), 124.

18 "Conference," *Herald of Truth* (May 1880): 91.

19 Enos E. Stauffer, *Die Briefe an David Stauffer* (Port Treverton, Pa.: Enos E. Stauffer, 1990), 737.

20 A. Martin Wenger, "The Church Service of the Mennonites of Lancaster County, Pennsylvania," *Mennonite Historical Bulletin* 2 (April 1941): 1-2.

21 Amos B. Hoover, *The Jonas Martin Era, Presented in a Collection of Essays, Letters and Documents That Shed Light on The Mennonite Churches During the 50 Year Ministry (1875-1925) of Bishop Jonas H. Martin* (Denver, Pa.: published by the author, 1982), 409.

22 Sandra Cronk, "Gelassenheit: The Rites of the Redemptive Process in Old Order Amish and Old Order Mennonite Communities." (Ph.D. diss.: Divinity School of the University of Chicago, December 1977), 157; see also 124-157.

23 Ibid., 155.

24 Ibid., 125.

25 Ibid., 156-7.

26 Copies of two doctoral theses on worship committees in the Bethel (KS) College Library are Gary Harder, "Touched by Transcendence—Shaping Worship that Bridges Life and Faith. The Worship Committee: An Idea Whose Time has Come" (St. Stephen's College, 1986); and Ronald A. Krehbiel, "A Study and Proposal of Congregational Involvement in Worship for a General Conference Mennonite Church" (San Francisco Theological Seminary, 1977).

27 Huub Osterhuis, *Zomar een dak boven wat hoofden*, 1968, trans. David Smith, ca. 1970, in *Hymnal: A Worship Book* (Elgin, Ill., Newton, Kan. and Scottdale, Pa.: Brethren Press, Faith and Life Press and Mennonite Publishing House, 1992), #1.

2

Concerning Coming Together

by Robert R. Miller

They spread their arms and beat their breasts, and mumbled during their prayers. No word they uttered could be understood as they continuously raised their eyes to heaven and sighed, "groaning and grunting like a tired old nag pulling a cart."[1]

This less than flattering account of sixteenth century Anabaptists at prayer characterizes the challenge of this essay: to suggest present-day patterns for worship that are both meaningful and faithful to the Anbaptist heritage. For all the richness and depth of our worship tradition, one has to wonder if some Anabaptist worship services today remind observers of that "tired old nag pulling a cart."

Worship

Worship has been defined in many ways. In the old English, *weorthscipe* (literally "worthship") has to do with "giving God the worth due God." James White defines Christian worship as "the deliberate act of seeking to approach reality at its deepest level by becoming aware of God in and through Jesus Christ and by responding to this awareness."[2]

For Anabaptists, the understanding of liturgy as both worship and work is central to their identity. William Willimon reminds us that "'worship' not only refers to that which cultically happens at a certain time and place but also to the Christian's whole existence. The Hebrew word 'Abad' ('to serve') is used for both work and worship."[3] Although often associated with specific orders of worship and in some cases, with the Eucharist itself,[4] the Greek word *leiturgia* is literally "the work of the people." As Ken Morse observes, "it can mean service to the world through the church just as properly as it can refer to acts of public worship."[5]

So, liturgy has a double meaning. And regretably, Anabaptists have a liturgical imbalance, having emphasized the work dimension to the neglect of the worship dimension. More than disconcerting, such an imbalance can be life-threatening. Rebecca Slough cites the Sojourner's community in Washington, D.C. whose "primary focus in the beginning was service and social justice. . .and they soon found they couldn't carry on that ministry without a strong worship life."[6] While contemporary Brethren and Mennonite communities are surviving, an underemphasis on liturgy as worship has contributed to their spiritual malnourishment. If they want to avoid the appearance of that "tired old nag pulling a cart," they must continue to hold both liturgical dimensions—worship and work—in creative tension.

The Anabaptist insistence that worship encompass all of life and not just the religious realm relates integrally to its understanding of sacrament. One key point of departure from the Catholic church was the Anabaptist rejection of sacrament as *opus operatum*, as having itself and alone the power to convey the grace of eternal life.[7] This was "not to deny the sacred in life but to see that all of life was under God's dominion and thus special."[8]

Lauree Hersch Meyer summarizes the understanding of Anabaptists in general and of Brethren in particular when she states, "Believing that Jesus is God's saving sacrament for the world, Brethren understand that membership in Jesus' body means that those baptized into Christ commit ourselves to life as sacrament."[9]

Worship in Congregational Life

In line with this holistic understanding, early Anabaptists were not nearly as inclined to perceive worship as distinct from the other activities of congregational life as some are today. Worship was everywhere.

> When the Anabaptists came together, they read the Bible, prayed, chose leaders, exhorted one another to be faithful in persecution, broke bread together, baptized, and debated with non-members in their midst. Each function was carried out under its own name and for its own sake, without any one being called worship.[10]

Worship was also the context for dealing with practical matters and congregational business as well as church discipline.[11] Given modern obsessions with privacy and individuality, would it be fair to suggest that what theological and ethical discipline there is in Anabaptist congregations today happens more behind closed doors than in the context of congregational worship? With congregational business relegated to separate business meetings and theological and ethical discipline relegated to near oblivion, at least some Anabaptist worship has become so compartmentalized and narrowly defined that we speak of it today as something we "go to" between 11:00 a.m. and 12:00 noon on Sunday mornings.

Without advocating a literalistic return to or reenactment of earlier patterns, it should be noted that the more separated worship becomes from the rest of life, the less inclined we will be to take it seriously and the less likely it will be to shape an authentically Anabaptist ethos in the years ahead. Both our individual piety and our corporate vitality will be diminished to the extent that worship becomes just one more activity to attend rather than a continual "giving God the worth due God." As John Rempel observes in describing the ethical dimension of Believer's church worship, "we worship God as fully in our scattered days as in our gathered hour."[12] Perhaps as much as anything else, it is the early Anabaptist understanding of worship, liturgy, and sacrament encompassing all of life that has distinguished the tradition and that must be faithfully preserved and applied in the years to come.

Traditional Worship Practice

Identifying traditional Anabaptist worship practice is somewhat speculative because the primary sources are so scarce. As someone has suggested, it's tough to write about the way you worship while running from cave to cave.

What evidence we do have suggests a very simple approach. Harold Bender noted that, "There can be little doubt. . .about its simplicity. . .it included basically, at least after the earliest days, Scripture reading, prayer, preaching, and singing."[13] He further observed, "The order of service and manner of worship in both Europe and America was always simple, sober, and nonliturgical, with emphasis on the sermon."[14] Brief attention will now be given to the traditions of Scripture reading, prayer, preaching, and singing as well as to the central ritual acts of traditional Anabaptist worship before examining some of the core principles they embody.

Scripture Reading. According to Harold Bender, "The high authority of the Bible. . .placed it in the very center of the service and the reading and exposition of it, or admonition from it, was the most important element."[15] For all the disagreement about Anabaptist worship, most would agree that the Bible must continue to be at the heart of corporate worship.

Comparing Brethren to the larger Protestant movement, Carl Bowman has noted that, "Direct individual interpretation of scripture may have been characteristic of mainstream Protestantism, but not of dissenters like the Brethren who were community-based in both their hermeneutic and ecclesiology."[16] While there may still be general agreement among Anabaptists about the centrality of Scripture and the necessity of a community-based hermeneutic, there seems to be agreement on little else regarding Scripture.

The Schwarzenau Brethren avoided the use of any creed, believing that it might constrain their search for new light upon the meaning of the Biblical text. As Paul Roth observes, the Brethren "have a centering on scriptures with an open mind. I think many of our congregations have forgotten, or maybe did not know that is the tradition out of which we came."[17] Could it be that a growing fundamentalism within Anabaptist congregations causes many to be more concerned with defending scriptural inerrancy than with looking for new light?

Prayer. Beyond the certainty that Anabaptists prayed when they gathered for worship, there is much uncertainty about its particular form. Whether the prayer was silent or spoken may have depended on the strain of Anabaptism with which each congregation identified; kneeling for prayer, however, seems to have been a common practice. The Lord's Prayer, as well as read or recited prayers, were frequently used along with the more spontaneous variety.

More to the concern of this paper is Ken Morse's observation that early Brethren "members were welcome to pray in public."[18] It is interesting to note that, at least among Brethren, prayer was perhaps the worship practice that most exemplified their theological convictions about the priesthood of all believers. It may at least be argued that in many Anabaptist congregations today, even this communal practice has largely been relegated to the clerical domain where pastors now pray on behalf of the people.

Preaching. Describing the traditional Anabaptist approach to preaching, Alvin Beachy observes that, in the Anabaptist sermon, "doctrine and theology [were] firmly subordinated to admonition. . . .Since they did know what God required of them, the problem was not lack of knowledge but lack of obedience. Therefore the function of the minister was to plead with his listeners to urge them to repentance, to love, to joy, to peace."[19] As we may no longer assume that many Anabaptists know what God requires of them in an increasingly secularized and biblically illiterate world, the challenge of preaching may now be twofold: lack of knowledge as well as lack of obedience.

The importance of preaching in traditional Anabaptist worship received early impetus from the first article of the Statement of Church Discipline (Berne, Switzerland, 1526-27), which reads: "Brethren should assemble several times a week if possible to be instructed in their faith and to exhort each other to remain faithful to the faith."[20] The most cynical assessment might suggest they have done little else in worship ever since.

Singing.

When Conrad Grebel argued from Scripture that there was to be no singing, he read Ephesians 5:19 and Colossians 3:16 against the tradition of chanting the Mass in a language no one understood. It was not a rejection of congregational singing, which had at that time not yet developed.[21]

That singing became an important practice of early Anabaptist worship is shown by the printing of at least five distinct Anabaptist hymnals by the 1560s.[22] It may be that the earliest Anabaptist gatherings included only instruction and prayer because, "Singing out as a group does tend to make a group meeting in secret more conspicuous."[23]

Once Anabaptists started singing, however, they did so with great seriousness. Kenneth Morse cites the Brethren Annual Meeting of 1848 which urged that, "Brethren should sing 'in the spirit, and in truth, and with solemnity,' that they should avoid 'light tunes which make us merry,' and that singing should 'tend more to the glory of God than to the tickling of the outward ear.'"[24]

Rebecca Slough suggests that the hymnal is a central symbol of Anabaptist worship in part because it provides opportunity for "setting words to music, and as a result, they can be appropriated into the human body, into the human mind, into the human experience in a different way." She also observes that congregational singing fosters an experience of unity in diversity, "provides a way for the group to move in common," and fosters democracy because no single voice dominates.[25] In increasingly diverse congregations with their increasing reliance on the professional pastor as "prime minister" and "CEO," these values of congregational singing should not be underestimated.

Central Ritual Acts

In addition to Scripture reading, prayer, preaching, and singing, central to Anabaptist worship have been the ritual acts of the Lord's Supper and baptism. Walter Klaassen notes that Anabaptists rejected all symbols except for the bread, wine, and baptismal water, "Only these three symbols are expressly mentioned in the New Testament, and beyond that they appealed to Jesus' words about worshipping God in spirit and in truth."[26] Perhaps as much as anything else, these symbols of faith, these acts of obedience and remembrance, have shaped and sustained Anabaptists.

The Lord's Supper. John Rempel states that the Lord's Supper was "the primal act of the church" which, according to earliest Christian records, "was the climax of worship and was in some places celebrated every week."[27] Robert Friedmann suggests that the Lord's Supper may have been the principle form of worship within the first decade of Anabaptism.[28]

While rejecting the Catholic understanding of the transubstantiation of the elements, Anabaptists still found meaning in the Lord's Supper by experiencing "Christ present in the people gathered around the table, not in the bread and wine."[29] This communal understanding of the Lord's Supper among early Anabaptists was so essential that it was not offered separately to individuals who were sick or even on their deathbeds.[30]

Dale Brown observes that "the [Lord's Supper] represents more than a mere togetherness; it is togetherness as a divine gift and an eschatological expectation. . . .By grace the community is granted a foretaste of the bond of peace which God wants for all people."[31] Rempel further notes that among Anabaptists "each service was an act of covenant renewal, of pledging to give our lives for others just as Christ had given his life for us."[32]

If all this is true, why then do Anabaptists observe Christ's presence among them, enjoy the foretaste of God's peace, and renew their covenant with God and each other so infrequently? Certainly there must be integrity in the observance, but do we take the Lord's Supper more seriously by observing it less frequently? If the Lord's Supper will continue to be "the primal act of the church," Anabaptists will need to consider ways to observe and experience its meanings more frequently while guarding against the kind of routinization that numbs their spirits and hardens their hearts to its transforming power.

Baptism. It has been playfully suggested that no matter what the text, Brethren preachers in the nineteenth century eventually came around to baptism.[33] More than anything else, baptism has marked the Anabaptist tradition as distinctive in terms of what they believe about it and have suffered because of it.

Lauree Hersch Meyer articulates the understanding of Anabaptists in general when she observes this about the Brethren: "Shaped by our Radical Reformation heritage, we view baptism as the liturgical mark of mature, intentional obedience to live in God's service. . . .We saw ourselves as a covenanted community in which all were ministers ordained into the priesthood by baptism."[34] John Rempel further notes that, "Even though. . .only occasionally enacted, the service of baptism constitutes the church."[35] If this is the faith, is not the practice of "institutionalizing" the baptism of pre- and early adolescent youth incongruous? Do we really expect any but the most spiritually mature of these children to grasp the meaning and implications of this decision we subtly but steadily pressure them to make?

In this time of declining memberships, numerically-oriented growth programs, and increasing disaffection of young people from the church, Anabaptists must take care not to adopt the kind of "survival mentality" that obscures the meaning of baptism and compels them to "get their children in" before they have the volitional strength to consider choosing otherwise. Perhaps, as Dale Brown suggests, the time has come to create a ritual that would "recognize the near-universal desire of adolescents to join the adult world"[36] and celebrate this rite of passage within the church without unduly pressuring for a decision to join the body as minister and priest.

Love Feast. While not universally observed among Anabaptist groups, brief mention should be made of the Brethren Love Feast, which incorporates a service of feetwashing, a fellowship meal, and the Lord's Supper into one liturgical drama. As William Beahm says of it, "The highest experience of our relation to God is integrally bound to our most intimate fellowship with one another. It symbolizes our faith with its vertical dimension toward God and its horizontal dimension toward one other."[37]

Perhaps the genius of the Love Feast, and the reason why it should not be excessively tinkered with, is this creative tension it maintains between the vertical and horizontal dimension of faith, the transcendent and immanent experience of the divine, the spiritual love of God and the concrete love of neighbor. To significantly alter the form of the Love Feast may be to weaken this tension and have us "fall off" on one side or the other (and there is little doubt to which side the Brethren will usually fall).

Earle Fike explains that as historically practiced, there were "little sermons" or expositions of scripture before the feetwashing, the fellowship meal, and the bread and cup.

> The love feast offers an opportunity to be traditional about ritual but contemporary in interpretation. You do the feetwashing and you do it in the same way its been done for years and years but the interpretation of that has to be in some ways contemporary or else people don't understand it.[38]

Paul Mundey suggests "re-visioning the love feast, experimenting with different forms to communicate the same vision and values."[39] Alternative forms, such as washing hands, can indeed be meaningful and are specially appropriate for persons who for medical and other reasons cannot wash feet. It may at least be argued, however, that there is an evocative meaning and power in these particular symbolic elements and acts that may not be fully conveyed in other forms. As Rebecca Slough observes, "If we're using shoddy materials we will get something out of it, but we will not discover the same kind of essential essence of the experience by using Kool Aid and cookies as we would if we were using bread and wine."[40]

Core Worship Principles

While one can infer many principles from the practices and rituals described above, several are particularly characteristic of Anabaptism. Duane Sider suggests that "what seems to run as a thread through Anabaptist writing and. . .practices as it concerns worship is a strong emphasis on the gathered body and the priesthood of all believers and the centrality of scripture."[41] To this may be added a fourth core principle, obedience.

The Gathered Body. The title of this essay, "Concerning Coming Together," is taken from a statement by a Moravian Hutterite leader, Peter Rideman. The title seems fitting because so much of what Anabaptist worship is about concerns their "coming together," the "gathering" of the community to encounter, honor, and be instructed by God revealed in Jesus the Christ.

For the early Anabaptists, "coming together" was itself an act of faith be-cause it made their "criminal" beliefs and practices more visible and themselves more vulnerable to arrest and persecution. But come together they did because their understanding of scripture and of the church compelled them to do so.

Dale Brown describes an Anabaptist "communal ecclesiology that affirms that no one comes to God apart from a brother or sister. It is impossible to separate our relationship with God from our relationship with one another."[42] Anabaptists gathered as a body for worship because they understood it was in their coming together that the presence and will of God was most fully mediated to them.

Dale Stoffer suggests that worship is "more than an I-Thou encounter. It's really a We-Thou encounter. It's not just us individually meeting God; its really the community of God's people meeting God together."[43] It should be noted that this theological understanding has at times degenerated into a sociological phenomenon. Floyd Mallott was known to comment that while the Catholics and Lutherans gather to worship God and the Calvinists gather to be instructed from God's Word, the Brethren gather to see one another.[44] As Stoffer cautions,

> primary focus begins with our relationship with God. That has got to be the founda-tion for that then becomes the motivation for true love toward the brothers and sis-ters and true commitment to the world. We distort the proper order if we begin with a community-centered or a world-centered worship experience."[45]

For whatever reasons Anabaptists have gathered for worship, they gather now in part to create and sustain the sense of community that in earlier times was created and sustained by their living together. Duane Sider observes that for Anabaptism in earlier periods,

> Worship didn't need to bear the responsibility of being a community-making activity, but I think we are seeing now that we no longer know how to make community or be community in the sense that we did when we were living in community. Worship now is needing to function as a community-making, community-forming activity in a way that it didn't at one point.[46]

"But then on the other side," Sider poignantly concludes, "just how much can Sunday morning bear?"[47]

The Centrality of Scripture. One meaning of "gathering," as defined by Webster's Dictionary, is "to wrap or draw around, as a garment."[48] That which Anabaptists "wrap or draw around" when they gather for worship is scripture. To talk about the centrality of scripture is to recognize that at the deepest level of reality, Scripture reveals the Word of God. It is this Word that Anabaptists at their best have sought to gather around. Understanding the true focus of worship to be God, scripture becomes the tangible symbol and resource that believers corporately gather around to experience God's presence and discern God's will.

As Kenneth Nafziger observes, this gathering around the Word of God vis-a-vis the words of scripture has significant implications for how and by whom worship is created.

> The congregation gathers around the Word. The people who were gathered in this non-hierarchical arrangement around the Word were really encouraged to use whatever gifts they [had] to. . .break open the Word of God. . . .There was this treasure here that required some effort to break. . .open and find out what the sweetness was that was in it.[49]

In coming together, there must be a center exerting its "gravitational pull" on the community so that the "centrifugal forces" of personal tastes, trendy styles, theological disparities, and social influences do not cause the worship of God to fly off in many different directions. For Anabaptists, that center has always been and must continue to be the Word of God as revealed in the words of scripture.

Priesthood of All Believers. The gathered body and the centrality of scripture have a great bearing on a third core principal of Anabaptist worship: the priesthood of all believers. If the body is to break open and discover the sweetness of the Word it has gathered around, it will require the gifts and authentic participation of everyone present, not just of those "ecclesiastically sanctioned" to do so. This seems to have been the case for early Anabaptists among whom "leadership was shared; services were held away from church buildings; expectations were clear that every member was a responsible adult who chose to follow Christ and share fully in the community of believers."[50]

As Nancy Faus observes, sharing fully in the community of believers must include sharing fully in its worship life. "Worship is meaningful when all in the faith community are invested and involved. Only when the worshipping community believes in the ministry of the laos (Greek for 'a body of people') can worship be the work the people of God do together."[51]

What Anabaptists believe about the priesthood of all believers and how they embody that belief in worship is sometimes incongruous. Jimmy Ross states that "nowhere should the doctrine of the 'priesthood of all believers' be more apparent than in our worship."[52] Yet it may be argued that nowhere is the priesthood of all believers less apparent.

Anecdotal evidence suggests that on any given Sunday morning in any given Anabaptist congregation, the pastor may open the service with announcements, conclude the service with a benediction, and assume responsibility for everything in between. (All this after planning the entire service within the isolation of an office with perhaps a call to the music director for approval of hymns and placement of the choir's anthem). To the extent that such worship exists in churches today, members are acting like anything but "priests" and worship is anything but the "liturgy," the work they do.

The cause of this congregational abdication is at least partially rooted in the development of the paid, professional ministry, which has encouraged a surrender of responsibility for worship to the pastor. If the *laos* is concerned about the quality of worship planned and provided by its pastors, perhaps it should consider reclaiming its biblical responsibility for worship rather than complaining about the pastor's Sunday morning "performance." As Tom Geiman put it, "If we are priests, then let us be priests in our worship."[53]

Obedience. A fourth core principle of Anabaptist worship was often referred to simply as obedience.

> The Anabaptists did not come from a week of irreligious, worldly living and expect a beautiful building and attractive liturgy to draw them to God. They insisted that the Christian walks with God constantly in holy obedience and expected their daily walk to come naturally to a climax in the fellowship of the gathered community of disciples.[54]

If worship for early Anabaptists was the offering of praise and prayer to God, it was also a means of seeking God's will in scripture and encouraging fellow believers toward higher levels of discipleship.[55] Jim Myer expresses the concern of many today when he states, "I just have a growing feeling that worship does not seem to lay serious claims on people's lives. More and more we disassociate the issue of the obedient life from worship."[56] Daniel Berrigan put it more tersely, "No one has been able to demonstrate that Christian worship leads, in any large or direct sense, to Christian conduct in the world."[57] This statement is a special challenge to Anabaptists for whom the ethical dimension of worship has been so central that it has often become the focus rather than a function of corporate worship.

James White suggests that obedient discipleship is a central concern and outgrowth of worship, but not the focus of worship itself.[58] When believers come to worship preoccupied with what they will do for God after worship, it becomes difficult to give "God the worth due God." Reflecting upon the effect of the strong Mennonite focus on obedience, John Rempel writes, "Mennonite worship can be downright dour and austere and graceless."[59]

One of the gifts Anabaptists may offer the larger church body is their stubborn insistence on the integral relationship between what is said in worship and what is done in life, between the encounter with God and the encounter with the world, between the honoring of God with music and words and the honoring of God with obedient lives.

Contemporary Relevance?

When asking about the contemporary relevance of traditional Anabaptist worship, a caution must be raised. As Jean Hendricks observes concerning her own experience,

> every stage in the tradition makes or adds to the symbols and I really reject someone saying that this tradition that was made a thousand years ago needs to be directly applied to me. . . .Too [easily] the basin and towel service motif becomes a doormat motif, especially for women. . . .Women serve. . .all the time and we do that because the church tells [us] to do it and there are these symbols that are held up so [we] do it some more.[60]

This statement implies the danger of assuming the tradition's validity and simply asking how it can be contemporized. Rather than merely updating or modernizing traditional worship forms, we must critically analyze them to determine their faithfulness to the biblical witness and their appropriateness for the present age. Rather than ask how we can transfer these forms into the twenty-first century, we must first ask which elements of tradition are essential and warrant transmission at all. What seems essential is not getting stuck on particular practices but rather looking beneath them for the principles they originally conveyed. As Kenneth Nafziger observes, "If all it was in the past was the clothes we wore or the habits we had when we came together to worship, it may not be worth keeping."[61]

Rather than simply ask how we can dress plainly or contemporize the "minister's table" in meetinghouses today, we should first ask what principles those practices conveyed in the culture of their day, whether those principles are still valid, and if so, how they can be meaningfully translated into the culture of our day. In the words of Paul Mundey, "The cultural form is not that which needs to be preserved, but the message transmitted through the conduit."[62] Richard Foster offers additional perspective when he states that "forms and rituals do not produce worship, nor does the disuse of forms and rituals. We can use all the right techniques and methods, we can have the best possible liturgy, but we have not worshiped the Lord until Spirit touches spirit."[63] Still, it should be recognized that, at least in some cases, "the medium is the message," and to cast out the cultural form (e.g. feetwashing) may also be to cast out or compromise the essential message.

Assuming some principles are essential and worth transmitting into the present age, and assuming some traditional worship forms can no longer bear the freight of meaning they once did for earlier generations, Anabaptists should be intentional and thoughtful about how they handle these treasures of their tradition. Neither those who plan nor those who participate in worship will be well served by clever and creative attempts to modernize form without consideration of the meanings changed or principles compromised in the process.

The Future in Light of the Past

In light of the above considerations, I offer these suggestions to assist in the creation of worship that is both faithful to the Anabaptist heritage and meaningful in the present age.

Attitude. The attitude with which believers approach worship is key. While Anabaptists have been excellent teachers of peace and service, missions and fellowship, and Bible study, "we have not taught worship." We even look down upon churches that have emphasized worship while slighting more "Anabaptist" matters of discipleship.[64]

If worship is to become what Rebecca Slough calls "the central action of the congregation,"[65] Anabaptists will have to grant it greater importance than they have heretofore. They will have to regard worship as an essential event rather than an auxiliary activity squeezed in between peace conferences and disaster relief.

Balanced Planning. How we regard worship is directly related to how we plan worship. Some worship resembles a scripted performance that tolerates little "interference" from the Holy Spirit. Other worship looks more like a people wandering in the wilderness. Concerning the latter, Kenneth Nafziger observes,

> For a while we talked about creative worship services and what that meant was that nobody planned anything. We just sort of stood up and let fall out what ever fell out. . . .I think that's probably a misuse of the word creative. God didn't create the world by just standing up and letting things fall out.[66]

Somewhere between a "scripted performance" and "letting things fall out" is an approach to planning that takes seriously the freedom of the Spirit as well as the human need for order and theme that tie the threads of worship into a seamless whole. John Rempel summarizes worship planning well by describing it as "staying close to the Holy Spirit in our preparations, then holding lightly to them so that we can also seize the moment."[67]

Group-Planned. However planning is done, the worship itself must emerge from the life of the congregation. Such worship reflects the community's *sitz im leben* without being circumscribed by it. Implicit in such worship is the work of a planning group whose individual experiences of the Holy Spirit and collective awareness of congregational life combine to create worship that is both authentic and engaging.

Believing as Anabaptists do that the Holy Spirit is most fully present and active in the gathered community, why does much of their worship planning occur in solitary isolation? No matter how thoughtful and engaged, the pastor remains an individual who simply cannot envision congregational life nor imagine worship possibilities the way a group can.

Without a doubt it is more difficult and time-consuming for five people to sit around a table and struggle with the Holy Spirit than for one to sit at a desk and struggle with the Holy Spirit within oneself. But worship emerging from the struggle of group process will be more authentic and engaging than that emerging from the privacy of the pastor's office.

Participatory. Like planning, participation should be broadened. With the exception of a time for the sharing of joys and concerns, participation in many services of worship today has been reduced to the singing of a few hymns and the speaking of a few litanies while the preacher and choir take center stage. Important as these are, they are not fully effective in drawing believers personally into the worship experience and engaging them experientially in the encounter with God.

If believers are to love God with all their heart, soul, strength, and mind (Luke 10:27), then they are to worship God with those capacities as well. If they are to worship God "in spirit and truth" (John 4:24), ways must be found to involve them, to engage them, to elicit from within them a personal response to the divine initiative. It may be a time of sharing; it may be an invitation to contribute during the corporate prayer; it may be an opportunity to respond to the sermon or a simple passing of the peace. If liturgy is to be the "work of the people," the faith community must work as it if it expects to be nourished and inspired by it. The Church must break out of its liturgical lethargy, overcome its fear of involvement, and move beyond a spectator mentality if it is to "give God the worth due God."

God-Focused. The Church of the Brethren worship book, *For All Who Minister*, describes the experience of many Anabaptist groups when it suggests that, "without a high liturgy, Brethren feel a sense of freedom in worship and sometimes put more emphasis on the communal dimension of worship, that is, the fellowship of those gathered together, than on the transcendent nature of worship, that is, the mysterious, omniscient God."[68]

Because of their communal ecclesiology and rural context, Anabaptists have historically done a better job of getting together and fellowshipping than, as Jim Myer puts it, getting down and honoring "the one who is great and mighty."[69] In a word, they have been better at offering pot-lucks than at offering praise.

Whatever the reasons for this, worship needs to focus on God—to praise "God for being God," [70]to acknowledge the difference between Creator and created, and to confess the distance between God's holiness and human sinfulness. For only as we more fully understand the radical otherness of God shrouded in ineffable mystery can we more fully appreciate the radical nearness of God wrapped in swaddling clothes. As Nancy Faus asks, "Where is God in this? And where are we, the gathered community? Instead of feeling good just being in worship together, we need to realize we have come together to worship God, who is both near and far, intimately with us and yet beyond us."[71]

Spirit-filled. The strength of the Anabaptist focus on following in Jesus' way may also be a weakness if it distracts believers from the presence and power of the Holy Spirit in worship. Those in the early church understood themselves "as being in relationship to God through Jesus Christ by the power of the Holy Spirit."[72]

While the presence and power of the Holy Spirit in worship means different things to different people, we can all sense in our beings when worship is filled with the Spirit and when it is not; when the congregation is animated by the Spirit and when it is not; when the people contribute their spiritual gifts and when they do not. As Jim Myer affirms, "When the evidence of the Holy Spirit is within us and directing our worship. . .then of course we have nothing to fear."[73]

If the Brethren tradition, a cousin of the sixteenth-century Anabaptists, has a particular gift to offer, it may be its pietistic focus upon the personal relationship with God. "Like other Pietists," Kenneth Morse observes, "the first Brethren protested the coldness of much public worship of their time and rejected the dogmatism of the official church."[74] John Rempel observes that "Brethren have a warmth and an intensity to their worship which spring from their pietistic roots."[75] In contrast, Rempel states that "persecution led to introversion and left a streak of melancholy in the Mennonite soul, which still sets the tone of worship and piety in traditional congregations."[76] While true to a much lesser degree in Brethren worship today, this concern for a more subjective, personal experience of God and the spiritual disciplines that nourish it are as elemental as concerns for community faithfulness and personal discipleship.

Spirituality is also tied to the Anabaptist understanding of the priesthood of all believers. It is a charge—something we need to work at and take seriously. Can believers realistically expect to be spiritually "dormant" all week long and then experience a spiritual "eruption" on the weekend? Like it or not, the experience of the Spirit's presence and power among us on Sunday morning may correspond rather directly to the cultivation of the Spirit *within us* throughout the preceding week. To repeat Duane Sider's question from an earlier context, "Just how much can Sunday morning bear?"

Spiritually-Gifted. "Each one of us has received a special gift in proportion to what Christ has given" (Eph. 4:7). If the pastors, choir, and music director are the only worship leaders week after week, it is questionable whether the community's spiritual gifts for worship are being identified and exercised to their fullest extent. Understanding these gifts or *charismata* as simply "endowments of special abilities" that strengthen, sustain, and upbuild the body of Christ,[77] and believing that "each one of us has received a special gift," are we to assume that only the church staff has been gifted for worship?

"Under his control all the different parts of the body fit together, and the whole body is held together by every joint with which it is provided. So when each separate part works as it should, the whole body grows and builds itself up through love" (Eph. 4:16). If liturgy is to be "the work of the people," if worship is to reflect a properly functioning body where all make their contribution to its unity and growth, those who are spiritually gifted in the leadership of worship must be continually called out and equipped to exercise those gifts. If worship in many congregations is not what we wish or believe it could be, perhaps it is because some of the body's parts are not working as they should.

Openness to God's Truth. It has been suggested that the last seven words of the church are, "We've never done it that way before." It may be argued this is true in worship as nowhere else in congregational life.

Philip Clemmens states that one of his "greatest concerns is that our worship would remain static," and he "senses among some people the veneration of practice rather than the. . .desire to worship God in God's fullness. . .with our fullness."[78]   As contemporary Christian musician John Fischer puts it so disturbingly and so well,

> The Spirit of God dances. He dances right under the noses of those who don't believe in dancing; and He dances right on by those who do. . . .His favorite dancing places are those where the keepers of the dance don't want him to go: on MTV, on drive-in movie screens, or on smoky stages with microphones that smell of whiskey. The Spirit of God loves sinners and dances best where life spills out on the floor.[79]

Believing that all truth is God's truth, we need to recognize and incorporate truth in worship in whatever form we find it. This is not to argue for the adoption of every new-fangled device that comes down the pike. It is to suggest that some of what comes down the pike conveys God's truth and is worthy of our use in worship, though it may defy our sacred/secular categories and disturb our cherished always-been-done-that-way manner of doing things. While less evident today, Dale Brown observes that "basic to the [Brethren] tradition has been a spirit of openness to changing forms and practices and to new light."[80]

Yet this spirit of openness must always be accompanied by a spirit of discernment. Theologian Dale Stoffer voices his concern "about a sort of generalized evangelicalism today that sort of picks up things from anywhere and everywhere without too much concern as to the theological foundations of those practices and ideas."[81] The same may be said of a "generalized liberalism" as well, for both are guilty of uncritically assimilating from popular culture whatever supports their causes and pleases their constituencies. The only thing that should concern Anabaptists more than the loss of their identity to the vicissitudes of popular culture is the loss of openness to accept God's truth wherever they find it and the lack of courage to follow wherever it leads.

New Rituals. If we believe that God is constantly doing a new thing in the world, the worship of God should affirm and reflect that conviction by developing new rituals to address the realities of modern culture.

With the divorce rate in our nation at about fifty percent, and with divorced persons increasingly filling sanctuaries, Anabaptists cannot continue to ignore in worship this very personal and painful reality. Just as the church provides rites of passage for marriage and death, it could also provide a rite of passage for those who experience death in their marriage. Given the tendency towards gossip and informal shunning in many congregations, a service acknowledging divorce may be an important step in the reconciliation of those involved and in their re-appropriation into the faith community. For it is in the worship of God, as nowhere else, that the whole community can suffer with its members, confess its own failure in relationships, and offer redemptive love.

To provide such a service is not to sanction or approve of divorce and thereby undermine belief in the permanence of the marriage covenant. It is simply to acknowledge that in spite of deepest convictions and best intentions, people fall short of God's commands and relationships sometimes die. When marital death occurs, an occasion for the expression of grief, confession, forgiveness, and love should be provided for those who sincerely desire it.

Multi-media. Most of us would agree that "we participate in worship through all our senses." Most of us would also agree that "worship has always been a multimedia experience."[82] Yet when it comes to incorporating various media into worship, many Anabaptists quickly revert back to a rational, word-oriented European tradition and "pull the plug" on anything that smacks of secular influence or modern technology.

Given that we now process information more audio-visually than ever before; that many regularly "exploit" modern technologies in work and leisure activities; that most enjoy the benefits of electronic media from the morning weather report to the evening news; and that many are deeply moved by drama in the theater, dance on the stage, and recorded music in the movies, why do we regard them with such suspicion in worship? If God could use the unlikely media of a manger and cross to proclaim "good news of great joy" (Luke 2:10), could God not use equally unlikely media to proclaim it today?

The Arts. Integrally related to the use of media is the use of the arts in worship. Duane Sider suggests that "our dedication to the moral life and to work and to plainness and to simplicity have not made it seem important for us to express ourselves artistically leaving basically only words and so worship has been very much word dominated in the Mennonite tradition."[83]

He goes on to observe with subtle delight that "its gotten squeezed . . .[into] quilts and colorful jams and jellies at fairs and certain kinds of clothing and certainly in music."[84] Suggesting, as this does, that humans must express themselves artistically, it is regrettable that, to a large extent, Anabaptists repress this artistic impulse in their worship of the Master Artist.

With regard to drama, many seem to have a negative, knee-jerk reaction because of the "secular" associations attached to it. But it is not as if drama in worship is a modern invention. Every time we baptize a believer, break bread with a sister, anoint a brother, wash the feet of another, confess our sins together, join our voices in song, or offer our first fruits to God, we dramatize the divine-human encounter. Like it or not, preachers and parishioners alike are actors in a sacred drama and the worship of God will be enriched in as much as Anabaptists carry on that dramatic tradition.

Paul Tillich states that "all arts create symbols for a level of reality which cannot be reached in any other way. In the creative work of art we encounter reality in a dimension which is closed for us without such works."[85] If in their worship of God, Anabaptists seek "to approach reality at its deepest level," if they "desire to worship God in God's fullness with our fullness," they must recognize art in its varied forms as an indispensable medium of God's character, grace, and truth.

Music. Given the importance of singing for Anabaptists, the question is not whether they shall continue to sing but how they shall sing in the future. Some will insist on a certain style of singing while others will insist on a particular genre of music or a specific body of hymnody. To be sure, style and genre must be considered with great care, for they will do much to shape Anabaptist identity and congregational life in the years to come.

It should at least be noted, however, that no particular style of singing, no particular genre of music, and no particular collection of hymns fully embodies, expresses, or exhausts the capacity to worship God. It may well be that both traditional a cappella hymns in four-part harmony and "scripture songs" in unison accompanied by a band will be required for all sorts and stripes of Anabaptists to worship God in the years to come. To insist on one or the other is to presume to know what God prefers, for it is to God and not each other that our music is finally offered.

Regarding taped music in congregational worship (a practice understandably repugnant to many musicians in the church), it should be remembered that in earlier years the organ, without which many congregations today would not presume to sing, was once forbidden in meetinghouses. Taped music, like other modern technologies, can be of service in the worship of God when used with discretion and integrity.

So long as music tends "more to the glory of God than to the tickling of the outward ear," it may be that the particular style matters more to humans than to God. Perhaps the challenge is to maintain a creative tension between the music that has nurtured those in the faith thus far and the music that will faithfully nurture future generations.

Preaching. In a worship class at Bethany Seminary years ago, Paul Robinson told a story about arriving late at a Sunday service one morning only to be "reassured" by the person next to him—"Don't worry. You didn't miss anything but the preliminaries. We're just ready for the sermon."[86] While preaching will continue to be a central act of Anabaptist worship, in the future it must be understood as one act of the worship drama rather than as the drama itself. If the worship experience rises or falls on the quality of the sermon, and if the quality of preaching within the Anabaptist tradition continues to be as uneven as it has historically been, we have reason to be concerned.

Walter Klaassen observes that,

> the Anabaptist rejection of the Protestant form of worship in which only one person preached must be seen basically as their criticism of the inadequacy of the Protestant doctrine of the priesthood of all believers. So far as they could see, the Protestant preaching services had none of the dynamic congregational process which they found described in 1 Corinthians 14.[87]

Ken Morse notes that in early Brethren meetinghouses, "elders and deacons sat on the same level with their brothers and sisters, seniority was recognized, and a presiding elder had authority to 'extend the liberty'" to other ministers.[88] Assuming all are ministers, assuming there is more than one person in each congregation who is spiritually gifted to preach, and assuming the Gospel is larger than any one pastor can comprehend and communicate, it is again time to "extend the liberty" to other members of the body in a more regular way, not just when the pastor is out of town.

Beyond the question about who will preach is the concern about how preaching shall be done. Ronald Arnett observes that the "mystery of God is not locked within the legalism of any dictated forms of proclamation but is found in a creative approach to tradition."[89] Duane Sider suggests that such a "creative approach" will mean paying attention to how people process what they hear.

> [Preachers] need to understand that people no longer organize their information along the lines of print like they did 30 years ago, but rather organize it audio-visually and that sermons need to find a way to recover an oral character rather than a print character. A lot of sermons that I still hear are essentially print pieces that happen to get spoken rather than oral pieces that happen to get written down.[90]

Good preaching, it has been said, covers a multitude of sins. Good preaching also covers a multitude of biblical texts during the course of a year. If Anabaptists claim to take the Bible as their guide for faith and practice, they must address the whole of scripture and not primarily the New Testament as they have tended to do. Just as nineteenth-century Brethren preachers "always" came around to baptism, so will Anabaptist preachers in the future keep coming around to their pet topics unless assisted to do otherwise. A flexible use of the lectionary can help avoid that temptation by disciplining the faith community to interpret present concerns in light of scripture rather than interpreting scripture in light of present concerns, as strictly topical preaching tends to do.

Prophetic. One of the quandaries of the modern pastor is how to speak a word of justice and a word of comfort, to challenge unfaithfulness while building relationships, to blend prophetic leadership with pastoral care (all this while ensuring job security). This may be a false dichotomy created by a false understanding of the pastor's role.

"The gifts he gave were that some would be apostles, some prophets, some evangelists, some pastors and teachers, to equip the saints for the work of ministry, for building up the body of Christ" (Eph. 4:11-12). This text indicates that pastors and prophets are different persons with different spiritual gifts and different functions within the body. There is a practical wisdom in this arrangement, for it does not ask ministers to walk the pastoral-prophetic tightrope and does not tempt congregations to evaluate their ministry on the basis of how much or how little they offend. However, as the job description of the professional pastor has expanded to encompass many of the functions originally shared among spiritually gifted members, she or he has increasingly merged the roles of pastor and prophet, perhaps to the church's detriment.

Whether or not the pastor is called to be a prophet, Anabaptism began as a prophetic movement and its offspring have always understood the prophetic character of biblical faith. Whether or not many congregations today understand the importance of prophetic worship is another question. As Warren Groff puts it, "Worship is the ringing alarm that awakens us from that sleep which allows us to drift with dominant cultural tendencies."[91] To sustain a prophetic witness in the world, the church must nurture a prophetic spirit in worship so that each can reinforce and revitalize the other.

Visceral. It has been said that Jesus came to take away our sins, not our minds. If we are to love God with all our mind as well as with all our heart, soul, and strength, then making worship as intellectually stimulating as possible is surely honoring God and this commandment. But as John Rempel observes, an "imbalance in our traditional worship was that the whole weight of our relationship with God rested on words and ideas."[92] Anabaptists have tended to worship God with the mind, the whole mind, and "nothing but" the mind while their hearts and souls have languished in exile and atrophied from disuse.

This was not the case for our Hebraic ancestors, whose worship took into account the whole breadth of human existence with all its joy, anger, and pathos. When "the Word became flesh," it laughed, cried, raged, doubted, and feared, expressing the whole range of human emotion. Does worship today with its emphasis, if not insistence, on good appearances, positive feelings, and therapeutic psychology, ignore the human condition and make a mockery of the One who was crucified by it? Is it any wonder that many who seek "to approach reality at its deepest level" do not seek it within some Anabaptist worship services?

Paul Tillich describes faith as "an act of the total personality. It is not a movement of a special section or a special function of [our] total being. They are all united in the act of faith."[93] If this is true, then Anabaptists can scarcely afford to disconnect them in worship as they have tended to do. The word "visceral" comes close to describing a quality of worship that transcends the dichotomy of mind and heart, intellect and emotion. Worship, if it is to "give God the worth due God," must do more than lightly tickle the intellect and superficially touch the emotion. It must reach down and grab worshippers in their viscera, where intellect and emotion are united and where there is no choice but to respond.

I am not clear how this visceral quality of worship is created. It may mean more stories and less dogma in preaching, more evocative images and less theological jargon in the liturgy, more honesty and less hypocrisy in confession, or more specificity and less generality in prayer. In these ways, we may at least begin to worship the Lord our God with all our mind, heart, soul, and strength.

Unifying. Ephesians 4 also exhorts believers to make "every effort to maintain the unity of the Spirit in the bond of peace" (Eph. 4:3). All that believers do within their services of worship, from the time they gather to the time they scatter, should be "body-building." Worship should have a unifying effect that mitigates against the centrifugal forces that continually pull them away from God and apart from each other.

While worship has at times divided more than united, Earle Fike observes that among the Brethren, "persons who cannot agree on the wording of an Annual Conference action will find themselves singing together, praying together, and in it all being lifted by the experience of worshipping God together."[94] While Anabaptists may forever disagree on matters theological, let them at least agree that in the worship of God, all of their sometimes important and frequently petty differences will be subordinated to the One who "has broken down the dividing wall, that is, the hostility between us" (Eph. 2:24). If they cannot do even this, is there anything they can do?

Inclusive. In describing the reconstruction of the Brethren tradition, Carl Bowman writes that "unity as harmony and acceptance has replaced unity as singleness and sameness—all are now welcome at the Lord's table."[95] Somewhere between a sectarian exclusiveness that welcomes only those who believe and behave similarly, and a radical inclusiveness that disregards belief or behavior, a creative tension must be found, one that expresses our best understanding of God's will in scripture and a genuine quest for new light. Such a tension will require integrity of all who participate and will acknowledge that the standards for participation must apply equally to all. Double-standards regarding who is and is not included in the body of Christ do not wash with God, and they do not ennoble efforts to worship God "in spirit and truth" (John 4:24). It may at least be argued that texts, such as the wedding banquet in Matthew chapter 22 and the great dinner in Luke chapter 14, indicate the jury is not yet in on who will ultimately be welcomed to the Lord's table.

Beyond the conscious decisions made about who's in and who's out, there are other ways inclusion and exclusion happen in the worship of God. A case in point is the exclusive language of the worship tradition. If in Christ Jesus "there is no longer Jew or Greek. . .no longer slave or free. . .no longer male and female" (Gal. 3:28), there can no longer be an insistence upon the masculine, white-European worship language that effectively excludes many women and minorities, thus undermining the unity of Christ's body. As Anabaptists become increasingly diverse and multicultural, worship language as well as worship style will need to reflect those realities while staying rooted in an Anabaptist ethos that gives identity and direction. Earle Fike expresses it well in stating, "if we are to welcome others from different cultures into our fellowship, we must learn to share their worship as well as invite them into ours."[96]

Language is also a barrier for children and youth. "Developmental studies have shown that the highly verbal style of Mennonite worship cannot usually meet the cognitive, emotional, or spiritual needs of children and youth."[97] Congregations must do better at involving children and youth in worship. At the very least, this will mean childrens' stories that are for children and not moral lessons for adults to overhear. It will also mean involving youth in worship throughout the year and not just on segregated Youth Sundays that imply their leadership is an aberration rather than an integral part of congregational life.

User-Friendly. An emerging model for evangelism is that of the *seeker-driven congregation* popularized by the Willow Creek Community Church in South Barrington, Illinois. According to Mike Overpeck, part of the pastoral team at a Church of the Brethren congregation modeled after Willow Creek,

> we try to understand why people are not going to church, then design a service around (our findings). We find they're not comfortable with singing. We provide the music for them. They're tired of people always asking for money. We don't ask. Everything is designed with the non-church person in mind, it is a non-participation service.[98]

With its lack of singing, participation, and call for giving, one might conclude it is a non-Anabaptist service as well. Dale Stoffer observes that the seeker-driven model for church growth, "has tended to give people what they want rather than what they spiritually need. So much of it is based upon perceived needs without calling people to some of our traditional Anabaptist commitments."[99] Agreed. However, it is also clear that this worship form is reaching a population that traditional Anabaptist services simply do not, and critics must overcome their suspicion (and perhaps jealousy) enough to acknowledge the good that is in it.

While the "seeker-driven" model clearly warrants critique, its emphasis on being "user-friendly" may warrant emulation. As Overpeck continues, "We avoid the usual religious terms. We explain the terms rather than use them. At Waterford we don't assume the people know the Bible stories. If we're to use one, we tell it."[100] While religious terms in worship need not be avoided, many congregations can do more to explain, interpret, and convey those religious terms in comprehensible language and media.

I deeply resonate with Paul Roth's fear that "we will let our worship and practices become so adulterated that we lose our center."[101] But I also fear becoming so concerned with the preservation of Anabaptist identity in worship and congregational life that we ignore those beyond our doors, discourage those who are knocking, and confuse those walking through them week in and week out.

Ecumenical. While it is important to maintain the distinctiveness of the Anabaptist worship heritage in as much as it continues serving God's purpose in the world, it is also important to recognize and nurture its many points of continuity with the larger Christian church. As Walter Klaassen suggests,

> In this twentieth century we no longer are fighting the battles of the sixteenth. Our Anabaptist ancestors were persecuted by Protestant and Catholic in the sixteenth century; today we have warm ecumenical relations with other churches. . . . The Roman form of worship and its simplification in the Lutheran and Anglican versions are our heritage as well. . . . It includes the twelve centuries from 325 to 1525 which we have in the past tended to exclude as one long, tragic error.[102]

One simple way of acknowledging and nurturing this shared heritage is observance of the Church Year. It is a well kept secret that Mennonites, until the turn of this century, were among the only Protestants in America following the Church Year, but later it fell into disuse among them.[103] If Anabaptists are to be reminded of their oneness in Christ with other believers, if they are to benefit from the treasures of the larger Christian tradition, if they are to consciously resist the intrusions of the cultural calendar,[104] they will need to observe in a flexible way the special days and seasons of the Christian year. For only as Anabaptists recognize the ties that bind them to the larger church will they gain a proper perspective and clarity on who they are, where they fit in, and what contributions they may continue to make to the upbuilding of Christ's body on earth.

Silence. In 1761 a Pietist leader described Brethren in eastern Pennsylvania as "zealous" in their worship, their preaching and praying occurring "with great clamor, as if they were hard of hearing." Hymns, he said, chased each other "as if they lacked [inner] silence."[105] Like that of their ancestors, much Anabaptist worship today is so filled with words and music that silence has become an uncomfortable accident that is carefully avoided.

Richard Foster suggests that "one reason we can hardly bear to remain silent is that it makes us feel so helpless. We are so accustomed to relying upon words to manage and control others."[106] As long as we control our worship of God, God will not control us, and quite frankly, most of us prefer it that way.

Just as the Lord was not in wind, earthquake, or fire for the prophet Elijah (1 Kings 19:11-12), so the Lord may not always be in sermon, hymn, or liturgy for us. As with Elijah, it may at times be only in moments of "sheer silence" that Spirit touches spirit and believers hear the Lord passing by. If Anabaptists are to truly hear the word of the Lord as did prophets of old, there must be moments in worship when they become silent to sense and to hear the Holy One in their midst. As much as God appreciates the "clamor" of adoration and praise, God may also appreciate the opportunity to get a word in edgewise.

Simplicity. With all that can be included in worship—from preaching to poetry, from drama to dance, from singing to silence—it is still imperative that Anabaptist worship today, like that of the sixteenth-century, retain a simple focus on God that will not be confused by a plethora of creative busyness. Simplicity in worship has a compelling quality all its own, as recognized by the

Old Order Brethren who have adhered to the traditional Anabaptist worship pattern for over a hundred years without change.[107]

Whatever simplicity means within the context of each congregation, a fundamental caution for Anabaptists of the coming century is that their worship should not "crowd God out."[108] For whatever crowds God out of worship, no matter how traditional, innovative, or "Anabaptist," is contrary to the purpose of "giving God the worth due God."

Conclusion

Richard Foster observes that "if we long to go where God is going and do what God is doing, we will move into deeper, more authentic worship."[109] Anabaptists of the sixteenth century counted the cost and paid a high price to go where they saw God going and do what they saw God doing. Perhaps a central question for Anabaptists of the twenty-first century is whether they will count the cost and pay the price for "deeper, more authentic worship."

These suggestions will, of course, apply to some Anabaptist communions more than others and are by no means guarantors of worship that is faithful to the heritage and meaningful in the present age. But if Anabaptist worship of the future is to look more to observers like people getting down and honoring the One who is great and mighty than like a "tired old nag pulling a cart," we will have to care enough to give it our very best.

1 Claus-Peter Clasen, *Anabaptism: A Social History, 1525-1618, Switzerland, Austria, Moravia, South and Central Germany* (Ithaca and London: Cornell University Press, 1972), 92, quoted in Edward N. Poling, "Worship Life in Sixteenth-Century Anabaptism," *Brethren Life and Thought* 37 (Spring 1992): 126.

2 The first definition is from *For All Who Minister* (Elgin, Ill.: Brethren Press, 1993), 3. The second is originally from James F. White, *New Forms of Worship* (New York: Abingdon, 1971), quoted in Kenneth I. Morse, *Move In Our Midst* (Elgin: Brethren Press, 1977), 12.

3 William H. Willimon, *The Service of God: How Worship and Ethics Are Related* (Nashville: Abingdon Press, 1983), 18.

4 Morse, *Move In Our Midst*, 55.

5 Morse, "Worship, Public," Donald F. Durnbaugh, ed. *The Brethren Encyclopedia* (Philadelphia: The Brethren Encyclopedia, Inc., 1983), 1373-4.

6 Rebecca J. Slough, interview with author, August 5, 1993.

7 Nancy R. Faus, "Lecture on Passages and Rituals," *Ministry*, October 7, 1982, Oak Brook, Illinois, 376.

8 Edward Poling, "Worship Life," 122.

9 Lauree Hersch Meyer, "Liturgy, Tradition, and Ministry in the Church of the Brethren," *Brethren Life and Thought* 34 (Autumn 1989): 205.

10 Alvin J. Beachy, "The Theology and Practice of Anabaptist Worship," *Mennonite Quarterly Review* 40 (July 1966): 166, citing John Howard Yoder, "Offhand Comments on Worship in Contemporary American Mennonitism," quoted in Poling, "Worship Life," 122.

11 Paul M. Miller, "Worship Among the Early Anabaptists," *Mennonite Quarterly Review* 30 (1956): 237, quoted in Poling, "Worship Life," 129.

12 John D. Rempel, *Planning Worship Services* (Elgin: Brethren Press, 1992), 14.

13 Harold S. Bender, "Worship, Public. Anabaptist," ed. Bender, *The Mennonite Encyclopedia: A Comprehensive Reference Work on the Anabaptist-Mennonite Movement*, 4 vols. (Hillsboro, Kan.: Mennonite Brethren Publishing House, 1955-1959), 985.

14 Harold S. Bender, "Worship, Public: Swiss-South German Tradition," ibid., 988.

15 Ibid., 984.

16 Carl F. Bowman, "The Therapeutic Transformation of Brethren Tradition," ed. Emmert F. Bittinger, *Brethren in Transition: 20th Century Directions and Dilemmas* (Camden, Maine: Penobscot Press, 1992), 44.

17 Paul Roth, interview with author, August 2, 1993.

18 Morse, "Worship, Public," 1863.

19 Alvin J. Beachy, "Theology and Practice," *Mennonite Quarterly Review* 40 (July 1966): 169, cited in C.D. Dyck, "Worship Patterns of Second Generation Dutch Anabaptists," quoted in Poling, "Worship Life," 125.

20 Robert Friedmann, *The Theology of Anabaptism, An Interpretation* (Scottdale, Pa.: Herald Press, 1973), 147, from "Statement of Church Discipline, Berne, Switzerland, 1526-1527," quoted in Poling, "Worship Life," 125.

21 Walter Klaassen, *Biblical and Theological Bases for Worship in the Believers' Church* (Newton, Kan.: Faith and Life Press, 1978), 11.

22 Bender, "Worship, Public: Anabaptist," 985.

23 Poling, "Worship Life," 126.

24 Morse, "Worship, Public," 1890.

25 Slough interview.

26 Klaassen, *Worship in the Believers' Church*, 12.

27 Rempel, *Worship Services*, 32.

28 Robert Friedmann, "Hutterite Worship and Preaching," *Mennonite Quarterly Review* 40 (1966): 6, cited in Poling, "Worship Life," 123.

29 Poling, "Worship Life," 130.

30 Ibid.

31 Dale W. Brown, "Worship," ed. Donald F. Durnbaugh, *The Church of the Brethren: Yesterday and Today*, (Elgin, Ill.: Brethren Press), 70.

32 Rempel, *Worship Services*, 32.

33 Brown, "Worship," 64.

34 Hersch Meyer, "Liturgy, Tradition, and Ministry," 205, 207.

35 Rempel, *Worship Services*, 31 .

36 Brown, "Worship," 67.

[37] *Pastor's Manual: Church of the Brethren* (Elgin, Ill.: Brethren Press), 28.
[38] Earle W. Fike, interview with author, August 2, 1993.
[39] Paul E. R. Mundey to author, July 15, 1993.
[40] Slough interview.
[41] Duane M. Sider, interview with author, July 15, 1993.
[42] Dale W. Brown, "A People Without a Liturgy? An Essay on Brethren Worship, Past and Present," *Brethren Life and Thought*, 31 (Winter 1986): 29.
[43] Dale R. Stoffer, interview with author, July 20, 1993.
[44] Floyd Mallott, cited in Brown, "People Without a Liturgy," 29.
[45] Stoffer interview.
[46] Sider interview.
[47] Ibid.
[48] *Random House Webster's Dictionary*, s.v., "gather."
[49] Kenneth J. Nafziger, interview with author, June 25, 1993.
[50] Poling, "Worship Life," 129.
[51] Nancy R. Faus, "Guest Editor's Introduction," *Brethren Life and Thought*, 31 (Winter 1986): 8.
[52] Jimmy R. Ross, "The Road Ahead," *Brethren Life and Thought*, 31 (Wint., 1986): 34.
[53] Thomas W. Geiman, interview with author, August 12, 1993.
[54] Bender, "Worship, Public." *Anabaptist*, 984.
[55] Ibid.
[56] James F. Myer, interview with author, July 13, 1993.
[57] Willimon, *The Service of God*, 16.
[58] James F. White, *New Forms of Worship* (Nashville: Abingdon Press, 1971), 51, quoted in Ross, "The Road Ahead," 33.
[59] Rempel interview.
[60] Jean L. Hendricks, interview by author, July 17, 1993.
[61] Kenneth J. Nafziger, interview with author, June 25, 1993.
[62] Mundey to author.
[63] Richard J. Foster, *Celebration of Discipline* (San Francisco: Harper and Row, 1988), 158-9.
[64] Philip K. Clemens, "What Do You Mean You Want Exciting Worship?" *Gospel Herald* 21 (May 1991): 2.
[65] Slough interview.
[66] Nafziger interview.
[67] Rempel, *Planning Worship*, 49.
[68] *For All Who Minister*, 4.
[69] Myer interview .
[70] *For All Who Minister*, 6.
[71] Nancy R. Faus, interview with author, August 10, 1993.
[72] Slough interview.
[73] Myer interview.
[74] Morse, "Worship, Public," 1373.
[75] Rempel, *Worship Services*, 17.
[76] Rempel, *Worship Services*, 19.
[77] C. Leslie Mitton, "Ephesians," eds. Ronald E. Clements and Matthew Black, *The New Century Bible Commentary* (London: Marshall, Morgan and Scott, 1973), XIX, 149.
[78] Clemens interview.
[79] John Fischer, *Real Christians Don't Dance* (Minneapolis: Bethany House Publishers, 1988), 123-4.
[80] Brown, "Worship," 77.
[81] Stoffer interview.
[82] *We Gather Together* (Elgin: Brethren Press, 1979), 160, 175.
[83] Sider interview.
[84] Ibid.
[85] Paul Tillich, *Dynamics of Faith* (New York: Harper and Row, 1957), 42.
[86] Earle W. Fike, "Worship in the Church of the Brethren: Moving From Past to Future," TMs, July 1992, Huntington, Pennsylvania, 1.
[87] Klaassen, *Worship in the Believers' Church*, 105.

[88] Morse, "Worship, Public," 1377.

[89] Ronald C. Arnett, "Logos In the Fellowship of Communication," *Brethren Life and Thought* 31 (Winter 1986): 49.

[90] Sider interview.

[91] Warren F. Groff, "Brethren at Worship: Questions of Fittingness and Adequacy," *Brethren Life and Thought* 31 (Winter 1986): 12.

[92] Rempel, *Worship Services*, 16.

[93] Tillich, *Dynamics*, 4.

[94] Fike, "Past to Future," 5.

[95] Bowman, "Therapeutic Transformation," 44.

[96] Fike, "Past to Future," 6.

[97] Rampogu Sampson Lemuel, "Worship, Public. (North America)," eds. Cornelius J. Dyck and Dennis D. Martin, *The Mennonite Encyclopedia* (1990), V, 946.

[98] Frank Ramirez, "The church that 'gives 'em what they want," *Messenger* (June 1993): 12.

[99] Stoffer interview.

[100] Ramirez, "What they want," 12.

[101] Roth, interview.

[102] Klaassen, *Worship in the Believers' Church*, 15.

[103] Sider interview.

[104] *For All Who Minister*, 21.

[105] Morse, "Worship, Public," 1375.

[106] Foster, *Discipline*, 100-1.

[107] Fred W. Benedict to author, July 31, 1993.

[108] Thelma Miller Groff, "Worship, Private," eds. Dyck and Martin, *Mennonite Encyclopedia* (1990), V, 943.

[109] Foster, *Discipline*, 161.

Conversation
ಕುಕು **V** ಚ೩ಚ೩

The Lord's Supper

"And he took bread and he broke it." This straightforward description of a simple act has sparked surprisingly diverse attempts to recreate it. Jeff Bach maps this variety of form and interpretation among Anabaptists. Some stressed commemoration, some Christ-like suffering, and some mystical union. Feetwashing, although commonly identified with Anabaptism, was by no means universal. Common threads across Anabaptist traditions include rejection of transubstantiation, rejection of ritual mediation by a priesthood, biblicism of form, and the linkage of the Lord's Supper with self-examination and discipline. By partaking of the Lord's Supper in homes using lay pastors rather than priests, Anabaptists "redefined the space of sacred ritual" by connecting it to ordinary life.

If Anabaptists historically differed about how to observe the Lord's Supper, Nadine Pence Frantz argues that its form nevertheless remains essential. Noting that Anabaptists, in their dual attention to the written Word and the living out of faith, unite "scripted" and "performative" traditions, she analyzes the performative character of the Lord's Supper—the ways in which it embodies faith. The Lord's Supper is seen not as a mere symbol or reflection of faith, but as something that itself shapes and reconstitutes faith. To alter the form (by removing elements such as the Holy Kiss and feetwashing) thus impacts upon the faith that is reconstituted through the ordinance. In a word, the ordinances are not to be taken lightly or tinkered with for casual or purely pragmatic reasons.

1

Incorporation into Christ and the Brethren: The Lord's Supper and Feetwashing in Anabaptist Groups

by Jeff Bach

No overview of Anabaptist beliefs and practices related to the Lord's Supper has been undertaken. Only recently has a monograph appeared which attempts to address the Lord's Supper in the thought of three particular Anabaptist writers and their communities.[1] While no survey of the topic is possible here, this article will offer a sampling of some Anabaptist writings and accounts of their observances of the Lord's Supper. The sample will suggest some of the range of practice and interpretation, or theology, of the Lord's Supper in the Anabaptist movement. The sixteenth and eighteenth centuries will receive primary concentration, since those mark times of some of the greatest changes in the Lord's Supper among Anabaptist groups.[2]

The choice of "Lord's Supper" to refer to the ritual reflects one of the favorite terms for it among Anabaptist groups, derived from Andreas Karlstadt's and Ulrich Zwingli's influences. The term "Lord's Supper" will refer broadly to that Christian ritual eating of bread and drinking wine (later grape juice by many), associated with the death of Jesus Christ, as reshaped in the Anabaptist movement.

Several, but not all, Anabaptist groups practiced a ritual of washing feet in conjunction with the Lord's Supper, some as a hospitality ritual. This overview will offer a glimpse of some variations of practice, interpretation, and significance of feetwashing among Anabaptist groups. The phrase "Love Feast" will refer to an expanded ritual of the Lord's Supper (i.e., bread and wine), feetwashing and a fellowship meal (*agape*, from which the term Love Feast, or *Liebesmahl*, originates) adopted by the Schwarzenau Brethren groups.

Rituals are special acts sometimes using unique, sometimes ordinary objects, gestures, or words. They are invested, intentionally or unintentionally, with extraordinary significance by an individual or group participating in them. Rituals are events that communicate and encode ultimate, transcendent meaning to participants. Yet at the same time, participants affirm, challenge, and modify those meanings. Rituals generally are effective because they are repeated (the polarity of preservation). However, every enactment presents opportunities for modification or change (the polarity of spontaneity). Rituals are dynamic events when they occur in the field between these polarities. When ritual behavior is dominated by preservation, it becomes static; when it is dominated by spontaneity, it can become so diffuse as to lose shared commonalities. In both cases, ritual is in danger of losing sufficiently shared meaning to remain symbolic communication. Ritual by no means belongs exclusively to the domain of "religion," that is, systems of thought and usually practice grounded in belief of transcendent and ultimate value or meaning. Indeed, some behavior that does not carry vocabulary explicitly associated with organized religion may be ritualistic.

Victor Turner has written of "ritual process," which creates transcendent moments of "communitas" when participants are bonded together in collective identity greater than the aggregate of the individuals involved in the ritual. Van Gennep has described ritual moments as times of "liminality," when traditional patterns and identities are temporarily suspended, to be followed by reintegrating the participants in a new (and renewed) social whole.[3]

In a study of the festival of Corpus Christi in the Middle Ages, Miri Rubin has observed that a ritual such as the mass, even when performed and interpreted by the priest who directs it, is nevertheless vulnerable to a plurality of interpretations by those who participate, who may respond with affirmation, challenge, or indifference. This range of meanings can reinforce ritual and the hierarchy who perform it as well as challenge the very authority structures that authorize the ritual. Rubin proposes that the church's ritual practice and teaching were simultaneously promulgated, performed, challenged, reemphasized, and reinterpreted among the combination of priests, theologians, civic authorities, pious laity, mystics, and heretics of the Middle Ages.[4]

These theoretical remarks raise the caution against seeking a uniform or normative practice or interpretation among them. This effort attempts to note commonalities and divergencies in ritual, suggesting a range of practices, interpretations, and changes within them.

The sources used are primarily writings about the Lord's Supper by leaders defending a particular Anabaptist view and practice. While Anabaptism itself tended to allow people to speak who were not the privileged of their day, we do well to remember that Anabaptists also privileged some voices and silenced others. Although reports of Anabaptist practices of the Lord's Supper in this period are rare, some effort will be made to compare practice and narrative.

Background

The Fourth Lateran Council of 1215 provided for the first time as church dogma the language of transubstantiation to define the "substance" of Christ's flesh and blood literally present in the "accidents" (outward appearance and properties) of bread and wine, the culmination of the mass upon the invocation of the words of consecration by a duly ordained priest. The same council also required communicating at least once a year. A worthy communion required beforehand oral confession before the congregation, true contrition, and adequate restitution or satisfaction offered for sins. Parishioners were understandably reluctant to communicate frequently. As the Middle Ages waned, the mass met a wide variety of responses, ranging from enthusiastic Corpus Christi processions, lay Eucharistic piety such as that of the Modern Devotion, humanists like Erasmus of Rotterdam who considered moral living to be as important as devout participation in the church's ritual life, and Sacramentarians like Cornelis Hoen who rejected outright the doctrine of transubstantiation.

Anabaptist Beginnings in Switzerland

Conrad Grebel and his associates in Zurich originally gathered around Ulrich Zwingli. Grebel and Zwingli were influenced in their reform views by humanists, including Erasmus, Johann Oecolampadius, Cornelis Hoen, and the reformer Andreas Karlstadt von Bodenstein.[5] Already in 1521, while Luther was at the Wartburg, Karlstadt had experimented with reform of the mass. He celebrated an "evangelical mass," dressed in academic gown rather than vestments, and offered communion in both kinds without requiring that communicants had confessed.[6] Luther squelched all of this upon returning to Wittenberg.

Karlstadt continued to develop his own theology and practice of the Lord's Supper while serving as pastor at Orlamünde, 1523-1524. By this time he had abandoned belief in real presence and the Eucharist as a means of grace. He called the Lord's Supper a commemoration, a sign pointing to Christ's redemptive death and entailing a spiritual communion of the body and blood of Christ. Karlstadt uniquely interpreted the words of institution—"this is my body"—to mean that Jesus was pointing to himself as he spoke. Karlstadt understood that Christ's physical body would be given on the cross for the disciples but not to them in the supper.

For Karlstadt, the Supper was a sign of loving fellowship among Christians. In contrast to his 1521 rejection of confession in preparation for communion, Karlstadt later insisted that communicants should indeed prepare for communion with self-examination, to see if they remembered properly the meaning of Christ's death commemorated in the bread and wine. Karlstadt even allowed the possibility of mutual correction and the ban. These views were published in a series of tracts during October-November 1524 in Basel, with funds raised by the Zurich radicals. The tracts attacked Luther's views on the Eucharist.[7]

In the same month, before Karlstadt's publications, Conrad Grebel wrote to Thomas Müntzer.[8] Calvin Pater has noted the similarities between Karlstadt and Grebel regarding the Lord's Supper that appear in this letter. Both rejected transubstantiation, the mass as a sacrifice and as means of grace. They rejected the ceremonial trappings of the mass. The Lord's Supper is a memorial to the death and resurrection of Christ. The eating is spiritual, so that by faith, the elements become "the communion of the body and blood of Christ," while

Christ remains bodily at the right hand of God. Both agreed that the Supper is a sign of believers' love and fellowship. (Grebel even called the Supper a "love meal.")[9]

Many of these commonalities were also shared with Zwingli, and beyond him, some with Erasmus.[10] It is difficult to establish precise priorities of influence. Certainly Karlstadt was the first to attempt an evangelical Lord's Supper. Similarities with Karlstadt appear in Zwingli's thought, yet the latter delayed altering the practice of the mass until 1525. More radical than Zwingli, Grebel insisted on only what he thought the Bible commands in observing the Lord's Supper. While Zwingli perhaps believed he was doing the same, he also supported his position with theologians from Christian antiquity, especially Tertullian, Augustine, and Ambrose. Grebel was more reluctant, though not unable, to do so.

Similarities, of course, do not necessarily prove dependence. However, Grebel's participation in the Zurich disputations (1523) show both strong influence from Zwingli as well as emerging disagreements. The 1524 letter to Müntzer reveals that Karlstadt also influenced Grebel. In this context, Grebel and his associates worked with scripture to develop their own implications for the Lord's Supper.[11] By late 1524, Grebel and his group were more willing than either Karlstadt or Zwingli to introduce and sustain a biblically oriented reform of the mass, which they called the Lord's Supper.[12]

Grebel wrote to Müntzer that by faith the bread "is the body of Christ and an incorporation with Christ and the brethren," to be eaten in love and unity. Believers would be "willing to live and to suffer for the sake of Christ and the brethren." Erasmus and Zwingli had stressed the Eucharist's character of displaying the corporate nature of the Church. Zwingli had even stated that Christians should offer their lives for one another.[13] Müntzer had stressed the need for an experience of internal spiritual suffering before believers could arrive at experiential knowledge of justification. By 1524, he advocated that the godly should destroy the godless with the sword.

The broader context of Zwingli's and Grebel's interpreting the Supper as a symbol of unity and willingness to die for fellow Christians was the political ties of the Swiss Confederation over against the Hapsburg empire. This style of confederating against an overlord spread at this very time into southern Germany and Austria in the unrest of commoners against their superiors, an influence that Thomas Brady has called "turning Swiss."[14] Already in 1524, however, Grebel insisted that willingness to die for fellow Christians precluded the possibility of killing in defense of fellow Christians or the Gospel. Neither Zwingli nor Müntzer shared this conviction.

Grebel called for ordinary bread at the Lord's Supper.[15] He also suggested that the Lord's Supper be observed in the evening, frequently, and in homes. Of course, the Swiss Brethren had no church building at their disposal.[16]

Grebel's reshaping of the Lord's Supper, inspired by Karlstadt, and sharing much with Zwingli, is a kind of sacramental iconoclasm. Grebel's relentless insistence on only what the Bible permits stripped away most of the elements of the mass, and reinterpreted what was left, namely the bread and wine, pastor and congregation. Grebel's restructuring represents a shift out of what traditionally was defined as sacred space, time, and objects (Sunday morning, church building, wafer and reserved chalice, along with priestly accouterments) and investing what was thought of as "ordinary" with the presence of the sacred (evening meal time, homes of believers, and ordinary bread and wine served to all communicants).

Grebel and Zwingli also differed in their understandings of the Church that partakes of the Lord's Supper. Early in the Zurich reform (1522-23), Zwingli had envisioned the practice of the ban and excommunication, prohibiting those who gave "public offense" from partaking until they mend their ways. Later Zwingli increasingly defined discipline as the prerogative of the city council and its enforcers to punish violators of the civically established religious order. He explained "binding and loosing" (Matt. 16 and 18 and Jn. 20) as preaching the Gospel, or leaving gross sinners to their sin until they repent.[17] His doctrine of predestination resulted in an invisible Church within a mixed congregation, partaking of the Supper. After January, 1525, the Swiss Brethren insisted that the Supper was for a visible Church whose members were baptized upon confession of faith and used the Rule of Christ, i.e., mutual discipline. In 1527 this view of the Church was more sharply defined at Schleitheim.

Balthasar Hubmaier

Balthasar Hubmaier was one of the best educated of the first generation of Anabaptist leaders. His order for the Lord's Supper (Nikolsburg, 1527) provides one of the earliest and most detailed examples of an Anabaptist liturgy for the ritual. While formal in organization and procedure, Hubmaier's order contains a rather simplified ritual, with ordinary bread and wine, eaten in commemoration of Christ's suffering and in a fellowship of love among Christians. Hubmaier laid out his observance in a dynamic interplay of a highly defined role, on one hand, for the officiating minister, still called a "priest," who directed the service, and on the other hand, a significant role for the congregation. For example, anyone in the congregation may add comments when the pastor preaches to interpret the Supper beforehand.[18] Each communicant must answer audibly to questions about the status of reconciliation and love, the "Pledge of Love," among the congregation.

The four questions pointedly asked to each communicant for oral response in the "Pledge of Love" are perhaps the most striking feature in this order. First, will members serve and subject themselves to God? Second, will they love and serve their neighbors with the help of Jesus? Third, will they offer and accept mutual admonition (discipline)? Fourth, do they desire to confirm this pledge publicly by eating and drinking the Lord's Supper as a living memorial?[19] These questions sharply defined the contours of loving fellowship.

In "A Simple Instruction" (1526), Hubmaier apparently rejected Zwingli's spiritualized interpretation of the words of institution, "this is my body." Zwingli, depending on the humanist Cornelis Hoen, argued that "is" really means "signifies," or, "This signifies my body." Hubmaier wrote that "is" means "is," so that "this bread must be the body of Christ." Yet in the same tract, Hubmaier stated that the bread is not "the body of Christ, except in remembrance." Although he resisted Zwingli's position, Hubmaier's views came closer to Zwingli than to any other reformer. Showing further signs of Zwinglian language, Hubmaier stated that the Supper is a memorial sign, a thanksgiving, which requires faith and love.[20] In formality of structure and the officiant's role, Hubmaier's Lord's Supper still reflected Roman Catholic ritual. In content and interpretation, it reflected a unique development of the influences of Zwingli and humanism.

Schleitheim

At the village of Schleitheim on the German-Swiss border, Anabaptists met in February, 1527, and reached a "Brotherly Union," consolidating the young Swiss and southern German Anabaptist movements. In many ways, the Schleitheim Confession's third article on the Lord's Supper echoed the views of Grebel. The Brotherly Union emphasized more clearly the role of the ban, or mutual discipline, in the Church. Schleitheim had a clear sense of the Church's "separation" from the "devil and the world."[21]

A document that circulated with the Brotherly Union, entitled a "Congregational Order" by its translator, John Howard Yoder, detailed more of the practice of the Lord's Supper. It was to be observed every time the sisters and brothers met. Worship meetings should also include a simple common meal. The Congregational Order envisioned the practice of community of goods, or at least a common fund. The Lord's Supper is a memorial of Christ's death, to remind believers how Christ died for them, so "that we might also be willing to give our body and life for Christ's sake, which means for the sake of all the brothers."[22]

Michael Sattler, who may have written the articles on the Lord's Supper, also wrote that Christ established this ceremony "primarily because [Christians] must suffer just like their head." Furthermore, "their death would not be their own but the Lord's." This identification with the Lord's suffering is not meritorious nor salvific, rather it is both the gift and cost of discipleship.[23]

The Brotherly Union and Sattler linked the commemoration of Christ's suffering to the bodily suffering of the sisters and brothers for each other. Offering one's life for them is offering up life for Christ' sake; their dying becomes Christ's dying. For Sattler, the suffering and ascended Christ is one, and is "really" present in the visible, disciplined congregation separated from the world. This congregation is Christ's body, spiritually and physically. For the

Swiss Brethren, the Lord's Supper thus connected the soteriological, ecclesio-logical, and ethical significance of Christ's death and resurrection.

Grebel, Hubmaier, the Brotherly Union, and Sattler all expressly tied the readiness of Christians to die for their sisters and brothers to the Lord's Supper and its commemoration of Christ's death. Certainly scripture, especially John 14-17, provided grounding for this connection. Zwingli had also emphasized the congregation as Christ's body and the Supper a sign of unity and love. Both Erasmus and Zwingli had drawn ethical implications from the Eucharist, including that Christians should offer their lives for one another.[24] Yet other influences may also lie behind this explicit connection.

The commoners' uprisings of 1524-25, often called the Peasants' War, produced many lists of grievances and articles of confederation. A significant element in many of these was the pledge to risk life and limb, and sometimes goods, for comrades in the uprising. Many communities adapted emergent evangelical thought, i.e., Lutheran and Zwinglian, and applied it to their social and economic grievances to create agenda for change and sometimes rebellion. This often accompanied anti-clerical sentiment.

The Allgäu Articles (February 24, 1525) began with a preamble in which the peasants pledged to "lay down life and limb for one another, for we are brothers in Christ Jesus."[25] The articles of the Black Forest peasants (May 1525), found among the papers of Balthasar Hubmaier after his flight from Waldshut, called for commoners to join together in "Christian union and brotherhood." Hubmaier at least helped to edit these articles, and perhaps he drafted them.[26]

The third article of the famous Twelve Articles of the peasants (February or March, 1525), which soon spread through many areas of unrest, called for equality between rulers and commoners. Yet the peasants denied anarchy, seeking rather to "live under the commandment of God."

> Christ has redeemed and bought us all by the shedding of his precious blood, the shepherd just as the highest. . . .We are to love God, recognize him as our Lord in our neighbor and do all that God commanded us at the Last Supper.[27]

The Lord's Supper appears in the third article of both the Schleitheim document and the peasants' Twelve Articles. What the latter had in mind by what God commanded at the Last Supper is not fully clear. Both documents, however, connected love of Christ and neighbor, and social equality to the Last Supper. For the Anabaptists who used the Congregational Order, the Lord's Supper was a ritual enactment of this paradigm of love and equality.

Hubmaier, Sattler, and Grebel were all active in areas of commoners uprisings. As James Stayer and others have pointed out, many who became Anabaptists had earlier been involved in some way with the Peasants' War.[28] This does not mean that the Peasants' War generated Anabaptism, nor that Anabaptism precipitated the Peasants' War. Grebel's letter to Müntzer, written on the eve of the uprisings, had called on Christians to die for one another in the context of his remarks on the Lord's Supper. The same letter, however, renounced violence. The parallels with the peasants' articles suggest that religious and social concerns were important to both movements. Anabaptists continued to alter the agenda and redefine the context in which to pursue it.[29]

The views of Grebel, Hubmaier, and Sattler on the Lord's Supper illustrate one way that concerns from the agenda of the commoners' uprisings continued in altered form after their suppression. The goal of an egalitarian, voluntary community with some level of shared resources lived on in practice among many of these Anabaptists.[30] All three carried over the commitment of some of the peasants that members of such a community must be ready to risk their lives for one another. Hubmaier was willing to grant that they might also need to bear the sword. Grebel and Sattler insisted that they must live and die defenselessly. Sattler expressed the clearest Christocentric foundation for love that risks life defenselessly for a neighbor. For all three, the Lord's Supper confronted Christians with a bond of love that compelled them to offer their lives for each other, in the way Christ's life had been offered for the forgiveness of sins. The Lord's Supper tied Christ's redemptive suffering to their bodily suffering for each other in the genesis and maintenance of an egalitarian community.

Anabaptist Mysticism: Hans Denck

Hans Denck, the Nuremberg school master, represents a quite different strand of Anabaptism, which was influenced by late medieval mysticism, the religious quest for an interior, unitive experience of the soul with God.[31] In his "Confession to the City Council of Nuremberg" (1525), Denck wrote that whoever valued self-mortification and avoided "blind trust in outward ceremonies" may "eat the living, invisible bread" and drink the "invisible wine from the invisible cup." Whoever drinks from the invisible cup becomes "drunk," meaning that they "know nothing" about themselves and "become deified (*vergottet*) through the love of God."[32]

In his so-called recantation shortly before his death in 1527, Denck called the Supper a "memorial" of the body and blood of the Lord. Believing in Christ is a spiritual eating of Christ's body that renews the soul. For Denck, drinking the wine is as if Christ says to the believer, "You will become fully one with me. I in you and you in me, just as food and drink mingle in some manner with the human body."[33]

Like Müntzer and his renegade, Hans Hut (whom Denck baptized), Denck believed that inward, spiritual suffering was necessary in order to be opened to an experiential encounter with the living, contemporary Christ. This suffering had little if anything to do with suffering for others or the suffering of the historical Jesus. Similarly, he was less worried about how to celebrate the Lord's Supper properly. Indeed, he granted that one could "live without outward bread where God's glory demands it." More important than keeping the outward ritual was appropriating the experience of the divine it represents. Denck's language is reminiscent of the Eucharistic piety of some medieval mystics. In such piety, union with Christ is enacted by consuming the physical elements of the Eucharistic elements and their absorption in the body. In a sense, the human body becomes one with the body of Christ through the Eucharist.[34]

Hans Denck represents a more overtly mystical interpretation of the Lord's Supper. He also stressed the spiritual appropriation of its meaning over the practice of the ritual.

Northern Anabaptism

Anabaptism in northern Germany and the Low Countries originated from the activity of Melchior Hoffman. Familiar with the views of Luther and Karlstadt, Hoffman developed a unique synthesis of many influences. By the time of his last meeting with Karlstadt in Strasbourg in 1530, Hoffman had adopted many of Karlstadt's views on the Lord's Supper.[35] Hoffman rejected Luther's view on the bondage of the will, adopted the heavenly flesh Christology, and moved further into that rarefied world of vision and prophecy. In the same year he sent "apostolic messengers" back to Friesland and East Friesland to baptize the elect in anticipation of Christ's imminent return (slated for Strasbourg, 1533).

Hoffman's most important work, *The Ordinance of God*, appeared in 1530 when his views had reached the final form for which he is remembered. In the work, Hoffman applied the imagery of marriage covenant between bride and bridegroom to baptism and extended it to the Lord's Supper. The Supper is like a groom giving a wedding ring (the bread) to the bride (a believer). Christ, the bridegroom "gives himself to the bride with the bread" and takes the wine and "gives to his bride with the same his true bodily blood."[36]

As the "bride" eats bread and drinks wine, "she has physically received and eaten the noble Bridegroom with his blood. She is in him, and again, he is in her." Hoffman continued, "the bodily Christ, who sits at the right hand of God, is in truth bodily her [the bride's] own and again, that she is bodily his, yes with flesh and blood. And the two are thus one."[37]

Hoffman qualified his language of union. Just as the ring is not the bridegroom himself, nor is he contained in the ring, Christ does not "corporally exist in the bread," and the "physical bread is not he himself." Yet the believer is one with Christ at the Supper. Hoffman described this by explaining how he believed the apostles understood Jesus' words and actions at the Last Supper.

> Through the bread and belief in the Word they should receive that body [Christ's] which sat by them there, that that same body should be their own which would be burned at the cross. And that theirs also was the physical blood which would be poured out from the cross.[38]

While Hoffman denied the bodily presence of Christ in the elements, he argued for Christ's presence in believers and identified Christ's suffering with theirs. Hoffman's expressions about union with Christ at the Supper clearly echo

Denck, whose influence Hoffman absorbed in Strasbourg. Yet Hoffman more clearly denied that the elements could transmit Christ's bodily presence.

Like Karlstadt, Hoffman also associated the ban with the Lord's Supper. If the "bride" (a believer) would break her "vow" (or commit spiritual adultery), then the Bridegroom (Christ) through his "apostolic emissaries" would "divorce her from his fellowship and would take from her the bread and wine."[39]

Hoffman's legacy was developed further at Münster by Bernd Rothmann. Melchiorite Anabaptism continued in three competing strands of Menno, David Joris, and the militant Batenburgers. Joris and the Batenburgers could conform to the ritual of the state churches, as well as forego communion. Joris, in particular, amplified the spiritualizing possibilities of Hoffman's views.

Bernd Rothmann

In 1533 Bernd Rothmann published his *Bekenntnis van beyden Sacramenten* (Confession Concerning Both Sacraments),[40] one of the longest Anabaptist treatments of the sacraments. Drawing on Zwingli's and Erasmus' explanation of a sacrament, Rothmann described it as an act carried out with an oath or special commitment. The act plus its object and oath constitute a sacrament.[41] Christians observe the sacraments because Christ commanded them and early Christianity practiced them.

For Rothmann, the Lord's Supper is a gathering of the faithful to commemorate Christ's death, remembering what Christ did by dying for sinners, and what debt of gratitude believers owe him. In a lengthy exposition of the words, "This is my body," he declared Zwingli's view closest to scripture and the apostles.[42] Faith and love are required among communicants. Like Hoffman and Karlstadt, Rothmann also considered mutual discipline and self-examination necessary preparations for the Lord's Supper.

According to Rothmann, "We should be willing, when demanded, to lose our lives for His name." Later the Münster Anabaptists would also kill for Christ's sake, like their Catholic and Protestant counterparts. Unlike Hoffman, Rothmann did not explicitly conclude that Christ suffers in the suffering of his followers. Rather, readiness to suffer is a measure of believers' love for Christ. Also, Rothmann envisioned community of goods as necessary for the congregation rightly observing the Lord's Supper.[43] James Stayer has pointed out how little the distribution of wealth really changed at Münster.[44]

Rothmann did not prescribe the ritual of feetwashing as part of the Lord's Supper, but he contributed to a rationale for it later among Mennonites. He saw Christ's washing the disciples' feet as a demonstration of his great love for them. Rothmann wrote that "it is vital that we, by loving each other, diligently study and seriously follow the example of our Master."[45] Washing feet in John 13 was an example of love to emulate, not a ritual to repeat. Rothmann also called the "Christian communion an *agape*, that is a meal for brethren, a banquet of love."[46] However, this was added interpretation of the Lord's Supper, not a meal distinct from the bread and wine.

Missing from this work are two important Melchiorite themes. The first is the strident iconoclasm often found in Hoffman's polemic against the Mass. The second is the apocalypticism endemic to Hoffman and so spectacular at Münster and in Rothmann's later writings. Frank Wray has suggested that Rothmann had not yet been influenced by Jan Matthijs,[47] who arrived soon after the *Bekenntnis* was published. However, Matthijs' apocalypticism came from Hoffman, whom Rothmann already knew and had met. Perhaps the *Bekenntnis* represents a brief moment of Rothmann's development before the Anabaptist kingdom.

Mennonites

The violent nadir of Münster in 1535 moved a secret sympathizer to both horror and compassion. Early in 1536, Menno Simons, a village priest in Pingjum, received baptism and became a contender for organizing the confused remnants of Hoffman's movement.

In the autobiographical section of his *Reply to Gellius Faber* (1554), Menno cited doubts about the mass during his second year as a priest as the original impetus toward Anabaptism. "It occurred to me, as often as I handled the bread and the wine in the Mass, that they were not the flesh and blood of the Lord."[48]

Of course, the memoirs were written much later, when Menno would have wanted to distance himself from Münster's lasting stigma. By naming Sacramentarian doubts, Menno could point to an influence prior to and other than Hoffman. Sacramentarian doubts would certainly have carried more respectable associations with humanists of the Low Countries. Yet this reference illustrates that questions related to the mass figured significantly in Anabaptist reform, even if baptism tended to draw more attention.

Much of Menno's theology of the Lord's Supper reflects influences from Karlstadt and Zwinglian thought, mediated in part by Hoffman and Rothmann's *Bekenntnis.*[49] With regard to spiritual communion with the body and blood of Christ, Menno more consistently maintained a dichotomy of outward and inward, that is, outwardly eating the elements while "the inner imperishable man of the heart eats in a spiritual sense the imperishable body and blood of Christ."[50] The outward elements could not mediate Christ's presence to believers.

Like Rothmann, Hoffman, and Karlstadt, Menno considered self-examination and congregational discipline through the ban as necessary preparation for the Lord's Supper. One needs to be "changed in the inner man, converted and renewed."[51] While Rothmann had stressed love for fellow Christians as necessary preparation for the Supper, Menno added a stronger emphasis on penitence and moral living. While Rothmann criticized the priests at mass for their lack of love for Christ, Menno criticized them for their immorality. Menno more stridently denounced the mass as "idolatry," echoing Hoffman's iconoclasm.

The theology of Menno is best understood in the context of late medieval penitential piety, according to Sjouke Voolstra. Even apocalyptic speculations and anticlerical sentiments were seated in a concern for proper penitence in anticipation of the last judgment.[52]

Menno's views on feetwashing belong in this penitential context. He wrote of feetwashing only rarely, usually as a metaphor for humility or cleansing. Once he referred to the act as a gesture of hospitality for visiting sisters or brothers.[53] Like Rothmann, Menno apparently did not consider feetwashing to be a part of the Lord's Supper. Yet he also contributed to the justification for the ritual when it finally was adopted by Dutch Mennonites.

The Mennonite views on the Lord's Supper represent an increasingly moralizing development of the Melchiorite tradition with emphasis on penitence. It marks a decided move away from the militant apocalypticism of Münster and the Batenburgers and away from David Joris' spiritualizing the legacy of Hoffman.

While echoing much of Menno, Dirk Philips also contributed uniquely to Mennonite practice and belief regarding the Lord's Supper. Dirk compared the believers' union with Christ at the Lord's Supper to the way ingested food is "transformed into the nature and becomes one being with the one who is fed," echoing the language of Hans Denck and Hoffman. Dirk continued, "so also true Christians are through faith in Jesus Christ completely united with him, incorporated in him, yes, transposed and changed into his nature and character."[54]

Even though Dirk repeatedly affirmed that Christ's body remained seated at the right hand of God, his understanding of Christ's presence with believers in the Supper has a higher profile than a Zwinglian memorial.

Perhaps Dirk's greatest contribution to Anabaptist ritual was securing the role of feetwashing at the Lord's Supper. In three different treatises he listed it as an ordinance marking the "true" Church. In "The Congregation of God," he explained a double significance of feetwashing. The first reason that Christ commanded the ordinance was "to give us the knowledge that he himself must cleanse us in the internal person and let the sin. . .be washed away by him."

The second reason for the rite was "that we should humble ourselves to one another."[55] Rothmann had seen Jesus' washing the disciples' feet as a symbol of love. Menno saw it as a metaphor for cleansing and perhaps as ritual of hospitality to offer traveling sisters and brothers. Dirk made it a ritual to reenact at the Lord's Supper in obedience to Jesus' command and example.

In the sixteenth century feetwashing was a part of the Maundy Thursday liturgy in which a priest washed the feet of twelve chosen people or perhaps of other priests, as Rothmann had mentioned, to dramatize the events of the Last Supper. Parishioners ordinarily would not have communicated at this service. Also, in the late Middle Ages some monastic communities still practiced a ritual of feetwashing as an act of hospitality for visitors, a legacy from the Rule of Benedict.

Only among the Dutch Mennonites did feetwashing persist beyond the sixteenth century. Later it was taken up by the Amish and Schwarzenau Brethren. Mennonites, who practiced it as a rite of hospitality, did it in homes (Waterlander Confession of Faith, 1577). As a hospitality ritual, feetwashing is mentioned in the Concept of Cologne (1591), Twisck's 33 Articles (1615), and in George Hansen's Flemish Confession of 1678 for the Danzig area.[56]

Dirk, however, clearly envisioned the ritual for the whole Church as a part of the Lord's Supper. This understanding also appeared in the Olive Branch Confession (1627), Jan Centsen's Confession of Faith (1630), the Dordrecht Confession (1632), and the First Prussian Confession of 1660. When Swiss Brethren ministers in Alsace subscribed to the Dordrecht Confession with the Ohnenheim Attestation (1660), they approved the ritual in writing, even if actual practice was slow to spread.[57]

There are no contemporary descriptions from the sixteenth century of how feetwashing was practiced. The *Mennonite Encyclopedia* assumes that generally pairs of participants (one washing, one drying) administered the rite to one or more persons sitting by. This has sometimes been called the "double mode." Many Anabaptist groups now practice what has been called the "single mode," in which one person both washes and dries the feet of the person seated adjacently. Then that person administers the rite to the next person and so on until all have participated. Men and women practiced the rite segregated by gender.

Dirk's two-fold interpretation of feetwashing was adopted in the Dordrecht Confession, although in reversed order. Representing ritually the spiritual purification and humility sought by penitents before approaching the Lord's table, feetwashing originated more as a penitential act than as a point of biblical obedience. Dirk grounded the practice with scripture but chose verses pertaining primarily to humility. Feetwashing as an act in imitation of the actions of Jesus was a secondary interpretation that developed later.

In contrast to the annual liturgical drama on Maundy Thursday, Mennonites who observed feetwashing with the Lord's Supper extended the ritual to the entire congregation each time the Supper was held. Humility and penitence were expected daily of all the congregation, not just a few.

Hutterites

Peter Riedemann's *Account of Our Religion, Doctrine and Faith* probably best presents Hutterite belief and intended practice in the sixteenth century and still serves that purpose today. Riedemann's views on the Lord's Supper reflect much of the Swiss Brethren inheritance from Zwingli and Karlstadt. For the communal Hutterites, the "partaking of the bread and wine of the Lord is a sign of the community as his body."[58] The Lord's Supper represented a sharing of Christ's body as common property of the community, just as they, through baptism became Christ's common property. Riedemann also stressed the necessity of unity for rightly observing the Supper.

Riedemann linked the suffering of Christ commemorated at the Supper to the suffering of his followers. Breaking the one loaf meant that believers "must bear the likeness of his [Christ's] death: be ready to die like him, if they would partake of his grace and become heirs of God."[59] This suffering is in imitation of Christ, more than a suffering with and for Christ's collective body in the sisters and brothers. The imitation of Christ motif may sound a distant echo of Hut's and Denck's mystical identification with Christ. Riedemann's views on the Lord's Supper represent a distilled mystical impulse from south-German-Austrian Anabaptism combined with the Zwinglian symbolism of Swiss Anabaptism in a crucible of enduring community of goods.

Pilgram Marpeck

Pilgram Marpeck, the civil engineer turned Anabaptist, tried to steer a course between the strict use of the ban by Dutch Mennonites, Hutterites, and some Swiss Brethren congregations, the militant apocalypticism of Münster, and the mandatory community of goods of Münster and the Hutterites. At the same time, he was keenly aware of the challenges of spiritualists like Schwenkfeld and criticism from the magisterial reform.

Marpeck used about two-thirds of Rothmann's *Bekenntnis* with additions to create the *Vermanung*, the longest and most detailed Anabaptist treatment of sacraments in the sixteenth century.[60] The remarks regarding the Lord's Supper will be limited here only to Marpeck's unique developments.

In his comments on the ban Marpeck rejected violence and distinguished sharply between the Old and New Testaments. He also qualified Rothmann's preference for community of goods. These points reflect an anti-Münster re-working of Rothmann's material. The third point also reflects anti-Hutterite polemic.[61]

Like Grebel and Schleitheim, Marpeck called for frequent communion (which Rothmann had not mentioned). In other writings, Pilgram Marpeck included feetwashing among the ordinances of the church and interpreted it primarily as a symbol of humility.[62] On these two points, Marpeck has mingled northern and southern Anabaptist influences.

Over against spiritualizers, Marpeck emphasized the importance of the gathered, visible Church as the body of Christ present on earth. Christ's trans-figured, ascended body at the right hand of God is represented on earth by the untransfigured body, the Church, apart from which no one comes to full faith. Stephen Boyd has pointed out that Marpeck extended the hypostatic union of the divine and human natures of Christ into his ecclesiology. For Marpeck, the Lord's Supper enacts that union of Christ's ascended body and Christ's body present in the gathered believers, the Church.[63]

Toward the Eighteenth Century: The Amish

In the last decade of the seventeenth century, a Swiss Brethren minister in Alsace, Jacob Ammann, questioned how vigorously his sisters and brothers were keeping the faith, and he is best remembered for enforcing a stricter interpretation of shunning (*Meidung*). Peter Giger, one of the objects of Ammann's rigor, also accused him of the innovation of holding the Lord's Supper twice a year instead of once.[64] Later, the charge was raised that Ammann's insistence on practicing feetwashing contributed to the Amish division of 1693. However, Ulli Ammann noted in 1698 that it became an issue only after the division was in progress, since neither Ammann's party nor the Swiss Brethren practiced the rite before the division.[65] While feetwashing and semiannual communion were not leading causes in the Amish division, they were among the distinctions separating the Amish from the Swiss Brethren.

One of the last letters about the Amish division, a memoir written in 1807, illustrates the death of the practice of feetwashing among western European Mennonites during the eighteenth century. Niklaus Wütrich suggested that Menno Simons, not the New Testament nor the apostles, introduced feetwashing. Yet in the same letter, Wütrich added that he could not find the ritual mentioned by Menno or by Jacob Ammann and could not find out "when feetwashing came into use after Christ."[66]

Wütrich could not find mention of feetwashing in eighteenth-century Mennonite statements of faith because the practice was already dying out in Europe.[67] Although it did go to Russia and North America with Mennonite emigrants, the ritual gradually disappeared from the home countries. No doubt accommodation to European culture and continued erosion of distinctive Anabaptist thought and practice in the seventeenth century contributed to this. For the Swiss Brethren, feetwashing had never been widely practiced and thus had a less secure place among their rituals.

Eighteenth Century Anabaptist Groups

Although the Peace of Westphalia (1648) formally ended the hostilities of the Thirty Years War, neither the violence nor the confessional war of words ended. Amidst the dogmatic fusillades of theologians and pastors, some voices of critique arose, calling for equal emphasis on moral living as on doctrinal correctness. This emerged first among the Reformed in the Netherlands under the influence of English Puritans living there. About a generation later it spread to German Lutheranism. In both traditions, sometimes groups of laity met in small groups for mutual edification. Some of those seeking renewal called for increased use of the Bible, rather than confessional statements of doctrine. Some of these people were interested in an affective response to grace, often speaking of spiritual rebirth. Although Philip Jacob Spener is often considered the originator of this current of critique and renewal, often called Pietism, the ingredients of pietistic renewal were present among the Reformed and Lutherans before Spener.[68]

The Schwarzenau Brethren

The Schwarzenau Brethren shared much with the Mennonites and Swiss Brethren in their views of the Lord's Supper. Many of the early Brethren had been Reformed, a tradition that shared some views in common with Anabaptist beliefs about the Lord's Supper. The New Anabaptists (Neu Täufer), as the Brethren were sometimes called, considered the Supper a memorial to Christ's death, as well as a celebration of love and fellowship. They also linked believers' readiness to suffer for Christ to the suffering commemorated at the Supper.[69] Communicants must be separated from the world and practice self-examination and the ban, if needed, in preparation for the Lord's Supper.

In addition to observing feetwashing at the Lord's Supper, the Schwarzenau Brethren added a unique contribution: the *agape*, or love meal. They had read of a meal in the practice of the early Christians in scripture, in Arnold's church history, and in his work on early Christianity, *Die Erste Liebe* (The First Love). While earlier Anabaptists had recognized two interpretations of the Lord's Supper, as memorial and love meal (some even using the term "love feast"), their practice had been to assign both interpretations to the one ritual eating of bread and wine.[70] The Schwarzenau Brethren insisted on holding the Lord's Supper only in the evening, since they pointed out, as others had earlier, that it was an evening meal (*Abendmahl*, the German word for the Lord's Supper). The Brethren also used strips of unleavened, pastry-like bread, recreating what they believed to be first-century practice.

The fires of Pietism added new energy to the interpretation of the Lord's Supper as a celebration of Christ's and believers' love. The Brethren eventually called their ritual a Love Feast. The first hymnal of the Brethren, produced in Europe in 1720, included a hymn for feetwashing, alluding to Psalm 133, as sisters and brothers "in faith and love uniting, like servants wash each other's feet."[71] The hymnal also included at least one hymn explicitly designated for the Love Feast.[72]

Ephrata

Johann Adam Gruber, an Inspirationist living in Germantown, wrote in 1730 (before the congregation had moved to Ephrata to create the Cloister) that the sisters and brothers of Conrad Beissel's congregation held "daily spiritual exercises and breaking of bread."[73] At Ephrata, Love Feasts were held for the whole community, for various dormitories of celibates or for householders, and for small groups by private invitation. Also Love Feasts were held in memorial of some of the dead members. Ezekiel Sangmeister, the Seventh Day spiritualizer and curmudgeon, complained that at Ephrata breadbreaking took place often, as if to effect reconciliation through the ritual and to reinforce Beissel's hold on the members.[74] At Ephrata the Love Feast was a central part of piety. The fellowship meal would have provided additional nourishment to the strict regimen of fasting. Sangmeister illustrates, however, that a diversity of opinions prevailed in the Ephrata movement.

Later comments about how Conrad Beissel officiated at Love Feast highlight differing attitudes toward ministry in rituals between the Ephrata Brethren and the Schwarzenau Brethren. Beissel visited the Seventh Day congregation at Antietam, which was still distributing the elements in the manner of the Schwarzenau group, or parent body. This entailed communicants' breaking the bread and sharing the cup to each other. Beissel officiated at Love Feast by breaking the bread and handing it and the cup to each communicant. Beissel was offended because the congregation believed that "all must be equals, and therefore they did not wish to allow any prerogative or privilege to any one person among them."[75] Beissel's practice returned to a more highly defined role for the officiant, corresponding to his view of his own ministry and the selected few he trusted to hold leadership.

Whether or not sisters among the Schwarzenau Brethren broke the bread and passed the cup to each other in the eighteenth century is unclear. By the nineteenth century, the practice was for a male elder to serve the bread and cup to the sisters. Not until the twentieth century did this pattern change in the Church of the Brethren, so that at Love Feast, sisters serve each other. Old German Baptist Brethren still retain the nineteenth-century (and perhaps older) custom.[76] The practice of the Schwarzenau Brethren illustrates a decided bias against an elite clergy, replacing it with a ministry situated in the priesthood of all believers administering the ritual to each other.

Brethren in Christ

In the Lord's Supper, the Brethren in Christ share with the Schwarzenau Brethren the practice of feetwashing, unleavened bread, and communicants administering the elements to each other. Brethren in Christ groups do not include a love meal—or "sacred supper," as they call it—as a part of the Lord's Supper proper because only the bread and the wine make up the communion meal. Traditionally, however, they have often served a fellowship meal at their gatherings before the Lord's Supper.[77]

The Brethren in Christ have emphasized self-examination and reconciliation in preparation for the Lord's Supper. While valuing the importance of restored relationships between sisters and brothers, they also emphasize self-examination as a time to assess assurance of experiential regeneration.[78]

The Brethren in Christ groups have tended to interpret feetwashing first of all as a sign of humility. They practiced the double mode of feetwashing until late in the nineteenth century, when some congregations began to adopt the single mode. Only in 1912 was the single mode formally adopted, while the double mode persisted in some places. The Old Order River Brethren continue to practice the double mode.

Among Schwarzenau Brethren, controversy over double or single mode emerged as an issue in the divisions of the 1880s. The descendant groups of these Brethren differ on which mode was brought from Europe. In the early nineteenth century, the double mode was the most widely practiced style of feetwashing. The Old German Baptist Brethren (sometimes called Old Orders) continue the double mode; most other Brethren congregations use the single mode.

Concluding Observations

The following observations hold true for all Anabaptist groups since the sixteenth century. All Anabaptists rejected the mass, a theology of bodily presence of Christ in the elements, and denied the sacrificial character of the mass as a means of grace. All rejected the *ex opera operato* understanding of a sacrament. Similarly they all rejected the mediation of the ritual through a sacerdotal priesthood, although some imagery from the concept of priesthood resurfaced in altered fashion in the Ephrata community. All Anabaptists offered communion in both kinds, and none used a wafer in the ritual.

Spiritualizing Anabaptists, such as Hans Denck and David Joris, were more willing to compromise on the actual practice of the Lord's Supper. They could either suspend the ritual or conform outwardly to communicating in state churches. Their interpretation of the Lord's Supper is harder to assess than that of other Anabaptist groups.

In rejecting the mass, many early Anabaptists, influenced in part by Karlstadt, brought the ritual of bread and wine out from the ecclesiastical boundaries that created a sacred distance between people and the elements. By bringing the Lord's Supper into homes, observed by lay pastors rather than priests, and offering bread and wine to all communicants, Anabaptists did not strip down what was holy. Rather, they redefined the space of sacred ritual by practicing it within the spaces of ordinary life. In a sense, they reinterpreted the sacred distance of a sacramental Eucharist into a sacred intimacy of the Lord's Supper.[79] This was in part due to the reality that Anabaptists almost never had church buildings at their disposal, but even Hubmaier's order, which provides an important counter-example if it was celebrated in a church building, called for radically reorganized seating and participation of the congregation even from Zwingli's Supper.

The Anabaptist insistence on preparation through self-examination and congregational discipline precludes the conclusion that Anabaptists in general had a casual attitude toward the Lord's Supper. They did, however, radically redefine the way in which they perceived it as holy.

Anabaptists were largely heirs to the Zwinglian interpretation of the Supper that it was a memorial of Christ's death and sign of the incorporation of the faithful into communion with the body and blood of Christ. The Corpus Christi [body of Christ] is not in bread and wine but among and in the people gathered to share it, the Church.

In contrast to Zwingli, Anabaptists drew very different conclusions about how the Church is the Body of Christ. In the Zwinglian/Calvinist reformation, the doctrine of predestination always made the gathered congregation an unknown mixture—as for Luther also—even though the Reformed sometimes used "discipline." After 1527 and 1536, it was clear that for Anabaptists there would be no Corpus Christianum (Christian society). For most Anabaptists, the gathered congregation was a visible Church through confessed faith, repentance, baptism, and regenerate living supported by mutual love and correction.

Anabaptists tended to use a more thorough-going biblicism in seeking the shape of practice and interpretation for the Lord's Supper than had Zwingli. Some added feetwashing to the experience, a practice which is still widespread, though not universal among Anabaptist groups. The groups descended from the Brethren at Schwarzenau added a love meal to articulate the ritual's character of fellowship and love.

Anabaptists worked out varying expressions for how Christ is present in believers. They all rejected the ability of the words of consecration of the mass to effect Christ's bodily presence in the elements. Usually Anabaptists substituted various scriptural passages about the Lord's Supper as words of institution. Denck used the mystics' language of an individual's personal union-deification with Christ while de-emphasizing the outward gestures and elements of the ritual. Other Anabaptists tended to stress the gathered congregation as the locus for Christ's presence. Dirk Philips could make use of language like Denck's, with the congregation in mind, although he repeatedly stressed Christ's session in heaven when interpreting the significance of the elements. Many other Anabaptists spoke of Christ's presence with believers as an "incorporation" or "communion" with Christ.

One way Anabaptists expressed Christ's presence with the community of the faithful was through suffering. This was often linked explicitly to Christ's suffering commemorated in breaking bread and sharing the cup. Particularly for the sixteenth-century south German and Swiss Anabaptists, who were influenced by the peasants' agenda, Christ was alive in the collective body of his disciples whose bodies suffered for him by giving their lives for each other. Except for Hubmaier, Münster, and the Batenburgers, giving up life for sisters and brothers excluded the possibility of killing for them. Although not as strongly focused on suffering, Pilgram Marpeck perhaps stated this most pointedly with his concept of the Church as the earthly body of Christ in hypostatic union with his ascended, divine nature.

During the *de facto* toleration in the Netherlands in the seventeenth century, feetwashing and even observance of the Lord's Supper declined among Dutch Mennonites. In Switzerland and areas where Swiss Mennonites fled, renewed persecution reinforced the identification of the suffering congregation with the suffering Christ.

This interpretation of the presence of Christ found a ready audience among the Schwarzenau Brethren in the eighteenth century as they pursued their biblically oriented reform apart from the legally established Reformed Church of their native territories. Identification with Christ's suffering was dramatized in the severe asceticism of the Ephrata celibates, who were removed from the possibilities of persecution present in Germany. By the time of the Brethren in Christ, this motif of sharing in Christ's suffering was being diluted.

Generally Anabaptists have practiced the ban with the aim of securing unity among believers when they come to the Lord's Supper. The legacy of this practice in Anabaptism has been to divide further the body of believers, so that unity was maintained on an increasingly smaller scale. Issues of authority, coercion, and personality have figured in all of these divisions. While Protestant or Roman Catholic unity in the sixteenth century is a myth, Anabaptists, nevertheless, have not achieved in practice the unity for which the ban was intended on a broad scale.

The ritual of feetwashing, gaining its toehold in Dutch Anabaptism, represents the expansion of a liturgical fragment symbolizing temporary humility into a practice of penitential cleansing and humility for all communicants in preparation for the Lord's Supper. Later, expanded interpretations justified the ritual as a biblical command and, especially in the eighteenth century, as an imitation of Christ's actions. Feetwashing as a ritual of hospitality died out during the seventeenth century although later it was revived briefly at Ephrata. By the nineteenth century, it had disappeared from western European Mennonites. It has continued to disappear from some Mennonite and Brethren groups in the twentieth century.

Although some sixteenth-century Anabaptists conceived of the Lord's Supper taking place at worship meetings that included a simple common meal, only the Schwarzenau Brethren tried to include distinct components for the meal of loving fellowship, or *agape* (the fellowship meal at Love Feast), and the memorial (the bread and cup) at the Lord's Supper. This addition represents a trend among the Schwarzenau Brethren and, in part, among Anabaptists to reform Christian ritual by expansion rather than the contraction typical of magisterial reformers.

As Miri Rubin rightly cautioned, ritual bears a plurality of meanings among those who participate, affirm, reject, or ignore it. The varieties of Anabaptism manifested a wide range in reshaping and reinterpreting the mass into the Lord's Supper. That heritage continues to be challenged by erosion of some practices as well as reaffirmed by continuation and new interpretations as the next century approaches.

[1] John D. Rempel, *Anabaptism and the Lord's Supper* (Scottdale, Pa.: Herald Press, 1993).

[2] This overview has been influenced by the theory of multiple origins of Anabaptism as a useful construct to account for variation without squeezing Anabaptists into a "normative" mold. Yet some persons and groups were omitted due to time and space limits. Considerably less attention will be given to spiritualizing Anabaptists (except Hans Denck), such as David Joris or the Batenburgers, because they often conformed in outward practice to the communion rituals of the legalized traditions of their territories.

[3] Victor Turner, *The Ritual Process: Structure and Anti-structure* (London: 1969), 140-65.

[4] Miri Rubin, *Corpus Christi* (Cambridge: Cambridge University Press, 1991), 3-10.

[5] Steffan Niklaus Bosshard, *Zwingli - Erasmus - Cajetan. Die Eucharistie als Zeichen der Einheit* (Mainz: Franz Steiner Verlag, 1978), 12-20, 31-3. Hereafter cited as *Eucharistie.* Bosshard discusses the development of Zwingli's eucharistic theology stressing primarily Erasmus' influence on him. Although Karlstadt drew some similar spiritualizing consequences from the humanistic tradition as did Zwingli, Bosshard sees little contribution to Zwingli from Karlstadt (pp. 50-2, 58). Both reformers, however, were reshaping the mass in response to similar influences from humanism. In contrast to Zwingli, Karlstadt was influenced by Luther and especially more by German mysticism. Karlstadt developed his Eucharistic theology in reaction to Luther, as well as under Luther's influence. Still there were enough parallels to Zwingli that Karlstadt could eventually settle (perhaps only reluctantly) for a place among the Swiss Reformed at Basel.

[6] James S. Preus, *"Carlstadt's Ordinaciones and Luther's Liberty, Harvard Theological Studies* 27 (Cambridge, Mass.: Harvard University Press, 1974), 10, 28-30.

[7] For a summary of Karlstadt's Eucharistic theology and its development, see Crerar Douglas, *Positive Negatives* (New York: Peter Lang, 1991), 117-51. My synopsis is based on Douglas' summary.

[8] Conrad Grebel, "Letter to Thomas Müntzer," ed. Leland Harder, *Sources of Swiss Anabaptism* (Scottdale, Pa.: Herald Press, 1985), 284-92. Hereafter cited as *SSA.*

[9] Calvin A. Pater, *Karlstadt as the Father of the Baptist Movements: The Emergence of Lay Protestantism* (Toronto: University of Toronto Press, 1984), 144-59. Although Pater may over-argue his points, he illustrates influences from Karlstadt to Grebel and his circle.

[10] Erasmus would have agreed that the Supper is a sign of loving fellowship among Christians. He would not have expected that meaning to exclude belief in the bodily presence of Christ in the elements.

[11] Pater relies heavily on one piece of evidence, namely Hegenwalt's reply in Luther's name to Grebel's correspondence to Luther. Pater assumes that because Hegenwalt indicated that Grebel would find his answer in Luther's answer to Karlstadt (*Against the Heavenly Prophets*), this means that Luther considered Grebel a disciple of Karlstadt and so should we. Luther was capable of lumping any number of enemies together in his denouncements without assessing their similarities or differences. Pater rightly points out the similarities between Grebel and Karlstadt, but those do not necessarily prove that Grebel is derivative of Karlstadt. Furthermore, Karlstadt's treatises on the Lord's Supper were published *after* Grebel's letter to Müntzer. Clearly, Karlstadt had been working out this theology before he wrote the tracts. However, it is unclear how much of this developing reform was transmitted to Grebel and associates before October 1524. The Zurich radicals helped pay for and disseminate Karlstadt's treatises, illustrating their affinity to the views expressed therein.

[12] "Second Zurich Disputation," and "Council's Mandate," in *SSA*, pp. 242, 251-2. Here Zwingli claimed that the city council had the authority to decide on the implementation of changes in the mass. The council decided not to introduce change, and Zwingli acquiesced.

[13] W. P. Stephens, *Zwingli: An Introduction to His Thought* (Oxford: Clarendon Press, 1992), 99. See also Bosshard, *Eucharistie*, 51-2.

[14] Thomas A. Brady, Jr., *Turning Swiss: Cities and Empire, 1450-1550* (Cambridge: Cambridge University Press, 1985).

[15] The testimony of Hans Ockenfuss includes an early account of Grebel and associates observing the Lord's Supper. According to Ockenfuss, "Grebel cut a loaf of bread and distributed it among them." See Harder, *SSA*, 343. It is significant that Grebel used ordinary bread, and that it was cut, rather than broken, probably to avoid resembling the fraction during the mass. Grebel protested during the Second Zurich Disputation against a host of "abuses" in the practice of the mass, including the wafer-like host, admixture, priests' placing the bread in the communicants' mouths, time of day for observing the Supper, as well as vestments, chanting, and the canon of the mass (*SSA*, 246-9).

[16] *SSA*, 287-8. These details reflect in part Grebel and his friends' unique contributions to the practice of the Lord's Supper, although Karlstadt's influence may stand behind some of them.

For instance, Karlstadt thought evening was the "more prefect" time of observance. He did not implement his more radical views.

[17] Ulrich Zwingli, *Commentary on True and False Religion*, ed. & trans. Samuel M. Jackson and Clarence N. Heller (Durham, N.C.: Labyrinth Press, 1981), 168-9; 172-4. See in contrast an example of Zwingli's earlier thought in his 67 Articles on the occasion of the First Zurich Disputation (Art 31-2), in which he permitted the congregation along with the pastor to impose the ban upon those who create "public offence." For an English trans., see Edward Peters, *Ulrich Zwingli. Selected Works*, edited by Samuel M. Jackson (reprint Philadelphia: University of Pennsylvania Press, 1972), 114. See also Stephens, *Theology*, 116-20.

[18] Balthasar Hubmaier, "A Form for Christ's Supper," eds. and trans. H. Wayne Pipkin and John H. Yoder, *Balthasar Hubmaier. Theologian of Anabaptism* (Scottdale, Pa.: Herald Press, 1989), 393-408, 395-6. Hereafter cited as *BH*.

[19] Ibid., 403-6.

[20] Balthasar Hubmaier, "A Simple Instruction," (1526) *BH*, 321-2, 331, 333-4.

[21] John Howard Yoder, ed. and trans., *The Legacy of Michael Sattler* (Scottdale, Pa.: Herald Press, 1973), 36-45. Hereafter cited as *LMS*.

[22] Ibid.

[23] Michael Sattler, "On the Satisfaction of Christ," in *LMS*, 112.

[24] Bosshard, *Eucharistie*, 51-2. See also Stephens, *Theology*, 94-9.

[25] Tom Scott and Bob Scribner, eds. and trans., *The German Peasants' War. A History in Documents* (Atlantic Highlands, N.J.: Humanities Press, 1991), 126. Hereafter cited as *GPW*. The peasants pledged to help each other seek justice and to "set life and goods and all that God has given us thereto, and to lay down life and limb, etc." In March 1525, leaders of the Whole Bright Band wrote to the town of Hofsteig to pressure them to join the movement. "Aid us in our Christian enterprise," wrote the leader, "and we will commit our lives, honor and goods to you as Christian brothers. You should do the same for us." p. 135.

[26] Ibid., 136. The Black Forest articles seek "Christian union and brotherhood" among the commoners, language that the Schleitheim articles also used, however, with new understandings, including pacifism and separation from the world. For a recent assessment of Hubmaier's role in the commoners' uprising of the Black Forest area, see James Stayer, *The German Peasants' War and Anabaptist Community of Goods* (Montreal: McGill-Queen's University, 1991), 63-72. For more discussion of Hubmaier's association with the articles see the introduction to the document provided with it by Scott and Scribner. See also Johannes Faber's testimony against Hubmaier's involvement with the peasants, "Vienna Testimony," in *BH*, 563-5.

[27] Stayer, *German Peasants' War*, 254-5.

[28] Ibid., 165-7.

[29] Ibid., 72-92.

[30] Arnold Snyder, "The Schleitheim Articles in Light of the Revolution of the Common Man: Continuation or Departure?" *Sixteenth Century Journal* 16 (1985): 424. Snyder offers some points of emphasis differing from Stayer.

[31] Werner Packull, *Mysticism and the Early South German-Austrian Anabaptist Movement, 1525-1531* (Scottdale, Pa.: Herald Press, 1977). For an opposing view, see, for example, Peter C. Erb, "Mysticism," *Mennonite Encyclopedia* (Scottdale, Pa.: Herald Press, 1989), V. Erb claims that by the emergence of Anabaptism, medieval mysticism had been "democratized" to refer to the experience of every believer with Christ, and thus no longer truly reflective of the mystical tradition of the Middle Ages.

[32] Hans Denck, "Bekenntnis für den Rat zu Nürnberg 1525," in Hans Denck, *Schriften. Teil 2, Religiöse Schriften*, ed. Walter Fellmann, *Quellen und Forschungen zur Reformationsgeschichte* 24 (Gütersloh: C. Bertelsmann Verlag, 1956), 25, hereafter cited as *HDRS*. The English translation used here is E. J. Furcha, ed. and trans, *Selected Writings of Hans Denck 1500-1527* (Lewiston, N.Y.: Edwin Mellen Press, 1989), 7-8. Hereafter cited as *SWHD*. Another translation is available in Clarence Baumann, *The Spiritual Legacy of Hans Denck* (Leiden: Brill, 1991). Baumann provides the German texts with translation.

[33] Denck, "Protestation und bekantnus," in Fellmann, *HDRS*, 109-10; and "Protestation and Confession" (1527), *SWHD*, 292-3.

[34] For just one of many possible examples, compare the Modern Devotion's Eucharistic piety. The Devotionalists wrote of spiritual and sacramental reception of the Lord. They considered "spiritual" communion, without actually receiving the host, an important devotion. See "John Brinckerinck on the Holy Sacrament," John van Engen, trans., *Devotio Moderna. Basic Writings* (New York: Paulist Press, 1988), 231-4.

[35] Pater, *Karlstadt*, 195-235.

[36] Melchior Hoffman, *The Ordinance of God*, eds. and trans. George H. Williams and Angel M. Mergal, *Spiritual and Anabaptist Writers* (Philadelphia: Westminster Press, 1957), 193-4, hereafter cited as *SAW*.

[37] Ibid., 194.

[38] Ibid., 195.

[39] Ibid., 196.

[40] Bernd Rothmann, *Bekenntnis van beyden Sacramenten* (1533), ed. Robert Stupperich, *Die Schriften Bernhard Rothmanns, Die Schriften der Müsterischen Täufer und ihrer Gegner* 1 (Münster: Aschendorf, 1970), hereafter cited as *Bekenntnis*. The quotations here will be based on the English of William Klassen and Walter Klaassen, who translated Marpeck's *Vermanung* of 1542, which is largely based on Rothmann's *Bekenntnis*. The translations have been checked against Stupperich's text.

[41] Ibid., 140-2. See also Bosshard, *Eucharistie*, 47. This was typical of a humanist understanding of a sacrament.

[42] Ibid., 180-1, 189. Occasionally Klassen and Klaassen have used "communion" for Rothmann's "Nachtmael." I have retained the word, "supper," for "Nachtmael" because it is closer to Rothmann's term and "communion" has a wide range of meanings.

[43] The quote is from Ibid., 182. See also 184-5.

[44] Stayer, *German Peasants' War*, 123-38. Stayer describes the communal economy of Münster as a "war communism."

[45] Rothmann, *Bekenntnis*, 176.

[46] Rothmann, 184. Rothmann noted that he was borrowing the quotation of Tertullian from Sebastian Franck's *Chronica*.

[47] Frank J. Wray, "The Vermanung of 1542 and Rothmann's Bekenntnis," *Archiv für Reformationsgeschichte* 47 (1956): 245.

[48] Menno Simons, *Reply to Gellius Faber*, ed. J. C. Wenger, trans. Leonard Verduyn, *The Complete Writings of Menno Simons* (Scottdale, Pa.: Herald Press, 1956, 1984), 668.

[49] These include beliefs that the Supper is a memorial, the need for faith and love in coming to the table, and a rejection of the mass as sacrifice, as means of grace and transsubstantiation.

[50] Menno Simons, *Foundation of Christian Doctrine*, ed. Wenger, *Complete Writings of Menno Simons*, 145-53. For the quotation, id., 153.

[51] Ibid., 144.

[52] Sjouke Voolstra, "True Penitence: The Core of Menno Simons' Theology," *Mennonite Quarterly Review* 62 (1988): 387-9.

[53] Menno Simons, "Final Instruction on Marital Avoidance"; and "Admonition on Church Discipline," ed. Wenger, *Complete Writings of Menno Simons*, 1061 and 417, respectively.

[54] Dirk Philips, "The Supper of Our Lord Jesus Christ," in his *Enchiridion*, eds. and trans. Cornelius J. Dyck, William E. Keeney and Alvin J. Beachy, *The Writings of Dirk Philips* (Scottdale, Pa.: Herald Press, 1992), 122-3.

[55] Dirk Philips, "The Congregation of God," ed. Dyck, *Writings of Dirk Philips*, 367.

[56] There is mention of feetwashing once in Hubmaier's congregation at Waldshut, but he did not refer to it in his later writings on the Lord's Supper. Sebastian Franck claimed in 1531 that the Swiss Brethren observed the ritual, but there is no other documentation for this. Despite their biblicism, the Swiss Brethren apparently did not institute feet washing. Heinrich Bullinger mentioned some "Apostolic Anabaptists" in Switzerland who practiced feetwashing, but it is unclear who these people were, if they existed. The Hutterites did not adopt feetwashing. See "Foot Washing," The *Mennonite Encyclopedia: A Comprehensive Reference Work on the Anabaptist-Mennonite Movement* 4 vols. (Scottdale, Pa.: Mennonite Publishing House, 1956), II, 347-51. There is surprisingly little written on the history of feetwashing, particularly in the sixteenth century.

[57] Ibid. For a text of the Ohnenheim Attestation, see John D. Roth, *Letters of the Amish Division: A Sourcebook* (Goshen, Ind.: Mennonite Historical Society, 1993), 145-6.

[58] Peter Riedemann, *Account of Our Religion, Doctrine and Faith*, Hutterian Society of Brothers (Rifton, N.Y.: Plough Publishing House, 1972), 82-5. Riedemann called the Supper a memorial to Christ's death, rejecting the bodily presence of Christ in the elements. Riedemann also required self-examination and mutual discipline (the ban) in preparation for the Lord's Supper.

[59] Ibid., 86.

[60] Pilgram Marpeck, *Admonition*, eds. and trans. William Klassen and Walter Klaassen, *The Writings of Pilgram Marpeck* (Scottdale, Pa.: Herald Press, 1978), 160-302. For an analysis of the similarities and differences between Marpeck and Rothmann, see Frank J. Wray, "The

'Vermanung' of 1542 and Rothmann's 'Bekenntnis'" in *Archiv für Reformationsgeschichte* 47 (1956): 243-51.

[61] Wray, "'Vermanung'," 247.

[62] Pilgram Marpeck, *Admonition*, ed. Dyck, *Writings of Pilgram Marpeck*, 271. See also ibid., 318, 340, 453; 79, 88.

[63] Stephen B. Boyd, *Pilgram Marpeck: His Life and Social Theology* (Durham, N.C.: Duke University Press, 1992), 118-25.

[64] Peter Giger, "Summary and Defense," ed. Roth, *Letters of the Amish Division*, 21.

[65] Ulli Ammann, "Summary and Defense," ibid., 98. Neither Jacob Ammann ("Summary and Defense," 1693) nor the Palatinate ministers who responded to him even mentioned feetwashing.

[66] Niklaus Wütrich, "Reflections on Shunning and Footwashing" (1803), ibid., 132, 138.

[67] See the article "Footwashing" in the *Mennonite Encyclopedia* for remarks on the decline of feetwashing in Europe.

[68] For the most recent, probably most balanced, and perhaps best statement of definition for Pietism, extending its scope from English Puritanism across central and northern Europe to America, see Martin Brecht, ed., *Der Pietismus vom siebzehnten bis zum frühen achtzehnten Jahrhundert*, vol. 1 of a projected four volume series, *Die Geschichte des Pietismus* (Göttingen: Vandenhoeck & Ruprecht, 1993), 1-10.

[69] A believer must be willing to "give his [or her] body, and even life, unto death, if it is demanded of him [or her], for the sake of Jesus." See Mack, 363.

[70] The Congregational Order of Schleitheim had called for a simple common meal at each meeting for worship, as well as observance of the Lord's Supper. However, the meal was not considered to be a part of the Supper. It is unclear how closely Swiss Brethren congregations followed the Congregation Order.

[71] A Hymn for Feet-Washing," trans. Ora W. Garber, no. 24 in *Geistreiches Gesang Buch*, in Durnbaugh, *European Origins of the Brethren*, 415-8. Part of this hymn appears set with a tune newly harmonized by Hedwig T. Durnbaugh in *Hymnal: A Worship Book* (Elgin, Ill.: Brethren Press; Newton, KS: Faith and Life Press; Scottdale, Pa.: Mennonite Publishing House, 1992), no. 451.

[72] "Love Feast Hymn," (no. 88 in *Geistreiches Gesang Buch*) trans. Ralph Schlosser, in Durnbaugh, *European Origins of the Brethren*, 413-15.

[73] Johann Adam Gruber, "Extract from J. A. Gruber's Letter from Germantown, 28 October 1730," printed in *Geistliche Fama* (1730), cited in Felix Reichmann and Eugene Doll, eds. and trans., *Ephrata as Seen by Contemporaries* (Allentown: Pennsylvania German Folklore Society, 1953), 3.

[74] Ezechiel Sangmeister, *Leben und Wandel des in Gottruhenden und seligen Bruders Ezechiel Sangmeisters*, originally published in Ephrata by Joseph Bauman, 1825-1827; trans. Barbara M. Schindler, *Journal of the Historical Society of the Cocalico Valley* 9 (Ephrata: Historical Society of the Cocalico Valley, 1979-1985): 17, 69. On p. 69 Sangmeister notes that in the mid-1760s, Love Feast was held every evening at Ephrata. At other times it was suspended altogether. Usually Conrad Beissel determined when the Love Feast would be held. Sangmeister decried Beissel's magic power (magia) over the community that was reinforced at Love Feast.

[75] Brothers Lamech and Agrippa, *Chronicon Ephratense* (1786), trans. J. Max Hark (New York: Burt Franklin, 1972; reprint of Hark's 1889 edition), 260-1.

[76] Marlene Moats Neher, "Julia Gilbert," *Messenger* (June, 1976): 20-4.

[77] Carlton O. Wittlinger, *Quest for Piety and Obedience* (Napanee, Ind.: Evangel Press, 1978), 63-8.

[78] Ibid., 65-6; 38-44.

[79] Some might suggest that a sacramental view of the Eucharist is indeed one of sacred intimacy, with Christ in the host that is consumed. Denck's language was close to this view but, of course, with a highly spiritualized view of "communion" with Christ. However, in the Catholic understanding of Christ's presence in the elements, the bread and wine are not really bread and wine any longer, only the "accidents" are there, and for this reason access to the elements has to be restricted. The Lutheran concept of sacramental presence is more complex with Christ's flesh and blood present "in, with, and under" the elements. Although the bread and wine remain that and Christ is present in them, they are no longer ordinary, and the change is dependent on a ministers' proclaiming the Word (the words of consecration) over them. For Anabaptists not the elements but the people are the locus of Christ's presence. While this was true for Zwingli, the "Body of Christ" was still invisible, since predestination made it impossible to know who among the communicants was elect.

2
The Lord's Supper:
Contemporary Reflections

by Nadine Pence Frantz

I want to argue for 1) a Believers' Church understanding of the nature of Christianity as a performative tradition as well as a scripted tradition; 2) an adequate understanding of the theological contexts of the times under examination (the sixteenth century and the twenty-first century); and 3) an explicit commitment to the Believers' Church affirmation that one does not truly know or understand God and God's actions in Christ until he or she has embodied a Christian life. Such an embodiment, I will argue, includes worship and ritual embodiment such as the Lord's Supper or the Love feast.

Christianity as a Performative Tradition

Within mainline Protestantism and a sizable majority of the Believers' Church traditions, it would be commonplace to hear different traditions typify themselves as "people of the Word." What they mean by this is that they are Christians whose self-definition and self-identity reside in some sort of relationship with the fact that they read the Bible. Although their interpretations of the Bible may vary from one to the other and their choice of key values and scriptures may differ radically, what these adherents share is a common orientation towards Christianity as "script-defined" or as a "scripted" tradition, i.e., one that is known and defined through the very act of reading and understanding the Bible. The force of this orientation is most seen in its missionary movement, which presupposes or imposes a culture of literacy before a proper understanding of the Christian faith is thought to be possible. In other words, when approaching cultures that are not script-oriented, the first task of the missionary is the teaching of the skills of reading and writing in order that the indigenous culture might "truly receive the word." Thus the very act of reading the scriptures is seen as constitutive of the nature of what it means to be a Christian.

Part of this orientation comes from a desire to make the Word accessible to every person rather than located within a literate elite or priesthood; it is a democratizing tendency. But another part of this orientation has reified the centrality of the text to such an extent that no other part of the Christian life seems constitutive of the faith, i.e., worship, service, peacemaking, baptism, etc.

An ability to read and recite certain texts becomes all that is needed, as if they are magical formulas.

Internal to the Anabaptist and Pietist movements that make up the Believers' Church tradition, however, is a self-corrective to this orientation. This corrective is the constant insistence that knowing and reading the Word are not enough but that doing the Word is the heart of the matter. This hermeneutics of obedience or mutual correlation of practice and knowledge is a strong center for the Believers' Church tradition and presses for an alternate way of understanding the nature of Christianity, one that also incorporates the "performative" orientation.

A performative understanding of the nature of Christianity has been more the center of the Catholic church whose foci are worship and the sacraments rather than the texts of the church. Yet, (to do a familiar Anabaptist line of argument and insist that they are neither Protestant nor Catholic) Anabaptists do not readily fit within the Catholic boundaries of understanding because their ritual, rather than being "empty," promotes "neighbormindedness." They hold onto the scriptures as direction for what they must do. So while Anabaptists are impatient with a Protestant orientation that makes reading the text the be all and end all of belief, they are just as uncomfortable with any hint that the church knows sufficiently what to do outside of the text. Thus, the Believers' Church tradition seeks to hold together both the scripted and the performative side of the Christian life.

In bringing to the forefront of our discussion a Believers' Church understanding of the performative nature of the church, the familiar list of its "doing" readily comes to mind: nonconformity, discipleship, simple life, peacemaking, accountability, service, etc. These I will leave to others. What I want to discuss under the list of "doings" is ordinances or rituals that (here we need to be a bit more Catholic) are as constitutive of the understanding of the relationship between God and humanity as is service, peacemaking, etc. To do this, I will refer to the Church of the Brethren materials about the love feast and Lord's Supper, working from them to make the analogy for the Mennonites and other Believers' Church traditions.

In 1932, Frederick Dove (a Brethren sociologist from Bridgewater College) noted this about Brethren love feasts:

> These love feast occasions are not without their influence in moulding culture patterns among the Brethren. It is safe to assume that they have been in large measure responsible for the spirit of humility and concern for one another which has always characterized the Brethren.[1]

Writing as a sociologist, Dove is interested in an understanding of the cultural changes of the Brethren. And though he does not spend a great deal of time analyzing them, he recognizes the influence of the ordinances on that culture. A social anthropologist, Clifford Geertz puts it this way:

> the dispositions which religious rituals induce thus have their most important impact—from a human point of view—outside the boundaries of the ritual itself as

they reflect back to color the individual's conception of the established world of bare fact.[2]

What both of these people are saying is that what is done in the marked times of ritual has an influence on what one does in ordinary time. The implication is that Brethren and Mennonite ordinances, their rituals, the way they "do" the Lord's Supper (and baptism, anointing, etc.), have as much to do with who they are and how they envision God's presence in the world as do times of action and service in the world. These rituals not only express understandings of God and the world (and who believers are to be in that world), but they also shape understandings of those very things. They act as a template or a pattern of the interaction of the divine and the human in this very material world. Actions in the Lord's Supper embody for participants and rehearse them in the manner of life that they understand God as desiring them to live. The acts pattern them in the way that they would hope to live.

This patterning goes beyond symbolic communication or stylized emotion.[3] It is a way of understanding through doing that is parallel to the epistemology of obedience that is present within the way the Believers' Church tradition approaches scripture. Worshippers learn who they are and what they are about through embodying the rituals; they are times of active self-knowing, both individually and corporately, and appropriation. They require the individual to let go of preconceived senses of his/herself and enter into the world of the ordinance—of the church. Knowledge is then gained not through a logical apprehension[4] of principles or message but through the slower, deeper process of action and appropriation—leading with the body rather than the mind. To quote Peter Nead (1796-1877):

> O! how solemn and instructive, to see the children of God seated at one table, united in the bonds of brotherly love, partaking of a repast which serves to remind them of that blessed time and state, when they, in common with other children of God, shall surround the table of their Lord in the Kingdom of Glory![5]

Thus ritual is a particular kind of doing. It is a highly dense set of actions that are marked in a way that ordinary actions are not. They are "enactments, materializations, realizations" of a particular religious perspective.[6] They demonstrate in material form the religious community's sense of how the divine and the human interact in the world—how God is present as humans as a community of believers. They are religious performances that embody the way worshippers believe in God and that contribute to the development of that understanding.

In using the language of performance, I realize that care must be taken not to imply that by calling it performance I mean that it is in some way false or put on. It is performance in the sense that it is marked as different from the ordinary and is highly dense in its character, as I noted earlier. It is also performance in the sense that it is marked with a sense of being observed. These actions are not private actions, not even when self-contained within a particular congregational setting. They are public and cultural in nature because what one does in them shapes who one is and how one will relate in the world. Ordinances are "that kind of doing in which the observation of the deed is an essential part of its doing, even if the observer be invisible or is the performer herself."[7] We watch ourselves do these actions in a way that we do not watch our other actions, and we do them as if they are meant to be watched—by the rest of the congregation, by the rest of Christendom, by God. It was common in the mid-nineteenth century for the Brethren love feast to have actual observers—outsiders who came to stand in their allotted space and "gaze upon the scene before them with eager and unflagging interest."[8]

Tom Driver argues that the double connotations of the word "perform" are not to be avoided. The verb, to perform, like its shorter but not simpler cousin, to act, is two-faced. On the one side these words mean "to do," while on the other they mean "to pretend." This ambiguity tells us much about the kind of actors human beings are.[9]

He reminds us that the element of pretending within ritual has some legitimacy. There is a sense that those who gather at the Lord's table are not being "real;" they are being "surreal" because they gather in a way that is not normal or ordinary in the world. Or, to put it the way that I prefer theologically, in gathering at the Lord's table, they enter into a commonality that God promises as more real than the brokenness that they feel in the surreal world. Juxtaposed against the brokenness and sin of the everyday human world, participation in the ordinance of the Lord's Supper requires "putting on" a new sense of what it might be like to have God fully present in the world and Christ fully present within the body of the community. The hope is that this "putting on" is not mere theatricality but also an active way of transforming ordinary, broken lives.

Speaking for the act of worship as a whole, John Rempel puts it this way:

> How can the hand of God be seen in our life as it is lived between an old and a new reality? Worship is the heightened vision, the pregnant symbol of our participation in God's presence in the world. In it the darkness that covers the earth is pierced by light. As worshipers we encounter God with "unveiled faces," as he really is. In his light, which is Christ, our world is illuminated. We see that we and the world are not doomed by our lost past but rescued from it. A new creation has begun. In worship we hear its promises and taste its reality.[10]

Johann Baptist Metz speaks of the delight in symbols and rituals as "praise of grace present within the senses."[11] Rituals are one of the ways that we transform past actions and present relations into new ones. They are the way we embody what it means to act differently towards each other.

This brings us finally to the theological questions of the way in which the Believers' Church believes Christ is present in the ordinance of the Lord's Supper and what that says about the structure of divine/human relations for the contemporary world.

Divine/Human Relations in the Lord's Supper

As Jeff Bach ably shows, during the Reformation (or reformations), the Anabaptist and spiritualist reformers rejected a theology of transubstantiation (or literal bodily presence) in regards to the elements of the Eucharist. The bread and the wine were not, as was claimed by the medieval church, the actual body and blood of Christ, changed in their essence but not in their accident. Nor did they subscribe to the concept of consubstantiation, as Luther proposed, in which the bread and the wine were not actually changed but Christ's body and blood were spiritually present alongside the physicality of the bread and the wine. Nor did they propose what Calvin later suggested, that the bread and the wine were the earthly instruments of the divine nourishment that took place in the taking of the Eucharist.

Instead, most called it a memorial meal or spoke of it as an ordinary meal and maintained that the presence of Christ was with the community in the taking of the meal rather than in the elements of the bread and the wine themselves. They affirmed the nearness of Christ at the Lord's Supper with those who participated in it, and spoke of the time as a "transcendent moment of fellowship with Christ."[12]

What they rejected in the Catholic sacramental and sacerdotal system was the idolatry that attends making physical things permanent carriers of the divine. In transubstantiation, the wafer and the wine forever changed into the body and blood of Christ, and elaborate procedures developed to care for the occasional careless drop or fallen wafer so that Christ's very body not be dishonored. Yet, Anabaptists did not choose to spiritualize the presence in the same way that Luther or Calvin did; they shifted the focus of the presence of Christ from the actual elements of the bread and wine to the community itself, still maintaining a sense that, in God's own good choice and power, Christ's presence could be known among the very material, very bodily, gathered community. The affirmation that Christ was still at the right hand of God served to remind the community that Christ's presence was not an automatic thing that was granted (the Supper itself was not efficacious), and that even when granted, it did not exhaust the fullness that was Christ. As John Rempel argues:

> Many Anabaptists sought to restore the human role in sacraments by applying the Latin word "sacramentum" to the church's response: in a sacrament believers pledge themselves to live out what God has promised them. Thus, in Balthasar Hubmaier's theology, the Lord's Supper becomes an oath in which believers pledge themselves to give up their lives for others just as Christ gave up his life for them.[13]

Thus, the sixteenth-century corrective addressed the question of idolatry that accompanies any system that places its trust in an outward thing—be it image, pilgrimage, or sacrament—as a means of salvation.[14] In our day, somewhere between the twentieth and twenty-first centuries, there is a different corrective to make.

The structures of divine/human relationship that accompany our times have a very different shape. Here in the United States, we are, in a sense, living out of the success of the magisterial Protestant structure that sets up a two-fold understanding of the world: a sacred and a secular. "To God [go] the holy days, to the world the plain ones."[15] Reinforced by the Enlightenment sub-ject/object split and the triumph of the Cartesian ego ("I think, therefore I am"), religious and spiritual matters have been relegated to a subjective, inner exis-tence or a transcendent, wholly-other spirituality. Reason, linear knowledge, and sense experience that can be physically duplicated have been set over against the "spiritual world" as if they are two starkly different realms which meet but do not touch or interact. It is Luther's world of Christ's presence alongside the physical elements which stand unchanged.

As in the movie "A Field of Dreams," in which a farmer whose father had played baseball plows under a whole field of crops to make a baseball field so that "he will come," the world of the divine is a disembodied one, free of physi-cality—of material life—and totally spiritualized. The material world is that plane of existence upon which we depend for our material existence, but it does not contain the divine in any actual form. One has to put on "the eyes of faith" to see the divine existing alongside the material form. Remember in "Field of Dreams" when Kevin Costner and James Earl Jones are the only ones in the crowd to see the message on the Fenway Park scoreboard? Eyes of faith, seeing things no one without faith will see.

A Lord's Supper that would be expressive of this dual-mindedness would be one in which participants would have little physical contact with each other—what Dale Brown calls "back-of-the-neck-communion"—the bread and the cup were special elements set aside for that special day (white cubes of Wonderbread?), and the stress of the theology would be on faith in God and the Bible which enables believers to see and know that Christ is true. Faith is essentially what makes it efficacious; "putting on the mind of Christ" would mean leaving secular/daily knowledge of life outside the door of the church and putting on a faith that "believes that all that God has said is true"—and somehow different in substance (or nonsubstance) than that knowledge from which believers must operate in daily life.

A Believers' Church corrective to this form would be a meal that shows the incarnational nature of God: that God is and can be among humans in their very material existence. Whether the supper is a full love feast or a bread and cup communion, it would seek to embody that Christ is present, found among us, and transforming our very material selves and communities. A powerful demonstration of this is the shift that has been made in the twentieth century from the closed communion to the open communion. Like the sixteenth-century forbears, it takes the focus off the elements of the communion themselves and shifts the question of the presence of Christ to that of the gathered body. But, unlike the forbears, for whom a closed communion was expressive of believers pledging their all to their Lord, a closed communion during these times only reinforces the sacred/secular split: "we are pure and can thus partake, you do not have proper faith and should thus stay home." When we welcome to the table all who confess Jesus as Lord—be they fully righteous in the eyes of all or not—we witness to God's grace of bringing together those who might differ or who may be at odds. This does not necessarily have to be accompanied by a dilution of the commitment to mutual discipline; what it does is make the embodiment of the supper the common ground from which to sort and disagree and talk as a church.

I agree with Jeff Bach that the trends of interiorization of the meaning of the supper and the disappearance of some of the physical acts associated with the meal, such as the holy kiss and feetwashing, represent a decay in the Anabaptist understanding and a homogenization with mainstream Protestantism. It reinforces the notion that God has nothing to do with materiality, nothing to do with the transformation of our physical existence, and relegates the presence of Christ to some sanctified, sanitary place in the sky whom we only need believe in to be saved. To do it all—holy kiss, self-examination, washing of feet, meal, bread and cup, hymns, and prayers for the community and the world—with those that participants get along with only by God's grace, would embody a transformed kind of togetherness, a gracious kind of community, that would be a welcome word to this world divided against its own soul.

The Ordinances in the Twenty-first Century

As we come to the beginning of the twenty-first century, the issues that face us—world destruction, mass starvation, ethnic wars and brutalities, and diseases such as AIDS—make the incarnation of God into this very needy world seem even more distant. More and more, people struggle with the idea of a purposeless world. All of life feels random, with no guidance or direction, with no ultimate foundation. There is a computer game called "Tetris." The objective of the game is to fill up the bottom space with a solid line of blocks that drop from the top of the screen. The challenge is that there are seven different shapes of blocks that drop, and they will only fit together in certain ways. And the blocks drop at random with the player only able to see one block ahead at any given time. The character of the 1990s feels much like this—that life is throwing odd shaped blocks with which we are to do something constructive, but they don't easily fit together, and we only know what is coming one block ahead at a time.

If we are indeed moving from a sense of a dual existence to a purposeless existence, the relationships that the Lord's Supper embodies and structures become all the more important. Observing the ordinances in the twenty-first century will be a declaration that it does matter what we do and that there is a larger purpose and a God to which everything and everyone is somehow connected. Perhaps Anabaptists should go back to a common loaf from which they all break, a common table at which all gather, a common cup to share with all who might come. The need will be to express the ever-present, incarnational God who cares about our condition, who cares about brokenness, and who cares about making right that which is not right. It need not be radically different from what the Believers' Church traditions have done before: a meal done in remembrance of what Christ once did for us, in remembrance of that death that put the end to all death, to mark that human suffering is not outside of the love of God. Preparation, the right hand of fellowship, feetwashing, the holy kiss, a common meal, the bread and cup, hymns and prayers—all would help our bodies pattern themselves in actions of connectedness and commonality.

To observe the ordinance of the Lord's Supper—to practice it, to do it, to perform the ritual, to get the body right with those around it; that is the way to truly know what it is to be a people of God, what it means for Christ to be present. That is the way to truly know what it means to proclaim that Jesus is Lord, redeemer, and savior. "The truth is that words are as physically rooted as arts and sacraments are."[16] And every time that believers act, that they embody, that they seek out rituals, they demonstrate the physicality, the materiality of what they mean and what they say. The incarnation was God coming to us in the person of Jesus who was called the Christ. And we are called to follow after him in our life as well.

There is no substitute for the performance of the ordinances; sitting and talking about it does not engender the same understanding. Telling about past experience does not require the same investment; reading the scriptures about the disciples at the Last Supper does not substitute for taking a place at the table. Christians must observe the ordinances themselves. They must do it to know and to understand the Christian life.

I want to conclude with another quote from Peter Nead:

Now, Feet Washing represents that course which we are to pursue. For instance—you observe, that in order to wash a brother's feet, you must bend or stoop yourself; and secondly, you brother gives his feet into your hands, and then you can wash them. In like manner, to gain, or have a brother cleansed from his trespasses, we must go in love and with great humility, and apprise our brother of his conduct, expostulating in an humble manner with him, and by so doing, it may be, that your brother will receive the admonition, and give himself into your hands, so that you can wash him from his trespasses, which is accomplished whenever a reconciliation takes place. Whereas, it may be, if you had not humbled yourself—that is, bent or stooped before your brother, he would not have acknowledged his fault—that is, given himself into your hands so that you might forgive—that is, wash him.[17]

The surest way of knowing that we worship a common God is to gather at a common table.

[1] Frederick Denton Dove, *Cultural Changes in the Church of the Brethren* (Elgin, Ill.: Brethren Publishing House, 1932), 150.

[2] Clifford Geertz, "Religion as a Cultural System," ed. Michael Banton, *Anthropological Approaches to the Study of Religion*, A.S.A. Monographs, no. 3, (London: Tavistock Publications, 1966), 35.

[3] John Rempel, "Christian Worship: Surely the Lord is in This Place," *The Conrad Grebel Review* 6 (Spring 1988): 104.

[4] Paul Ricoeur, "Appropriation," ed., trans., and intro. John B. Thompson, *Hermeneutics and the Human Sciences: Essays on Language, Action and Interpretation* (Cambridge: Cambridge University Press, 1981).

[5] Peter Nead, *Theological Writings on Various Subjects; or a Vindication of Primitive Christianity as Recorded in the Word of God* (Dayton, Oh.: B.F. Ells, 1850), 145.

[6] Geertz, "Religion as a Cultural System," 29.

[7] Tom Driver, *The Magic of Ritual: Our Need for Liberating Rites that Transform Our Lives and Our Communities*, (New York: Harper, 1991), 81.

[8] H. R. Holsinger, *History of the Tunkers and the Brethren Church* (Oakland, Cal.: Pacific Publishing, 1901), 249.

[9] Driver, *Magic of Ritual*, 80.

[10] Rempel, "Christian Worship," 101-2.

[11] Johann Baptist Metz, *The Emergent Church: The Future of Christianity in a Postbourgeois World* (New York: Crossroad Books, 1981, trans. Peter Mann), 52-3.

[12] Jeff Bach, "Incorporation into Christ and the Brethren: The Lord's Supper and Feetwashing in Anabaptist Groups." Paper presented at the conference on Anabaptism:A Heritage and its 21st Century Prospects (September 29-October 2, 1993).

[13] Rempel, "Christian Worship," 103-4; emphasis mine.

[14] Ibid., 106.

[15] Ibid., 115.

[16] Judith Rock and Norman Mealy, *Performer as Priest and Prophet: Restoring the Intuitive in Worship Through Music and Dance* (San Francisco: Harper and Row, 1988), xx.

[17] Nead, *Theological Writings*, 132-3.

Conversation
ॐॐ VI ॐॐ

Language and Symbolism

Using Psalm 16 to frame his reflections, Gerald Shenk recalls the images and markers of his Mennonite past, finding them collectively important, if not always forming a coherent pattern. He describes, occasionally with humor, the importance of symbolic markers and expresses appreciation for those that shaped his heritage. He calls not for the preservation of specific symbols that have lost their vitality, but for the recreation of a symbolic legacy that continues to confront human institutions with a holy community.

Ronald C. Arnett underscores the importance of language to the maintenance of a faith community. Traditional, sedentary societies might have been able to reproduce moral commitments without relying heavily upon verbal explanation, but mobility requires modern faith communities to articulate their commitments if they are to be effectively transmitted. Conforming to cultural patterns is insufficient; members must hear why the faith is important.

Religion, therefore, goes beyond belief and action to encompass the words, cadences, sights, sounds, and stories of the faith community. Writing from their Mennonite and Brethren perspectives, respectively, Shenk and Arnett concur that linguistic and symbolic markers are fundamental for a strong faith community.

1

The Lines Have Fallen
in Pleasant Places

by Gerald Shenk

I hope to remind everyone, each in their own tradition, of lines and cadences from the past. And so, at the outset I want to cite Psalm 16. I first checked it in the version that was accessible to me, and then I had to go back and look it up in the version that echoed from my childhood. I'll give that one first (KJV):

> Preserve me, O God: for in thee do I put my trust.
> O my soul, thou hast said unto the Lord, Thou art my Lord:
> my goodness extendeth not to thee;
> But to the saints that are in the earth,
> and to the excellent, in whom is all my delight.
> Their sorrows shall be multiplied
> that hasten after another god:
> their drink offerings of blood will I not offer,
> nor take up their names into my lips.
> The Lord is the portion of mine inheritance and of my cup:
> thou maintainest my lot.
> The lines are fallen unto me in pleasant places;
> yea, I have a goodly heritage.
> I will bless the Lord, who hath given me counsel:
> my reins also instruct me in the night seasons. (Ps 16:1-7)

And I'll take from the NRSV the line from verse six:

> "The boundary lines have fallen for me in pleasant places;
> I have a goodly heritage."

Recently, I came across a bit of banter on the Mountain Stage, a public radio folk music show from West Virginia, which made me aware again of the ambiguity of symbols. A guest had brought in a recipe or perhaps an actual example of the "wet-bottom shoofly pie." It only took a few snickering remarks by the host to make me feel defensive enough to turn the radio off. How dare they tamper with my culture's artifacts like that?

Suddenly I felt like the fellow depicted by Appalachian scholar Loyal Jones in his "Brier Sermon": hurrying down the road to get away from his "backward background," he kept meeting people from the cities who were coming out to snatch up every bit of the laid-back lifestyle they could retrieve. The biggest loss was like a betrayal, even an assault when this Appalachian hears his own music coming back to him over television from a slick performer in New York.

And although I personally have virtually no family nor even friendship ties with individual Amish persons, it feels like a violation to me when I come across a caricature of them on a popular show like Saturday Night Live. Like Ross Perot's ears, anything unique or outstanding enough to merit cartoon attention gets tweaked without mercy in the public media. In this mass society, it is an affront to persist in the distinctives of a subculture. To resist the melting pot in language, dress, or even food is a subversive action. To take that resistance further, into realms of social and economic patterns, even sexual behavior and family mores, is perceived as outright political defiance. (Try having more than three children.)

Our symbols were supposed to be for our own use, obeying us without objection and conveying just exactly whatever freight of meaning we required of them. But, there is no avoiding it: our symbols become such fixed patterns that they are almost able to communicate on their own. Like Garrison Keillor's big old dog who had just caught a huge fish but it flopped back into the stream and got away, those symbols act like they are on the verge of speech!

Somewhere between the Amish and the Mormons, Anabaptists still have some clarification to do. Perhaps you have made a collection, as I have, of the more glaring misperceptions by outsiders. *Newsweek* recently had this one; see if you can untangle it.

> A young Jewish woman from Washington at a summer science camp at the University of Wisconsin discovers bewilderment and ignorance of religious traditions among this mixed group of young scholars. One friend, hearing that another came from a large family, asked, "Oh, are you a Mormon?" That person almost indignantly objected, "No, we dress normal!" Took it as a reference to Mennonites, and denied it vigorously. All she knew of Mennos was that they dress "weird."[1]

Gospel Herald reported the remark from a men's magazine some months ago, which advised beard-wearers to trim their beards every day, "unless you want to look like a Mennonite."

And this isn't confined to our own culture and the confusions and ignorance of our own society: my brother reported to me that in Bolivia, mention of the word Mennonite brings the response: "good cheeses, good cheeses!"

A tricky thing about being identified by your symbols is that other people can use them also, sometimes in ways that confine and restrict you. Early in my graduate program, I made the momentous choice to acquire a simple computer (a Commodore 64). Exulting in my accomplishment, I distributed the first of many research papers produced on it just three days later. But my bubble of enthusiasm almost burst, when in the following session another doctoral colleague reported back from discussion with his wife that "Mennonites are not supposed to have computers."

Similarly, a recent article by Shirley Kurtz in western Maryland describes the unique advantages of being the only Mennonites within a wide surrounding area, the only ones who get to define what being Mennonite really is. Her daughter "learned" from a school teacher that Mennonites can't use electricity, television, or modern transportation, etc. Just as helpful is the frequent "knowing" claim that tea and coffee are forbidden to us as well. People know Mennonites by their symbols, they think. In fact, it seems that this is the most they are willing to learn about us.

Sometimes even accurate information about us can seem quite strange, played back as the perception of outsiders. It was unforgettable for me in 1983, traveling with a group from Mennonite Central Committee in then Soviet Central Asia, to find a local Soviet official for religion trying to verify the accuracy of what he had found on Mennonites in his encyclopedia as he prepared for our visit. Is it true, he asked with a sly grin after all our queries on Soviet religious policies, that you practice the ritual called "leg-washing"? (There is usually not a separate term for foot in Slavic languages).

Both for better and for worse, Mennonites are known by their symbols. Symbols aid them in naming and communicating the values of their heritage to new generations (they hope). But, symbols also wear out; they no longer express us. We receive them as condensed and potent signs of connection to meaning that was made earlier, on our behalf. So even while symbols may preserve us, we can preserve them only by conscious decision. Even a "people of preservation"—to borrow the phrase—cannot take its symbols for granted.

This review of an Anabaptist heritage in language and symbolism might best be captured by scenes from childhood memories, a time when perceptions might (mythically) converge. Sights, sounds, smells, actions, categories all came from a sub-cultural complex that bespoke a common heritage. The origin of the patterns and their minute differences from one branch to another may have been deliberate or accidental, but they all signified something. It was not mere happenstance if a buggy wore a purple top, or if a bishop's son bore a long tie into the communion service during the mid-1960s. Only groups like these could make the length of a skirt hem or the width of a hat brim something that signified cooperation (or otherwise) with the teachings and norms of a faith community.

Let me give you the picture: a hot, sultry September Saturday afternoon. The church windows are open; smells of hay and cows waft through. The sermon is long; it followed a stumbling devotional. The music is our prayer-book and our liturgy. We sit in separate sections, informally marked off for males and females, for young and old. The bench is getting sticky; the old varnish softens in the heat and sweat. Dress is simple, even more than usual. Uniformity is encouraged because this is the season for communion. A personal inventory has been taken to determine whether this body is ready to partake together. Discipline problems have been identified. This is council meeting, preparatory service. If as a small child you are not fortunate enough to be able to sit still that long, some kindly grandparent nearby may slip you one of those round pink candies that only appear in such dire straits. Otherwise, you sit, you kneel, you sit, stand, and pray just like the grownups.

But, there is more to it than this. What about the unspoken? Isn't there a rumble underground that moves along with deep power, only rarely coming up to find visible or perceptible expression? What about kinship, ties of blood, racial loyalties, cultural patterns ingrained as deep as prejudices? What are the risks we know without speaking of them? How do we tell when our very well-being as a faith community is in jeopardy?

Standing outside the meetinghouse with the men in their small circles, as they quietly comment on weather, crops, and current events, I overhear a conversation about the elections in progress. Campaigns are underway, candidates are being chosen, and their merits are being obliquely debated. One sudden concern: a candidate has been chosen from a Catholic background. Will this affect our schools? What about taxes, freedom of religion, and our right to speak up in public? Will there be an unfair advantage given to our rivals?

Or yet another scene: a city meetinghouse with streams of our people converging. Calm, orderly, normalcy: except for the noisy protester in the street outside with a bullhorn and a crowd he has convinced that these Mennonites are naive or even politically dangerous for bringing their foreign visitors from the Soviet Union. It is an enactment of parable; it is a demonstration that a child could grasp, of love for enemy, of ties that rise above the barriers and boundaries of nation and state.

These, too, are some of the rhythms and patterns of a godly life, pursued in the company of the faithful, a holy and peculiar people forming Christian communities wherever they are found. We have a goodly heritage, as my grandfather used to say. "Our lines have fallen in pleasant places." (Psalm 16:6)

I had originally welcomed this invitation, expecting to enjoy a leisurely time of picking through the ancient pathways of our peoples, reviewing their patterns and sifting through to test for current significance. The impossibility of accomplishing such a preposterous task grew on me gradually, however, to the point where I feel compelled to make a cautious disclaimer of sorts.

These symbols—the rituals, the language, the cadences, the rhythms of patterned and godly lives—are there in a way that exists in memory and somehow exists above or beyond individual ability to carry that freight. If there's one thing you cannot do, it is to be a traditional Mennonite by yourself. Another virtually impossible task is to start a traditional congregation today. These things don't work. Anabaptists can always go the other way, but they cannot recreate traditions from whole cloth.

And I find it mind-boggling to contemplate this when I realize how much wholesale social change I have witnessed in my own generation on this precise point of visible and otherwise perceptible patterns. I am completely puzzled by how those choices were made, and how we would ever hope to replace them by anything like a functional substitute.

I know those patterns. They come down through various permutations. But I do not see the trade, the calculation, or the exchange: with what have they been replaced?

I am impressed with the work of Mary Douglas, a leading British anthropologist who pays serious attention to religion. For her, change as change is of little interest. So things change? Everything changes. Things like these are constantly eroding under the pressures. Change is not a surprise; let's rather pay attention to the patterns, the evidence for patterns of things that endure.

These groups are still moving in patterns that somehow fit those beliefs, we contend, and continuities are of greater interest than the superficialities of merely abandoning externals. There is an order among us, whether old order, new order, or somehow re-order. Wouldn't it be a radical act to work at establishing or re-establishing those traditions full-blown today? What does it take to recapture the essence of these communities when external circumstances have become so obviously different?

Anabaptists still need strong communities of faith, solid institutions, and leadership. Our rhetoric may become richer or poorer, our overall economic positions wax or wane, but we must spend most of our energy in maintaining an awareness of the spiritual conditions for life together in faith. Will our protest have a focus? Does our commitment match our rhetoric? Can we call forth the coming generations to follow and join us and then extend the paths of discipleship among their own peers? What patterns of organization will be required to sustain that journey?

I want to conclude with Robert Bellah's observation, a conviction, no less:

> The Reformation, especially in its Calvinist and sectarian forms, reformulated the deepest level of identity symbols, which as in all traditional societies were expressed as religious symbols, in order to open up entirely new possibilities of human action. God's will was seen not as the basis and fulfillment of a vast and complex natural order that man must largely accept as it is—the conception of me-dieval Christianity as of most traditional religion—but as a mandate to question and revise every human institution in the process of building a holy community.[2]

May this be our heritage.

[1] Chana Schoenberber, "Getting to Know About You and me," *Newsweek* (September 20, 1993), 8.

[2] Robert Bellah, *Beyond Belief*, cited in Sara Little, *To Set One's Heart* (John Knox Press, 1983), 9.

2

Language of the Faith and Every Day Life

by Ronald C. Arnett

In the beginning was the Word, and the Word was with God, and the Word was God. He was in the beginning with God; all things were made through him, and without him was not anything made that was made. In him was life, and the life was the light of men. The light shines in the darkness and the darkness has not overcome it.[1]

"In the beginning was the Word" is a familiar Christian text. The Word as sacred is fundamental to the Judeo-Christian tradition. The question that guides this essay is "what is the everyday importance of the Word?" Is language of the faith simply a form of religious piety, an outdated practice, and act that carries little significance for a modern world? My aim is to offer a practical understanding of the relationship between everyday life and the language of the faith. With support from a number of religious and secular authors, I contend that the health of the Christian community is at risk unless we find ways to reclaim a meaningful connection between language and everyday Christian life.

Viktor Frankl's *Man's Search For Meaning* makes a powerful case for the importance of language in a time of stress. Frankl, his family, and many others cast out from Hitler's Germany were faced with enduring and making sense out of horrendous crimes. Frankl's observation was that those with a language and philosophical system out of which life could be understood and interpreted had a greater chance at survival. Those with a language that helped explain and bear such humiliation and devastation were aided in their quest for survival as much, if not more, than the hardiest men and women with great physical strength. Frankl states,

whenever there was an opportunity for it, one had to give them a *why*—an aim—for their lives, in order to strengthen them to bear the terrible *how* of their existence. Woe to him who saw no more sense in his life, no aim, no purpose, and therefore no point in carrying on. He was soon lost. We had to teach the despairing men, that *it did not really matter what we expected from life, but rather what life expected from us.*[2]

Language was needed to teach another that meaning could be found even in the midst of suffering. It was not just the practical action of men and women of courage that assisted survival; the quiet courage of teaching one another the importance of finding a why for life was deeply needed. Frankl and others often used a spiritual language to make sense out of their plight.

Of course, it is good to do practical work, to engage in practical action. The point of the above material from Frankl, however, is that the why of practical faith comes not from action but from language that teaches us the significance of such a faith. A practical faith only concerned about the "how" can ignore that which nourishes the reason for our actions.

Using farming as an example, we need people who know how to farm well—people of action. We also need people who love the earth and tell us why the hours of toil are significant. Such people add nobility and reason to the task beyond survival. Such poets of life and language give us a why to sustain our practical how in the midst of long and demanding hours of labor.

Using the church as a point of comparison, we might suggest that as the work of the church becomes demanding, we need assistance from those who help frame reasons for why such work is worthy of time and effort. The task of this essay is simply to remind us that the language of why is necessary when we meet the practical demands of how a task is to be done, particularly when the task is unpleasant.

Introduction

My premises in this article are three-fold: 1) a practical faith is a significant contributor to the development of religious community, 2) people of a practical faith are often skeptical of religious language; it can be misused, and 3) religious language is needed to support the long term contribution of a practical faith, with full knowledge that pious language can be used as a screen for inappropriate behavior.

Practical Faith

A practical faith manifests itself in action and service. It is this call to a practical faith that makes the Brethren significant contributors as a people of faith. Brethren, as historically practical people of faith, have put their faith into action through Heifer Project, Brethren Volunteer Service, On Earth Peace, and a ministry of service and action.[3]

The rural connections of the Brethren have given them important insight into a life of faith that nourishes growth and practical results. For crops to grow healthy and without weeds, they need work and attention. A life of faith has kinship to the rural roots of the Brethren; attentive work is needed in the shaping of lives and those around them in a life of faith.

Being a practical people, Brethren have sometimes been skeptical of words and language. They have been more concerned about how a person lives than the flowery language used to describe the action.

All of us have been to a church or organization that makes claims that are not followed, generating mistrust and cynicism in the membership. In short, practical people are often justly worried about rhetorical exaggeration. In the words of Andy Murray's song, it is important to be a "full measure man";[4] in this case, a farmer who can be trusted to bring the "full" amount of grain to the mill. According to Murray, a man or woman who spends less time talking and more time cultivating and harvesting grain is a hero of everyday honesty. It is the behavior, not words, that signals trustworthiness.

Language Misused

It is little wonder that a practical people of faith might not be known for a large number of philosophers and theologians. Most Brethren heroes are people of action like Dan West, Anna Mow, and M. R. Zigler, to name a few. Each in his or her own right made scholarly contributions, but their work as missionaries, preachers, and spiritual leaders of action carved a place for them in our hearts. Thus it should not surprise us when language is looked at with a skeptical eye by a practical community of the faith.

Language can be misused. We fear those who might be interested in religious language for its own sake, not as a guide for faith put into action. It is possible to use words that are not followed, laying groundwork for cynicism in the Church. *The Cynical Americans* suggests that cynicism is fueled by unmet high expectations.[5] Language that holds a sacred view of the world that is behaviorally ignored or contrary to what actually happens is a sure tried way to generate interpersonal cynicism within the Church. Sissela Bok, in *Lying: Moral Choice in Public and Private Life*, puts in print what those skeptical of grandiose use of language intuitively understand. "Trust and integrity are precious resources, easily squandered, hard to regain. They can thrive only on a foundation of respect for veracity."[6]

This concern about language is pointed to by James, suggesting that we hold our tongues before sharing our counsel with another, is born of the knowledge that words can be misused. People often say things they later regret.

> Let every man be quick to hear, slow to speak, slow to anger, for the anger of man does not work the righteousness of God. (James 1: 19-20)

> Be doers of the word, and not hearers only, deceiving yourselves. For if any one is a hearer of the word and not a doer, he is like a man who observes his natural face in a mirror; for he observes himself and goes away and at once forgets what he was like. (James 1: 22-24)

> If any one thinks he is religious, and does not bridle his tongue but deceives his heart, this man's religion is in vain. (James 1: 26)

The tongue can use language to deceive. The old cliché that actions speak louder than words guides the theology of James and often a practical people of faith.

Practicality Misused

People of a practical faith are correct in assuming that words need to be used with caution. We all know people who have been hurt by others using words in careless ways that direct people in problematic directions. In order to compensate for this recognition of language misuse, a practical people of faith place significant emphasis on behavior. We want to see a person "walk the walk, not just talk the talk." We judge another by the fruits of his/her actions.

This focus on behavior is an important counter to language misuse, but like what it attempts to correct, the focus on behavior can be misused as well. We can become so centered on the practical and so distrustful of language that we cannot teach anyone, unless they are willing to spend a lifetime observing our behavioral culture.

Have you ever tried to learn from a skilled artisan who has no words for what he or she is doing? Learning from someone under such conditions is very challenging, particularly in a verbal culture. One is expected to rub shoulders with such a person long enough to learn their trade. Such learning has and continues to have a place. But in a transient culture in which we may not live close to the same people for a lifetime, such a learning style is increasingly problematic and at best partially functional.

The more urban, mobile, and diverse the mix of people that compose the Church of the Brethren, the less likely a practical focus on learning, skeptical of language and based on interpersonal interaction, will be effective for new members. If it attempts to bring into its midst individuals who are unfamiliar with small town interaction patterns, relational connections, and/or rural social values, they may not have the patience needed to learn about its culture. They will want to hear from it what is important and why.

The denomination should not be surprised at its Annual Conference when "new" members of the Church of the Brethren stand up and say, "We need a creed. What does this Church stand for anyway?" I am committed to our non-creedal position as a Church and would not support a change. Yet on the other hand, I am sympathetic to those impatient with a Church that expects learnings to emerge primarily through rubbing shoulders with one another. How are those who have not lived in a Brethren community their entire lives, gone to camp, attended Annual Conference, and graduated from a Brethren college, to learn about the Church?

Let me state once again that a practical style of learning based on rubbing shoulders with another is and continues to be significant. My contention is not to downplay the importance of such an orientation. The point is that a practical focus can be overdone if we do not acknowledge the changing world in which we must minister. In a world of diversity, words need to reach out to one another, explaining the why and the significance of behavior.

Without a language base tied to practical learnings, we may figure out how to do the task and still miss the point of the exercise. The master laborer may not be able to tell us why a task is important to do, even though he or she may know in his or her own heart. The person functioning as the apprentice may not learn for many years why a particular skill is an important way to invest a life. We might ask, "Why be a member of a particular church when any denomination will seemingly do?" When we observe what a particular group does, we might ask, "Why is such action significant?"

It is said that for many small businesses, the first generation builds the financial base and the reputation for a company. A vision guides the reason for making business "good." The next generation manages the funds but talks nothing about why the business is important other than to generate income for the family. When this middle generation passes the baton to the next generation, it receives a business but no heart for why the business is important. They continue to be interested in making money, but their lack of love for the enterprise unknowingly permits the business to atrophy. At this point, decline begins. This third generation only concentrates on the practical, and the language for why a particular business deserves time and effort is absent in the everyday conversation and management.

Practical Theology

Practical theology is interested in whether or not something works, accomplishes a particular action, is consistent with proclamations of faith, and results in religious behavior that makes a difference in everyday lives of people. Luther referred to James as an "epistle of straw." He was concerned about the focus on good works. It is my contention that we live in an era when the practical fruits of the faith need to be encouraged. We need theologians and laity willing to roll up their sleeves and work. A practical theology that makes a difference in one's own life and the lives of others is significantly needed.

The focus on practical theology is not new or novel. Its foundation is in James, the life of Christ, the works of St. Augustine, and the recent writings of such people as Dietrich Bonheoffer, Martin Luther King, Jr., Stanley Hauerwas, and Robert Bellah. The words of James have meant that we are to carry forth our faith into everyday interaction. The way in which we work, play, eat, associate with friends, and treat our families is not an extension of the faith; such actions need to reflect the faith in action.

A practical theology that makes a difference is central to the faith of the Brethren and is crucial in this essay. Without a recognition that my first and foremost concern is practical theology, the potential contribution of this essay will be by-passed. The notion of practical is not questioned in this essay; it is at the heart of a Brethren faith. My suggestion is for us to broaden what we consider practical.

The question that propels the remainder of this essay is as follows: Is there more to a practical theology and a practical faith than behavioral patterns? My suggestion is yes—language is a practical necessity for any communion wanting to pass on its view of the world in an increasingly diverse and transient culture.

Practical theology that connects Word and behavior is the heart of the epistle of James.

> Be doers of the word, and not hearers only, deceiving yourselves. For if any one is a hearer of the word and not a doer, he is like a man who observes his natural face in a mirror; for he observes himself and goes away and at once forgets what he was like. If any one thinks he is religious, and does not bridle his tongue but deceives his heart, this man's religion is vain (James 1: 22-24, 26).

In the connection of Word and action, both language and behavior are viewed as part of a practical faith.

Language as Practical

The position of many Brethren is that a practical theology of service needs to be sustained and nourished. The world is still in need of a faith tied to action. The point of this essay is that such an orientation does not continue without support of language as well as behavior. Brethren need language to remind them what kind of people of the faith they are to be. They require a language that connects them to their creator, reminds them who they are, and points a direction for behavior consistent with the faith.

As pointed to above, to be a practical people of faith without a language base to describe one's action requires reliance solely upon continuity, such as a lifestyle that results in little change from generation to generation. A rural or small town community where people live and work with one another in similar ways from year to year does not require a language to explain what is already expected. Behavioral tradition and the "habits of the hearts," or mores of the group, as Bellah states, sustain the people.[7]

However, when a group is being newly constructed or when transience moves people in and out of the group on a regular basis, a way to explain the behavior becomes more essential. In short, a focus on language becomes more important as mobility enters the life of a people.

If people living life in traditional behavioral patterns have not developed a language that introduces and explains what their everyday life of faith means, then the group is less likely to inform others about themselves, taking on the characteristics of an exclusive culture. A church culture with little emphasis on language to explain or make sense out of everyday life is a closed culture. Such a church culture will have enormous difficulty in recruiting new members, unless by happenstance the behavioral characteristics of a new member approximate the actions of the traditional group.

The importance of language to keep a group open is of particular importance to a group that rejects the call for a creed. Without a creed there is a temptation for small groups to develop into behavioral cliques that include or exclude people based more on behavior than attitudes of faith.

The sacredness of the Word is fundamental to the health of the Christian community if that community is to offer an arm of connection to those unsure of the mores and actions of a people. My stress on the importance of the Word is not a novel concept; the emphasis on the importance of language as a practical tool for making contact with others beyond sectarian behavioral guidelines might, however, be more unique.

James William McClendon, Jr., in an excellent book on theological ethics, states a point about Baptists that applies to Brethren, at least to a degree.

> The Baptists in all their variety and disunity failed to see in their own heritage, their own way of using Scripture, their own communal practices and patterns, their own guiding vision, a resource for theology unlike the prevailing scholasticism round about them [a commitment to a practical theology]. The basic failure was baptists' distrust of their own vision, their common life, their very gospel; whereas it might have been the resource for their theology, and theology in turn the means of exploring that gospel, revitalizing that life, focusing that vision. We need to do this by acknowledging the rich resources for theology in the narrative common life of that vision.[8]

When we focus primarily on the practical, limited to behavioral characteristics, we can miss understanding what makes us unique. We may exhibit the behavior and have little understanding of why such an act of faith is worthy of being done. One of the values of a year abroad for students is not only to learn about other cultures but to discover the uniqueness of their own heritages.

A practical faith so focused on getting something done needs a language base to remind others and itself of the unique contributions offered by a group of people. Those committed to a practical faith tradition may consider it a waste of time to discuss the faith when the real contribution is made in the doing of the faith. There seems to be little reason to be in conversation about faith when one is so busy trying to carry out the life tasks guided by a faith commitment. It is to such a group that the epistle of James is directed. "Count it all joy, my brethren, when you meet various trials, for you know that the testing of your faith produces steadfastness. And let steadfastness have its full effect, that you may be perfect and complete, lacking in nothing " (James 1:2-4).

Imagine such a sermon bringing in new converts! James was speaking to those already convinced about the way and the path. He was on target for those already convinced of a particular position. What do we do, however, with those who have yet to make a life decision that will guide their practical action of the faith? In addition, what do we do when others want to understand why a particular action or behavior is important? It is necessary to have a language base that makes sense out of actions in such a fashion that others can understand.

The people of the church need to be in conversation about the foundation of their action; a language of faith undergirds the action of faith. Giles and

Coupland in *Language: Contexts and Consequences,* state the shaping nature of our language.

> Language . . . is a crucial factor in intergroup relations to the extent that the social meanings of its many, and sometimes very subtle, forms are salient, complex and diverse. Our social lives are built around the symbolic functioning of language; in our language we give life, meaning and value to our relationships, allegiances, institutions and, of course, ourselves; the social conditions that structure all of these again find their shape in the language we use.[9]

Granted, language can be misused, ignored, and offered as a smoke screen for devious behavior. However, language is still the tool that must be used to shape who and what we are. A person who meets with a group and states one position publicly and then articulates another privately is still shaping people. In such a case, the language of the faith expressed in public is countered by private discourse.

The private language shapes the language of the people who discover that public pronouncements are merely nice statements that carry little conviction. In such instances, it is not language that we should question; it is the incongruence between public and private positions. Language shapes a people, and when public statements are found to be of no value at the private level of interaction, questions should be raised. But Anabaptists should not give up on the value of language to define who they are. Anything can be misused, including an excessive focus on behavior.

Mary Gore Forrester concludes her book on *Moral Language* with a simple reminder, "moral truth is determined by the most widely and tenaciously accepted moral beliefs."[10] Moral beliefs do not emerge out of a vacuum; they are carried in the lives and stories of a people through language. Language is the carrier of both moral and immoral belief structures. Whatever belief structure emerges and begins to move a people will be carried by their everyday language. Where sacred language has been left behind, it is not surprising that the sacred is being forgotten in everyday life. Just as an arm placed in a cast begins to wither and no longer offers strength previously connected with its use, language that once sustained a people will grow weak and unable to motivate when not used.

There is now a body of secular literature that points to the need for a sacred view of the Word, not out of religious piety, but out of a conviction that ignoring a language of faith in the church community has not worked, at least according to Robert Bellah, Alasdair MacIntyre, Stanley Hauerwas, and Vernard Eller. Our concentrated efforts on interpersonal behavior have left the meaningfulness of community to whom we know rather than what we believe and why we believe it.

A "good old boy" system is based on a practical behavioral network. It is important to have friends and relatives in the church, but if it is to grow, it must explain how and why it does what it does. When congregations begin to invite storytellers into worship, they become less concerned about who they are connected to and more interested in a language of the faith that reminds them of their sin, the mind of Christ, the importance of the scriptures, and discerning the Bible together. They are then open to anyone wanting to take the scriptures seriously. Behavior is important, but we have no creed. There is no one way of acting that we can claim as interpersonally correct. But, the importance of language, the need to take the Word seriously, this Anabaptists can expect of one another as they join in Christian community.

[1] Jn 1:1-5. The Revised Standard Version is used throughout essay.

[2] Viktor Frankl, *Man's Search for Meaning: An Introduction to Logotherapy* (New York: Pocket Books, 1974), 121-2.

[3] See Ronald C. Arnett, "Brother James: The First of the Brethren?" *Messenger* (February, 1989): 14-5, 23-4, 26.

[4] Andy and Terry Murray, "Grandaddy Was a Farmer," *Goodbye Still Night*, Recording (Elgin, Ill.: Brethren Press, 1978).

[5] Donald L. Kanter and Philip H. Mirvis, *The Cynical Americans: Living and Working in an Age of Discontent and Disillusion* (San Francisco: Jossey-Bass, 1989), 3.

[6] Sissela Bok, *Lying: Moral Choice in Public and Private Life* (New York: Vintage Books, 1978), 262.

[7] Robert Bellah, et al., *Habits of the Heart: Individualism and Commitment in American Life* (Berkeley: University of California Press, 1985).

[8] James Wm. McClendon, Jr., *Systematic Theology: Ethics* (Nashville: Abingdon Press, 1986), 26.

[9] Howard Giles and Nikolas Coupland, *Language: Contexts and Consequences* (Pacific Grove, Cal.: Brooks/Coles Publishing Company, 1991), 191, 199.

[10] Mary Gore Forrester, *Moral Belief* (Madison: University of Wisconsin Press, 1982), 175.

Conversation
ಜಾಜಾ VII ಲ೮ಲ೮

Nonconformity

The two kingdom theology—that persons either stand with Christ in God's Kingdom or oppose God and live in the kingdom of darkness—was at the heart of traditional Anabaptism. According to Steven M. Nolt, assimilation with larger Protestantism has blurred the boundaries of this distinction. Mennonites embraced mainstream practice by adopting institutions from the other kingdom while keeping them "Mennonite." Mennonite Mutual Aid, for example, became an alternative to the traditional rejection of life insurance, and Wayfarers and Torchbearers were scouting equivalents. Brethren, too, were influenced by mainstream trends, especially turn-of-the-century revivalism and liberalism. They gradually redefined nonconformity in inner and spiritual terms, and began to "live with one foot in each kingdom." For example, Brethren rejected the separate life in favor of the simple life; those who practiced simplicity "lived as larger society did, only less so." Nolt adds that in making these shifts both communions remained true in part to their heritage; Brethren drew on Pietism to emphasize the personal side of faith, and Mennonites continued to view the church as a community, only their community had become much like the rest of society.

Dale Stoffer agrees that major movements in larger Protestantism—revivalism, fundamentalism, and classical liberalism—damaged the commitment to nonconformity, specifically by increasing individualism and decreasing accountability to the community of believers. The result has been an imbalance in mission, where "evangelism," in some cases, and "social service," in others, is overemphasized, while a third prong, "living witness", is consistently neglected. Stoffer calls for redressing this imbalance. The Anabaptist heritage, he says, is strongest when Brethren and Mennonites commit to all three.

1
Reinterpreting Nonconformity:
Mennonite and Brethren
Thought and Practice

by Steven M. Nolt

Nonconformity is not a term of common currency among members of today's Church of the Brethren or "old" Mennonite Church.[1] Yet less than a century ago it was an assumed part of church life and thought. During the twentieth century the two fellowships reinterpreted certain theological themes, swapped cultural assumptions, and recast their visions of nonconformity to surrounding society. Both groups have reworked their understanding of nonconformity along somewhat different lines. Nevertheless, both churches originally drew their understandings and practices from similar roots. Sharing much in common, their experiences offer related but divergent examples of believers wrestling with their relationship to the world around them.

Anabaptism and Nonconformity

Nonconformity was the application and logical extension of the Anabaptists' radical ontological dualism, which historian of Anabaptism, Robert Friedmann, called "the heart of the implicit theology of Anabaptism."[2] This dualistic two-kingdom theology was unique, not in its separating human experience into vying parts, but rather in the particular parts themselves. Whereas many avenues of Christian thought had run a line of demarcation between the flesh and the spirit, the inner and the outer, or faith and works, the Anabaptists saw the great divide between the church and the world. The Christian stood wholly with Christ in God's kingdom, while those opposing God lived wholly in the kingdom of darkness. Humans did not find themselves internally divided into physical and spiritual halves nor were their vocational choices of another order from their devotional activities. They were completely members of God's kingdom or they were totally outsiders. The kingdoms neither converged nor overlapped. The true followers of Christ lived as strangers and pilgrims, as citizens of another kingdom than that which governed and controlled their surrounding society.

Within Anabaptism the Swiss Brethren and Hutterian Brethren emphasized this sense of kingdom separatism most completely. The Schleitheim Confession of the Swiss Brethren clearly bears the stamp of two kingdom dualism. Written in 1527, it was one of the earliest theological statements from an Anabaptist pen and one of the most enduring and influential in later Mennonite history. Although the confession does not represent every channel of sixteenth-century Anabaptist thought, it does exemplify that stream which nourished most later South German and Swiss Mennonites.

Schleitheim speaks in exclusive, stark, either/or terms. There is no middle ground or room for compromise in the Seven Articles. In discussing the communion table of the Lord's Supper, the conveners of Schleitheim announced that no one can be

> partakers at the same time of the table of the Lord and the table of devils. All those who have fellowship with the dead works of darkness have no part in the light. Thus all who follow the devil and the world, have no part with those who have been called out of the world unto God. All those who lie in evil have no part in the good.

In eloquent and uncompromising language the Confession drew a pointed distinction between the competing kingdoms. Explicitly the Swiss Brethren declare that

> there is nothing else in all the world and all creation than good or evil, believing and unbelieving, darkness and light, the world and those who are [come] out of the world, God's temple and idols, Christ and Belial, and none will have part with the other.[3]

The Anabaptist experience of persecution and harassment at the hands of civil authorities and state church clerics heightened their sense of being a separate people. From the perspective of an Anabaptist on the way to execution, the two kingdoms were clearly and self-consciously alienated from one another. For their part, the Anabaptists' certainly sought to disentangle themselves from any compromise with the world, as well.

Because the Anabaptists viewed salvation and regeneration as transferring one completely from one kingdom to another, they expected that Christians would feel tension with the world in all aspects of life. Salvation was not simply redemption for a disembodied soul at some future point in time; rather salvation was God's gift of wholeness beginning now. God graciously blesses the church not only with salvation from eternal separation but also from the desire for self-defense and the need to possess large numbers of material goods. For the Anabaptists there was not salvation in works, as some opponents charged them with teaching; rather, good works, nonresistance, and lives of simplicity and humility were salvation. They were gifts of satisfaction and sufficiency graciously provided by God.

Radical Pietism of the late seventeenth and early eighteenth centuries drew on certain Anabaptist emphases including those of the gathered, separated church and seriousness of personal discipleship. The regeneration of sinners was not only an inner subjective experience but the transforming power of

God's grace in the believer's life changed that life and those around it. Unlike many of the Continental Pietists, the Brethren radicals who gathered in Schwarzenau in 1708 were convinced that the inner Word demanded definite outward expression. The faithful observance of the ordinances and the church as the committed, visible body was one of the most important testimonies to the active presence of God's indwelling Spirit.

Rather than simply understanding the Christian experience in an inner-outer, or spirit-flesh distinction, the Brethren also had a dualistic sense of being an identifiable, separate body. In Alexander Mack's words, the "church is separated from the world, from sin, [and] from all error." Corporately the Brethren became a united, visible "body or the church of Christ" which "still walks outwardly in a state of humiliation in this wicked world."[4] Mack understood the church to be a separate people, nonconformed to their surrounding society, humble, and self-denying. Later Brethren elder Matthew M. Eshelman (1844-1921), writing an extensive treatise on Dunker nonconformity, emphasized the holistic nature of redemption and separation from the world. Salvation, he wrote, was "like leaven, it leaveneth the whole lump." No aspect of the Christian's life was unredeemed; no part of the Christian's life could be in conformity to the world. "The whole mind, opinion, judgment, sentiment, courage, belief, choice, desire, purpose, inclination, remembrance, and spiritual nature must undergo a change," Eshelman argued. All of life "must be conformed to the perfect law" of God.[5]

Nonconformity in North America

Upon immigrating to North America the Brethren and so-called "old" Mennonites found themselves in a friendlier social environment. Civic and religious toleration, for the most part, marked their first century and a half in the New World. The line between church and world was less clear now. Surrounding society no longer worked so hard to keep itself separate from the Anabaptists' heirs. It fell almost entirely to the Dunkers and Mennonites themselves to maintain the boundary between the two kingdoms. No longer facing the hostility of European Christendom, Mennonites and Brethren developed a theology of humility. Meek yieldedness and individual submission replaced the themes of physical persecution and suffering. Humility became an increasingly important emphasis in both groups during the first three-quarters of the nineteenth century. The Mennonites, it seems, drew much of their inspiration from Pietist sources.[6] Mennonites wrote of weakness and spiritual poverty. Dunkers referred to themselves as "fools for Christ's sake."[7] Members had to withdraw consciously from a largely democratic society in which they were now invited to participate.

Both groups emphasized plain dress and simple housing. With notable exceptions, members of both churches stayed away from large-scale business ventures and investments. Dunkers upheld the venerated "ancient order of the Brethren."[8] Meanwhile "old" Mennonites published and read articles warning against "Amusements" and "Fashion at Church."[9] The fellowships also taught noninvolvement in worldly organizations, secret societies, and many public corporations. Such entanglements represented the "unequal yoke" that the New Testament warned against and threatened to bridge the two kingdoms, compromising Christian separation. Worldly associations might also require the swearing of oaths, filing of lawsuits, or participating in frivolous parades and parties, all of which would have meant disobedience to New Testament commands and conformity with the patterns of the world. Typically, Brethren and Mennonites also avoided political involvement, as well, hoping to keep from mixing too much with the kingdom of this world. Supported by their humility theology, Mennonite and Brethren nonconformity upheld the two-kingdom dualism.

During the last three decades of the nineteenth century both churches experienced a major division in their ranks. The fracturing was different in each case, owing to the groups' respective organizations. The Brethren felt national schisms, while the Mennonites underwent a series of regional rendings. In both cases significant minorities withdrew from their parent body, uncomfortable with innovations in church life and practice. The Brethren also suffered the loss of the progressive wing of their denomination. Ultimately the conservative seceders hoped to maintain the "old order," including a commitment to a strict two kingdom worldview. The dissenting conservers sensed that the larger Brethren and Mennonite bodies were becoming more accustomed to living as members of both kingdoms.[10]

Yet for much of the 1800s, Mennonites and Brethren had successfully maintained a principled nonconformity to surrounding society. Both in theory and practice, it held faith and life together. Growing as it did out of a two-kingdom worldview, nonconformity applied to all aspects of one's life. There was no provision for doctrinal nonconformity without an accompanying physical-social separation. Nor could one engage merely in Sunday morning social dissent. Nonconformity was a daily practice which informed work, dress, entertainment, family, education, and financial decisions. Nonconformity brought all of life under a single principle. It integrated all of life and bore witness to the Anabaptist view of salvation itself, which was both present and future, spiritual and physical, personal and social.

Thus, changes in Mennonite and Brethren understandings of nonconformity involved theological shifts accompanied by a practical reorientation of actions and emphases. Before and after the turn of the twentieth century, both the "old" Mennonites and the Church of the Brethren experienced a reworking of certain doctrinal understandings. Those changes, coupled with the social and material upheavals among church members themselves, and set against the background of a rapidly evolving industrial host society, resulted in a reinterpretation of nonconformity among both groups.

Reinterpretation Among the Mennonites

Among "old" Mennonites (and the Amish Mennonites with whom they later joined) changes in religious attitudes and approaches began surfacing during the late nineteenth century. A period of sudden and rapid institution building and church program creation mirrored the broader reorganization of American society. The industrial trusts, labor unions, state university systems, and numerous private societies that grew up during America's Gilded Age exemplified the growing organization and rationalization of larger society. The progressive spirit of optimism which leaned heavily on faith in education, exploration, and scientific progress, led Americans, including American Christians, to create an organized institutional world.

Mennonites were not exempt from the pull of late 1800s activism. An entire generation of the church introduced periodicals, regular book publication, schools, mission boards, old people's homes, orphanages, urban church work, Sunday schools, conferences, and a continent-wide biennial general conference. Mennonite institutional activists adopted an aggressive stance towards the world, speaking in terms of "conquering" and "advancing" for God. In 1895 one Mennonite activist commented characteristically, "Our people are going to be a power for Christ such as we hardly realize."[11]

But the young workers did more than copy formal church structure from surrounding Christendom. They also opened themselves to wider Christian thought and imbibed American Protestantism, speaking in new ways about the very relationship of God and humanity. Salvation itself took on new meaning for many Mennonites with significant consequences for nonconformity and the Christian's relation to the world. Whereas soteriology had been understood in a larger, more life-encompassing way, salvation gradually came to have narrower implications. Like their Protestant neighbors, Mennonites began to speak in terms of a "plan" of salvation: a forensic transaction with the divine that one could chart schematically. According to these new patterns of thought, salvation had clear implications for the afterlife but was much more nebulously connected to anything in the present. A personal relationship with God affected one's earthly life in more of a secondary way; primarily, it freed one from the terror of the future.

Among the consequences of this shift in salvation thinking was a funda-mental shaking of the two kingdom foundation of Mennonite nonconformity. The new approach to personal salvation focused almost exclusively on the indi-vidual's relationship to heaven, on the one hand, and hell on the other. Not that earlier Mennonite notions of salvation did not include a future home in paradise, but then the intensity of focus was as much on the redeemed earthly life as on the realm beyond. At the turn of the century when the influential Mennonite thinker Daniel Kauffman (1865-1944) wrote a book on nonconformity, he began, as one might expect, with a section entitled the "Two Kingdoms." But, surprisingly, that section turned out to be a description of the Last Judgment! The two kingdoms were reduced simply to eternal states and the ancient Anabaptist dualism became merely a future distinction. Only after one died, Kauffman wrote, would one "finally reap the rewards" of Christian discipleship.[12]

The new concepts of salvation ultimately eviscerated the practice of nonconformity by robbing it of its essential connection to God's will and work in the Christian life. Whereas Mennonites had understood salvation as encompassing all of life here and hereafter—a salvation from the vanities and violence of the world as much as salvation from eternal torment—salvation now had less to say about the choices and chances one took in the present. Obedience was still important, to be sure, but it was no longer so closely and obviously tied to one's standing with God.

Mennonites attempted to rework their traditional understandings of nonconformity in light of their new salvation outlines. The most notable effort at linking the two was one that employed a two-part model. First, preachers and teachers presented the "plan of salvation." Next they presented the "restrictions" of the Christian life. The restrictions included practices traditionally associated with nonconformity: plain clothing, nonresistance, non-swearing of oaths, and teaching against unequal yokings in associations and secret societies. Employed in Kauffman's influential doctrinal books, the salvation-restrictions distinction was widely used by North America's "old" Mennonites.[13] By the 1940s it had become an assumed part of church thought across the denomination.[14]

Placing any doctrine or practice under the negative rubric of "restrictions" did little to excite sympathy for it, but more detrimental to the practice of nonconformity was the obvious disconnection between the salvation "plan" and the "restrictions" themselves. In fact, the death knell of historic nonconformity among Mennonites sounded when the church divided the Christian's most fundamental relationship to God from the everyday choices of daily discipleship. The rationale for remaining separate from the world soon evaporated. "I do not put any religion in the attire of the body, so far as salvation is concerned," Mennonite mission advocate George L. Bender (1867-1921) said in an address in which he made a pained attempt to defend plain clothing. Salvation for Bender was "the pearly gates" and "golden streets" of heaven. Such an understanding of salvation was not effected in the least by his coat collar, Bender admitted, yet he struggled to tie his people's historic understandings with their modern revisions.[15]

In the end Bender and his church proved unable to make a convincing link. Although it took another generation or two for the "salvation with restrictions" model to lose all convicting moral authority, traditional Mennonite nonconformity was on the way out. Yet separation from the world was not completely dead. Instead it was being reinterpreted in noticeably different terms.

While the theological legacy of turn-of-the-century Mennonite activism ultimately gutted the foundation of traditional nonconformity, another legacy of that period replaced the separatism that was lost. Making full use of their growing organizational world, twentieth-century Mennonites practiced a type of "institutional nonconformity." Creating church-based or affiliated institutions became the major Mennonite strategy for dealing with the onslaught of cultural change during the twentieth century. By building Mennonite organizations that would engage in activities similar to those of their worldly counterparts, Mennonites could grant a measure of flexibility and latitude of freedom while still maintaining some distance from the world itself. Giving tacit approval to innovations and progressive movements by channeling those energies through a church group permitted Mennonite leaders to offer a "both/and" response to the demands of their acculturating membership and their historical and theological commitment to some sort of church/world dualism.

Typical of the new institutional nonconformity was the Mennonite response to involvement in financial insurance. The church had long argued against the purchase of commercial insurance plans, especially life insurance programs, that church leaders feared would detract from the Christian's need to lean on sisters and brothers in times of hardship. Additionally, membership in a broad-based insurance program tied one financially to the lives and lifestyle of the non-Christian world, clearly a situation involving an "unequal yoke." Insurance companies also brought law suits in court and cultivated a sense of fear of the future and of death.

As Mennonite men returned from their years in Civilian Public Service during World War II, the church searched for a way to make home mortgage and business loans available to them. However, the resulting plan known as Mennonite Mutual Aid became more than a post-war reentry program for demobilized COs. It also took to selling insurance policies. Insurance with a Mennonite twist suddenly allowed members to individually plan for their own personal financial security, avoid connections with the world, and preserve key Mennonite traditions, such as mutual aid. Church leaders could now openly advocate church-based insurance while still discouraging members from taking out commercial policies. In 1951 as Mennonite theologian J. C. Wenger was making a "Plea for . . . Nonconformity to the World," he could also unreservedly endorse insurance coverage through Mennonite Mutual Aid. In Wenger's view, MMA was "obviously created by Christian people, for Christian purposes, and operating on Christian principles."[16] The company provided services that were worldly-wise yet operated within the context of the church. Finally Mennonites could have insurance and be nonconformed, too.

In a similar vein several years earlier, Mennonite economist Carl Kreider seemed to advocate nonconformity when he warned Mennonites against buying stocks and civil bonds. Such investing was "inconsistent for Mennonites," he said. Yet, Kreider's investment caution was decidedly different than that of his nineteenth-century forbears. For them, financial speculation itself was worldly, a part of the other kingdom to which Christians did not belong. For Kreider, however, the problem with investment was that heretofore there had been no

Mennonite means of investing one's wealth. There had been no institutional equivalent acceptable to Mennonites. Now, Kreider informed his readers, things stood much better. "Our church organizations such as the Mennonite Board of Missions and Charities and the Mennonite Board of Education have plans whereby individuals with money to invest can purchase annuities." Happily, "These annuities bear favorable rates of interest" and permitted the conscientious church member to make a significant donation to "worthwhile causes."[17] Institutional nonconformity handily made room for once frowned-upon activities while keeping innovations within the framework of the church.

Similarly, Mennonite schools served as alternatives to worldly universities. Higher education was redeemed when it assumed—symbolically and physically—Mennonite garb. Studying at a Mennonite college was deemed appropriate and even, in time, beneficial. American Mennonites developed liberal arts institutions, not Bible schools. Thus, they gave left-handed approval to larger society's assumptions about proper education but still maintained some distance from larger society's quadrangles. Like other private schools, Mennonite colleges evolved into professional, accredited institutions, but they continued to operate within the Mennonite community. They were the same, yet different from their secular counterparts. Families guardedly permitted exposure to otherwise questionable subject matter, provided it occurred within the context of a church school.[18]

Institutions worked together in granting one another legitimacy. The Mennonite hospitals, psychiatric care centers, and retirement homes that sprang up largely during the post-war era expressed a Mennonite desire to serve neighbors and the church community and, in many cases, sanctified Mennonite professionalism encouraged by Mennonite colleges. Mennonite young people could pursue higher education with ambition and approval, knowing that they could use their education in acceptable, approved Mennonite-related institutions. Parents and church leaders who might have expressed caution toward higher education a generation earlier now endorsed professional pursuits since a degree would not necessarily drive a young person away from the church but, in fact, enabled young adults to work in a Mennonite setting.

Among other examples of institutional nonconformity were efforts such as the Wayfarers and Torchbearers programs, begun in 1957 and 1958. These children's clubs were self-conscious Mennonite alternatives to Girls Scouts and Boy Scouts. And, beginning in 1955 "old" Mennonites organized the first of many credit unions as a church alternative to local banking. In all, Mennonites created an amazing array of institutional alternatives to larger society. By practicing institutional nonconformity, late twentieth-century Mennonites have in many ways remained a people apart while maintaining lifestyles little different from their neighbors. They are able to send their children to Mennonite colleges, save through Mennonite credit unions, buy insurance, invest earnings, find employment, and plan vacations—all through Mennonite institutions. In 1989 a church member profile discovered that while convictions regarding personal nonconformity, such as attitudes towards dancing or gambling, continue to weaken, Mennonite commitment to institutional nonconformity, such as support of church schools, periodicals, and so on, remains relatively high.[19]

Modern Mennonite institutional nonconformity is significantly different than its nineteenth-century precursor. Mennonite institutions exhibit little two-kingdom dualism. Frequently they function much like other secular organizations. The services which Mennonite institutions perform are often only somewhat distinguishable from those of their worldly counterparts. Nor have Mennonites been able completely and convincingly to connect their theology and their institutions in a way as integral as nineteenth-century nonconformity brought faith and practice together. Mennonites have reinterpreted nonconformity in such a way that separation from the world occurs at the organizational rather than ontological level.

Some Mennonites have speculated on the demise, or at least radical remaking, of many Mennonite institutions during the early twenty-first century.[20] Such speculation may not be idle. Since Mennonite institutions functioned primarily as alternatives to organizations in larger society, as these Mennonite creations become more like their secular twins, their own reason and purpose for existence diminishes.

Reinterpretation Among the Brethren

As the Brethren approached the twentieth century, they too stood heir to a tradition of radical nonconformity. An Anabaptist dualism of church and world had soaked deeply into the daily life and thought of most Dunkers. Influential nineteenth-century elder and writer Peter Nead summed Brethren assumptions when he described the church as "the people of God" who "are a distinct and separate people from the world—that is they are of another character and party, engaging in a calling which is opposed to the sinful maxims, customs, and practices of the world."[21]

Following the stormy upheavals and schisms of the early 1880s, the German Baptist Brethren experienced remarkable expansion and reorganization. Like the Mennonite activists described above, young Dunker leaders established new institutions and programs. Although the Brethren never created an institutional world like that of the Mennonites, their achievements were noticeable. The continuance of a church periodical, the publication of tracts and books, the establishment of several colleges, the beginning of foreign and urban missions, and the creation of Sunday school and mission boards all filled the late nineteenth and twentieth centuries. Additionally, aggressive evangelists drew scores of new converts into the church, increasing the group's size noticeably.[22]

The rapid growth of the church and its accompanying geographic spread raised new challenges to the Brethren dualistic worldview. Although the church continued to call converts out of the world and into the church, they needed to be more congenial in their attitudes towards the other kingdom. Some mission workers believed that Brethren dress standards, for example, hindered church outreach. Such a high and impenetrable wall of separation between the church and the world retarded efforts at evangelism. These workers pressed for a more flexible boundary between the two kingdoms so as to invite easier cross-over. Furthermore, the Brethren faced questions regarding the speed with and degree to which new converts should adopt the "order of the Brethren" after conversion. Did salvation exist apart from a nonconformed life? Some were beginning to think so, and they suggested that the plain order of the church might be less than essential to the Christian life.

The "dress question," as it was called, served as the lightening rod for debate on the purpose and practice of nonconformity. As queries and concerns mounted, church leaders searched for some strategy to handle the impending crisis. In the midst of the scramble for a way through the thorny question, Elder Henry C. Early (1855-1941) of Virginia's Shenandoah Valley provided a rein-terpretation of traditional Brethren nonconformity which rechanneled Brethren thinking significantly.[23]

Invited to present a bicentennial address as Moderator of the 1908 Annual Meeting, Early emphasized Brethren commonality with other Protestants. When he mentioned nonconformity, he did so under the creative new designation of "the simple life." The elder spoke of separation from the world as a "means to an end, not an end in itself." He had recast nonconformity in a means and ends, methods and purposes mold. The means, in this case plain clothing, were not nearly so important as were the ends toward which they worked. Early succeeded in defusing the explosive dress question by devaluing the importance of dress itself. He separated the actual wearing of clothing from the inner purposes of the wearer. In so doing, he radically reinterpreted Dunker notions of nonconformity.

Previously Dunker thought had linked the inner and outer so closely (whether the issue was baptism, dress, or the Love Feast) that to sever them would destroy the meaning of both. Now, outer forms became incidental means. The distinction between the church and the world was giving way to a more fundamental dualism between means and ends, between outer activities and inner purposes. Moreover, the idea of the simple life itself ignored the older dualism. The difference between the simple life and the worldly life was only a matter of degree, not fundamental distinction. In short, the difference between the kingdoms was now quantitative, not qualitative. Persons living simply lived as larger society did, only less so. There was no qualitative divide between the simple and the life of excess. Presumably the evolutionary principle built into the idea of the simple life would permit limited involvement in any activity or behavior provided such involvement was quantitatively less than that of surrounding secular culture.[24]

By 1911 other Brethren authors had picked up on the idea of the simple life and the means-ends dichotomy. As a framework for discussing issues or viewing the relationship between the church and the world, two kingdom nonconformity was quickly relegated to the perimeters of debate and eventually dropped altogether. That year a committee, chaired by Early, delivered a report (later approved) which lifted the threat of disfellowship from those who disregarded prescribed church dress standards. Significantly, the report employed the phrase "simplicity of life," "simple life," and "the simple Christian life," as well as the assumption that fixed principles may be separated from less-than-ultimate means. The committee's report also asked ministers "to see that the simple life in general is taught and observed."[25]

Five years later the reinterpretation of the simple life as a reformulation of nonconformity was widely accepted and received something of an official blessing. The General Sunday School Board included the topic as one of several doctrines to be included in a commissioned book for youth and young adult instruction. The book, *Studies in Doctrine and Devotion*, published in 1919, did include a passing reference to nonconformity. It even instructed young readers to "hear the church" in matters of separation from the world "even if not quite able to see the need" since the church as the body of Christ "has the right of administration." The book's major attention to Christian separation, however, came under the title of "The Simple Life." Although half the content dealt with "Christian Adornment," the author sought to broaden the subject, in line with its evolving reinterpretation.[26]

The simple life, the book said, was "the spiritual principle of the inner life." While the author pressed the importance of the simple life, he gave precious few examples of application. Even under the heading "Some Specific Teaching on the Dress Question" came only general statements about modesty that likely would have been acceptable to a variety of Christian groups. The simple life, it seemed, was not so simple after all. It involved weighty personal decisions and choices. Members were permitted their "individual tastes," the book said, but should somehow avoid fashion.[27]

With the "dress question" apparently settled, the doctrine of the simple life drew less attention and discussion. Certain quarters of the church continued to stress a simple living that recalled nonconformity, but for the most part the principle of means and ends fostered by the church's reinterpretation allowed congregations and even individuals to choose their own means. According to one scholar, teaching on the simple life "languished" and "received no new substantive content."[28] With no external measuring stick of faithfulness, simplicity became a largely relative matter.

In a further reinterpretation during the 1930s and 1940s, Brethren writers began to substitute the "spiritual life" for the simple life. The spiritual life was even less closely connected with identifiable practices or taboos. Cultivating a spiritual life further encouraged a personal dichotomy of inner and outer. Any sense of a church-world dualism was replaced with an inner struggle to discipline the "soul." Such discipline could not be judged or evaluated by fellow believers. Nor did it have much to say about one's life with others.

Highly personal and subjective, it had narrowed the all-encompassing principle of nonconformity into a private formula for life with God.

As Carl Bowman has written, the "'spiritualization' of the simple life fit well with the affluence and economic expansion of the late 1940s and 1950s when America was broadly perceived as the 'affluent society' par excellence, where the 'good life,' free from the scourge of poverty, existed in abundance." As church members adapted to American middle class life, they enjoyed their newfound lifestyle while remaining separate and simple in thought and personal devotion.[29]

Individual decision regarding appropriate behavior has resulted in a rather wide variety of practice among today's Brethren. Uniformity is gone, however. Even members who self-consciously choose to live simply do so for a variety of personal reasons, not all of which are closely tied to traditional nonconformity. Those who maintain a lifestyle markedly out of step with their surrounding culture are not always convinced that such a choice is for everyone. They would argue that individuals need to come to such an understanding on their own.

The *Brethren Profile Study* conducted in 1985 revealed current Brethren understandings of their sense of separatism from and involvement in the world. Seventy-four years after Annual Meeting granted liberty in matters of dress, individual choice resulted in a retreat from plainness. Should Brethren dress more simply than the average American? Twice as many said no as replied favorably. In addition, some forty percent of respondents believed that it is appropriate for Brethren to enjoy "the same lifestyle as other Americans." The triumph of the spiritual life left few outward Brethren identity markers. When asked if "there is any important way in which the Church of the Brethren seems different. . .from other 'mainline' Protestant churches," fifty-six percent of the respondents said, "Not really."[30]

As the Brethren reinterpreted nonconformity, they heightened their sense of the subjective. Nead's call for uniformity of custom and habit was foreign by the late twentieth century. Instead, the Brethren had chosen to recast separation in inner-personal and spiritual terms. Their lowering the wall of separation between the church and the world did allow more members of "the other kingdom" to enter the church. But, it also permitted some members to live with one foot in each kingdom and, ultimately, blur the division entirely. Frequently without the help of fellow travelers, each Christian was left with the individual responsibility of seeking first the Kingdom of God.

Conclusion

As they reinterpreted their respective understandings and practices of nonconformity, both the Brethren and the Mennonites discarded the foundation of traditional Anabaptist nonconformity: the two-kingdom world view. Perhaps this signified their ultimate acculturation into a Western democratic society.

Mennonites and Brethren felt a part of both kingdoms; indeed, judged by their lives they were part of both kingdoms. Perhaps they had always been more a part of both than they realized or admitted.[31] Yet their self-conscious living in both worlds marked a loss of part of the Anabaptist heritage to which they were heirs.

But, both remained true, in part, to their respective heritages of faith. The Brethren reinterpretation drew on Pietist roots and emphasized the personal nature of the Christian experience. Separation from the world became more of an inward spiritual reality. Cultivating the private spiritual life often replaced a critique of surrounding society. When Brethren social or economic choices did run counter to the ways of the world, such choices grew out of personal conscience. Individuals acted autonomously, taking singular stands against injustice or materialism.

The Mennonites reinterpretation, too, drew on their traditional understandings of the church as community, the body of Christ which transcended the individual. However, the corporate reality of the church often became the reality of the church corporation. The larger church community remained strong and highly visible, but it assumed the organizational face of a modern institution. Mennonites had preserved the notion of the importance of the group in priority to the individual. Church institutions certainly were larger than the lone Christian. In fact, one could give oneself up to the maintenance and preservation of church institutions much as earlier martyrs had yielded themselves and gave themselves up for the faith.

Perhaps both groups need to rediscover that piece of their heritage that was lost. For the Brethren, perhaps a new vision of the corporate church acting and living as an incarnate body would creatively unleash the power nurtured by personal spirituality. For Mennonites, a new sense of personal regeneration might re-energize church institutions, allowing them to be truly the alternatives they were meant to be.

¹ But see a few contemporary examples, such as the back cover of Donald F. Durnbaugh, ed., *Church of the Brethren: Yesterday and Today* (Elgin, Ill.: Brethren Press, 1986), which states that the denomination "is widely known for its heritage of nonconformity"; Doris Janzen Longacre, *Living More With Less* (Scottdale, Pa.: Herald Press, 1980), 51-60; and John D. Roth, "Let's Reclaim Nonconformity," *Festival Quarterly* 16 (Winter 1990): 15-7.

² Robert Friedmann, *The Theology of Anabaptism: An Interpretation* (Scottdale, Pa.: Herald Press, 1973), 36.

³ John Howard Yoder, trans. and ed., *The Legacy of Michael Sattler* (Scottdale, Pa.: Herald Press, 1973), 37, 38. For the continuing influence of this confession in twentieth century Mennonite circles, see Beulah Stauffer Hostetler, *American Mennonites and Protestant Movements: A Community Paradigm* (Scottdale, Pa.: Herald Press, 1987).

⁴ William R. Eberly, ed., *The Complete Writings of Alexander Mack* (Winona Lake, Ind.: BMH Books, 1991), 66.

⁵ Matthew M. Eshelman, *Nonconformity to the World, or a Vindication of True Vital Piety* (Dayton, Oh.: Christian Publishing Association, 1874), 59, 60.

⁶ Joseph C. Liechty, "Humility: The Foundation of Mennonite Religious Outlook in the 1860s," *The Mennonite Quarterly Review* 54 (January 1980): 5-31; see also Theron F. Schlabach, *Peace, Faith, Nation: Mennonites and Amish in Nineteenth Century America* (Scottdale, Pa.: Herald Press, 1988), 95-105.

⁷ For example, see Eshelman, *Nonconformity*, iv.

⁸ Dale R. Stoffer, *Background and Development of Brethren Doctrines, 1650-1987* (Philadelphia: Brethren Encyclopedia, Inc., 1989), 104, 108, 112, 113; and James H. Lehman, *Old Brethren* (Elgin, Ill.: Brethren Press, 1976), 139-60.

⁹ See the extensive listing under "Dress and External Conformity" in Steven L. Denlinger, ed. and comp., "Glimpses Past: Annotations of Selected Social and Cultural History Materials" in *Herald of Truth, Gospel Witness,* and early *Gospel Herald* (Lancaster, Pa.: Lancaster Mennonite Historical Society, 1985), 8-21.

¹⁰ A comparative look at the Old Order divisions (along with those of the Amish and River Brethren) is in Beulah Stauffer Hostetler, "The Formation of the Old Orders," *The Mennonite Quarterly Review* 66 (January 1992): 5-25. More Detail on the divisions themselves is in Schlabach, *Peace, Faith, Nation*, 220-9; and Stoffer, *Background and Development*, 133-64.

¹¹ George L. Bender, "Simplicity and Uniformity of Attire: How Successfully Advanced," *Herald of Truth* 32 (February 15, March 1, 1895): 68. On late nineteenth and turn-of-the-century Mennonite activism in general, see Theron F. Schlabach, *Gospel Versus Gospel: Mission and the Mennonite Church, 1863-1944* (Scottdale, Pa.: Herald Press, 1980), 31-53, 83-8. On the era's effect on salvation understandings, see J. Denny Weaver, "The Quickening of Soteriology: Atonement from Christian Burkholder to Daniel Kauffman," *The Mennonite Quarterly Review* 61 (January 1987): 5-45.

¹² Daniel Kauffman, *A Talk With Church Members* (Dakota, Ill.: J. S. Shoemaker, 1900), 9-11.

¹³ Daniel Kauffman, *Manual of Bible Doctrines* (Elkhart, Ind.: Mennonite Publishing Company, 1898), especially in the book's subtitle as "Setting Forth the General Principles of the Plan of Salvation,. . . and Pointing Out Specifically Some of the Restrictions Which the New Testament Scriptures Enjoin Upon Believers"; Daniel Kauffman, *ed., Bible Doctrine* (Scottdale, Pa.: Mennonite Publishing House, 1914), 457; and Kauffman, ed., *Doctrines of the Bible: A Brief Discussion of the Teachings of God's Word* (Scottdale, Pa.: Mennonite Publishing House, 1928), 490.

¹⁴ Although slow to appropriate the new terminology and distinction, eventually even the more tradition-minded Lancaster, Pennsylvania, Conference Mennonites had adopted it. See "Statement of Christian Doctrine and Rules and Discipline of the Mennonite Church, Lancaster Conference" [adopted 1943], Lancaster Mennonite Historical Society Library and Archives, Lancaster, Pa.

¹⁵ Bender, "Simplicity," *Herald of Truth* 32 (n.d.) 60, 61, 67, 68.

¹⁶ John C. Wenger, *Separated Unto God: A Plea For Christian Simplicity of Life and for a Scriptural Nonconformity to the World* (Scottdale, Pa.: Mennonite Publishing House, 1951), 238. On Mennonite Mutual Aid's beginnings, see "The Birth of Mennonite Mutual Aid," *Mennonite Historical Bulletin* 39 (July 1978): 4-6.

¹⁷ Carl Kreider, "The Christian Attitude Toward Investments," *Gospel Herald* 37 (February 9, 1945): 900, 901.

¹⁸ Donald B. Kraybill, *Passing on the Faith: The Story of a Mennonite School* (Intercourse, Pa.: Good Books, 1991), 185-7, offers an interesting example of institutional nonconformity from the history of a Mennonite high school. In this instance, the sponsoring church body strongly discouraged attendance at theaters, yet allowed the school to offer a course in drama and produce school plays. While some older constituents claimed that acting itself was worldly

and ethically questionable (given the aura of untruth surrounding role-play), most patrons believed that school plays were acceptable because they were directed and performed by Mennonites for a church audience.

[19] J. Howard Kauffman and Leo Driedger, *The Mennonite Mosaic: Identity and Modernization* (Scottdale, Pa.: Herald Press, 1991), cf. 192-202; 151, 177, 132-4.

[20] John A. Lapp, "Can Our Institutions Supply the Glue to Hold Us Together as a Peoplehood?" public lecture, April 20, 1993, The People's Place, Intercourse, Pa.

[21] Peter Nead, *Theological Writings on Various Subjects, or a Vindication of Primitive Christianity as Recorded in the Word of God* (Dayton, Oh.: B. F. Ellis, 1850), 122. A sampling of Brethren nonconformity standards is in D. L. Miller, et al., eds., *Revised Minutes of the Annual Meetings of the German Baptist Brethren* (Mount Morris, Ill.: Brethren Publishing House, 1899), 78-81, 117-37, 155, 167-6; and Roger E. Sappington, ed., *The Brethren in the New Nation: A Source Book on the Development of the Church of the Brethren, 1785-1865* (Elgin, Ill.: Brethren Press, 1976), 253-328.

[22] Various articles in *The Brethren Encyclopedia*, 3 vols. (Philadelphia: Brethren Encyclopedia, Inc., 1983); and Donald F. Durnbaugh, "Recent History," ed. Durnbaugh, *Church of the Brethren*, 29-30.

[23] Emmert F. Bittinger, "The Simple Life: A Chapter in the Evolution of a Doctrine," *Brethren Life and Thought* 23 (Spring 1978): 107-8.

[24] Earlier this kind of reasoning had been publicly repudiated by the author of a Brethren tract entitled "Plain Dressing." The author argued that such thinking would permit one to wear a simple silk dress, simple jewelry, or simple dress hats, when the real problem was silk, jewelry, and dress hats in any form. See *The Brethren's Tracts and Pamphlets, Setting Forth the Claims of Primitive Christianity* 1 (Elgin, Ill.: Brethren Publishing House, 1900).

[25] *Minutes of the Annual Meeting of the Church of the Brethren* (July 6-8, 1911), 4-5.

[26] D. W. Kurtz, et al., *Studies in Doctrine and Devotion* (Elgin, Ill.: Brethren Publishing House, 1919), 193-4.

[27] Kurtz, et al., *Studies*, 174-87; a discussion of clothing fills pages 180-7.

[28] Bittinger, "The Simple Life," 114. The important mid-century volume, William M. Beahm, *Studies in Christian Belief* (Elgin, Ill.: The Brethren Press, 1958), did not include a discussion of the simple life. It spoke only in terms of the personal spiritual life.

[29] Carl F. Bowman, "Beyond Plainness: Cultural Transformation in the Church of the Brethren from 1850 to the Present," (Ph.D. diss.: University of Virginia, 1989), 640.

[30] From a synopsis of the survey findings, Carl F. Bowman, "Brethren Today," ed. Durnbaugh, *Church of the Brethren*, 220. The full report of the study appeared as Carl F. Bowman, *A Profile of the Church of the Brethren* (Elgin, Ill.: Brethren Press, 1987).

[31] In 1958 Mennonite graduate student J. Lawrence Burkholder challenged Mennonites to assume some degree of "social responsibility." He questioned whether Mennonites actually can live a separate life with any ethical seriousness. Burkholder has written that "reality became for me ambiguous and could be described only by the use of paradox. Having been brought up with a two kingdom theology, polarity itself was no problem." But he discovered as well "that reality is itself ambiguous and that separation from the world is illusory in the ultimate sense." Not surprisingly, Burkholder's dissertation was rejected by the Mennonite institutional establishment of the late 1950s. It has been published more recently as J. Lawrence Burkholder, *The Problem of Social Responsibility from the Perspective of the Mennonite Church* (Elkhart, Ind.: Institute of Mennonite Studies, 1989), iv. In further reinterpretation of two kingdom theology since Burkholder, Mennonites no longer easily equate the kingdom of God and church. Instead many hold that the church is only one part of the kingdom which in turn encompasses much more than the visible Christian body.

2
Nonconformity: Archaic Ideal or Timeless Essential?

by Dale R. Stoffer

In the concluding remarks of his presentation at the "Brethren in Transition" Conference at Bridgewater College in 1991, Carl Bowman observed, "if yesterday's battle was to overcome sectarianism and carry Christianity into the world, perhaps today's is to rediscover the lines separating Christ from culture and to excavate the non-mainline elements of the Brethren vision."[1]

What Bowman proposed as a contemporary challenge for the Brethren holds likewise for many who share the Anabaptist heritage. What are the lines of demarcation between the people of God and the world? How should the Anabaptist commitment to nonconformity be expressed today? Or is nonconformity simply a part of our heritage that should be quietly and unceremoniously laid to rest?

In this essay I explore first, the roots of nonconformity and its importance for contemporary expressions of Anabaptism; second, reasons for the lessened commitment to nonconformity and difficulties in its continuing application; and third, observations and proposals regarding a contemporary expression of nonconformity.

Roots and Importance of Anabaptist Nonconformity

When dealing with matters of Christian life and practice, I find it a good discipline to remind myself of their theological underpinnings. All too often purely pragmatic cultural reasons dominate our adoption or rejection of particular church practices, especially here in America.

The Anabaptist view of nonconformity had several important roots. First and foremost, nonconformity grew from a Christological and, derivatively, a biblical rootage. Because of their wholehearted devotion and discipleship to Christ, Anabaptists were willing to follow the teaching and example of Christ and His apostles explicitly. This biblicism led them to take most seriously Christ's call for an exclusive attachment to Him and his Father (Mt. 7:24; 8:18-22; 10:34-39) and Paul's admonition not to be conformed to the pattern of this world (Rom. 12:2). Because we follow in the footsteps of Christ, we will be different from the world.

We need likewise to be reminded of the point that J. C. Wenger makes in his classic statement on nonconformity, *Separated unto God*. In this work, published in 1951, he calls the plain churches back to an historic and biblical understanding of nonconformity. But he chooses the above title to stress that separation unto God is foundational to nonconformity.[2] The concept of separation unto God is really the positive side of nonconformity from the world.[3] The two must be kept together to avoid distorting the concept of nonconformity. For, by neglecting separation unto God, believers run the risk of replacing this spiritual foundation with those things that are properly expressions of nonconformity: particular styles of dress, the peace witness, and various ethical commitments. By neglecting separation from the world, we can develop a spiritualized approach to nonconformity that allows us to feel at home in the world as long as our personal relationship with God is "sound." Wenger further connects this twin truth with a theme basic to the Anabaptist view of the church: we are the people of God. As he states, "The conception of the people of God as being separate from the world and belonging exclusively to the Almighty is found throughout the Bible."[4] This understanding of the church as God's holy people separated unto God and from the world was a second root of the Anabaptist call to nonconformity.

A third root derives from this Anabaptist view of the church and God's exclusive claim upon his people. The Anabaptist world view was dominated by the concept of the two kingdoms: the kingdom of Christ and the kingdom of this world. In dualistic fashion, they held that one could be a citizen of only one of these kingdoms, either the kingdom of light, life, faith, hope, love, and peace or the kingdom of darkness, death, disillusionment, despair, anger, and war. The true disciple of Christ will choose to be conformed to Christ and his ways, not the world and its ways.

Finally, nonconformity is rooted in the Anabaptist view of salvation. Because of their stress on regeneration and the radical transformation that occurs through the power of the Spirit, the Anabaptists were quite optimistic about the ability to live the Christ-like life. Wenger notes the link between the new birth and nonconformity when he states: "Nonconformity to the world is the natural outcome of having been born again and of being alert to the spiritual issues which confront Christians living in a given culture."[5]

I hope the answer to the question of whether contemporary Anabaptism can quietly discard nonconformity as a quaint relic of the past is obvious. Only by radical surgery on the Anabaptist doctrines of Christ, the church, and salvation can nonconformity be excised. However, the result hardly deserves the name Anabaptist.

Reasons for a Lessened Commitment to Nonconformity and Difficulties in its Continuing Application

Just for fun I did a search of the American Theological Library Association's Religion Database to see how many articles were written on nonconformity in religious periodicals since the 1950s. Nonconformity was such a popular topic that the database did not even bother using it as a subject heading! I had to look up the word "conformity" to find relevant articles, but only four or five of the forty-six listed titles dealt with nonconformity. By comparison there were 890 titles listed under modernity and 264 under acculturation. You may interpret what this means, but it does at least indicate that nonconformity is not a popular topic. What are the reasons for a lessened interest in and commitment to nonconformity among the Anabaptists? Here I will be treading some of the same ground that Steve Nolt ably covers. I will do so only in summary fashion, but this discussion is necessary in order to make any meaningful observations and proposals.

Clearly, the reasons for the undermining of nonconformity among many sharing the Anabaptist heritage are varied. Sociological, political, economic, and theological developments have played a part. The initial impetus for moving away from historic Anabaptist nonconformity resulted from the influence of the progressive spirit that swept America in the latter part of the nineteenth century. Interestingly, the first wave of progressivism moved Mennonites and Brethren in conservative directions: the revival movement, home and foreign missions, and Sunday Schools. The next wave, however, during the early twentieth century moved Mennonites and Brethren in the direction of classical liberalism and the social gospel. In both cases the reason for moving into contemporary culture was based on a sense of mission. Those taking a more conservative tack felt that in order to be effective in advancing the gospel, it was necessary to keep pace with the times and utilize any means developed by modern culture that would aid this cause. Those taking a more liberal tack felt that in order to address the pressing social issues of the day, the church had to move fully into the contemporary culture by embracing the modern worldview.[6] Note that in both cases, advancement into the modern world was seen as a means to an end. We may rightly ask, however, whether present-day Anabaptist heirs to these two perspectives have become so at home in the contemporary setting that the original mission, whether conservative or liberal, has become blurred.

Once Mennonites and Brethren came under the influence of revivalism, fundamentalism, liberalism, and evangelicalism, these movements contributed to the erosion not only of the external vestiges of nonconformity but its theological foundations as well. Revivalism, fundamentalism, and classical liberalism, each in its own way, elevated the individual while depreciating the importance of accountability to the community of faith. Both revivalism and fundamentalism also viewed salvation as a once-and-for-all past event that occurred at the time of confession of faith. This view was at odds with the traditional Anabaptist view of salvation as both a past event and a lifelong process but also severed any vital connection between conversion and the Christian life, between justification and sanctification. To suggest that a life of nonconformed discipleship to Christ was required of every Christian was considered just another form of works-righteousness. This, I might add, is the background to the Lordship salvation debate occurring within fundamentalist circles today.

Steve Nolt observes how traditional nonconformity has been reworked during this century to make it more palatable to Anabaptists who have become more at home in the world. Mennonites have developed institutions that parallel those found in society while Brethren (here Nolt relies on the work of Carl Bowman)[7] have spiritualized and individualized nonconformity by recasting it as the simple life and, later, as personal spirituality.

Another difficulty in maintaining a traditional approach to Anabaptist nonconformity has been political. It is one thing to adhere to the doctrine of the two kingdoms in a monarchy or a setting in which one has no political voice. It is more difficult to hold this doctrine consistently in a democracy in which one is, by definition, part of the political process. For example, by the mid-1800s some Mennonites and Brethren had already become part of the political process by exercising their right to vote, and even some Old Order Amish today will vote in elections that have issues of local importance. Recently, Mennonites and Brethren of both a liberal and conservative theological persuasion have shown how far they are from a two kingdom perspective by using political lobbying techniques to try to sway political policy on a variety of issues. In so doing they seem to be working from the assumption that the answers to social and cultural ills are to be found through political means.[8] It is true that Brethren and Mennonites in the past would appeal to the state on issues that had special significance for maintaining their way of life, especially regarding the doctrine of nonresistance. But, they appealed as those who understood that they were outside the political arena; theirs was a prophetic voice calling the state to live according to the mandate God had given it. They never confused the mandate of the church with that of the state by calling the state to live according to church principles or by using the techniques of the state to further the cause of the church.

A serious difficulty that has arisen for progressive Anabaptists during the past fifty years has been the problem of transmission of the Anabaptist life, especially nonconformity. The Anabaptist core values used to be transmitted through the church and family-oriented culture; this was especially true prior to the mid-1800s when the German subculture dominated among Brethren and Mennonites. As progressive Anabaptists moved into the mainstream of modern America in the late 1800s and throughout this century, they became vulnerable to cultural forces that directed society away from the church as the social center of the community, toward an increasingly secular world. Additionally, with the trend toward the nuclear family, these Mennonites and Brethren could no longer rely on the traditional means of inculcating Anabaptist values, the church and home. What had formerly been learned by experience in the community of faith now had to be learned cognitively before it could be put into practice.

This new process poses several challenges for progressive Anabaptists. First, we are not used to learning this way. Have you ever tried to explain what a Mennonite or Brethren is to someone who knows nothing of these movements? It is extremely difficult to describe a style of life; you have to experience it to understand it. Given the fact that most progressive Anabaptist churches, whether conservative or mainline, have been influenced by social and religious movements that have weakened their Anabaptist lifestyle, it is questionable whether people can learn what it truly means to be Anabaptist in many of these churches. Second, because many churches failed to realize that their youth were not learning what it meant to be Anabaptist, one or two generations of progressive Anabaptists have arisen who have only a vague notion of what the Anabaptist faith and lifestyle is all about. All this means that those who are progressive Anabaptists must be far more analytical and intentional about understanding and living their faith if they are to pass it on to the next generation. They can no longer assume they know what it means to be Anabaptist because much of what they have learned by experience has been an Anabaptism diluted with elements from revivalism, fundamentalism, liberalism, and evangelicalism.

I am not so naive as to believe this can be corrected by simply turning the clock back to the sixteenth century for the Mennonite faith or the eighteenth century for the Brethren. Anabaptists must come to terms with their modern setting. This is true even of the Old Order Amish. But the first task in rediscovering the Anabaptist faith, including nonconformity, is to understand the original heritage. Only then should we take the next step of asking how the Anabaptist heritage can be lived out in the contemporary world. This likewise gives a standard to determine where contemporary Mennonites and Brethren have strayed from Anabaptist principles and mixed them with other religious or cultural concepts.

Observations and Proposals regarding a Contemporary Expression of Nonconformity

You may expect me to be quite negative about the possibilities of developing a contemporary expression of nonconformity. In one area I am. Due to the influence of individualism and pluralism, I doubt that progressive Anabaptists will ever again express nonconformity in such visible, external ways as dress, personal appearance, and styles of homes, vehicles, meetinghouses, etc. But, as I stated at the outset, I believe that nonconformity is essential to an Anabaptist and biblical faith, and I believe there are ways that nonconformity can continue to be expressed, even by progressive Anabaptists.

An intriguing observation was made at the Amish Society Conference held recently at Elizabethtown College. In the opening address for the conference, Marc Olshan suggested that the Amish can teach us "English" the importance of developing a "personal Ordnung" or order of life. This personal Ordnung would enable us to set limits in our lives that would free us from cultural forces that entice us to want and do more. In his response to this presentation, Stephen Ainlay observed that "personal Ordnung" is an oxymoron; Ordnung is a community commitment and loses all sense of meaning if it is individualized.

This exchange has important implications for a contemporary application of nonconformity. It is presently unrealistic to expect that progressive Anabaptists can arrive at consensus on an external expression of nonconformity. Yet, if nonconformity and Anabaptism, as well, are to continue, modern Anabaptists must develop a new consensus about and commitment to the core values of the Anabaptist faith and life. One of the important truths of the Anabaptist and classical Pietist traditions is that the inner must always precede the outer; that is, inner, spiritual commitments are necessarily prior to the outward expressions of faith. The inner life gives meaning and vitality to the outward. (I believe the weakening of the Anabaptist vision in this century has been due to a diminishing commitment to the core principles upon which Anabaptist life and thought were built.) But Anabaptism goes on to say that these inner commitments cannot merely be individual. God's desire is to form a people who will visibly and corporately represent Him in the world. This means that there must be a corporate dimension to these core truths that develops as both individuals and the church freely own them. In this way these truths or principles are able to shape and regulate all actions and beliefs.[9] Only at this point, with the development of a consensus about the core principles of Anabaptism, can discussion begin about the external expression of nonconformity.

But, the important question remains: from what source do these principles derive? Without consensus on the source, any attempt to build agreement on the basic principles of Anabaptism, including nonconformity, will fail. The source should be the same one the early Anabaptists and Brethren utilized: their commitment to Christ led them to obey the teaching and example of Christ and the apostles, that is, Scripture, especially the New Testament.

As I stressed at the beginning of this essay, the foremost foundation for nonconformity is Christological. It is Christ through his Word who reveals God's purpose for us and what our stance toward the world should be. I may be biased, but I believe Scripture does in fact stress the very points that serve as the foundation for Anabaptist nonconformity. God's ultimate purpose is to form a people for His own glory. He calls us to an exclusive commitment to Him and his Son, Jesus Christ. Christ, as the head of the church, sets the agenda for the church. He very clearly establishes that the way of God's people is radically different from the way of the world. See, for example, the Sermon on the Mount in Matthew 5-7 and John 15:18-19; 17:14-16. Through the experience of regeneration and the inner working of the Holy Spirit, God provides the spiritual resources necessary for living transformed lives, ever growing in Christlikeness. God's sovereign purpose, Christ's example and exclusive claim on our lives, and God's spiritual provisions all point to the fact that believers, as Christ's disciples, are to be distinct from and nonconformed to the world and its values.

I am firmly convinced that progressive Anabaptists must take seriously the doctrine of the two kingdoms once again. Though its radical dualism poses a problem in a democracy, the issue even for those in America is, who sets the agenda for our lives—Christ or culture? Unless Anabaptists work from the conviction that separation to God calls them to be separated from the world, there is little need to continue to talk about nonconformity. Timothy George has rightly observed one of the essential components of the original Anabaptist vision. He states:

> The Anabaptist vision is a corrective to the ethics of the mainline reformers. It reminds us that to sanctify the secular must never mean simply to sprinkle holy water on the status quo but always to confront the culture with the radical demands of Jesus Christ.[10] Let not our desire to be part of the modern world cause us to forget our identity and mission.

I do not believe it is necessary or profitable to detail how nonconformity should specifically express itself among Anabaptists who have progressed into modern culture. The specifics will follow if members take seriously Christ's radical claims on them, that He sets the agenda for the church, and, therefore, the doctrine of the two kingdoms.

There is, however, an additional point that needs to be made about nonconformity. I suggested it earlier when I detailed the reasons for a lessened commitment to nonconformity. Nonconformity is directly tied to the understanding of the mission of the church. As long as nonconformity was linked to the traditional Anabaptist view of the church and the doctrine of two kingdoms, it remained an unquestioned principle. But, when the mission of the church began to be seen almost exclusively as either evangelism or social witness, commitment to nonconformity weakened. It is also true, though, that nonconformity can be so emphasized that the call to certain forms of mission can fail to be heard.

Within the Anabaptist and Brethren traditions, the mission of the church has been viewed in three ways. The first way is what I call "living witness." Here mission is viewed in an existential sense; as the individual and especially the church live out the radical message of Christ, they present a counter-cultural witness to the world. The emphasis is much more on being than doing. The Old Order groups would model this form of mission.

The second form of mission is evangelism. Mission is understood in an activist sense and somewhat individually. The church is sent to a lost and dying world to share the gospel of salvation by grace through faith in Jesus Christ.

The third form of mission is social service. Mission again is perceived in an active sense, but the emphasis is on responding not only to individual cases of need but also to larger social needs. Structural evils in society that perpetuate various social ills are also confronted.

Each of these forms of mission has biblical support and each has been present in the Mennonite and Brethren heritages. The Mennonite and Brethren heritages have been strongest when they maintained a commitment to all three. When these movements have gravitated toward only one form, problems have arisen. When living witness became dominant, they tended to ignore the surrounding culture and to be content with keeping quietly to themselves. When some progressive Anabaptists emphasized evangelism in the late 1800s, concern for nonconformity diminished as they sought to utilize modern techniques of outreach, and they developed a wary attitude toward social service because of its association with liberalism. When in this century social service became the dominant form of mission among other progressive Anabaptists, nonconformity quietly disappeared along with evangelism in the wake of concern for pluralism and inclusiveness.

Commitment to all three forms of mission is essential if nonconformity is to play a continuing role in contemporary Anabaptism and if progressive Anabaptists are to be agents of redemption spiritually, emotionally, physically, and socially. Without commitment to living witness and its accompanying doctrine of two kingdoms, nonconformity passes into oblivion. But nonconformity must not be so emphasized that modern Anabaptists forget the biblical mandate for sharing the good news of redemption and compassion to a lost and hurting world. Admittedly, there is a tension among these three forms of mission. That is why we generally gravitate toward one of the three. However, because all three are firmly rooted both in Scripture and the Anabaptist heritage, we must not follow a path of least resistance that sidetracks us from any of them.

The challenge that faces the church today is the same one that has challenged it in every era: how to maintain uncompromising fidelity to Christ and His Word and, likewise, how to communicate its faith effectively to the contemporary culture. Mennonite historian Grant Stoltzfus has observed that most religious groups have undergone profound changes in the American experience. He states:

> The changes have been on the whole in the direction of blending with the American culture with its strong pressure toward conformity. It would appear that only those religious groups (or elements within the groups) are able to survive and fulfill their mission who do two things: (1) They retain and pass on their faith in its essentials; (2) they are able to make wise and safe adaptations to a changing world in order to live effectively in it and to communicate effectively with it.[11]

What is the continuing prospect for nonconformity? Much depends upon the willingness of progressive Anabaptists to respond anew to the exclusive claims of Christ and rediscover and reapply the Anabaptist view of the church and its doctrine of two kingdoms. This obviously means that modern Anabaptists must acknowledge the radical difference between the church and the world. In the process they may have to relearn some of the lost vocabulary that is part of their heritage: obedience, self-denial, discipline, trials, and even suffering. Are they ready to go this far? I frankly don't know. It may be that they have become so at home in American culture that they cannot divorce themselves from it.

There are some positive signs, however. There is among Anabaptists a growing openness to and appreciation of forms of mission other than the one in which they were raised. Those who stress evangelism have come to see the importance of social witness and vice versa. Both of these groups are even showing greater fascination with the living witness model of Old Order groups. Second, the secularizing forces in American society continue to move culture away from traditional Anabaptist values. As American culture becomes more violent, more willing to use coercion and force, as families continue to fracture and individuals demand their rights over the good of society, culture itself may force the church to define itself in counter-cultural ways. The Anabaptist faith can have a powerful witness in a fractured, alienated, disillusioned culture. Rather than jettisoning nonconformity as a relic of the Anabaptist past, I would challenge progressive Anabaptists of both conservative and mainline persuasions to reconsider its central importance to Anabaptist faith. Let us be self-critical enough to realize how both conservative and mainline Christianity have eroded key emphases of our faith. And let us wrestle anew with the biblical call to develop a counter-cultural, nonconformed life and faith that provides a living witness to the gospel of Jesus Christ but also enters redemptively into the lostness and brokenness of our culture.

[1] Carl F. Bowman, "The Therapeutic Transformation of Brethren Tradition," ed. Emmert F. Bittinger, *Brethren in Transition: 20th Century Directions and Dilemmas,* (Camden, Maine: Penobscot Press, 1992), 53.

[2] John C. Wenger, *Separated Unto God* (Scottdale, Pa.: Herald Press, 1951), vii.

[3] J. Denny Weaver, "Is the Anabaptist Vision Still Relevant?" *Pennsylvania Mennonite Heritage* 14 (January 1991): 7.

[4] Wenger, *Separated Unto God,* vii.

[5] Ibid., ix.

[6] For examples of these two perspectives in the Brethren movement, see Dale R. Stoffer, *Background and Development of Brethren Doctrines, 1650-1987* (Philadelphia, Pa.: Brethren Encyclopedia, Inc., 1989), 144, 151-2.

[7] For Carl F. Bowman's discussion of these points, see his "Beyond Plainness: Cultural Transformation in the Church of the Brethren From 1850 to the Present" (Ph.D. diss.: University of Virginia, 1989) and idem, *Brethren Society: The Cultural Transformation of a "Peculiar People"*, (Baltimore: Johns Hopkins University Press, 1995).

[8] A recent book on hermeneutics has mistakenly assumed that the position on church-state relations taken by many progressive Anabaptists today is the same as the historic position. The work states: "Anabaptists frequently took these commands [the ethical demands of Jesus in the Sermon on the Mount] as seriously applying to public life and to all people on earth, so they renounced all violence and became pacifists. But Jesus nowhere teaches that his Kingdom principles should form the basis for civil law." Ironically, it goes on to say: "We will not attain wholeness in this life, but we can arrive at a measure of maturity. Jesus' standards should be our constant goal. His ethic is for **all** believers, not just a select few. But inasmuch as his ethic is also primarily for **believers**, we dare not impose it on those outside the faith. We cannot expect unbelievers to follow or appreciate God's will. We must not try to coerce an unregenerate world to conform to his standards." This latter statement summarizes very well what is actually the historic Anabaptist position, one still maintained among Old Order groups. See William W. Klein, Craig L. Blomberg, and Robert L. Hubbard, Jr., *Introduction to Biblical Interpretation* (Dallas: Word Publishing, 1993), 335.

[9] For a similar point, see Weaver, "Vision," 6.

[10] Timothy George, *Theology of the Reformers* (Nashville: Broadman Press, 1988), 322.

[11] Grant M. Stoltzfus, *Mennonites of the Ohio and Eastern Conference* (Scottdale, Pa.: Herald Press, 1969), 281.

Conversation ৪৫ VIII ৫৫

Membership

Donald F. Durnbaugh reminds us that Brethren and Mennonite membership expectations historically focused on conversion, commitment, discipleship, and discipline. As Mennonitism matured, it developed formal methods, including catechisms, for impressing these expectations upon baptismal candidates. Brethren, on the other hand, relied more upon informal processes for instruction— families, worship, personal relationships, and "general absorption" of the culture. Pietism, suggests Durnbaugh, compliments the Anabaptist notion of membership by adding the "required individual response" to the communal component of membership. He points out that heart-felt faith, often considered to typify Brethren, was also central for Mennonites and that the theology of humility, usually associated with Mennonites, also applies to the Brethren.

John David Bowman doubts that modern Anabaptists can reclaim quickly their traditional assumptions for membership. Seeing little challenge to the tradition from larger Protestantism—which shows increasing interest in many Anabaptist practices (including anointing, communal discernment, feetwashing, and nonviolence)—Bowman concedes that this lack of challenge only deepens the dilemma of Anabaptist definition. A more serious threat than other faith communities is modern individualism. Group affiliations have lost their centrality as sources of personal identity as a free market attitude towards membership has transformed evangelism into marketing and commitment into consumer preference. Under these conditions, reinstatement of church discipline and a return to adult (post-adolescent) baptism are unlikely.

1

Membership and Indoctrination in Anabaptist Churches

by Donald F. Durnbaugh

This presentation, in venerable homiletic fashion, has three parts. The first section addresses membership and indoctrination in Anabaptism, the second membership and indoctrination among Brethren, and the third, the relation of Anabaptist and Pietist thought on these two issues. By necessity, it will be more suggestive than complete, intended to continue the discussion rather than conclude it.

Membership and Indoctrination in Anabaptism

Membership. Reference to major sources of information about Anabaptism reveals that the term "membership," as such, barely appears. It is not listed in the original four volumes of *The Mennonite Encyclopedia* although dealt with in a general way under the topic "Admission"; this was written, as were so many other articles in that valuable reference work, by its editor, Harold S. Bender (1897-1962). The extremely comprehensive *Mennonite Bibliography* (1977), with over 28,000 entries of books and articles, has not one listing under "membership" nor do the cumulative indexes of *The Mennonite Quarterly Review*. Likewise, search in the indexes of the published volumes of the series *Mennonite Experience in America* (1985 ff.) also resulted in blanks. Such recent valuable monographs as John L. Ruth's *Maintaining the Right Fellowship* (1984) and Beulah Stauffer Hostetler's *American Mennonites and Protestant Movements* (1987), both focusing on the Franconia Mennonite Conference as "the oldest Mennonite community in North America," are equally devoid of mention.[1]

A helpful clue for the direction both of research and understanding comes from the supplementary fifth volume of *The Mennonite Encyclopedia* (1990). Here the seeker is led from "membership" by cross reference to "church membership" although the actual article consists not of probing theological analysis but rather mainly of descriptions explaining how new members are received into Mennonite fellowships, the emergence of categories such as "associate member," and reports on demographic and sociological studies of those belonging to Mennonite congregations. Utilizing this clue, and returning to the *Mennonite*

Bibliography, one finds over forty listings under "church membership." But here, too, the result is less than helpful. Most are small articles in Dutch Mennonite periodicals, discussing problems such as the method of accepting members coming from Dutch Protestant bodies.[2]

One concludes, first, that formal discussion of membership has low priority among Anabaptists and their direct descendants, the Mennonites. Second, to gain deeper understanding, one needs to look at Anabaptist understandings of church and discipleship. This should not surprise us because those in the Anabaptist tradition may be defined as believers who reject the formalistic and legal concepts of church membership by virtue of infant baptism, creedal adherence, or territorial residence, and who, by contrast, accept Jesus Christ as Lord and master, whom they as disciples seek to follow. Discussion of membership, therefore, almost immediately leads to consideration of those "naming the name" and "walking the walk" as opposed to creedal allegiance or ecclesiastical preference.[3]

The classical source here is the Brotherly Union or Schleitheim Confession of 1527, widely (if not uniformly) accepted as a constituent charter of Anabaptism. It emerged as a guideline for believers from the congeries of early dissenters, striking a midcourse between the rejected territorial churches on the right and the erratic and irregular radicals on the left. The first two of the seven articles, it will be recalled, spoke to church membership in dealing with baptism/initiation and banning/discipline:

> Baptism shall be given to all those who have been taught repentance and the amendment of life and [who] believe truly that their sins are taken away through Christ, and to all those who desire to walk in the resurrection of Jesus Christ and be buried with Him in death, so that they might rise with Him.

> 2) The ban shall be employed with all those who give themselves over to the Lord, to walk after [Him] in His commandments; those who have been baptized into the one body of Christ, and let themselves be called brothers or sisters, and still somehow slip and fall into error and sin, being inadvertently overtaken. [Then follows a sentence on the procedure of Matthew 18: 15ff.] But this shall be done according to the ordering of the Spirit of God before the breaking of bread, so that we may all in one spirit and in one love break and eat from one bread and drink from one cup.[4]

Church order, beginning with baptism of the sister and brother and continuing with corrective discipline, is based on conversion. The Anabaptists were those "bible believers" who undertook to follow Jesus Christ in deed and in truth, which, as they understood it, required substantial amendment not only of belief but also especially of life. It is this ecclesial grounding that pushes discussion of Anabaptism rapidly into the ethical arena.

The organization of the useful anthology, *Anabaptism in Outline* (1981), is instructive. This compendium presents from the sources an overview of Anabaptist affirmations on basic Christian tenets. It begins with a chapter on "Jesus Christ [as] God's Revelation," then proceeds through "The Work of God in Man," "The Holy Spirit," "Cross, Suffering, and Discipleship," "The Church,"

"Church Order," "The Bible," and on through other topics such as "Church Discipline" to conclude, fittingly, with "Eschatology." A typical confession of faith orientation is that of Menno Simons, writing ca. 1537:

> By this counsel we are all taught that we must hear Christ, believe in Christ, follow his footsteps, repent, be born from above; become as little children, not in understanding, but in malice; be of the same mind as Christ, walk as he did, deny ourselves, take up his cross and follow him; and that if we love father, mother, children, or life more than him, we are not worthy of him, nor are we his disciples.[5]

It is commonly acknowledged that Harold S. Bender presented a classic description of early Anabaptism in his address on "The Anabaptist Vision," published in 1944. Among many quotations used, he noted with approval the assessment of Max Goebel (1811-1857), the magisterial German scholar of Pietism:

> The essential and distinguishing characteristic of this [Anabaptist] church is its great emphasis upon the actual personal conversion and regeneration of every Christian through the Holy Spirit. They aimed with special emphasis at carrying out and realizing the Christian doctrine and faith in the heart and life of every Christian in the whole Christian church.[6]

Interestingly, in Bender's delineation of the genius of Anabaptism—a discussion that follows the descriptions by Goebel and other observers—he bypasses the foundational theme of conversion to focus on the Christian praxis in his three point outline: 1) the essence of true Christianity as discipleship; 2) the church as a brotherhood; and 3) an ethic of love and nonresistance. In a valuable but somewhat overlooked article (1973), C. J. Dyck asserted that church-based benchmarks, such as those listed by Bender, though accurate in their own way, are actually secondary rather than primary. He maintained that "the experience of regeneration, the nature of the new life in Christ, was basic to all other considerations."[7]

A dozen years after his landmark article, Bender himself came to a similar conclusion. In an article on "The Anabaptist Theology of Discipleship" he wrote:

> For a time I thought, with others who perhaps still think so, that the central controlling idea of Anabaptism was the concept of the Church. Yet with all its power and historic significance it seems to me not to be the ultimate idea. In a sense, is not the concept of the Church also a formal concept? The character of the Church is determined by something beyond the Church itself, for it ultimately derives from the concept of the nature of the Christian experience and the Christian life. The concept of the Church is actually a derivative idea.[8]

Membership, therefore, in the Anabaptist line focuses on the conversion and life commitment of convinced believers. It is now necessary to look at the corollary of membership, that is indoctrination.

Indoctrination. If "membership" proved to be a questionable term for Anabaptists, "indoctrination" is even less appropriate, and, unsurprisingly, fails to appear as such in Anabaptist/Mennonite reference works. A movement that arose in reaction to institutions and establishments will not easily accept a term that implies dogma, creedalism, and formalism. However, if we take it in the broader sense of teaching (Matt. 28), training, and preparing for membership, then it can, within limits, be used.

By the nature of the case, the early Anabaptists were scarcely in a position to adopt regularized and specific methods of teaching. Everything we can glean from the early internal and external accounts demonstrates intense but informal seasons of teaching and instruction, often necessarily held in secret. The pattern of instruction is reminiscent of the "barbes" or teaching elders of the Waldensians of the twelfth century and later (with whom the Anabaptists have often been linked); these traveled about, often in the guise of merchants, to inform and succor their bands of followers. As the Dutch Reformed scholar Leonard Verduin (fl. 1956) reminded us, early Anabaptist leaders were often called *Winckler*, or people "who gather in some corner or secluded place, for purposes of religious exercises."[9]

Accounts of Anabaptist meetings, wrung by torture from imprisoned converts, describe visits by leaders who gathered small groups for instruction. Considerable effort was taken to provide those wishing baptism with basic biblical understandings, as well as orientation to specific congregational practices and expectations. This pattern is continued to this day in the customary practice of the Old Order Amish, when young men and women are given instruction prior to their baptisms. The somewhat similar Hutterian Brethren, to the contrary, have institutionalized religious instruction in their German schools and Sunday schools, as well as in six-to-eight week prebaptismal sessions.[10]

After the fiercest fury of oppression passed in the sixteenth century, it was common for beliefs to be taught within the surviving Anabaptist/Mennonite families and passed down from generation to generation. It was customary for copies of sermons and edifying letters to circulate, often the only means to perpetuate the faith when leaders had been removed by force. Again, elders of the Amish and Hutterian Brethren followed this pattern with church orders and sermons handed on from those senior in the ministry to those junior. The role of hymns as a means of instruction is also noteworthy among Anabaptist groups, as in the lengthy martyr hymns in the *Ausbund*.[11]

Anabaptists were not opposed in principle to a more formalized method of instruction, if circumstances permitted. They often utilized summaries of belief, known as confessions of faith. It has long been observed that the classic Hutterian document, the *Rechenschaft* or *Confession of Faith* (1565) by Peter Riedemann (1506-1556), took its initial structure from the Apostles Creed. The typical Anabaptist approach was to encourage the creation of many confessions of faith but to oppose the adoption of creeds, eternally binding upon all. It was in The Netherlands that Anabaptists, there first called "Menists" and then "Mennonites" after their teacher Menno Simons, enjoyed sufficient toleration and prosperity to issue a number of stated confessions of faith; the oldest is considered to be that of the Dutch Waterlanders of 1577. The confession, evidently written by P. J. Twisck (1565-1636) in 1617 and published in 1660, has been called the oldest fully developed confession of faith, as many of the earlier efforts (including that of Schleitheim) focused on points of contention and did not attempt to be complete doctrinal statements.[12]

In the seventeenth century a considerable number of confessions of faith were produced, particularly in the Low Countries. The most famous is the Dordrecht Confession (1632), often reproduced in Europe and North America. Although more strict than some, it has been used more widely than any other. Many of these confessions were intended to provide the basis for uniting divided fellowships by finding areas of common agreement.

Such confessions could be and were used for catechetical purposes, perhaps imitating the practice of the more established churches, such as the classic Small and Large Catechisms of Martin Luther. The authors of the lengthy article on "Confessions of Faith" in *The Mennonite Encyclopedia* explain:

> The Anabaptists never attached the weight to creeds or confessions given to them by the remainder of Christendom; they were Biblicists who produced a large number of confessions, not as instruments to which the laity or ministry subscribed *ex anima*, but as instructional tools for the indoctrination of their young people and as witnesses to their faith for distribution in society or as a means of better understanding between differing groups.

A favorite catechism notable for its pietistic flavor was the often-issued *Christliches Gemüthsgespräch* by Gerrit Roosen (1612-1711), first published in 1732 in North Germany and in 1769 in North America.[13]

In summary, Anabaptist-Mennonite indoctrination began as informal but intensive preparation for baptism and consequent church membership of new converts; it was gradually transformed over the years into a more systematized and formal instruction for young people. As Mennonite bodies came to enjoy greater freedom in Northern Europe and North America, their pedagogical approach became more and more similar to that of other denominations.

We turn now to consider the same themes—membership and indoctrination—among the Brethren.

Membership and Indoctrination among the Brethren

Membership. Brethren largely drew upon Anabaptist/Mennonite church understandings as they organized their young movement in the first decade of the eighteenth century; therefore, much of what has already been stated can stand for their position as well. The difference is that they were more profoundly shaped in their beginnings by Pietism than were the Mennonites, for whom that influence came later. As this dialectic will form the basis for the concluding discussion in this article, the theme can be passed over for the moment.

Insights into the early Brethren understanding of membership can be discerned in the open letter they sent to Pietists in the Palatinate just preceding the first baptisms in late summer, 1708. Noting that they had left "all sects" because of malpractices concerning "infant baptism, communion, and the church system," they announced that they intended to follow the command of Christ to be baptized. When they referred to the teaching of Peter to the multitude (Acts 2) at the time of Pentecost—"Repent, and be baptized every one of you in the name of Jesus Christ"—they understood themselves to be under the same mandate. Of course "obviously disorderly persons" could not be accepted for baptism if they were "without true remorse and repentance."[14]

Following such baptism would come church order ("an exact relationship") and brotherly and sisterly discipline. "When a person does not better himself, after faithful warning, he must be expelled and cannot be treated any more as a brother." The group at Schwarzenau who became the first Brethren were very clear in their commitment to dedicated and disciplined membership. The language of the earliest and best description of these events, that of Alexander Mack, Jr. (1712-1803), reveals this. He wrote:

> Under these circumstances some felt themselves drawn powerfully to seek the footsteps of the primitive Christians, and desired earnestly to receive in faith the ordained testimonies of Jesus Christ according to their true value. Finally, in the year 1708, eight persons consented together, to enter into a covenant of a good conscience with God, to take up all the commandments of Jesus Christ as an easy yoke, and thus to follow the Lord Jesus, their good and faithful shepherd, in joy and sorrow, as his true sheep, even unto a blessed end.[15]

Although there are few extant records of the early years of the Brethren in Europe, everything we know correlates well with this picture of covenanted and committed Christianity. The records preserved in colonial America sound the same note. As in Schwarzenau and Krefeld, so in Germantown and Amwell church discipline was the most noticeable outworking of this kind of membership. It affected even the families of church leaders, as revealed in preserved correspondence and in observations by outsiders. In his admiring portrait of the Brethren, the Universalist Elhanan Winchester (1751-1795) remarked:

> The Tunkers or German Baptists take the Scriptures as their only guide on matters both of faith and of practice. [So] adverse are they to all sin, and to many things that other Christians esteem lawful, that they not only refuse to swear, go to war, etc., but are so afraid of doing anything contrary to the commands of Christ that no temptation would prevail upon them ever to sue any person at law, for either name, character, estate, or any debt, be it ever so just.[16]

Indoctrination. Again, the lack of records for the initial period of Brethren history precludes detailed understandings of the practice of the teaching of the young. Indeed, for a time the early Brethren had imbibed the tenets of Radical Pietism that held normal marriage and childbearing wrong for true Christians, holding out celibacy or companionate marriages as far superior. By their account, they had to work past these misunderstandings to come to their own position, which they then sought to perpetuate among converts.[17]

One of the first publications of the Brethren, that of Alexander Mack, Sr., had an instructional slant. This was Mack's *Rights and Ordinances* (1715) cast in the form of dialogue between father and son, in which information was passed on regarding the new movement. For several reasons this should not, of course, be thought of as a catechism. It did not cover all of the important points of doctrine but rather devoted itself to the controverted parts of the Brethren belief. Further, in using the dialogue form, it followed a well-worn pattern for didactic writing with which the Brethren were undoubtedly familiar.[18]

Alexander Mack, Jr., the most prolific writer among the Brethren in colonial America, did compose material that was directed to the young. Several of his numerous poems were dedicated to youth in the church. In unpublished literary remains held in the Abraham Harley Cassel Collection at Juniata College is a long catechetical manuscript devoted to doctrinal instruction of young people.[19]

Judging from minutes of the Yearly Meetings of the early nineteenth century, no extensive teaching or training was considered necessary prior to baptism. A query of 1837 asked: "When persons desire to be received by baptism into the church, if it be necessary to instruct them before baptism [on] the taking of oaths, going to war, and the like, that according to our view it is forbidden in the gospel?" The answer recommended that such candidates be visited "if possible" before the baptism "and by all means ought to be previously instructed" on such points and on nonconformity to "the fashions of the world in apparel and the like." Their willingness to renounce such things must be evident before baptism took place. The procedure was regularized in a Yearly Meeting minute eleven years later by requiring the examination of the applicant by two or more ministers and a statement before the church council of willingness to adhere to the Brethren discipline.[20]

It was not until quite late that the Brethren came to depend upon instruction in the Sunday school and in special membership classes as preparation for baptism. For much of Brethren history instruction was an informal process through family influence, attendance at church services, and general absorption of the Brethren way by participation and observation.

Interaction of Anabaptism and Pietism

The interrelationship of Anabaptism and Pietism as it bears upon the question of responsible membership and methods of instruction does, in fact, does hold special importance. The issue suggests the ongoing tension between community expectations and loyalties and the inescapable moment of individual choice in conversion and subsequent membership for members of Believers' Churches.

The dichotomy was posed most sharply by Robert Friedmann (1891-1970) in *Mennonite Piety Through the Centuries* (1949); he held that Anabaptism represents community and Pietism individualism, with the two seen as opposing poles of spirituality. It will be recalled that Friedmann saw Pietism as an escape hatch for Anabaptists weary of persecution. To evade conflict, they modified a rigorous ethic of discipleship by accepting a milder, less confrontative form of religious commitment in Pietism, with its withdrawn, inward-looking orientation toward the status of the individual soul.[21]

Insofar as Mennonites moved toward Pietism, for Friedmann they abandoned the narrow path of Christian discipleship for the less rigorous highway of sentimental devotion. They rejected the "bitter Christ" whose demand led to suffering, and sought the "sweet Christ" of Pietist suasion. Necessary fellowship was to be found in the conventicles of the like-minded Pietists, who came together for mutual edification, rather than in the harried congregations of the persecuted Anabaptists who found renewed strength and inspiration for their contention with the world in their conclaves of bible study and mutual admonition.

Many scholars have wrestled with this concept, including those seeking to understand the emergence of the Brethren as a separate religious identity. There is a kind of consensus that Brethren have been at their best when the rigor of Anabaptism has been tempered by the zeal of Pietist devotion. The "order" of Anabaptism is balanced by the "ardor" of Pietism. Yet, it is important to guard against making this dialectic too pointed. We recall that the genesis of Anabaptism was found in the conversion of the Swiss Brethren. Any number of historians have pointed out the similarities and historical connections of the two movements, Anabaptism and Pietism. Carl Bowman's book *Brethren Society* is the latest reminder that the two movements have much in common and that over-polarization masks the way in which the two are complementary rather than antagonistic.[22]

How can the themes of membership and indoctrination be related to this debate? Given the basic Anabaptist definition of the church as a body of gathered believers, the role of the community is self-evident. In the same breath, however, one remembers that the voluntary character of Anabaptism demands the initiative of the adult believer expressing the ardent desire to join the fellowship. Logically, Anabaptists held to the role of free will in the process, over against the predestinarian views of Luther and especially the double predestination of Calvin and later Calvinists. Luther was concerned to protect his teaching of justification as the unmerited gift of God's grace with no synergistic admixture of individual effort, and Calvin the awesome authority and might of God.[23]

If Anabaptism represents the communal pole of membership, then Pietism represents the required individual response and initiative. The two are thus seen as complementary and needed. Vernard Eller commented on the earlier quoted description of Brethren beginnings:

> Notice, also, the expression of the dialectic as it appears in the younger Mack's description of how Brethrenism was founded. 'Felt powerfully drawn,' 'passionately yearned,' and 'opened to them in their hearts' are all Radical Pietist phrases describing inner experience. And yet in each case this phrase is coupled with an Anabaptist emphasis on outward obedience: 'the footsteps of the first Christians,' 'ordained testimonies of Jesus Christ,' 'obedience in faith.'

In this reading, both tendencies are needed and both, rightly understood, are equally valid. Where they reside in "creative tension," there is balance and authenticity.[24]

Some historians have indicated that this blending of Anabaptist community and Pietist warmth was substantially the attraction explaining the marked movement of North American Amish and Mennonites toward the Brethren in the late eighteenth and early nineteenth centuries. It was also during this period that numbers of Mennonites, caught up in revivalism, transferred their allegiance to the United Brethren and to the River Brethren (later Brethren in Christ). This has been studied carefully by Richard MacMaster and Theron Schlabach in their volumes in the *Mennonite Experience in America* series. MacMaster explains that—unlike the stereotyped portrayal of the Mennonites of the era as spiritually dead and tradition-bound—Mennonites were quite comfortable with the themes of rebirth and personal experience. It was rather their informal structure of church polity that permitted easy egress by the Wesleyan revivalists.

Pietism, in MacMaster's reading, was a major component of American Mennonites, as evidenced in the popularity of Christian Burkholder's *Useful and Edifying Address to the Youth on True Repentance and Saving Faith* (1804), the title of which evidences Pietist-like concerns. It is, however, MacMaster's understanding that the Mennonite appropriation of Pietism, particularly in the form of humility, did tend to omit the foundational Anabaptist expectation of and emphasis upon suffering. Theron Schlabach, in continuing the discussion for the nineteenth century, agrees that Mennonites were clearly imbued with Pietist values. He sees the shift more positively than had Robert Friedmann, indicating that Pietism may well have "filled a vacuum left by changes within Anabaptism and Mennonitism." Moreover, he muses, "perhaps Mennonites accurately sensed that their own tradition lacked some important ingredients for a full-orbed, fully-developed Christian faith."[25]

Both MacMaster and Schlabach theorize that Mennonites creatively derived from the Pietist input a theology of humility. A change in emphasis was needed because in the free air of America's religious openness and economic opportunity, they did not in fact live under oppression, as in Europe, so a theology of suffering was scarcely credible. Focusing on humility, with its logical corollaries of nonconformity and avoidance of the world, was an apt way of fencing off the world. Conversion remained central, but the fruits of conversion could be discerned clearly; the question became: were humble traits and attitudes in evidence in the lives of the people? Schlabach believes that this emphasis allowed Mennonites and Amish largely to escape the otherwise dominant pressure to conform to regnant Protestant individualism. This Pietistic orientation had its weaknesses, but it "offered an authentic substitute for the suffering theme that America had removed from Mennonite experience" and, further, "helped Mennonites and Amish keep a vision of discipleship."[26]

With some modification, this interpretative measure can be placed upon the Brethren of the nineteenth century as well. The attitude of humility, if not always the precise word, could be used to summarize the Dunker ethos. One did not, for example, put oneself forward as a candidate for ministry, for that would be proud and a guarantee that one would never be chosen. Homes and furnishings, to say nothing of the meetinghouse, should exhibit restraint and lack of ostentation.

The love feast itself, in particular the ordinance of feetwashing, was interpreted as a lesson in humility. Peter Nead's discussion in *Theological Writings on Various Subjects* (1866), links the humbling posture of the feetwashing with the process of church discipline.

> In like manner, to gain, or have a brother cleansed from his trespasses, we must go in love and with great humility, and apprize our brother of his conduct, expostulating in an humble manner with him, and by so doing, it may be, that your brother will receive the admonition, and give himself into your hands, so that you can wash him from his trespasses. Whereas, it may be, if you had not humbled yourself—that is, bent or stooped before your brother [in feetwashing], he would not have acknowledged his fault.[27]

In a section on "Non-conformity to the World," Nead wrote that "the riches, honors, and pleasures of the world are very tempting, and that the people of God be not overcome, let them be humble, keep down at the feet of Jesus and [then] they are safe." Plainness of apparel and adornment is the more appropriate if one considers "that our bodies were originally taken from the earth and will return to the earth again." For, stated Nead, "This solemn truth should teach us humility."[28] Comparable attitudes can be gleaned from innumerable pronouncements of the Annual Meeting on specific lifestyle issues among the Brethren during the course of the nineteenth century.

Conclusion

We have briefly surveyed Anabaptists, Mennonites, and Brethren in considering the themes of membership and indoctrination, concluding with some comments on the interrelation of Anabaptism and Pietism.

There are several possible learnings we can take from this appraisal. One is that because so many of these problems concerning meaningful membership and effective indoctrination are still to be with us, there is little hope of true solutions. We would do better to get about our business without wasting time on historical reflections. The other, which I share, is that gaining historical perspective on contemporary issues does, in reality, have value. One consideration is that guidance may be found in reviewing the struggles, achievements, and failures of those who have gone on before. Hints at least of helpful and less helpful approaches may be discerned by the thoughtful. The second is that all truly important issues are not time-bound and retain relevance across the centuries as they repeat themselves in somewhat different manifestations. It would be shortsighted to avoid contact with prior experiences that might well provide, if not answers, at least fruitful ways to pose problems that can suggest possible, if partial, solutions. Such at least is the perspective offered here.

[1] Harold S. Bender, ed., *The Mennonite Encyclopedia: A Comprehensive Reference Work on the Anabaptist-Mennonite Movement.* (Scottdale, Pa.: Mennonite Publishing House, 1955-1959); Nelson P. Springer and A. J. Klassen, eds., *Mennonite Bibliography* 2 vols. (Scottdale, Pa.: Herald Press, 1977); Richard K. MacMaster, *Land, Piety, Peoplehood: The Establishment of Mennonite Communities in America, 1683-1790* (Scottdale, Pa: Herald Press, 1985); Theron F. Schlabach, *Peace, Faith, Nation: Mennonites and Amish in Nineteenth-Century America* (Scottdale, Pa.: Herald Press, 1988); James C. Juhnke, *Vision, Doctrine, War: Mennonite Identity and Organization in America, 1890-1930* (Scottdale, Pa.: Herald Press, 1989); John L. Ruth, *Maintaining the Right Fellowship* (Scottdale, Pa.: Herald Press, 1984); and Beulah Stauffer Hostetler, *American Mennonites and Protestant Movements: A Community Paradigm* (Scottdale, Pa.: Herald Press, 1987).

[2] Leland D. Harder, "Church Membership," ed. Bender, *Mennonite Encyclopedia* V; *Mennonite Bibliography*, 1631-1961 (1977), 64ff.

[3] Useful discussions of the meaning of church membership in Anabaptism are in Cornelius J. Dyck, *An Introduction to Mennonite History*, (Scottdale, Pa.: Herald Press, 1993, third ed.), 133-50; and J. Denny Weaver, *Becoming Anabaptist: The Origin and Significance of Sixteenth-Century Anabaptism* (Scottdale, Pa.: Herald Press, 1987), 113-41.

[4] John H. Yoder, ed., *The Legacy of Michael Sattler* (Scottdale, Pa.: Herald Press, 1973), 36-7.

[5] Walter Klaassen and others, eds., *Anabaptism in Outline: Selected Primary Sources* (Scottdale, Pa.: Herald Press, 1981), 99.

[6] Harold S. Bender, "The Anabaptist Vision," ed. Guy F. Hershberger, *The Recovery of the Anabaptist Vision: A Sixtieth Anniversary Tribute to Harold S. Bender* (Scottdale, Pa.: Herald Press, 1957), 37.

[7] Cornelius J. Dyck, "The Life of the Spirit in Anabaptism," *Mennonite Quarterly Review* 47 (1973): 312.

[8] Harold S. Bender, "The Anabaptist Theology of Discipleship," *Mennonite Quarterly Review* 24 (1956): 26, cited in Myron S. Augsburger, "Conversion in Anabaptist Thought," *Mennonite Quarterly Review* 36 (1962): 243.

[9] On the Waldenses, see Giorgio Tourn and others, *You Are My Witnesses: The Waldensians Across 800 Years*, ed. Frank C. Gibson (Turin: Claudiana Editrice, 1989); and Leonard Verduin, *The Reformers and Their Stepchildren* (Exeter: Paternoster Press, 1964), 160.

[10] John A. Hostetler, *Amish Society*, (Baltimore: Johns Hopkins University Press, 1993, fourth ed.), 78-9; and John A. Hostetler, *Hutterite Society* (Baltimore: Johns Hopkins University Press, 1974), 236.

[11] Hostetler, *Amish Society*, 227-33.

[12] Peter Ri[e]deman, *Confession of Faith: Account of Our Religion, Doctrine and Faith* (Rifton, N. Y.: Plough Publishing House, 1970); Leonard Gross, *The Golden Years of the Hutterites* (Scottdale, Pa.: Herald Press, 1980), 196-7; and Christian Neff, J. C. Wenger, and Harold S. Bender, "Confessions of Faith," ed. Bender, *Mennonite Encyclopedia*, 679-86.

[13] Neff, "Confessions of Faith," 679.

[14] Donald F. Durnbaugh, ed., *European Origins of the Brethren* (Elgin, Ill.: Brethren Press, 1958), 115-20; and idem, *Brethren Beginnings: The Origin of the Church of the Brethren in Early Eighteenth-Century Europe* (Philadelphia, Pa.: Brethren Encyclopedia, Inc., 1992), 22.

[15] Henry Kurtz, *The Brethren's Encyclopedia, Containing the United Counsels and Conclusions of the Brethren, at Their Annual Meetings. . .*(Columbiana, Ohio: author, 1867), 22-3.

[16] Donald F. Durnbaugh, ed., *The Brethren in Colonial America* (Elgin, Ill.: Brethren Press, 1967), 326. Winchester was concerned to counter the charge that the doctrine of universalism made for antinomian wickedness by pointing to the evident morality of the Brethren, who believed in universal restoration.

[17] See the discussions in Floyd E. Mallott, *Studies in Brethren History* (Elgin, Ill.: Brethren Publishing House, 1954), 40; and Donald F. Durnbaugh, "The Genius of the Early Brethren," *Brethren Life and Thought* 4 (Winter, 1959): 11-3.

[18] [Henry Kurtz, ed.]. . .*Rights and Ordinances of the House of God. . .* (Columbiana, Ohio: author, 1860), 1-111, bound with *Brethren's Encyclopedia* (1867); for the latest English translation, see Durnbaugh, *European Origins*, 344-405.

[19] Some of Mack's compositions are presented in Samuel B. Heckman, *The Religious Poetry of Alexander Mack, Jr.* (Elgin, Ill.: Brethren Publishing House, 1912).

[20] Kurtz, *Brethren's Encyclopedia* (1867), p. 190; [1837], 38; [1848].

[21] Robert Friedmann, *Mennonite Piety Through the Centuries: Its Genius and Its Literature* (Goshen, Ind.: Mennonite Historical Society, 1949); his argument is summarized on pages 72-7.

[22] Much of the discussion among Brethren scholars on this point is summarized by Vernard Eller, "On Epitomizing the Brethren: A New Approach to an Old Problem," *Brethren Life and Thought* 6 (Autumn, 1961): 47-52. A thorough, historically and theologically informed interpretation is in Dale R. Stoffer, *Background and Development of Brethren Doctrines, 1650-1987* (Philadelphia, Pa.: Brethren Encyclopedia, Inc., 1989), 5-63. The latest discussion is in Carl Bowman, *Brethren Society: The Cultural Transformation of a "Peculiar People"* (Baltimore: Johns Hopkins University Press, 1995). The best study of Brethren historiography, with a good overview of the Anabaptist/Pietist discussion, is Rainer W. Burkart, "Die Kirche der Brüder. . .: Geschichte ihrer Erforschung vom 18. Jahrhundert bis zur Gegenwart" (Master's Thesis: Friedrich-Alexander-Universität Erlangen-Nürnberg, 1986), 36-63.

[23] For discussions of Anabaptism and free will see, among others, Robert Friedmann, *The Theology of Anabaptism* (Scottdale, Pa.: Herald Press, 1973), esp. 58-77; Jan J. Kiwiet, "The Theology of Hans Denck," *Mennonite Quarterly Review* 32 (1958): 3-27, and his *Pilgram Marbeck: Ein Führer in der Täuferbewegung der Reformationszeit* (Kassel: J.G. Oncken Verlag, 1957); and Thor Hall, "Possibilities of Erasmian Influence on Denck and Hubaier in Their Views on the Freedom of the Will," *Mennonite Quarterly Review* 35 (1961): 149-70.

[24] Eller, "On Epitomizing the Brethren," 50.

[25] MacMaster, *Land, Piety, Peoplehood*, especially 159ff., 165ff., 226-8; Schlabach, *Peace, Faith, Nation*, especially pp. 30ff., 87ff. (quotation, 91).

[26] Schlabach, *Peace, Faith, Nation*, 105.

[27] Peter Nead, *Theological Writings on Various Subjects: or a Vindication of Primitive Christianity As Recorded in the Book of God* (Dayton, Oh.: author, 1866), 132-3.

[28] Ibid., 123-4.

2

Membership Expectations

by John David Bowman

How might Anabaptists reclaim their traditions regarding church membership for the future? The assignment is formidable. First, this article is to address four questions in light of the traditions defined by Durnbaugh. These questions are as follows:

1. Can Anabaptists retain traditional expectations for members, including congregational discipline, and still be tolerant, democratic, and ecumenical?

2. Can modern Anabaptists reconcile the individualism of modern society with the communal emphasis of traditional Anabaptism?

3. To what extent do, or should, pre-adolescent membership classes and other commonly used methods of bringing new members into the fellowship retain the Anabaptist heritage?

4. How can the faith community affirm the belonging of pre-adolescents to it while preserving the emphasis on adult believers' baptism and membership?

It seems most reasonable to focus on these one at a time while recognizing there will be some overlap.

I

Can we retain traditional Anabaptist expectations for members, including congregational discipline, and still be tolerant, democratic, and ecumenical?

This, like the other questions, opens many corridors that beg to be explored before a satisfying response can be determined. Perhaps we will do best to focus upon some clarifying and preliminary questions. Here are but a few.

Which Anabaptist tradition shall we claim for our study? Shall we consider as a measuring standard the Anabaptism of the sixteenth century, the eighteenth century, or that of fifty years ago? It would seem sociologically and historically unrealistic to assume a static tradition. Still, the similarities and differences through the ages could, perhaps, inform us of underlying principles beyond the obvious forms. It may be that these underlying principles, if they are present, could be more essential to the study before us than the age-bound traditions themselves.

A related question asks, "What shall be the guidelines by which we define *Anabaptist tradition*? Our answer could lead us down some remarkable paths of discovery. For example, will these guidelines be the various actions of the

Anabaptists? If so, how are we to separate that which was culturally popular from that which was central to the unique Anabaptist perspective? The use of wine and unleavened bread in communion is less a testimony to Anabaptism than to Christianity since it was, and is, an expression of the Roman Catholic, Eastern Orthodoxy, Lutheran, and Reformed traditions.

Perhaps, we should suggest the guidelines of our definition be that which was uniquely Anabaptist. If so, we must challenge the assumption that church discipline, including the ban, was a purely Anabaptist tradition. The ban was in evidence among not only the Anabaptists, but Catholics, Calvinists, and Lutherans. This leads me to wonder why Alexander Mack so rigorously defended the ban. Was his a response to a few within his circle of influence who wanted to discontinue the ban? Was church discipline on the wane in general and was his part of a wider effort to maintain its effects?

As we sort out the guidelines of our definition, are we being sufficiently careful to sort out the difference between those traditions which are culturally dictated from those rooted in theological considerations? Ought we maintain a culturally formed tradition with the same zeal as a theologically informed tradition? Consider, for example, the pre-scientific view of scripture prevalent among the early Anabaptist leaders. Was that an historically determined perspective or a result of carefully informed theological reflection? When attempting to apply this tradition to future projections, can we realistically expect congregations to return to a pre-scientific world view in the name of tradition?

How much of what we consider Anabaptist tradition would be different if those leaders would have emerged in another time? So much has happened since the sixteenth century. Even our words and phrases carry different meanings and rely upon different conceptual assumptions; consider, for example, what can be meant by the word *true*.[1] Menno Simons and Alexander Mack lived in times when the prevailing church traditions were little more than Roman Catholic, Lutheran, Reformed, and a few additional movements. Now, not only are we faced with over two hundred denominations and thousands of non-denominational megachurches but subgroups within denominations, such as ethnic groups. We live in a dramatically more pluralistic society than theirs.

Recently, at an Old Order baptism, a minister looked up from the river to the bank and noticed how all looked alike as they observed the proceedings. "How uniform we are," he said. "It is a sign of our unity as members of one body." All white faces dressed in identical clothing. Is this also an Anabaptist tradition of church membership? If not, what shall be the sign of Anabaptist unity today?

Can we retain traditional Anabaptist expectations for members, including congregational discipline, and still be tolerant, democratic, and ecumenical?

The question causes me to wonder, why is Anabaptism threatened by twentieth century ecumenism? The traditions that set it apart from other church groups are less distinctive today. The peace witness is now embraced by the Presbyterians and the United Church of Christ as well as many sub-groups in a variety of denominations. Adult baptism is championed by a multiplicity of Baptist groups. In 1969, I heard Presbyterian William Barclay declare to a Scottish congregation that infant baptism was indefensible. Our concern for egalitarian servant leadership style is shared by others. Even the Roman Catholics are now suspecting the papal authority ought to rest in collective wisdom of Cardinals rather than any individual Pope. Other groups are awakening to the power of the ordinances of anointing for healing and feetwashing, which have often been thought unique to the Anabaptist tradition. Even the passion for a community hermeneutic is being discovered in non-Anabaptist circles as evidenced in Lyman Coleman's Serendipity groups, Faith at Work events, and movements like *Cursillo*[2] that are gaining power within the life of many denominations.

It is increasingly difficult for Anabaptists to discover their reason for being. As the virtues they have cherished become embraced by increasing numbers of other traditions and as other traditions are assimilated into their church experience, might it be that if they listened harder, they could hear the master saying, "Well done thou good and faithful servants. Enter now into the wider church fellowship God has prepared in part through your efforts." Or is this the time to reassess what they still have to offer to the world and to the Church of our Lord? Perhaps they should regroup into a new sectarian movement.

With all these questions in mind, let me attempt to address the first query more directly. If we utilize the traditions highlighted by Durnbaugh, we can give at least a preliminary response. I glean from his article the following two traditions of Anabaptism related to church membership:

> Church membership is based upon a conversion which requires the substantial amendment of conduct, primarily, and of belief.

> Church discipline is a tool of the church to facilitate the maintenance of Christian conduct which springs from the regenerated heart.

The former tradition assumes adult baptism, which will be addressed later. The latter invites us to reflect upon what tools might be employed today to help maintain lives of conduct springing from regenerated hearts. While one of these tools, the use of the ban, is discussed below under the second query, we can affirm here that due to the psycho-social complexities of our era, the church will need to employ a mixture of tools to help maintain conduct which springs from regenerated hearts. This variety of tools should neither rule out nor insist upon the use of such extreme measures as excommunication. The purpose of the tools needs to be the focus rather than any specific tool. It is not the forms but the Spirit that informs God's people. Having begun reflections upon the relationship of the group to the individual in discipline leads to the second query under consideration.

II

Can we reconcile the individualism of modern society with the communal emphasis of traditional Anabaptism?

Membership cannot be addressed apart from understanding how the Anabaptists thought about the Church. And since Durnbaugh invites the Radical Pietists to join us, their understanding of the Church, also, will be vital to our considerations since they have influenced both Mennonite and Brethren groups.

German Pietism emerged in the last quarter of the seventeenth century as a result of influences from English Puritanism and Dutch Reformed Pietism. Their *collegia pietatis*, or schools of piety, were meetings for the purpose of prayer and Bible study. For the most part, these groups attempted to reform the state churches from within. Some of these Pietists came to believe they must separate themselves from the corruption they saw in the church and in the clergy. This group became known as the Radical Pietists.[3] Citing Christian Burkholder, Durnbaugh clarifies that Pietism has been "a major component of American Mennonites."[4]

Elsewhere, Durnbaugh states, "The best way to understand the early Brethren is to see them as a Radical Pietist group which appropriated an Anabaptist view of the church."[5] The Church of the Brethren and the Mennonite groups of America have been influenced by both Anabaptism and Pietism.

Keeping in mind the caution of Carl Bowman, echoed in Durnbaugh's paper, that we ought not over-polarize the two movements of Pietism and Anabaptism, we will now consider how these two movements viewed the Church.

If I read Dale Stoffer correctly, German Philadelphianism's ideal of the Church prevailed as the normative understanding of the Church for the Radical Pietist movement. "They perceived the church as an *invisible fellowship of true believers* which transcended confessional and national boundaries, which was bound together by brotherly love, and which waited expectantly for the inbreaking of Christ's Spirit."[6] This understanding of an invisible church grew out of a disgust for perceived corruption of the New Testament ideal for the Church. Jacob Boehme, one of those who first inspired the Pietist movement, stressed this view. Boehme "distinguished between the Church of Abel, the invisible and universal church composed of those who are experientially united with God whether they may be living or dead, and the Church of Cain, the church visible in history."[7] The role of Abel, in this scheme, is to prophetically warn and attempt to reform Cain.

Menno Simons and Anabaptists in general, however, insisted on the visible and pragmatic nature of the church. Menno declared that "the community of God, or the church of Christ, is an *assembly* of the pious, and a *community* of the saints" who are disciples of Christ.[8] The Anabaptist hermeneutical process

was closely tied to its understanding of the Church. Both Brethren and Mennonite groups embrace a hermeneutic of community: trusting the Holy Spirit to
work most effectively and authoritatively through the community as it seeks to
discern rightly the meaning of scripture, or, as Brethren might say, "the Mind of
Christ."

In light of the dialectic of visible and invisible church, I have to wonder
about the possible connection between the Radical Pietist suspicion of the
organized church and modern rejections of the church. While attendance in
worship decreases, polls show vast numbers of Americans believe in God and
many consider themselves to be Christian. Is this a resurgence of a Radical
Pietism or merely a *Shelahism* as described by Robert Bellah in *Habits of the
Heart*? I suspect the latter, yet what is the difference? Perhaps, the increasing
number of "independent" churches are closer to the Pietist's perspective, but are
they?

As for the Anabaptists, was their approach to the church communal or
covenantal? Was the bond of community the common world view, or was it the
covenant which led to a community-shared world view and subsequent
interpretation of faithfulness?

Modern individualism may not have to mean the destruction of community.
Our society is in process of seeing the limits of individualism. This is evidenced
in the popularity of authors such as Scott Peck, Robert Bellows, and similar
more recent writers. Perhaps, even the Lake Wobegon stories give evidence of
the need for community rather than individual orientation. Baby boomers notwithstanding, individualism is coming to the end of its reign although it will not
disappear from the scene entirely. How might we tap into a blend of individualism and community which enhances faithfulness? Is such a thing possible?

The relationship of individual to community is at the heart of church
discipline as we have come to think of it. How is the church to discipline its
members? If we lived in a first-century dyadic[9] psycho-social culture, the ban
would be a most effective tool to bring a person back into compliance with
group norms.

Ours, however, is a mind-set far removed from the dyadic. Our identity is
not found in the group to which we belong. How much interference from the
church will you or I tolerate in our faith walk? If my congregation insists upon
displaying an American flag in the sanctuary, which I consider an idolatrous
violation of the second commandment, how am I to respond faithfully?

We live in a competitively oriented world which, like it or not, is shaping
church life. Churches are afraid of getting into the red with either membership
or budgets. As a result, they offer increasing numbers of choices. These congregations are treated like stores by potential and current members. "If one
church doesn't treat me right," says the parishioner, "I'll go next door." The
church that does not buy into the free-market paradigm can expect increased
conflict and dwindling numbers. Being small, or large, does not necessarily
mean being faithful, yet people are concerned when their support shrinks.

How, then, are we to reconcile current understandings of the relationship between individuals and groups with a model of discipline rooted in the dyadic paradigm of Matthew 18:15-22 and 1 Corinthians 5:1-5 and cherished by tradition? It would seem impossible unless we alter our understanding of the nature and boundaries of the church community. This brings us to the third query.

III

To what extent do (or should) pre-adolescent membership classes and other common methods of bringing new members into the fellowship conform to the Anabaptist heritage?

Commonly used methods of bringing people into the church have, for the most part, been borrowed from Protestant evangelical churches. Modern Protestant evangelicalism is at odds with an Anabaptist approach to church life. Most of these church bodies approach the world and church from a radically different perspective. Theirs is a view that sees the world filled with people who are Christian but just don't know it. The church's task is to help them become active. Church growth models currently being advocated within the Church of the Brethren appear to be out of this model. Smile, invite the non-church member to worship, assign them some jobs like taking up collection, and you've "evangelized" the person. Once in the church, they will grow to ever increasing degrees of spiritual maturity.

Anabaptists have tended to assume that a major decision has to be made about radical life-changing discipleship. You can still invite the non-church members to worship and assign them jobs to do, but you don't so quickly grant the kiss of fellowship to those who have not yet made the life altering decision for obedient following of the Master into covenantal ministry. This is in sharp contrast to the most current manual for church leaders in the Church of the Brethren which asserts that "Baptism is a beginning. It is understood not as something completed but as the start of the Christian's pilgrimage of faith." [10]

Anabaptists could say that baptism and membership are the start of ministry. An Anabaptist might agree that it was the beginning of discipleship but hardly the start of faith! Such a statement blurs the boundary between church and society which was a hallmark of the visible church of the Anabaptists.

If embraced, this new doctrine will make it increasingly difficult to reclaim baptism as an action of radical choice in repentant response to God's love and will press us toward an ever younger age for baptism as we discover the faith of little children. Who, today, is seriously interested in reclaiming adult baptism? With rare exception, it is a dying notion. The final query, however, presupposes we currently adhere to adult baptism and want to preserve it.

IV

How can we affirm the belonging of pre-adolescents to the community while preserving the emphasis on adult believer's baptism and membership?

Most congregations in the Church of the Brethren tradition have a membership class taught to junior-high aged people with the expectation, stated or implied, that following the class, students will "join church." I have witnessed and heard about high pressure tactics used to manipulate youth into the water when they did not feel ready. The pressure comes from pastors, parents, peers, and Sunday School teachers. Any effort to shift baptism to an older age frequently is met with significant opposition and is undermined easily.

As pastor at a congregation several years ago, I worked on membership issues with the Juniors (fifth and sixth graders) as assigned by my overseeing commission. It was clear to the students that they were not ready for baptism. After considerable conversations with parents, commissions, and even the congregational business meeting, we arrived at a mutual understanding that we would allow the age to be raised. Each year from then on, I continued to work with the congregation. It meant that apart from adults and older youth few were baptized. Many church leaders became nervous with the move toward adult baptism, yet it appeared to become accepted. Years later, when I returned to that congregation, I discovered that the new pastor was again baptizing Juniors.

Issues of preparation for membership are further exacerbated by the increasing secularization of society and this new social legacy to novitiate members. Most membership classes today are painfully inadequate for the task because they are based upon an assumption that is no longer valid, that people basically understand what it means to be a Christian.

I recently interviewed some new members who were adults transferring from another church or were baptized. They completed the membership class but said they really did not understand the basics of the faith and did not know even elementary information about the Bible.

Should we assume children grow up in a Christian, or a secular society? The issue has less to do with prayer in school than prayer, conversation, and Bible study in the home and church. High school teachers tell me that students can no longer grasp most literature because they are ignorant of the biblical allusions permeating the classics. The culture in which we live is changing, and we can no longer assume the faith fundamentals will be understood prior to church membership classes. Neither a couple hours of coffee and conversation nor a thirteen-week course in Brethren or Mennonite heritage will suffice. Perhaps, we should embrace a period of waiting as is done in the Nigerian *Ecclyesiyar 'Yan'uwa a Nigeria* [11] which has a potential member become a "Waiter at the Gate" until she or he is prepared for membership.

So how might it happen that we take seriously pre-adolescent spiritual awakening without resorting to baptism? It is being done already. I can document one situation. In the Manchester Church of the Brethren, twelve-year-old people are invited to select an adult mentor who will spend a year of direct one-to-one nurture, including an apprenticeship in spiritual development.

When it is clear a youth feels the need to respond to a spiritual awakening, she or he may call for an experience akin to the one we believe is behind Jesus' childhood temple experience. The Brethren in North Manchester call it the "Eighth Day Service"[12] after Anabaptist references to the eighth day of creation and after Alexander Mack's use of circumcision, an eighth-day experience, as a metaphor for awakening faith. This is a covenantal service in which the youth is formally recognized by the church as one who now holds a new position within its life. The youth is now able to take communion but not vote on congregational issues. During the years following the Eighth Day service, the youth pledge to work with greater intentionality on faith issues in preparation for the full yoke of covenantal ministry and discipleship, signified by baptism and the life beyond baptism. Junior and Senior High people, regardless of membership status, are visited annually by church leaders for a spiritual inventory. Each time they are asked to review their progress—their faith life successes and failures—since the last conversation. Each year the youth are asked to establish a goal to ensure future growth.

This model has only been in effect for four or five years, but its continuity following a pastoral change suggests it maintains value in congregational life, as well as in the lives of the individual youth asking for the experience. Will this be the answer we seek? Probably not.

The Eighth Day Experience was first proposed in a Church of the Brethren Annual Conference authorized manual on church membership. Since then, the newest pastors' manual not only omits reference to this previous manual, but it contains a different pre-adolescent service whose form is unlikely to move us toward adult baptism. Resistance to mixing maturity and baptism is significant.

So, now that we have looked at the key questions shaping the discussion, how might Anabaptists reclaim their traditions regarding church membership?

While a design might be created to project some adaptation of Anabaptist traditions concerning membership into the future, this writer suggests that there are yet too many preliminary issues still pleading for clarification. A congregation here or there might take up the challenge on one or more of the traditions, but charting a course is unlikely at this time in light of the needs: to turn the momentum from a several-decade drift from Anabaptist ways, to overcome the inertia of those too weary or content to challenge the status quo, to agree which of the membership traditions are specifically Anabaptist, and to develop clarity regarding a list of traditions worthy of preservation.

Perhaps, further discussion of these questions will yield greater intentionality about the way God would have Anabaptists walk in the coming century.

1 This allusion is discussed more fully in Willard Swartley's article, "Uses and Authority of Scripture: Contemporary Applications and Prospects" in this volume. He suggests that before the enlightenment, "true" could refer to that which was true to relationships as well as that which was true to the five senses while only the latter carries the word's meaning today.

2 *Cursillo de Christianidad* is a movement active since the late 1940's and is known under a variety of names: Episcopalians know it as *Tres Dias*, Methodists refer to The Emmaus Walk, and Lutherans call it *Via de Cristo*. A group of Brethren Church and Church of the Brethren members are developing an Anabaptist version known as the Way of Christ.

3 C. David Ensign, "Radical German Pietism," ed. Donald F. Durnbaugh, *Brethren Encyclopedia* 3 vols. (Philadelphia: Brethren Encyclopedia Inc., 1983), II, 1079.

4 Durnbaugh, "Membership," 14.

5 Donald F. Durnbaugh, ed., "Early History," *The Church of the Brethren: Past and Present* (Elgin, Ill.: The Brethren Press, 1971), 11.

6 Dale R. Stoffer, *Background and Development of Brethren Doctrines: 1650-1987* (Philadelphia: Brethren Encyclopedia, 1989), 21-2. Emphasis added.

7 Ibid., 20.

8 Menno Simons, "Reply to Gellius Faber," 734, ibid., 54.

9 Bruce J. Malina, *New Testament World: Insights from Cultural Anthropology* (Atlanta: John Knox Press, 1981), 53ff.

10 Earle W. Fike, Jr., *For all Who Minister* (Elgin: Brethren Press, 1993), 130.

11 "Church of the Brethren in Nigeria" is the translation. Actually, '*Yan'uwa* literally means "Children of the same mother," thus including both male and female.

12 John David Bowman, *Invitation to the Journey* (Elgin, Ill.: The Brethren Press, 1990), 54.

Conversation
 හහ IX ශඋශ

Ministry

Steven C. Ainlay and E. Morris Sider describe variations in the Anabaptist ministry over time and space. Ainlay cautions that traditions alter as history and geography change, making modifications in the heritage inevitable. As he surveys the ministerial norms of the Amish, Hutterites, Brethren, Mennonites, and Brethren in Christ, he discovers that the old order groups—Amish and Hutterites—have generally maintained a traditional ministry based on personal relationships and inherited authority. The other Anabaptist communions, which became more modernized, eventually developed forms characterized by rationalization and professionalization.

Sider reminisces about his father, a Brethren in Christ minister in Ontario, and asserts that despite the distance in time, the traditional model of ministry represented by his father still has value. Although Sider acknowledges that larger, suburbanized congregations may find this pattern less helpful, he believes that ministers who serve long-term, are self-supporting, and belong to the community they serve can significantly contribute to modern congregations. Thus, he urges seminaries and denominational leaders to offer alternatives for the ministry that include traditional components.

1
Ministry in the Anabaptist Tradition

by Steven C. Ainlay

Theological, Historical, and Sociological Perspectives

Reviewing the heritage of the Anabaptist ministry is a daunting task given the complexity of the early Anabaptist movement and the multiplicity of forms that Anabaptism has taken over the past four hundred years. Nevertheless, it is an important discussion to have because it speaks directly to the theme of this volume.[1]

Debates over the role of the minister, from the sixteenth century to the contemporary scene, revolve around questions concerning the distinguishing features of the Anabaptist movement (that is, what distinguishes it from other Christian groups and movements) and get to the heart of what it means to be an Anabaptist. Behind many of these debates lies this central question: Do ministerial practices conform in any meaningful way to the Anabaptist vision or are they contrary to it? Furthermore, within many of the groups tracing their roots back to the sixteenth-century Anabaptist movement, the role of the minister has been transformed over the last century by the very forces that have made questions of Anabaptist identity so urgent: individualism, bureaucratization, professionalization, etc.

Warning: The Search for Heritage May Be Hazardous to Your (Individual and Collective) Health

At the outset, I would note that examining one's heritage and its relationship to contemporary social arrangements is risky business. One risk is probably self-evident: contemporary arrangements—whether ministerial patterns, economic arrangements, models of church polity, etc.—may be at odds with the heritage uncovered. This sort of discovery can prompt changes in the way things are done or the way in which people think of themselves. Witness the effects, for example, of Harold S. Bender's "Anabaptist Vision" on Mennonite life during the second half of the twentieth century.

There is another, less evident risk to the business of "heritage hunting." The search for one's heritage will always be an exercise in what some social psychologists call "retrospective interpretation." Because we are inescapably bound to our own historical era and our own geographical location, we can never fully capture the vantage point of those who came before or lived elsewhere. This methodological problem has proved troublesome to sociologists, anthropologists, and historians alike. It is relevant as well for those who engage in "heritage hunting." Persons or groups looking for their heritage risk weaving together a story which highlights those aspects of the past that legitimate their priorities, priorities always located in the present. At the same time, other aspects of the past—which Max Weber might have included in his category of "inconvenient facts"—are dismissed, minimized, or altogether ignored. In other words, there is seldom one "heritage" waiting to be discovered.

By way of example, the "rural life movement" of the 1930s and 40s comes to mind. During this period, Mennonites were still rural, with eighty-two percent living in rural areas (compared to fifty-three percent for Americans as a whole). Many Mennonites worried about the urban encroachment into their world and the increasing tendency of Mennonite young people to venture into the urban environment. They worried about the intrusion of such modern innovations as the telephone, automobile, and radio, which gave people living in rural areas too much access to cities and urban culture. They worried, too, about the effects of secular education. Mennonite writers made various attempts to convince their readership that the "heritage" of Mennonites was rural and that the exposure to the urban/non-farming way of life constituted a violation of that heritage.[2]

The rural life movement was just one manifestation of what Michael Yoder has termed the Mennonite "rural bias." Yoder observes that "most Mennonites of European origin, until well into the twentieth century, assumed that the Christian life is best lived in a rural community."[3] This assumption was grounded in both theological concern (Mennonites believed that rural life offered protection from persecutors and exposure to worldly forces) and historical understanding. Scholarship in recent decades has, however, challenged the notion that the Anabaptist movement was rural in origin. It has documented that the original Anabaptist movement was neither rural nor urban but reflected the heterogeneity of sixteenth century middle Europe, showing that the movement was originally composed of a cross-section of society, including noblemen, teachers, lawyers, and other professionals, a goodly number of artisans, and peasants, who, after all, made up ninety percent of the population. Only when the movement was driven out of the cities and towns by persecution did it become a truly rural peasant movement. Thus, as we are all at risk of doing, the rural life movement selectively recalled the Anabaptist heritage.

The retrospective interpretation of the past is not just or even mostly a matter of bad scholarship. All of us, no matter how thorough or well-honed our investigative skills, face a past which can only be seen retrospectively. It is more a matter of the politics of identity (individual or group) and the desire to legitimate one's view of life or one's plans and hopes for the future. Historians, sociologists, theologians, and the like are not immune from this "legitimating process" but can, in fact, be key players as members of the so-called "culture elite."[4]

None of this is meant to suggest that there is little value in "heritage hunting." It is simply to remind ourselves of the tendency we have to streamline our histories and the potential repercussions (sometimes repressive) that our retelling of the past may have for other people. This cautionary note seems particularly important when discussing ministerial models, given the difficult positions in which many ministers have found themselves—oftentimes pulled by competing constituencies holding diametrically opposed notions of the Anabaptist heritage—during the transitions of the last century.

Having said this, my goal here is not to establish the fundamental "truths" of Anabaptism but rather to identify elements of the Anabaptist tradition which form a sort of cultural bedrock upon which discussions of the ministry have been and continue to be built. My argument will be that "crises" in the ministry have resulted (and continue to result) primarily from the pressures that modernization exerts on religious leadership positions, leading to a more rationalized system of authority that seems to be in tension with long-standing Anabaptist themes.

The Role of the Minister Among Early Anabaptists

The Mennonite historian, C. Henry Smith, once described the early Anabaptist attitude toward the ministry in the following manner,

> they did not have a specially trained and supported ministry. Like the missionaries in the primitive church, ministers were to live by the labor of their own hands. The ministry was to be regarded as a labor of love. *Hirelings* was a term often applied to the state clergy. Benefices and fat livings were as frequently criticized as any other practice among the established institutions. Ministers were chosen by the congregation from among their own number. The first leaders, of course, were highly trained men, converts, for the most part, from the Catholic priesthood or university graduates. But after these had been killed off and the Brethren had been dispersed, there were few trained leaders.[5]

As Smith pointed out, early Anabaptism challenged the traditional role of the Catholic clergy. For some early Anabaptist leaders, like Menno Simons, this was a matter of both theological and personal concern. Ordained to the Catholic priesthood in 1524, Menno served as a parish priest for twelve years and then joined a small group of Anabaptists under the leadership of Obbe Philips (the Obbenites).[6] Menno's disenchantment with the Catholic church and its teachings was gradual, but he was eventually pushed from the Catholic priesthood because of doctrinal doubts he had concerning transubstantiation and baptism and pulled by the inspiring example of Anabaptists who willingly died for their faith. Sometime during the winter of 1536-37, Menno accepted a call to lead the Anabaptist brotherhood in northern Holland. He found little in the role of the Catholic priest upon which to model his new ministry. Speaking of the "Popish priests" of his day, he wrote in 1539,

> we openly declare that the mission and vocation of your preachers are not of God and His Word but of Antichrist, the dragon, and the beast, that they are not called to preach the Word of the Lord by the Spirit of God and the church, but by their bellies, as were the priests of Jeroboam to worship the golden calf; that they do not enter by the right door; therefore we dare with God's Words to testify that they are thieves and robbers.[7]

Menno's view of the ministry developed over the years and his most thorough treatise on the subject appeared in 1554 under the title "Reply to Gellius Faber."[8] Faber (or Jelle Smit), an ex-Catholic priest, published an attack on the Anabaptists in 1552. Simons felt obliged to respond and in doing so detailed his own conversion as well as his view of the ministry. Simons writes a virtual job description for the Anabaptist minister when he suggests

> It should be observed for what purpose the true preachers are called; namely, that they should teach the Word of the Lord correctly, right use their sacraments, lead and rule aright the church of God, gather together with Christ and not scatter, console the bereaved, admonish the irregular, seek the lost, bind up the wounded, ban those that are incurable, without any respect of persons whether great or small; and solemnly watch over the vineyard, house, and city of God, as the Scriptures teach.[9]

According to Russell Mast, Menno viewed the ministry as what has been termed a "set apart" ministry but recognized, in a manner consistent with Paul, that various members of the church would have different gifts.[10] Thus, he did not see the "call to preach" as something available to everyone. According to him, ministers must be persons of "unblamable life," who have no thought of their own gain.[11]

Menno was also quite specific about the nature of the preaching which the minister should pursue. Consistent with the primacy of scripture that, again, gave the Anabaptist movement a sort of *raison d'être*, he insisted that the minister should focus his message on the gospel. Menno urged,

> This command and word, I say, Christ commanded all true messengers and preachers to observe, saying, Preach the gospel. He does not say, Preach the doctrines and commands of men, preach councils and customs, preach glosses and opinions of the learned. He says, Preach the Gospel.[12]

But, even though early Anabaptists rejected the role of the Catholic priest and writers like Menno Simons articulated their view of the ministry, a ready solution to the ministerial "problem" proved elusive, and a number of models emerged. This owed, in part, to the persecution that took away so many young leaders. It also owed, in part, to the disorganization that inevitably followed the migration of Anabaptist groups fleeing torture, death, and economic hardship. It also owed, again in part, to the chiliastic tendency of the early Anabaptists: with the end so near at hand, what need was there for a thoroughly conceived organizational structure?[13]   Finally, it owed to the fact that the Anabaptist movement had different regional constituencies. Thus, Swiss-South German Anabaptists developed models of leadership that were distinct in some ways from those in the Netherlands and in other areas.   Even within regional Anabaptist movements, various names and functions of ministers were used.

Early Anabaptists in the Netherlands, for example, used terms such as "bishop" and "elder" (*oudste*), "baptizer" (*doper*), "preacher," "deacon," and "purse bearer" (*buydeldrager*), "servants" (*dienaer*), and "servants of the poor" (*armendienaer*) to refer to those who performed ministerial functions.[14]   They did not draw sharp distinctions between the offices during this time of persecution and, not surprisingly, congregations experienced some disorganization.   By 1545, however, they began to sharpen the definition of offices and functions: elders (whose task it was to baptize, administer communion, perform marriages, ordain elders, preachers and deacons, and to ban), preachers (whose task it was to preach and/or read the Scriptures in the meetings), and deacons were clearly distinguished from one another (with preachers chosen from among the deacons and elders chosen from among preachers).   Ordination was by laying on of hands.   Schisms within Anabaptism in the Netherlands led to the further proliferation of ministerial models.[15]   Among a number of these groups, the distinction between elder and preacher was no longer observed by the seventeenth century.

By way of another example, Harold Bender observed that among the Swiss-German Anabaptists considerable responsibility was given to the bishop-elder in each congregation.[16]   By 1565, at the time of the Strasbourg Discipline, the threefold ministry of bishop-elder, preacher, and deacon was well established although the number of people occupying these offices varied by congregation and region.

The Ministry From a Believers' Church Perspective

Several themes running through the early Anabaptist Weltanschauung provide a backdrop for understanding their conception of the minister's role: the primacy of scripture, the church as Gemeinde, and Gelassenheit.[17]

The Primacy of Scripture. In summarizing the "Anabaptist Vision," Cornelius Dyck begins by noting that Anabaptists were committed to "letting the Bible be the final rule in faith and practice."[18]   This "primacy of scripture" meant many things to the Anabaptists.   Among other things, it meant that they rejected both the primacy of ecclesiastical hierarchy of the Catholics and the primacy of political authority to which they felt Zwingli and other reformers were committed.[19]

For some of the early Anabaptist reformers the primacy of scripture was precisely what prompted their rejection of many elements of Catholic teaching and even propelled them beyond the mainline reformation groups.   Harold Bender captured the importance of scriptural authority for Menno Simons in his brief biographical sketch of the reformer. Bender noted that Menno Simons was indebted to Luther for his insight that following God's commandments could never lead to eternal death, an outcome promised to heretics who deviated from fundamental teachings of the Church. As Bender described Menno's thinking,

> When Menno Simons accepted Luther's view and dared to deny the dogma of tran-substantiation as held by the Catholic Church because the Scriptures did not teach it, he found a way out of his doubts and struggles, a way to free his conscience and deliver his soul from eternal death. But in so doing he entered upon a road that would inevitably lead him out of the Catholic Church, for to follow the Scriptures in all matters of conscience was to forsake the fundamental principles of Catholicism. In making his decision on the mass, however, Menno did not follow Luther's teach-ings on this point; rather he developed his own interpretation of the Lord's Supper; he did not become Lutheran in any way. What he was always grateful to Luther for, was the fundamental principle of the authority of Scripture as over against any hu-man authority.[20]

Menno himself spoke of the primacy of Scripture without equivocation. Writing around 1540, he observed,

> We certainly hope no one of rational mind will be so foolish a man as to deny that the whole Scriptures, both the Old and New Testament, were written for our instruc-tion, admonition, and correction, and that they are the true scepter and rule by which the Lord's kingdom, house, church, and congregation must be ruled and governed. Everything contrary to Scripture, therefore, whether it be in doctrines, beliefs, sacra-ments, worship, or life, should be measured by this infallible rule and demolished by this just and divine scepter, and destroyed without any respect of persons.[21]

Thus, the teachings of Scripture for Menno Simons and other Anabaptists proved more important than the doctrinal or political priorities of the times. As Harold Bender put it in his "Recovery of the Anabaptist Vision," early Anabaptists "preferred to make a radical break with the fifteen hundred years of history and culture if necessary rather than to break with the New Testament."[22]

Church as Gemeinde. A number of writers have emphasized that the concept of a body of believers, or the priesthood of the laity, was an important part of the Anabaptist movement.[23] While some writers question whether or not the early Anabaptists recognized a priesthood of all believers or merely the diversity of special gifts in the church, it is clear that they conceived of themselves as a *Gemeinde*, a body or community of people who voluntarily joined to share a common life.[24] Harold Bender, writing on the Anabaptist conception of the church, noted that

> one of the most characteristic features of Anabaptism is its church concept. The church (Gemeinde), according to the Anabaptist, is a voluntary and exclusive fel-lowship of the truly converted believers in Christ, committed to follow Him in full obedience as Lord; it is a brotherhood, not an institution. It is completely separated from the state, which is to have no power over the church; and the members of the church in turn do not hold office in the magistracy. There is to be complete free-dom of conscience, no use of force or compulsion by state or church; faith must be free.[25]

Bender concludes that this Anabaptist emphasis on church as "brotherhood" carried an "anti-hierarchical emphasis," which meant that the clerical nature of church offices had to be minimized and lay participation and responsibility given a high priority.[26] This idealized Anabaptist church organization had a distinctly egalitarian emphasis, leaving little room for the Catholic hierarchical model of clergy leadership and required that the role of a minister be reconsidered and remodeled.

Gelassenheit. Although it has had many meanings, the term *Gelassenheit* has come to signify much of the early Anabaptist-Mennonite spirit. It continues to be an important theme in most Anabaptist groups and for some, like the Amish, it has become a near hallmark.[27] In writing of the term in the *Mennonite Encyclopedia,* Robert Friedmann noted that "self surrender," "resignation to God's will," "yieldedness to God's will," and "self-abandonment" are among the numerous expressions of the concept. Hans Denck may have popularized the idea among early Anabaptists and summarized the idea effectively when he said, "There is no other way to blessedness than to lose one's self-will."[28] Gelassenheit provided a language for understanding martyrdom and the costs of discipleship in the early Anabaptist experience.[29] Gelassenheit made the self-aggrandizement, the power of one individual to exercise her/his will over another, problematic and, therefore, added to the difficulty of finding an appropriate leadership model for the ministry.

An Emergent Heritage

While these themes that shaped the early Anabaptist view of the ministry remain salient to understanding ministerial models operating among Anabaptist groups today, they have been modified and transformed as other theological, sociological, and historical forces have been encountered and appropriated.

Among the most important of the theological encounters was the one between Anabaptism and Pietism. Gelassenheit may have taken on a somewhat different meaning than was originally intended, given the strong influence of humility theology from Pietism on various Anabaptist groups. Theron Schlabach has noted that adequate research on the roots of humility theology remains to be done (although his own work certainly moves us quite far along in this regard).[30] There can be little doubt that Anabaptists brought Pietist teachings with them from Europe, and the humility theology that runs through their experience owes much to this.

The Anabaptist embrace of Pietism and its humility theology meant that Mennonites lost much of the confrontational mood of early Anabaptism. It also became an important way for Anabaptist-Mennonites to set themselves apart from the individualism, enterprise, and aggressive nationalism they found in America. Schlabach notes that making humility a central theme in their lives allowed them to prove themselves separate from "human greed, self-aggrandizement, and war."[31]

But Pietism was not the only influence—theological or other—that complicated the development of Anabaptist ministerial models. Persecution brought geographic mobility, and moves to Russia, Canada, the United States, Paraguay, and other places brought in their wake cultural collisions and mergers. Anabaptists have been changed through encounters with fundamentalism, evangelicalism, Pentecostalism, etc. Similarly, the societies that received the Anabaptist pilgrims were to go through profound changes themselves, which had an effect on the shape of the Anabaptist ministry. The story of what must be seen as the emerging Anabaptist ministerial heritage has, therefore, many chapters, reflecting the various Anabaptist groups and their unique histories.

The Minister's Role in Various Anabaptist Groups

Since the sixteenth century, the history of Anabaptism has been one of triumph in the face of adversity. But it has also been a history of internal turmoil and schisms (or, for the more positive spin, "renewals") which led to the development of new religious groups. Among other institutional problems, each group faced the challenge of developing patterns of ministry that were true in some respect to the concerns of early Anabaptist leaders and that fit their own organizational, regional, and doctrinal purposes. Similarly, the various Anabaptist groups have faced very different environmental imperatives. Some have remained largely rural, set apart from some of the most powerful modernizing forces in society. Others have "neared" the modern world. The result is that over the four hundred years of Anabaptist history, various arrangements have been accommodated in the different groups. One could not hope to survey all of the developments in all the groups, but we can at least capture glimpses of the unfolding of ministerial roles.

The Amish. In the Amish, we find the three themes discussed earlier—the primacy of scripture, church as Gemeinde, and Gelassenheit—to be played out, perhaps most clearly of all Anabaptist groups, in the role prescribed for the ministry. John Hostetler describes the nature of Amish ministerial leadership in the following manner:

> Among the Amish—who have rejected coercive powers as worldly, and who cultivate humility, obedience, and simplicity—the selection of leaders is a delicate process. One who is chosen to lead must not seek either authority or power, but in reality he is placed in position where he must exercise both. In selecting candidates for office members look for humility and evidence of good farm and family management. Any forwardness or idiosyncratic tendencies are quickly detected. An Amishman would never prepare himself for the vocation of preacher, nor would he announce that he felt called of God to prepare for the ministry, as members of evangelical groups would do. Attending a seminary would be a sure sign of worldliness and reason for excommunication, for it would indicate a loss of humility and the development of ego. The Amish method of using nominations for election and selection by lot helps to prevent manipulative power and personal ambition.

Authority is widely distributed among all members so that no single leader or sub-group will have all the power.[32]

Donald Kraybill discusses the various ministerial roles of the Amish in his book, *The Riddle of Amish Culture.*[33] Kraybill reports that there are three leadership positions (*Diener* or "servants") within Amish districts: the bishop (*Voellinger-Diener* or minister with full powers), minister (*Diener zum Buch* or minister of the book), and deacon (*Armen-Diener* or minister to the poor). These positions are all held by males and are viewed as servants of God and congregation. The bishop is the spiritual head of the church and officiates at baptisms, weddings, communions, funerals, and members' meetings of the congregation. He also bears primary responsibility for enforcing church regulations, including recommendations to the congregation on excommunications. The Amish minister, or preacher, has primary responsibility for preaching but also assists the bishop in providing spiritual direction to the congregation. Deacons read scripture and lead prayers in worship services. They have other, less public, responsibilities that include helping the ministers and bishop investigate violations of church regulations and supervising marriage plans of members. None of the Amish leaders are formally trained, and they earn their livings through farming or other typical Amish occupations.

Amish ministers are selected by "lot."[34] Kraybill describes the selection process as follows:

> The lot "falls" on the new minister with only a few minutes of warning. A slip of paper bearing a Bible verse is placed in a song book. The book is randomly arranged with other song books, in a number equal to the number of candidates. Seated around the table, the candidates each select a book. The bishop in charge says: "Lord of all generations, show us which one you have chosen among these Brethren." The candidates then open the books, looking for the fateful paper. The lot "falls on the man as the Lord decrees." The service is packed with emotion. Like a bolt of lightning, the lot strikes the new minister's family with the stunning realization that he is about to assume the high calling of ministerial responsibilities for the rest of his life. In the spirit of Gelassenheit, the "winner" receives neither applause nor congratulations. Rather, tears, somber silence, and sympathy are extended to the new leader and his family, who must bear the heavy burden of servanthood as they give themselves up to the church.[35]

Kraybill notes that this selection process is "astute" given that it not only solves the problem of succession but affirms basic community values. He continues,

> Once again, personal desires are surrendered to the common welfare. The leader and his family yield to the community "by giving themselves up" for the larger cause. No perks, prestige, financial gain, career goals, or personal objectives accrue to the officeholder. Although it would be haughty to seek ordination, some individuals may privately hope for the office, or at least enjoy the respect given their role after ordination. Core values are reaffirmed, for only local, untrained men are acceptable candidates. The permanency of the lot underscores the durability of commitment and community. The entire ritual is a cogent reminder that leadership rests on the bedrock of Gelassenheit.[36]

Hostetler adds that "even though the community might view the man chosen as less qualified than another nominee, the members are satisfied with the result because the choice was God's."[37]

The Hutterites. The Hutterites are organized into *Leuts,* which are administratively separate from one another. Each *Leut* has its own senior elder and consists of multiple colonies.[38] Hutterite ministers—the first and second preachers—are among the limited number of baptized men who form the colony council.[39] The first (or head) preacher holds the highest leadership position, but his actions are subject to review by the council. Hostetler and Huntington capture the extent and complexity of the preacher's role, describing it in the following manner.

> The preacher receives no formal training prior to his election. He is elected by lot from nominations by his own colony (with the aid of other colony delegates). He is ordained to exercise full powers only after several years of proven leadership. A preacher must have the ability to be conservative in religious values but progressive in work and economic affairs. Good handwriting is an asset since he must transcribe sermons. He must be able to exert authority wisely, since he is expected to carry out the collective will as well as God's will. His role encompasses total as well as specific responsibility. Ideally he refers all weighty matters to the council. His religious duties include conducting church services and funerals as well as performing marriages and baptisms. He hears personal problems, voluntary confession, and administers punishment for sins. He must interpret the present in terms of the past. He must oversee the life-long indoctrination of his people and the spiritual tempo of the colony. He has a direct interest in seeing that the colony schools are functioning properly, but his relating to the teachers is informal. He has the responsibility for smoothing over difficulties that arise between members. He keeps a record of births, marriages, and deaths, which reflect concern both for their history and marital patterns and keeps travel records when members leave the colony for trips. The preacher is intimately concerned with the economic well-being of the colony. He keeps an eye on the activities of the householder to insure that the colony is run efficiently enough to provide for its people's needs and for future expansion. He also countersigns checks with the householder. The preacher is both guardian of traditions and spokesman for the colony in its "foreign affairs." He must remain vigilant against the *Weltgeist,* the spirit of the world.[40]

Both first and second preacher have responsibility for leading the worship services.[41]

Both the Hutterites and the Amish have intentionally distanced themselves from the modern, secular, pluralized world that surrounds them. As Don Kraybill notes of the Amish, they have "culturally bargained" with that world, leading to some accommodations. Nevertheless, they have preserved long-standing patterns of ministerial leadership far more tenaciously than have those Anabaptist groups that have cut somewhat different bargains with the world.

The Mennonites. Each of the Mennonite groups has a somewhat different history and each developed somewhat different understandings of the ministry. While Mennonites once shared the threefold pattern of Anabaptist ministry that persists among the Amish (bishop, preacher, and deacon), many have moved away from this understanding.[42] Depending on the extent of their exposure to various forces of modernization (urbanization, education, exposure to mass media, non-farm occupations, etc.), they have sometimes adopted patterns of ministry that more closely resemble mainline Protestant denominations. Notably, some Mennonite groups have moved quite far in the direction of the single pastor leadership model. Others have tried to experiment with models that retain some of the characteristics of shared leadership yet conform to bureaucratic principles. The bottom line is that any attempt to generalize about the Mennonite conception of the ministry risks obscuring important differences within the Mennonite world or Mennonite history.

Having said this, it appears that through the eighteenth century there was more uniformity when compared to growing differences in the nineteenth and twentieth centuries. Some of the saga of the Mennonite ministry has been traced through the *Mennonite Experience in America* series. Richard MacMaster, in the first of three books in the series, details Mennonite life during the eighteenth century. While it is not entirely clear just how ministerial responsibilities were divided, eighteenth-century Mennonites used the three-fold leadership model of elder, or bishop, preacher, and deacon.[43] As with the Amish today, the authority of preachers was limited compared to that of the elder. Ministers were often secured through a process that involved balloting to pick eligible men and the lot for the final selection. MacMaster notes that ministers during this time were not paid and congregations often chose prosperous men to lead them.[44] Because of their commitment to humility theology, they also allowed the lot to fall on people who considered themselves too poor. Richard MacMaster reports on the case, for example, of Martin Boehm, who in 1756 was chosen by lot to serve a congregation south of Lancaster, Pa. Upon picking up his songbook in the lot procedure and before he knew he had received the lot, Boehm began to tremble and thought "Lord not me. I am too poor."[45] Ministers worked in a variety of occupations: farmers, millers, weavers, blacksmiths, etc.[46]

During the 1800s, moves toward "modernizing" the church and the role of the Mennonite minister met with various forms of resistance. Theron Schlabach reports that in 1889 Old Order partisans went into a newly built meetinghouse in eastern Lancaster county and ripped out the new pulpit that had been installed there, leaving in its place a traditional "singers' table." As Schlabach explains it, "to them a high pulpit was a sure sign that Mennonites wanted to be like the proud, popular churches who set their clergy above and apart from their congregation."[47]

Eastern Pennsylvania provided the ground for the Oberholtzer reform movement.[48] This movement not only contributed to a major schism but it led to experimentation with new forms of ministry. John H. Oberholtzer (d. 1895) was a popular preacher and arguably the most important mid-nineteenth-century Mennonite church reformer. He protested "slow tongued" ministers, rigid authority, and what he perceived to be fixations on clothing and external trivia. He advocated deeper internal piety and urged Mennonites to become less separatist. Correspondingly, Oberholtzer and his followers chose to be more "in the world" culturally. They also advocated salary for ministers.[49] Ultimately, the Oberholtzer movement combined with other progressive Mennonite groups to form the General Conference of Mennonites in North America. Some, like the Lee County (Iowa) Mennonites, already had trained and salaried pastors by mid-nineteenth century.[50] From the beginning, then, the General Conference Mennonites were more "progressive" in their view of the ministerial role.

In 1868, while the new conference was quite young, the General Conference quickly moved to establish in Ohio the Wadsworth Institute, whose purpose was, as Schlabach observes, "to produce ministers more able to explain God's Word in a way to bring people to a 'personal living experience,' promote Mennonite unity, and be a 'means toward the spread of the Gospel'."[51] The school lasted only ten years, but it became a sort of symbol and even "myth" of Mennonite forays into higher education.[52] It also provided a precedent for future Mennonite experiments in biblical and seminary education.

Some thirty years after the closing of Wadsworth, the General Conference Mennonites again established a school for educating its ministers at Bluffton College in Ohio. Mennonite Seminary began in 1914 as a department within the College but in 1921 became a separate institution, Witmarsum Seminary. Witmarsum lasted only ten years with its strongest years in the mid-twenties.[53] Between 1915 and 1931 one hundred and forty people, representing all districts of the General Conference plus a number of other Mennonites, registered for courses at the seminary. Its faculty combined the talents of people from both General Conference and "Old" Mennonites. John Ellsworth Hartzler, who served as its President, embodied this hybrid, having left the Presidency of Goshen and Bethel Colleges. Hartzler, a progressive in the Old Mennonites, had long been interested in seminary education.[54]

Other Mennonite groups resisted the modernizing of the ministry. The Old Mennonite Church, the largest of the Mennonite groups in North America, lagged behind the General Conference Mennonites in the development of seminary education. Church leaders worried about the effects that such education would have on the role of the traditional Mennonite minister and on Mennonite life as a whole. Daniel Kauffman, who has been termed the "reigning Bishop" of his time and who served as editor of Mennonite Publishing house in Scottdale, Pennsylvania, stood in staunch opposition to Mennonite seminary education. In 1913 Kauffman noted

> We are not at all enthusiastic over the idea of establishing a Mennonite theological seminary under any circumstances. In fact, we share the conviction of the great body of our people that such an enterprise would be a hindrance rather than a help to the cause for which we stand. If we are to judge from what seminaries have done for other denominations, we may reasonably expect one among us to encourage the removing of ancient landmarks which we hold dear. It would lead to the lowering of the standards of our ministry from a free to hireling basis. It would revolutionize our way (which we believe to be the scriptural way) of calling men to the ministry. It would discourage rather than encourage that kind of humility and spirituality which we believe to be conducive to the greatest good in the spiritual uplift of the

people. Recognizing the fact that the average seminary of today is tainted more or less with that form of "advanced thought" which has properly been termed "thinly veneered infidelity," the thought of the connection [that] there would of necessity be between them and the leadership of our church is not comfortable.[55]

Despite the opposition of such leaders, however, the "Old" Mennonites began providing biblical and theological education through their church colleges in the first half of the twentieth century. In 1934 Goshen College (IN) began offering a Th.B. degree and a decade later established a separate Bible School within the college.[56] In 1946 Goshen College Biblical Seminary became an institution in name as well as fact. In 1938 the "Old" Mennonites also opened a second seminary at Eastern Mennonite College (VA), offering a Th.B. degree.

The Mennonite Brethren also eventually developed programs for Bible and theological training. They offered Th.B. and B.R.E. degrees at Tabor College (KS) and at the Mennonite Brethren Bible College (Winnipeg, Manitoba) and in 1955 established graduate theological education at the Mennonite Brethren Biblical Seminary (Fresno, CA). By the 1960s seminary education and the idea of full-time, paid ministers was becoming an accepted part of Mennonite life although some conferences persisted in their resistance to the idea.

The Brethren in Christ. According to Morris Sider, the history of the Brethren in Christ ministry can be divided into three periods: 1) ca 1780 (their founding) to the mid-1880s; 2) the late 1880s to the 1950s; and 3) the 1950s to the present day.[57] During the first period, their ministerial model conformed rather closely to the Amish/Mennonite model of that time. Ministers were unpaid and did not receive formal training; they had multiple ministers whose appointment was lifelong; and the congregation issued the call to ministry. The Brethren in Christ differed from other Anabaptist groups in the process by which they selected new ministers. Owen Alderfer suggests,

> From the beginning, as far as we know, ministers were chosen by ballot by the Brethren. Origin, Confession of Faith, and Church Government (published in 1901) describes the method of election leading to ordination: the need for a minister is indicated and a planned election is announced. On the given day, appropriate Scriptures are read, a charge is given, and all members vote. Election is based on plurality. A question of majority versus plurality for election had come to the General Conference in 1885, but "majority" was not accepted. In case of a tie, lots were cast to determine who the Lord would choose for office.[58]

Thus, the use of the lot was always more restricted than in Mennonite or Amish practices.

As Sider observes, this model was intended to be consistent with the "Anabaptist hermeneutic" in which members bore a corporate responsibility for determining the meaning of God's Word.[59] Martin Schrag points out that there was an attempt at this time to conform to the notion of a "priesthood of all believers."[60] Sider notes that this first period was influenced heavily by Pietism with its emphasis on the small group, or conventicle, and on personal, individual religiousness. He also points out that the Brethren in Christ were not yet oriented toward having professional evangelists. In fact, with the Mennonites, they shared the concern that full-time professional ministers could be "dangerous." Hirelings would not be, among other things, free to preach the truth but would instead be forced to placate their supporting constituency.

During the second period, a number of things began to change. For one, the call to the ministry shifted from corporate to personal.[61] Again, this shift also occurred in most Mennonite groups although perhaps a little later (e.g., this shift did not begin until the late forties or early fifties for "Old" Mennonites). The Brethren in Christ also developed specialized ministries—evangelistic and missionary—and began to provide formal training for these specialized ministries and congregational ministries as well.[62] This led to the establishment of church schools, such as Messiah College, founded in 1909, and boards that guided the training of persons for the ministry (i.e., the Ministerial and Examining Board was established by the General Conference in 1951; the Ministerial Credential Board was established in 1964; and the Board for Ministry and Doctrine was established in 1984).[63] Schrag notes that Brethren in Christ efforts to establish their own seminary were stymied for a number of reasons (such as the denomination's smallness). Its historical roots in divergent theological traditions made it hard to find a home in the seminaries of other groups.

Since the 1950s, Sider observes, the Brethren in Christ have introduced even more dramatic changes in organization, doctrine, and lifestyle.[64] Again, similar to the Mennonite experience, many ministers are now trained, employed full-time as ministers, and have come to the ministry because of a personal call. These changes have been accompanied by organizational restructuring. In 1957 the Brethren in Christ did away with the traditional functions of the local bishop, who oversaw one or two congregations, with that work being assumed by the pastor, and the single pastor model seemed to gain new legitimacy. Relaxation of rules governing lifestyle have also changed the expectations placed on minister as both model and enforcer.

The Church of the Brethren. From the end of the American Revolution until the mid-1880s, the Brethren went through what has been termed a "wilderness period." Dale Stoffer suggests that this designation refers to both their geographical and cultural location in America.[65] During this time, Brethren migrated into new territories, removing themselves further from the urban centers of the east coast.

During the wilderness period Brethren utilized a "free ministry," a model of church leadership that seemed well-suited to their way of life. As Stoffer describes it,

> Their free church or believer's church pattern included the "free ministry" (unpaid, self-supporting ministers), worship in homes, and lack of formal liturgy. Ministers were elected by the congregation so a church seldom lacked an elder for any more than a brief period of time.[66]

During the early part of the nineteenth century, Brethren congregations operated with two officers: the minister and deacon. They were elected for life (unless removed from office by the congregation). The functions of minister and deacon were not unlike those of the minister and deacon in other Anabaptist groups of the period. Around the middle of the nineteenth century, the Brethren developed a "three-degree ministry." Stoffer describes this ministry as follows:

> On occasion the church would call a promising young man to the ministry of the first degree. His responsibilities included: 1) preaching when given "liberty" by the older ministers, 2) conducting a meeting if none of the elders were available, and 3) preaching at funerals. If he showed himself faithful during this trial period, he was advanced to the second degree. Besides his former duties, he now could 1) make his own "appointments," i.e., arrange to preach at a certain preaching point on a given date, 2) administer baptism, 3) take the counsel of the church concerning the admission of an applicant for baptism if the elder was absent, 4) serve communion in the absence or at the request of an elder, and 5) perform marriage. Upon the faithful execution of these responsibilities, he could then be advanced by the congregation to the third degree or full ministry (only those advanced to this level were ordained with the laying on of hands). The so-called elder or bishop could not only perform all his former prerogatives but also 1) preside at any council meeting whether in his home congregation or in another, 2) give the charge to ministers and deacons in order to install them, 3) serve on the Standing Committee of Yearly Meeting, 4) ordain other elders, and 5) share equal status with all other elders, except where appropriate to defer to elders with seniority.[67]

Stoffer points out that because the elders often traveled between congregations, they provided a social and religious link.

Like the Mennonites, the Brethren have experienced a number of important schisms during their nearly two centuries of existence. During the late 1800s (1881-83), the church experienced a "double schism." Those who were to become The Old German Baptist Brethren felt that the church was innovating too much in response to increasing urbanization and industrialization of American life and tried to protect the old simplicity and fraternity which they feared was disappearing. At the same time progressive elements within the denomination separated, feeling that the mainstream was hopelessly reactionary, and formed the *Brethren Church*. This "double schism" played an important part in the development of ministerial patterns among the Brethren.

What Oberholtzer was to the Mennonite church, Henry R. Holsinger (d. 1905) may have been to the Brethren.[68] Holsinger was born in Pennsylvania, a direct descendent of Alexander Mack. He joined the church in 1855 and entered the ministry in 1866. He was involved in a number of publishing activities and eventually became the publisher of the first weekly periodical devoted to Brethren interests, *The Christian Family Companion*. As Donald Durnbaugh has recently noted, Holsinger was concerned with "sweeping away the rubbish of tradition." Among his plans for specific church reform, Holsinger advocated training for ministers at schools of higher education and regular financial support for ministers.[69] These calls for a trained and supported ministry contributed to the schism within the Brethren.

Opponents to Holsinger's reforms resisted the idea of an educated ministry. An educated ministry, they believed, would in turn lead to ministers who would preach for hire (here a distinction was made between a "paid" ministry and a salaried ministry, the latter being more problematic).[70]

Conservatives were outraged at Holsinger's reforms and the seeming tolerance of the Brethren mainline. At the Annual Meeting of 1880, conservatives demanded that a number of recently permitted innovations, including colleges, Sabbath schools, and supported pastors, be denounced.[71] When the Annual Meeting failed to respond forcefully enough to satisfy these demands, the conservatives were lost. Two years later, Holsinger was disfellowshipped leading to the loss of the progressives in 1883.

Holsinger's push for an educated ministry was realized in 1888 when Ashland College received a new charter. Stoffer, quoting the charter, notes that the school saw the training of Christian ministers to be among its major functions.[72] The progressive Brethren Church pushed ahead on other fronts as well, welcoming women to the ministry by the end of the nineteenth century.[73] Stoffer reports that over twenty women entered the ministry in the last decade of the 1800s and first decade of the 1900s. While surely not a tidal wave, this was in stark contrast to developments in other Anabaptist groups at that time. The more "conservative" Church of the Brethren (the largest Brethren group) accepted salaried pastors and women in the ministry more slowly.

Retaining the Vision in a Credentialed Society

Sociologically speaking, none of this story of the development of Anabaptist ministerial models is all that surprising. That the Amish and Hutterites have been able to preserve ministerial models that conform fairly closely to the expectations of their sixteenth century predecessors is as predictable as the fact that most Mennonites, Brethren in Christ, and Brethren have developed models of ministry that more closely conform to those of mainline Protestantism.

The change in Anabaptist ministerial patterns might well have been anticipated by Max Weber.[74] Weber, one of the so-called "classical" figures in sociology, distinguished between three types of authority—each of which represents a basis upon which the legitimacy of leadership is established. According to Weber, modern society is increasingly characterized by "rational" (or rational-legal) authority. By this, he meant that the legitimacy of one's leadership is actually based on impersonal rules that are legally enacted and contractually established. Weber contrasted this mode of legitimacy with two others. "Traditional" authority, by comparison, is based on the sanctity of tradition. In this case, legitimacy is not to be found in rules but rather in particular people who inherit it or are given it by some higher authority. Rational and traditional authority differ from the third type—charismatic authority—in that the later relies on a legitimacy that is based on the individual's exceptional ethical, heroic, or religious virtue. Each of these types of authority provides a basis for leadership claims, yet each has very different implications for both leader and those who are led. To put the shift in leadership patterns in the various Anabaptist groups into Weberian terms, there has been a movement from traditional to rational-legal authority with seminaries and church bureaucracies playing key roles in the professional training and certification inherent in this process.

Theron Schlabach has suggested that changes called for by the Oberholtzer reform movement in the Mennonite church, including changes in the ministry, reflected this process. Schlabach observes,

> Some of Oberholtzer's reforms are clear examples of what scholars have seen within Western society's process of modernization. According to students of modernization, pre-modern authority is largely personal rather than attached to constitutional systems and documents, except perhaps to some ancient and sacred documents which personal authorities then guard and interpret. Also, traditional authority lies with persons more than with the offices they hold. Modern authority, by contrast, is precisely as Oberholtzer was demanding. It is "rationalized"—that is, formally defined, deliberately spelled out, limited by constitution, and not left to personal discretion. It rests on documents, such as constitutions and minutes.[75]

As Weber anticipated, modern authority has also come to rely on another sort of document: credentials. So much is this the case that some cultural critics, such as Randall Collins, complain that modern society has become a "credentialed society."[76]

What can be said of Oberholtzer can also be said of changes introduced among the Brethren in Christ during their second and third ministerial periods and of Holsinger's reforms among the Brethren. Of course, in the final analysis even the most conservative elements within each of these groups has accommodated to the pressures toward modernization.

The sociological point would be that these different conceptions of authority are not merely randomly distributed in populations but rather can be predicted. What Peter Berger has called "carriers" of modernization seem to precipitate the shifts in authority patterns.[77] Among these carriers, we would certainly include industrialization, urbanization, bureaucratization, the growth of mass media, and education. To the extent that Anabaptist groups have contacted and participated in these carriers, their claims to authority have, by necessity, shifted.

Sider, speaking of developments among the Brethren in Christ, notes that the professionalization of the ministry was an inevitable outgrowth of the professionalization of the membership.[78] When congregations consisted mostly of farmers, an untrained ministry was acceptable, but as members moved in increasing numbers into business and the professions, their expectations for ministers inflated. But again, this could be said of the Mennonites and Brethren as well. Only the Amish and the Hutterites have successfully resisted the influences of modernization and have retained non-rational authority structures.

For groups like the Brethren in Christ, the forces of modernization have been compounded by the influence of other theological traditions that emphasize ideas in seeming contradiction to the Anabaptist themes discussed earlier. Owen Alderfer, for example, has pointed out the "burden" of Anabaptism for the Brethren in Christ.[79] Alderfer notes that whereas their evangelical tradition stresses individualism, Anabaptism stresses community, and inasmuch as evangelicals have used the organizational models of business, Anabaptism is built on notions of brotherhood. Such differences in theological orientation have led to tensions within the Brethren in Christ conception of the ministry and are not easily reconciled.

From the standpoint of the various Anabaptist groups that have "modernized" their ministerial models, such sociological reasoning provides little consolation. Even those who are sympathetic and even promoters of various aspects of the new professional ministerial models have expressed concerns. When all is said and done, these concerns emerge from apparent contradictions between the Anabaptist premises upon which traditional conceptions of the ministry were founded and the logic of the modern world.

Among Mennonites, by way of some examples, J. Lawrence Burkholder has questioned whether it is indeed possible to hold onto the traditional Mennonite tenets of lay responsibility, lay initiative, "brotherhood," the "priesthood of all believers," and the "preacherhood of all believers" in the face of an emerging professionalized ministry.[80] Leland Harder maintains that the new leadership model has created tendencies toward inhumane hiring and recall policies that seem antithetical to Mennonite church teachings.[81] Menno Epp believes that the single pastor model has increased the pressure felt by ministers.[82] He argues that congregations develop heightened and unrealistic expectations for their professionally trained pastors, leading them to exit the ministry altogether. As I suggested at the outset, these complaints all spring from the fundamental tension that exists between the idea of a professionalized clergy and the three themes of Anabaptism discussed earlier.

Mennonites are not alone in their concern with new ministerial forms. Sider has cautioned that the pragmatic accommodation of bureaucratic forms and increased professionalization has created a threat that the Brethren in Christ are "in the danger of being like everyone else."[83] If this happens, Sider queries, "is there any justification for the existence of the Brethren in Christ Church?" Furthermore, Sider, like Epp, wonders if the new model of ministry has not created greater tensions between pastor and congregation. Schrag asserts that the centralization of congregational decision making in the hands of pastors and church boards has taken away responsibility from the congregation, especially in the choosing of ministers, thereby threatening the fashioning of a common life, a "community body life."[84] Luke Keefer has cautioned that the single pastor model can be harmful to congregational life, arguing that "power vacuums tempt aggressive personalities to try to grasp the reins of a congregation" (although Keefer believes careful credentialing may reduce this risk).[85]

These concerns with the modern ministerial model share something in common with the concern that Anabaptists have always had about leadership within the tradition. Since the sixteenth century, those connected with the Anabaptist movement have sought ministerial models that were true to its biblical orientation, its emphasis on the community of believers, and its commitment to yielding self to some greater authority. This was true in the sixteenth century, and it continues to be true as we near the close of the twentieth century. As we move into the twenty-first century, the challenge will undoubtedly remain much the same.

With each passing generation, the search for appropriate ministerial models becomes, in some ways, more and more complicated as today's "cutting edge" is tomorrow's "heritage." Already today, many Anabaptists struggle with the single pastor "tradition," a radical idea earlier in this century. Of one thing we can be certain: tomorrow's Anabaptists will feel compelled to make sense of their heritage, too, but their heritage will be somewhat different from the one we consider today. Theirs will include not only the three-fold lay ministerial model and the "traditions" of single, professional ministries but will include shared leadership models and the like as well.

[1] The author would like to acknowledge the support of the Lilly Endowment (Grant #900760).

[2] Among other publications aimed at assisting Mennonites during this period was a book entitled *Mennonite Community Sourcebook*, edited by Esko Loewen. Lowen's book tried to help Mennonites become aware of the resources for preserving and fostering rural life. A chapter by Ralph Hernley which appeared in Lowen's book, entitled "Community Life," pointed to the trends causing disintegration of community life: materialism, urbanization, industrialization, secularization, modern education, communication, and transportation.

[3] Michael Yoder, "Rural Life," *Mennonite Encyclopedia* (Scottdale, Pa.: Herald Press, 1990), V, 778.

[4] See James Davison Hunter's review of the importance of "culture elites" in his *Culture Wars* (New York: Basic Books, 1991).

[5] C. Henry Smith, *Smith's Story of the Mennonites*, fifth edition revised and enlarged by Cornelius Krahn (Newton, Kan.: Faith and Life Press, 1981), 15.

[6] Harold Bender, "A Brief Biography of Menno Simons," in Menno Simons, *The Complete Works of Menno Simons* (Scottdale, Pa.: Mennonite Publishing House, 1956), 4.

[7] Simons, *Complete Works*, 163.

[8] Menno Simons, "Reply to Gellius Faber," ibid., 625-781. The actual title in the original was "A Plain Reply to a Publication by Gellius Faber, Minister at Emden, Which in 1552 (if I do not mistake) He, Sad to Say, Put to Press to the Disgrace of the Pious Children of God, to the Increase of their Cross, to the Ensnarement of the Simple, and to the Comfort and Strengthening of the Impertinent."

[9] Ibid., 649.

[10] Russell Mast, "Menno Simons Speaks Concerning the Ministry," *Mennonite Quarterly Review* 54 (April 1988): 106-16. Mast insists that Simons did not have in mind the "priesthood of all believers" here but saw the ministry as separate, with special talents that not all members could possibly share.

[11] Simons, "Reply to Gellius Faber," 665.

[12] Menno Simons, "Foundation of the Christian Doctrine," *Complete Works*, 165.

[13] In *Smith's Story of the Mennonites*, 28., C. Henry Smith discusses the chiliastic tendency among early Anabaptists.

[14] N. van der Zipp, "Ministry (Netherlands)," *Mennonite Encyclopedia*, III, 699.

[15] Van der Zipp discusses the differences that emerged; see 700-1.

[16] Harold S. Bender, "Ministry in Switzerland, South Germany, France and North American Groups of This General Background," *Mennonite Encyclopedia*, III, 703.

[17] I have noted elsewhere that some of these themes are important to understanding the difficulty that Anabaptists have with the concept of power, but they are equally important to understanding the uniqueness of the Anabaptist ministry (in large part because the role of the minister and issues of power converge). Stephen C. Ainlay, "Mennonite Culture Wars: Power, Knowledge, and Cultural Elites," a paper presented at the Elizabethtown College Conference on Power: Its Use and Misuse in Anabaptist, Mennonite, and Brethren Communities, Elizabethtown, Pa. July 1993.

[18] Cornelius Dyck, *An Introduction to Mennonite History* (Scottdale, Pa.: Herald Press, 1981), 136.

[19] Smith, *Smith's Story of the Mennonites*, 4.

[20] Harold Bender, "A Brief Biography of Menno Simons," 6.

[21] Simons, "Foundations of Christian Doctrine," 160.

[22] Harold Bender, "The Anabaptist Vision," ed. Guy Hershberger, *The Recovery of the Anabaptist Vision* (Scottdale, Pa.: Herald Press, 1957), 41.

[23] Calvin Redekop, *Mennonite Society* (Baltimore: Johns Hopkins University Press, 1989), 65.

[24] Mast, "Menno Simons Speaks."

[25] Harold S. Bender, "The Church," *Mennonite Encyclopedia*, I, 594.

[26] Ibid., 597.

[27] Don Kraybill notes that while Gelassenheit is an abstract concept, it has specific meaning for groups like the Amish. He observes, Gelassenheit "carries a variety of specific meanings: self-surrender, resignation to God's will, yielding to God and others, self-denial, contentment, a calm spirit. Various words in the Amish vocabulary capture the practical dimensions of Gelassenheit: obedience, humility, submission, thrift, and simplicity." See Donald Kraybill, *The Riddle of Amish Culture* (Baltimore: Johns Hopkins University Press, 1989), 25. Kraybill goes on to note that for the Amish, "yielding the right way, God's way" has implications for all levels of experience: personality, values, symbols, structure, and ritual, (26). Similarly, the notion of self-surrender is central to the Hutterite understanding. John

Hostetler and Gertrude Huntington note that "self-surrender, not self-development, is the Hutterite goal. The communal will, not the individual will, becomes important. The good of the majority governs the stages of life from birth to death." See John Hostetler and Gertrude Huntington, *The Hutterites in North America* (New York: Holt, Rinehart, and Winston, 1967). For other Anabaptist groups, the effects of Gelassenheit on the external signs of life may not be as evident as it is for the Amish and Hutterites but it is still powerful. Calvin Redekop, in his book, *Mennonite Society*, insists that it remains very important to understanding Mennonite life today.

28 Robert Friedmann, "Gelassenheit," *Mennonite Encyclopedia*, II, 448. Friedmann notes that Pietism gave Gelassenheit a somewhat more mystical quality, suggesting the goal of "unperturbed calmness of the soul."

29 Calvin Redekop argues that the fact that the *Martyr's Mirror* occupied such a place of central importance in Mennonite families for centuries points to the continued importance of the concept (92). Robert Friedmann, however, concluded his entry on Gelassenheit in the *Mennonite Encyclopedia* by noting that "present-day Mennonitism [he was writing in 1956] has lost the idea of Gelassenheit nearly completely; yet with the recovery of the ideal of discipleship also Gelassenheit may be revived" (449).

30 Theron Schlabach, *Peace, Faith, Nation: Mennonites and Amish in Nineteenth-Century America* (Scottdale, Pa.: Herald Press, 1988), 29.

31 Ibid., 96.

32 John Hostetler, *Amish Society* (Baltimore: Johns Hopkins University Press, 1980, third ed.), 108.

33 See Donald Kraybill's discussion of the three positions in Kraybill, *The Riddle of Amish Culture*, 79 ff. Hostetler also details these positions in *Amish Society*, 109.

34 Kraybill, *The Riddle of Amish Culture*, 110.

35 Ibid.

36 Ibid.

37 Hostetler, *Amish Society*, 113.

38 Hostetler and Huntington, *The Hutterites in North America*, 3; see also John Hostetler, *Hutterite Society* (Baltimore: Johns Hopkins University Press, 1974); and John W. Bennett, *Hutterian Brethren* (Stanford, Ca.: Stanford University Press, 1967).

39 They are part of a concil of five to seven men. The first and second preachers together with the holdholder, field manager, German school teacher, and one or two other men hold these key positions. Hostetler and Huntington, *Hutterites in North America*, 27.

40 Ibid., 28.

41 Ibid., 34.

42 For a brief review see *Leadership and Authority in the Life of the Church, A Summary Statement* (Scottdale, Pa.: Mennonite Publishing House, 1982). This statement was adopted by the Mennonite Church General Assembly held at Bowling Green, Ohio, August 11-16, 1981.

43 Richard MacMaster, *Land Piety, and Peoplehood: The Establishment of Mennonite Communities in America 1683-1790* (Scottdale, Pa.: Herald Press, 1985), 200.

44 Ibid., 196-7.

45 Ibid., 199.

46 Ibid., 198.

47 Schlabach, *Peace, Faith, and Nation*, 224.

48 Ibid., 118 ff.

49 Ibid., 120.

50 Ibid., 128.

51 Ibid., 132.

52 See ibid. on the mythical quality of Wadsworth, 135.

53 Samuel Floyd Pannabecker, *Ventures of Faith: The Story of Mennonite Biblical Seminary* (Elkhart, Ind.: Mennonite Biblical Seminary, 1975).

54 See Stephen Ainlay, "The 1920 Seminary Movement: A Failed Attempt at Formal Theological Education in the Mennonite Church," *Mennonite Quarterly Review* 64 (October 1990): 325-51.

55 Daniel Kauffman, "A Proposed Union Seminary," *Gospel Herald*, (July 24, 1913): 257-9.

56 See John Umble, *Goshen College: 1894-1954* (Scottdale, Pa.: Mennonite Publishing House, 1955).

57 E. Morris Sider, "History of Ministry in the Brethren in Christ Church," *Brethren in Christ History and Life* (April 1992): 81-9. See also Martin Schrag, "A Response to 'History of Ministry in the Brethren in Christ Church," *Brethren in Christ History and Life* (April 1992):

90-5; Owen Alderfer, "Ministry in Brethren in Christ History," ed. E. Morris Sider, *We Have This Ministry: Pastoral Theory and Practice in the Brethren in Christ Church* (Nappanee, Ind.: Evangel Press, 1991), 61-81.

[58] Alderfer, "Ministry in Brethren in Christ History," 63.

[59] Sider, "History of Ministry in the Brethren in Christ Church," 82.

[60] Schrag, "A Response to 'History of Ministry in the Brethren in Christ Church'," *Brethren in Christ History and Life* (April, 1992): 91.

[61] Alderfer, "Ministry in Brethren in Christ History," 70.

[62] Sider, "History of Ministry in the Brethren in Christ Church." Again, the Mennonites seem to have had a parallel development here. The training of missionaries was an acceptable idea far earlier than the training of people serving home congregations. Likewise, one could acknowledge a personal call to the mission field far earlier than one could acknowledge a personal call to serve as a congregational minister. This has been emerging as a clear distinction in my own interviews with people who graduated from Goshen College Biblical Seminary between the years 1934-1954. See additional discussion of the Brethren in Christ search for appropriate educational opportunities for the ministry in Carleton O. Wittlinger's *Quest for Piety and Obedience: The Story of the Brethren in Christ* (Nappanee, Ind.: Evangel Press, 1978), 433-40.

[63] Schrag, "Response to 'History of Ministry'," 91

[64] Sider, "History of Ministry in the Brethren in Christ Church."

[65] Dale Stoffer, *Background and Development of Brethren Doctrines, 1650-1987* (Philadelphia: Brethren Encyclopedia, Inc., 1989), 99.

[66] Ibid.

[67] Ibid., 102.

[68] Donald Durnbaugh has pointed out this comparison. He also likens aspects of Holsinger's approach to John Funk, especially his role in publishing. See Donald F. Durnbaugh, "Henry R. Holsinger: Individual Defiance of Institutional Authority in the Late 19th Century," paper presented at the Conference on Power: Its Use and Abuse in Anabaptist, Mennonite, and Brethren Communities, Elizabethtown, Pa., July 1993. See also Stoffer, *Background and Development of Brethren Doctrines*, 133ff.

[69] Durnbaugh, "Henry R. Holsinger," 5.

[70] Stoffer, *Background and Development of Brethren Doctrines*, 134.

[71] Durnbaugh, "Henry R. Holsinger," 14.

[72] Stoffer, *Background and Development of Brethren Doctrines*, 136.

[73] Ibid., 170.

[74] Max Weber, *Theory of Social and Economic Organization*, ed. Talcott Parsons (Glencoe, Ill.: Free Press, 1947).

[75] Schlabach, *Peace, Faith, and Nation*, 123.

[76] Randall Collins, *The Credentialed Society* (New York: Academic Press, 1977).

[77] Peter Berger, Brigette Berger, and Hansfried Kellner, *The Homeless Mind* (New York: Basic Books, 1973).

[78] Sider, "History of Ministry in the Brethren in Christ Church."

[79] Owen Alderfer, "Anabaptism as a 'Burden' for the Brethren in Christ," eds. Terry Brensigher and E. Morris Sider, *Within the Perfection of Christ* (Nappanee, Ind.: Evangel Press and Brethren in Christ Historical Society, 1990). For a discussion of the theological influences on the Brethren in Christ notion of the ministry, see Martin Schrag.

[80] J. Lawrence Burkholder, "Theological Education for the Believer's Church," *Concern* 17 (1969): 10-32.

[81] Leland Harder, *The Pastor-People Relationship* (Elkhart, Ind: The Institute of Mennonite Studies, 1983).

[82] Menno Epp, *The Pastor's Exit* (Winnipeg, Canada: Canadian Mennonite Biblical College Publications, 1984).

[83] Sider, "History of Ministry in the Brethren in Christ Church."

[84] Schrag, "Response to 'History of Ministry'," 91.

[85] Luke Keefer, "The Training and Credentialling of Ministers," ed. E. Morris Sider, *We Have This Ministry: Pastoral Theory and Practice in the Brethren in Christ Church* (Nappanee, Ind.: Evangel Press, 1991): 140-55.

2
Anabaptist Ministry

by E. Morris Sider

Stephen Ainlay describes several basic elements of the historic Anabaptist ministry and has shown that over the course of years diversity developed in the practice of this ministry, the extent of diversity depending on the group involved. The situation is similar when we attempt to identify what the present and future ministry of Anabaptist-related groups should be.

I wish to begin to examine the subject by describing the ministry of my father. His ministry, covering the years from the late 1920s to the late 1950s, retained much of the character of the historic Anabaptist ministry. Then I want to determine why modifications to this kind of ministry occurred and to ask whether a ministry such as that of my father is possible, even desirable, for the future. Finally, I shall make a few suggestions for preserving elements of the historic Anabaptist ministry. In doing so, I shall be raising more questions than answers, but in discussing the questions we may work together toward the answers—in good Anabaptist fashion.

My father, Earl Sider, grew up in Ontario, Canada, in a home of much piety. Family worship, Bible reading, prayer at both the beginning and the end of meals, and more were part of the family's daily routine. So was singing; in the summer the parents and their six children frequently gathered on the porch of their house to sing, and neighbors would sit on their porches to hear them.

Given such a family background, it is not strange that eventually all the children would be active in some phase of Christian service, including my father. He attended Messiah College (then more a Bible school than a college), where he was among the school's first students. My mother also attended the college at the same time. Shortly after their graduation they married and returned to live on my father's home place, where they helped with the farming and prepared to take over a 100-acre farm which had been given to my father by his parents while he was still a child.

Meanwhile a small congregation made up of farmers had begun near the small village of Cheapside, some thirty miles to the west. For several years ministers from neighboring congregations took turns preaching in the Sunday services held in the homes of the members. Eventually the congregation requested a permanent pastor to live among them.

They chose my father. He was well known to them; in fact, he was related to several of the members. They and others in the congregation had associated with him in church activities such as love feasts, Bible conferences, and district and provincial council meetings. Thus, when the congregation looked for a pastor, they chose someone essentially from their own number in an Anabaptist version of the call to pastoral leadership.

My father accepted the call; he would have considered rejection a failure of Christian duty. He and Mother loaded their possessions and their first child, my sister (then a baby), onto a wagon on a rainy day and rode behind horses to their new home in the West.

With no income or savings, their choice of housing was necessarily limited. Certainly the first house they lived in was below the average level of their parishioners. A farmer in the community (not a member of the congregation) offered them an old house, recently used to raise turkeys, at a low rent. Together with one of my aunts, my parents scrubbed the house, put on paint and new paper, and settled in for their first years of ministry.

For an income my father did what his parishioners did—manual labor. For the first few years he hired out to farmers, some of whom were his parishioners, as a day laborer. Later he became a painter and later still also a farmer. He taught both trades to his three sons. The hardest work I have ever done was to tar the large roofs of high, hip-roof Ontario barns—alongside my father—using a six-inch brush on hot days so that the tar would spread well.

My father worked at such manual labor all his life. He never received a salary as minister, and, of course, never had the benefit at retirement of a denominational pension plan (that came into effect the year following his retirement). Occasionally he received a so-called love offering from the congregation, but even as a child I was more impressed by the smallness than by the love of the offerings.

Again, we can see in my father's ministry a version of historic Anabaptist ministry, namely, the bi-vocational ministry, in which he lived among the people, worked with his hands as they did, and lived on their income level. In short, he identified with his people in virtually every possible way.

He also conducted the services of the congregation according to another element of Anabaptism with significant participation by the laity. The mid-week prayer meetings were always held on a rotating basis in the homes of members (cottage prayer meetings we named them). Services on Sunday included much congregational singing and the giving of testimonies, or experiences, as they were often called. Members frequently read the Scriptures and offered extemporaneous prayers. My father provided leadership, but it was minimized by the active role of members in the life and services of the congregation.

In all of this, my father had a highly effective ministry. One measure of its effectiveness was the relatively large number of young people sitting under his ministry who eventually went into some kind of church or service ministry as pastors, church college professors, missionaries, medical people, church leaders (including the present moderator of the Brethren in Christ Church), a Mennonite

Central Committee administrator, and more. This despite the fact that the congregation remained relatively small.

His effectiveness was, I think, in part because he identified closely with his people, as I have suggested. It was also effective because he pastored out of a heart of great love, which I like to think is also part of historic Anabaptist ministry. He even loved those who gave him the most difficulty; he was prepared to remain—over many years—to work with them and to make them better people. Once, in teenage exasperation, I asked Daddy why he didn't call in the bishop of the district to "silence" those difficult people. His reply was, "Morris, I can't do that. I love them."

There was, finally, a community counterpart to my father's ministry to the congregation. In his occupation as a painter, he did business with the people of the Cheapside area virtually on a daily basis. In doing business he did pastoral work at the same time. In those days in the rural communities of Ontario, a person received the noon meal from his or her employer. Working with my father, I ate with him at the table of these community people; even as a young person I was fascinated by how he ended the conversation during the meals on some kind of spiritual note.

This meant that in time he became something of a community pastor, conducting marriages and funerals for people outside the congregation and, especially following retirement, preaching in the pulpits of other denominations. An elderly, non-church couple told me this summer that years ago when their first child died, my father left his painting as soon as he heard the news to come to be with them in their sorrow and that he conducted the funeral without charge.

I have recently been putting together some stories about my father's effective ministry in the community. Perhaps my favorite is the story about his painting the large roof of a barn for a farmer who lived about eight miles from our house. Unfortunately, for some reason the paint came off the roof too soon. The owner was angry. He came to our place to demand that Daddy do something about this disaster. My father's response was to get more paint and to repaint the roof without charge. The instructive sequel to the story came some time later, following the death of the owner. His son came to our house after the funeral to tell Daddy that his father had become a Christian before he died and that this happened because of my father's conduct in repainting the roof.

So what I have been trying to say through the story of my father is that the vision that was historically Anabaptist relative to the ministry could result in a highly effective ministry. Through this example we can, I hope, better visualize how an earlier model worked and use it as a point of comparison for what follows.

Now an important question to consider is whether this model, as good and as effective as it surely was for my father, is a viable model for today and in the future. Again I must state what will become obvious, namely, that I have more questions and observations than definitive answers.

From where I stand—in the Brethren in Christ Church—the answer to the question that I have raised seems for many people to be that the historic form of ministry is no longer effective, or at least is less effective for most situations. I suggest that there are some reasons for this response, most of them obvious.

One of the reasons is the changing concept of pastoral leadership. And, one of the reasons for this change is the model now frequently used for leadership. Congregations have been in the process, I suggest, of changing leadership from a model based on community and the pastor being part of the community to a model based more on corporate business structures. This, it seems to me, has all sorts of implications for the ministry.

It is no accident that such a change has been occurring. In earlier years, congregations were rural and agriculturally based, as was my father's congregation. In such situations, community is (or at least was) the almost natural mode for various aspects of life. For traditional Anabaptists the scriptural basis for church community was surely supported, in a sociological sense, by the rural setting.

But, times have changed in this as in most other ways. Anabaptists have ceased, along with the rest of Canada and the United States, to be mainly rural people. Instead they have moved off their farms, and in so doing many have become business and professional people. Frequently the laity who exert strong influence in congregations come from such people, who bring with them, consciously or unconsciously, a view of the presumably more efficient leadership modeled by business and the professions. Such a model, of course, has implications for all church life, certainly for the ministry.

One of the obvious consequences is the promotion of a professional ministry. Business and professional members understandably want their counterpart as ministers. My observation is that even non-professional and non-business members often prefer a person well-trained and performing in a professional manner. Thus, a professional pastor is brought to the congregation, perhaps without its having a direct voice in the choice, as is increasingly the case among Brethren in Christ.

And, of course, the professional pastor is supposed to earn his money by doing what he was hired to do, to lead. A sense of following rather than participating on the part of the congregation frequently results. Such a tendency is accentuated by seminars and other programs, sometimes conducted by so-called experts outside our Anabaptist-related groups, that declare that the pastor has the vision and must do what is necessary to have that vision fulfilled. I have even heard it said in Brethren in Christ circles that the minister should be seen as a sort of chief executive officer (CEO). We have, with this attitude, moved a considerable distance from the kind of pastoring done by my father, from an Anabaptist approach to the ministry to more of a Calvinist concept that images a strong pastor model.

An extension of this development is the professionalization of the church program, including the services. A professional pastor understandably will want to have a professional program. But the degree to which the program becomes professionalized will likely correspond to the degree to which participation by members is minimized. An illustration may be found even in music. A professional pastor and his or her professional congregation will want to have good music, which often means "special singing" by a music group or choir. A study which I have begun of Brethren in Christ church bulletins dating from the 1940s (when congregations began to use bulletins, undoubtedly a sign in itself of an increasingly professional approach to worship) shows what we could conclude even without the research: the number of songs or hymns sung by the congregation (audience participation) declines in proportion to the amount of special singing in a given service.

A concern to extend outreach also has the potential to move Anabaptists away from the historic model of the ministry. (Here again, I argue from my Brethren in Christ experience, but I think I detect the same tendency, if not so vigorously pursued, in other Anabaptist-related groups.) What I hear goes something like this: if what Anabaptists have is so good, surely they should be persuading others to accept what they have. One may name this as one wishes, but basically it is a call to evangelism. So far, so good; we can, and indeed should, agree to this proposition because, as we know, evangelism was part of early Anabaptism as well as Pietism.

But, I sense that often the conviction is that present church life, including the ministry, is not up to this task. The historic forms, it is thought, emphasize maintaining the group rather than pursuing an aggressive evangelism that goes out into the highways and byways to compel people to come to the Anabaptist feast. I suppose there is a certain historical explanation to this maintenance mode; the long years of persecution, of being the quiet in the land, of being different and separated—all promoted maintenance rather than aggressive expansion.

But, the thinking goes, evangelism in our diverse culture needs to be more aggressive, more flexible, and look less like Anabaptism if it is to be effective. The danger of this thinking to historic Anabaptist ministry is that in moving to this style of evangelism, the methods and organizations of other non-Anabaptist groups will be copied, including the role and methods of the ministry. That may not be bad, but it may not be the historic Anabaptist mode.

Finally, a third contextual problem for an Anabaptist-style ministry is individualism (that sounds almost like a truism). We are all well aware that society is highly individualistic, in some contrast to earlier years when the natural bent of Americans to individualism was softened by the need for agricultural people to cooperate in many aspects of their work. Such individualism, caught from the surrounding culture, has clearly increased in Anabaptist circles (certainly it has in mine) as they have moved away from their agricultural backgrounds. Where the world has its Yuppies, the Mennonites, according to Emerson Lesher, have their Muppies.

This, I think, has significant implications for the ministry. Among the implications is the likelihood that the pastor will be less willing to take a small salary—let alone no salary—or remain with the congregation to work through difficulties, as my father did in his ministry of thirty-one years. Instead, because it is personally advantageous, he or she may leave for greener or more comfortable pastoral fields. In this I am reminded of the minister who, when he accepted a call from a large congregation, made it clear that he would leave at the first sign of trouble; he would not put up with any nonsense. Conversely, not infrequently the laity, when they consider that their individual tastes or needs are not being met, leave for another congregation or perhaps even denomination. That, of course, has other kinds of implications for the pastor.

Given these situations and problems, can we retain the historic Anabaptist model of ministry? Or should we be realistic and acknowledge, with William Wordsworth, that our times are too much with us, thus we should be looking for other, more effective, more comfortable models? I have no definitive answer to that question. What I do have are a few observations—most in the form of further questions—that bear on the issue.

First, how much of the historic Anabaptist-style ministry is actually scriptural, and how much of it is mainly cultural and historically conditioned? Stephen Ainlay in the preceding paper suggests that there are historical reasons why the ministry took the shape that it did even before modern times. And, of course, we recognize that much of what we do and how we think on other levels is culturally conditioned. Thus, should Anabaptists not make some greater effort to determine what is in fact scriptural about their ministry and hold to that, while being willing to lay aside what is cultural and thus perhaps out of date? There is, after all, no one clear church polity laid out in Scripture; in the Bible, one may find congregational, presbyterial, and episcopal tendencies if one looks for one's favorite polity.

Second, and relatedly, how much should pragmatic considerations govern our form of ministry? Again, one may argue that a certain pragmatism necessarily governed the early shape of Anabaptist ministry. There may have been no other choice than the maintenance mode. Should modern Anabaptists allow the same reasoning for themselves? The reasons for a maintenance mode at the very least are less strong now than earlier. Reaching people and nurturing them is, after all, what we are about. If this requires some shifts from the historic approach, is it not a point of Scripture, also of wisdom, to make such shifts?

Third, and somewhat conversely, should we not be saying that there is much in the historic ministerial practice that is sound, and thus worthy of preserving? Let me illustrate by reference to the so-called Baby Boomers. I hear much talk in my circles about the future of the church being with the Baby Boomers, thus we must adjust our program, including the ministry, to what they want. What they want, however, are quick decisions, greater individualism, and the kind of leadership in the church that they know in their world of work. But, our historic thinking, which we shall all agree has scriptural support, is that

Christians should not necessarily have all that they want. Perhaps precisely what Baby Boomers need is what they do not get in the world, including Christian community and servant leadership from the ministry. The historic position in such matters may be a good corrective.

And fourth, is there not some merit in a variety of styles of ministry within an Anabaptist framework? Stephen Ainlay has shown already that Anabaptists have various versions. Could we agree that from group to group, within groups, and according to locality and situation, there exists a variety of workable models built on the historic approach to ministry?

I like to think, for example, that there is still room for the kind modeled by my father: bi-vocational, close identity with the people, and long-term commitment to the congregation. But, other congregations that are larger and less rural, with members who are professionals and business persons, may very well require an adaptation of that model. I'd like to see a variety of models encouraged by seminaries and church leadership, including the more traditional models that now seem to be tender vines on the Anabaptist branches.

The overriding concern, I suggest, should be how well Anabaptists maintain the concept of the priesthood of believers and its concomitant Anabaptist emphasis on the community of believers. Professionalizing the ministry has the potential to move them in an opposite direction. While I doubt that for most groups this trend will be reversed in the near future, there are ways in which the trend may be minimized and thus a greater sense of community developed.

One way is to make greater use of the lay ministry. Congregations and pastors should discern and call persons from among them who could serve in meaningful ways, including preaching. In the same sense, they should encourage those who on their own initiative are led to serve in leadership roles in the congregation.

Relatedly, as Martin Schrag, a colleague of mine at Messiah College, now retired, has said over the years, community is promoted by common interests. His point is that by taking up causes or activities on which all—laity and pastors—can work together on a relatively equal footing, professionalization of the ministry can be minimized.

A further way of promoting congregational community is for the pastor to de-emphasize her or his central role. Eugene Peterson tells about the great release he felt and what a blessing it was to his ministry when he discovered that he did not need to be the chairman of every committee in his congregation. Indeed, he did not need to be on any committee at all; the work of the congregation could be done just as well by the laity, and he could be a better pastor by having more opportunity to develop the spiritual side of his ministry. Such action would surely go some distance in minimizing the growing tendency of congregations and our various groups toward the centralization of authority, which is inimical to our historic beliefs about the ministry in particular and church polity in general.

Perhaps in the end the most important factor in promoting a style of ministry with Anabaptist overtones is the frame of reference out of which the minister works. If it is out of an Anabaptist mindset, the ministry is more likely to develop in that tradition. Even a professional ministry need not stand outside the tradition; indeed, professional pastors, given the mindset, may very well all the better be able to recognize and appreciate the gifts of the people in their congregations and to engage their parishioners with them in the work of the church. Such professional pastors may be among the best prepared to model for their people the thinking, lifestyle, and kingdom activity that is the historic tradition. The ongoing task of Anabaptist groups is to instill such a mindset into their present and future pastors.

> Thus saith the Lord, Stand ye in the ways and see, and ask for the old paths, where is the good way, and walk therein, and ye shall find rest for your souls. (Jer. 6:16)

Conversation
ഇൽ X ൝യ

Yieldedness
& Accountability

Donald B. Kraybill and Fred Benedict examine the rhythm of traditional Anabaptism: Gelassenheit, or yieldedness. Kraybill's description of this tradition emphasizes its pervasive influence on daily life, governing speech, demeanor, dress, and worship style. Participation in the community takes priority over personal needs and individual expressions. Fellowships that practice yieldedness expect members to defer to community traditions and collective wisdom. Meekness and patience are prized—worshippers, for example, sing hymns slowly to show that they wait on God rather than demanding immediate divine action.

Fred Benedict, from his Old Order perspective, delivers a gentle but powerful affirmation of yieldedness and accountability, which he calls the "Anabaptist spirit." Like Kraybill, he concludes that yieldedness forms the heart of the Anabaptist tradition. He links yieldedness with separation from the larger society and exhorts modern Anabaptists to remain separate from its pulsing cadence. The more faithful believers are to Jesus' teachings, declares Benedict, "the more uncomfortable" they are in their worldly surroundings. He therefore calls for resistance to modernity and a "conscious adoption of a pre-modern mindset."

1

Yieldedness and Accountability in Traditional Anabaptist Communities

by Donald B. Kraybill

Gelassenheit: Giving Up and Giving In

In many ways this discussion of yieldedness and accountability summarizes some of the themes in earlier presentations in this volume. In the allotted space it is impossible to trace in detail the various manifestations of yieldedness in historic Anabaptist communities as well as those that persist in Old Order communities today. Rather than focusing on a specific historical period or dealing in depth with a particular community, I will offer an interpretative framework for understanding the importance of yieldedness in the Anabaptist tradition. I will occasionally present samples or traces of yieldedness from the historical sources, but the thorough and meticulous job of documenting this ubiquitous theme in the original sources will need to be left to others. I propose that the theme of yieldedness was a pervasive and shared theme in the social, cultural, and religious experience of all Anabaptist related groups.[1] It of course also appears, perhaps in other guises, in other religious traditions as well.

The notion of yieldedness is rooted in the German word *Gelassenheit*. The word is rarely found in the writings or on the lips of the religious offspring of the Anabaptists in recent centuries. It was used at times by early Anabaptists and is most widely found in the Hutterite source materials.[2] Although not formally used by many Anabaptist groups, the meaning of Gelassenheit was woven into the social fabric of their communities. Gelassenheit is pregnant with many meanings but suggests a sense of yieldedness or submission to a higher authority. It also carries a variety of specific meanings, including self surrender, resignation to God's will, yielding to God and others, self denial, a calm spirit, contentment, and an acceptance of the "giveness" of one's circumstances.[3]

In the words of Peter Walpot written in 1571, may God

grant you and all who seek it the grace to deny your selfwill, your flesh and your life and bring your reason captive into the obedience of Christ. Then you will not run in uncertainty or fight as one who merely thrashes in the air. You will discipline your body, bringing it into true submission, and, through selfrestraint, enter in at the narrow gate and walk the narrow path leading to life. But men are tested in the furnace of Gelassenheit as gold is tested by fire which in due time will test and purify everything.[4]

Following Cronk,[5] who has done the seminal work on Gelassenheit, we can conceptualize it along two dimensions—religious and social—both of which entail internal and external dimensions. Medieval mystics talked of internal submission to God's will. The Anabaptists talked of giving themselves up to God's will. This internal spiritual struggle was an attempt to lay aside selfish ambitions and devote oneself wholly unto God. But for the Anabaptists the struggle was not merely an internal spiritual one, it also had external consequences. The notion of discipleship, so central to Anabaptist understandings of Christian faith, meant following the way of Jesus in daily life regardless of the consequences, which might include suffering and persecution.[6] Indeed, the martyr's death was the paradigmatic expression of Gelassenheit in which one completely gave oneself up to God's will. In the words of one martyr, Michael Sattler, "Christians are fully yielded and have placed their trust in their Father in heaven without any outward or worldly arms."[7] Such self abandonment for the sake of God's kingdom was at the heart of the notion of Gelassenheit.

But, as Cronk has demonstrated, Gelassenheit was not only a spiritual attitude or personal willingness to abandon one's life for the sake of the kingdom; it was embodied in the ritual and symbolism of congregational and community life. In other words, Gelassenheit entailed not only giving up; it also meant giving in to siblings, leaders, tradition, and to the Ordnung of the Christian community. The code words for the social expression of Gelassenheit became obedience, humility, simplicity, submission, meekness, and lowliness. The meek and lowly Jesus, who was willing to walk to Golgotha without balking or resisting and who called his disciples to love even their enemies, was the model for community behavior. The posture of submission or yielding to the higher authority of leaders, ordnung, tradition, and community values regulated the entire spectrum of socio-religious life from body language to social organization, from personal speech to symbolism. Gelassenheit was the fulcrum, the fundamental principle, upon which the whole social system rested. The conceptual distinction between religious and social is somewhat dubious and artificial because the two were woven together. To resist human authority was to resist God. To deviate from community standards of propriety was to violate divine precepts.

The ways of Gelassenheit are difficult to comprehend in modern life, saturated as it is with personal ambition, greed, and dreams of self-fulfillment. Indeed, in many ways Gelassenheit is the antithesis of individualism. Whereas modern culture values self achievement, personal advancement, and public recognition, Gelassenheit calls for self-denial, surrender, and the yielding of one's life to others. In a community regulated by the principles of Gelassenheit, the community, not the individual, is the primary unit of social significance. Talk of individual rights, civil rights, and personal ambition—common assumptions and parlance in modern culture—flies in the face of the ways of Gelassenheit.

Yieldedness heralds the virtues of duty, obligation, and obedience and calls for self-surrender to the interests of the larger community. Although talk of yieldedness sounds repressive to modern ears, it carried a redemptive paradox in Anabaptist teaching for the followers of Christ were called to lose their lives in order to save them, to die to the flesh in order to be victorious in spirit.[8] Likewise, those who submit to the dictates of a redeemed community not only serve their neighbors but ultimately acknowledge their dependence and trust in God. Gelassenheit is thus a spiritual/social process that recycles individual energies into community capital, a recycling that is empowered by the words of Jesus, the blood of martyrs, the teaching of the church, and the authority of elders.

The gradual loss of Gelassenheit in many Anabaptist communities has involved a shift from a religious fatalism of sorts to a growing emphasis on control. The posture of submission means that one yields to whatever life brings. The stance of individualism, by contrast, takes control of things. It takes the initiative, displays leadership, and engages in strategic planning, birth control, career planning, and assertiveness training. Such a controlling and planning mentality is a modern one, shaped by an enlightenment and scientific world view. By contrast, Gelassenheit takes things as they come and in quiet resignation accepts them as part of divine providence.

Human behavior needs regulation. A tightly ordered community regulated by the principles of Gelassenheit provides communal and traditional controls to direct social behavior into proper channels. When these older communal systems crumble in the face of modernization, individuals must exercise greater control over their behavior. Individualism, in other words, is a necessary survival skill for those living in the modern world beyond the boundaries of traditional communities.

From a sociological perspective, Gelassenheit offers a comprehensive program of social control that funnels individual energy into constructive community goals. The values and rituals of Gelassenheit channel the individual into prescribed paths that enhance the community and arrest debilitating expressions of individualism that might threaten the welfare of the community. All groups—from armies who hope to win wars to modern corporations trying to beat the competition—must find ways to harness individual aspirations and replace personal goals with corporate ones. Endowed with the power of religious legitimation, the ways of Gelassenheit were able to transform individual energies into the service of the church community.

The principle of Gelassenheit provides an integrative framework for understanding and interpreting a wide array of social and religious practices in traditional Anabaptist communities. Its conceptual elasticity enables us to see an underlying logic that ties together a variety of disparate practices from taboos on lightening rods to solos in church services, from the rejection of photographs to the rites for ordaining leaders. Such an analysis runs the risk of stretching the

conceptual elasticity of Gelassenheit too thin by spreading it over all socioreligious life. And, while this is indeed a hazard, I contend that Gelassenheit is a
root principle that enables us to see, understand, and integrate a vast array of
phenomena from a single point of reference.

I offer several observations before exploring five dimensions of
Gelassenheit.

1. The formation of "old order" communities (Old German Baptist Brethren, Old Order Amish, Old Order Mennonites, and Old Order River Brethren) in
the late nineteenth century resulted largely because the habits of Gelassenheit
were threatened by technological changes, the emergence of bureaucracies, the
rising expressions of individualism, and the inroads of Protestantism, which
carried new understandings of salvation.[9]

2. The ethos of Gelassenheit has been preserved to some extent in many of
the Old Order groups today, who practice the habits of yieldedness. The Hutterites with their commitment to communal property practice the essence of
Gelassenheit by requiring the individual to give up material goods for membership in the community. While the Old German Baptist Brethren and the Old
Order Amish tend to verbalize the call to yieldedness more than the Hutterites,
the two former groups have not structured the material patterns of Old Order life
to the extent that the Hutterites have.

3. The assimilation of so-called mainstream Anabaptist groups—the
Mennonite Church, the Brethren in Christ, the Brethren Church, the Church of
the Brethren and the General Conference Mennonite Church—can be read as a
gradual erosion of Gelassenheit and a growing embrace of individuation. Some
traces of the ethos of Gelassenheit remain in all of these groups, but for the most
part these faith communities have replaced an emphasis on self-denial with a
celebration of the giftedness of individual members. Such a transformation is
certainly not a full embrace of a hedonistic culture because the gifts of
individuals are affirmed for their contribution to the church community, but,
nevertheless, the focus is on the individual rather than on the community.

4. The posture of yieldedness is contingent upon membership in strong
communities that are culturally separate from the larger society. Persons who
are immersed in the individualism of modern life will find it difficult, even repressive and suffocating, to embrace the ways of Gelassenheit. In other words,
a certain amount of individualism and assertiveness is necessary in modern
society if one is to function successfully outside the bonds of an integrated community. Yieldedness, thus, only works in the context of an orderly community.

I want to briefly explore five dimensions of Gelassenheit in the heritage of
Anabaptist communities and show how yieldedness manifested itself in these
five domains of personal and community life. I cannot delve into detailed
illustrations in any of the communities but merely hope to provide suggestive
examples that point to the significance of yielding across the spectrum of
socioreligious life. In a general sense the historical period is the mid-nineteenth
century, but as noted above, many of the patterns persist even today in the Old

Order groups. The depth and width of Gelassenheit varied, of course, from community to community. It was deeper and wider in the Swiss/South German stream of Mennonites than in the Dutch/Russian cultural stream. It was also deeper and wider in the Amish cultural stream than in the German Baptist Brethren tradition. But, nevertheless, it was operative to some extent in all the cultural streams flowing from the Anabaptist heritage.

Beliefs: Waiting on Divine Providence

The world view of Gelassenheit emphasizes yielding to and waiting upon divine providence rather than taking charge of and working out one's own redemption. Salvation is a collective experience that unfolds as one participates in a redemptive community. Unlike the evangelical mindset that in an individualistic fashion emphasizes personal salvation, personal conversion, personal evangelism, personal devotions, and so on, the Gelassenheit understanding of salvation entails participating in the orderly life of a redemptive community. Participation in the community takes priority over individual experience and the verbalization of individual beliefs.

Moreover, redemption in this perspective involves waiting. "Salvation," said one Old Order Mennonite leader, "is a gradual project." It occurs over a lifetime as one learns the lessons of humility in the community. Unlike some evangelical thinking, salvation does not occur in a single miraculous moment that serves as the once and for all turning point. Salvation is not the product of a rationalized process of means and ends, a calculated mindset that views conversion as a means to eternal life. There is no "plan" of salvation that one must follow in order to be saved. Rather, one waits patiently on the mercies of God to refine one's life through trial and tribulation as well as pain and suffering so that it will become acceptable to God.

Such gradual redemptive projects are also rather quiet. There is little verbalization about the feelings or experience of salvation. Rather there is quiet attention to the behaviors that are expected and fitting for membership in a redeemed community. One's life and work give testimony to the quality of one's faith, not slippery words and fickle emotions. In other words, behavior is the most trustworthy evidence of redeemed living.

Finally, one yields in humility to the wisdom of God who determines the final outcome. Thus, it is impossible to know if one is saved. Indeed, it is down right arrogant to make such an assertion because only God knows about these things. One simply seeks to live faithfully according to the bestowed tradition, leaving the ultimate outcome in the hands of a loving God. Lack of enthusiasm for missions and evangelism is a natural consequence of the Gelassenheit world view. To try to convert someone is not only theologically arrogant but is an attempt to control things, unbefitting the humility of yieldedness.

Values: The Complexity of Simplicity

The values of Gelassenheit guide personal behavior as well as cultural norms. The code words of virtue are plainness, simplicity, obedience, humility, lowness, and meekness. These are often paired against their opposites—fancy, complexity, disobedience, pride, high, and haughty—which are proscribed. Obedience is the supreme virtue, the tangible expression of a yielded life. Children learn to give up and give in at an early age. They learn to lose themselves, to yield to the larger purposes of family and community. Children are expected to obey parents and teachers without question, women are expected to listen to men, who in turn follow the guidance of church leaders, as ministers heed the counsel of elders or bishops. Obedience to one's respective authorities reflects a willing and yielded heart that is also yielded to God. Disobedience to the authorities of the community is tantamount to rebellion against the will of God.

Pride and humility, longtime vice and virtue, have often been juxtaposed in historic Anabaptist communities.[10] Schlabach and Liechty have described[11] in detail the theology of humility that developed in the nineteenth century among North American Mennonites. The many proscriptions against expressions of pride were typically directed at manifestations of individualism. Mennonite leader Daniel Kauffman, writing in 1914, said, "Self denial is the essence of the Christian religion and life." Indeed, his book of Bible Doctrine had a fifteen-page chapter devoted to self denial as well as a chapter devoted to humility, which he defined as "lowliness of mind, modesty, meekness, submissiveness and freedom from pride and arrogance."[12] Humility was a socio-religious value that arrested attention seeking behavior and encouraged yieldedness. The many pleas for plainness, simplicity, humility, and self-denial were religiously legitimated means of fostering the spirit and behavior of Gelassenheit.

The personality traits of Gelassenheit include self-denial, gentleness, slowness, patience, and a quiet spirit. Large families helped to nourish these traits as children learned to wait in line, share food, rooms, clothing, and parental attention. The spirit of Gelassenheit is reflected in a gentle body language, a slower pace, quiet demeanor, gentle chuckle, measured response to a question, and thoughtful deference to someone else's opinion. A tame, gentle, and patient self is the preferred personality type. Boisterous laughter, swift action, and a cocky spirit supplant the ethos of yieldedness. John Hostetler[13] has shown the significant role and use of silence in Amish culture.

Nonresistance, based on the words of Jesus, "resist not evil" (Matthew 5:39), was a dimension of Gelassenheit that was widely and deeply shared by all the North American Anabaptist related bodies in the nineteenth century. The nonresistant stance embodies the essence of Gelassenheit in its willingness to take whatever comes: verbal assault without retort, bodily injury and violence without retaliation, property damage without commensurate revenge, and financial exploitation without litigation. In the final analysis, Gelassenheit is "defenselessness," the willingness to absorb malice and leave vengeance up to God. The rejection of the use of force in all dimensions of personal, social, and political life was the defining trademark of all the groups flowing from the Anabaptist tradition and led some of them to be called "defenseless," "nonresistant bodies," etc.[14]

Nonresistance led to the rejection of litigation and public office holding activities, which often became a test of membership. The nonresistance posture penetrated all dimensions of social life, personal behavior, interpersonal relations, business relationships, and, of course, political life. There were many lapses from the noble ideals of nonresistance, and the church used some force when it excommunicated and shunned members but, nevertheless, it was the ideal, the paramount value to which members were admonished again and again. With powerful religious legitimation underscored by the example of Jesus, non-resistance wrapped personal, social, religious, economic, and political factors into a single cultural package.

Ritual: From Baptism to the Ban

Yieldedness is most likely to thrive within sectarian communities that create strong internal moral orders and that emphasize explicit boundaries of separation from the world. Gelassenheit, in other words, declines with the rise of denominationalism. Historically, baptism and the ban were the entrance and exit respectively to congregational life. Applicants for baptism were expected to turn away from worldly habits and yield to the expectations of the community's ordnung. Especially at baptism they were expected to conform to the order, or Ordnung, of the community. The specific expectations took many different forms in the various communities and, of course, varied by historical period, but nevertheless there were explicit standards of conduct to which the individual was expected to yield. The sectarian community had high expectations, and it was difficult to enter. Denominations, by contrast, are rather easy to enter because they set few behavior expectations but rather ask for vague affirmations of Christian faith that permit individuals to interpret and practice their faith according to their own preferences.

Denominations, due to their tolerance of individual diversity, rarely expel persons. In other words, it's hard to get expelled from a denomination except for a rather heinous offense. Traditional Anabaptist groups, in sectarian fashion, however, were quite willing to excommunicate or disfellowship those who were unwilling to yield to the ordnung of the community. All of the groups banned such excommunicated persons from communion or the Lord's Supper, and some also socially avoided or shunned errant members, hoping that they would eventually return to the fold. The process of church discipline in all the traditions pivoted on the three-step process of Matthew 18. An expression of remorse, a compliant attitude, and the presentation of a "yielded front" by the offender were critical determinants to a successful outcome of the process. The belligerent, the haughty, and the arrogant—those who readily abandoned the traits of Gelassenheit—were banned from the fellowship.

Between baptism and the ban stood the ritual of communion and/or the Love Feast. Baptism came but once in a lifetime and upright members were never banned, but the twice-a-year observance of the Lord's Supper was an important integrative event that reinforced the moral order and encouraged yieldedness in congregational life. Gelassenheit carried expectations for accountability prior to the observance of communion. The deacon's visit to each household in the Brethren tradition or the preparatory and "self examination" service in the Mennonite heritage were ritualized moments that emphasized the importance of giving up selfish desires, rooting out sin, and submitting to the ordnung of the community so that the communion could celebrate the congregation's oneness and unity.

And in those instances when the congregation was not at peace, communion would be postponed until unity was restored. In any event, the preparation for communion and the service itself emphasized the importance of being broken and crushed. As grains of wheat are broken to make bread and as grapes are crushed to make wine, so the individual must be purged of self will in order to build up the unity of the body. In the words of the Hutterian,[15] "We who are many are one loaf. Like grains of wheat we have yielded up all we are and live together in Christian community." Such brokenness articulates the deepest meanings of Gelassenheit. A single, common cup symbolized the unity that was possible in the yielded community.

The footwashing service that was incorporated into the communion service also embodied Gelassenheit in the willingness of members to kneel or stoop over in order to wash the feet of brothers and sisters. Footwashing has tended to decline in the twentieth century with the rise of individualism. The communion table of course was only open to those in "close" fellowship who were willing to uphold the ordnung of the community. By contrast, in denominational settings a "bread and cup" communion is offered as part of a Sunday morning service to anyone who professes Christian faith regardless of affiliation or daily practice. Such "convenience communions" are open without a lengthy self-examination or the bothersome footwashing.

Baptism, communion, and the ban were major ritual enactments of Gelassenheit, but there were many other expressions of it as well. Kneeling is the posture of Gelassenheit. Kneeling for baptism, footwashing, ordination, congregational prayer, and, in the Amish tradition, for a serious confession also signaled the humble posture of Gelassenheit. Kneeling for congregational prayer, typically two times during a worship service, was the norm in many Anabaptist groups. With the rise of individuation, kneeling for congregational prayer declined and has for all practical purposes disappeared in the worship services of the mainstream groups.

A cappella singing in unison, at sluggish pace as still practiced in Old Order services, set the mood for Gelassenheitan ethos of waiting and patience. Furthermore, it prevented individuals from receiving special attention for their ability to sing parts, let alone solos or in special groups. The use of solos, quartets, and choirs was strongly frowned upon in some traditional circles for fear they would lead to "performances" that would call attention to individuals or special groups and cultivate pride. Such displays of vain glory would also detract from the sense of "waiting on the Lord," which is underscored by the slow cadence of unaccompanied unison singing. In some traditions the song leader simply sat among the congregation and led with his voice from his seat. And applause, so foreign to the spirit of Gelassenheit, was unthinkable in a worship service.

The historic patterns of leadership downplayed the notion of individual calling and highlighted the servant role of the leader. Amish youth, for instance, are asked at baptism if they are willing to serve in a leadership capacity if called by the congregation. The ordination of leaders embodied the spirit of Gelassenheit, especially in those traditions which used the "lot" to select leaders. In the election process used by various Brethren groups and in the lot procedure, the congregation calls (nominates) members and then elects them or, in the case of the lot, selects them by a divine lottery of sorts. Serving without special training or pay, ordained leaders are expected to give themselves up as servants to the congregation.

Speaking without access to prepared notes prevented preachers from showing off their knowledge and underscored the giving up even their innermost thoughts to divine direction. The humility of the preacher was even more accentuated in some traditions by the custom of deciding who would preach at the very beginning of the church service. In some Old Order traditions preachers engage in a brief rite of Gelassenheit at the beginning of their sermon by saying how unworthy they are to bring the sermon and that they can only pass on what the Lord lays on their heart. In all of these ways the rituals of leadership emphasized the yieldedness of leaders to the Lord and to the congregation. These patterns are, of course, quite different from professional models of ministry where self-selected candidates pursue a pastoral career with remuneration.

Symbols: Lightening Rods and Likenesses

A variety of symbols, and in some cases their rejection, articulated the meaning of Gelassenheit in the nineteenth century. Many of these symbolic manifestations continue to embody yieldedness in Old Order communities today. Numerous groups taught against the use of lightening rods because they symbolized an erosion of trust in God. In like manner, life insurance was stringently forbidden by numerous communities because it symbolized an acceptance of individual planning and control that contradicted simple trust in God. The stance of yieldedness expected a simple faith in the providence of God as well as an unwavering commitment to dependency on the faith community instead of taking charge of one's own life and looking out for oneself.

Photographs or "likenesses," as they were called in the later nineteenth century, were forbidden by many groups because they called attention to the individual and fostered pride in ways that were contrary to the humble spirit of Gelassenheit. Jewelry of all sorts—earrings, breastpins, finger rings, wrist watches, and in the words of the 1857 German Baptist Brethren Annual meeting, "jewelry in general"—was forbidden.[16] Jewelry was not merely a symbol of worldliness, it highlighted and accentuated the charms of individuality and mocked the spirit of yieldedness and thus threatened the well being of an orderly community.

All of the groups emphasized the importance of distinctive garb in the nineteenth century. A symbol of nonconformity to the larger world, distinctive patterns of dress also symbolized in the most fundamental way the spirit of Gelassenheit for they signaled the individual's yieldedness to the community.[17] Dress-related issues often became contentious at baptism or in preparation for the Lord's supper, the peak moments of yieldedness. Dress was a fundamental expression of Gelassenheit because it symbolized the giving up of the right to self expression via dress and signaled compliance to the ordnung of the community. In modern life dress is a crucial tool of self expression, used day after day to make statements about one's individual tastes. However, in the Old Order community dress functions in the opposite manner. It symbolizes the rejection of individual choice and the endorsement of communal standards, the very heart of a submissive spirit.

Social Architecture: Small Scale Style

Gelassenheit was also embedded in the very structure of things, the social architecture of Anabaptist communities. Apart from large families there was a general preference for small scale organization in nineteenth-century Anabaptist communities. This preference continues to persist in Old Order communities today. In the recent words of an Amishman, "Our discipline thrives on the man walking behind the plow, not the man traveling all over the country trying to build a superstructure." Organizational structure was also to be modest and humble. Large bureaucracies, centralized organization, and large businesses might place too much power and control in the hands of one person and could lead not only to arrogance but to the abuse of power. Small congregations, fluid and flexible organizational patterns driven by tradition, were preferred over centralized and rationalized bureaucracies. The penchant for small scale, local organization was undoubtedly one of the factors behind the resistance to the formation of a general conference in the Mennonite Church in 1898 and the relative absence of centralized and bureaucratized organizational expressions in Old Order communities today.[18] Thus, from egos to organizational structure the ethos of Gelassenheit favors smallness.

Summary

I have contended that the principle of Gelassenheit provided a cultural logic that underlay and integrated the moral order of many Anabaptist communities in the nineteenth century. The religious and social commitment to yieldedness shaped the world view and beliefs, harnessed personal behavior, structured cultural values, regulated religious ritual, manifested itself in the acceptance and rejection of symbols, and shaped the structure of social organization. The ethos of yieldedness that pervaded the cultural and social organization was ultimately grounded upon and legitimated by religious values, a commitment to the ways of the meek and lowly savior. For a multitude of reasons and in a variety of ways these habits of Gelassenheit became woven into the cultural fabric of many nineteenth-century North American Anabaptist communities. They supported and reinforced an ecclesiology that encouraged and expected members to yield to the collective wisdom of tradition and the gathered community. The stance of Gelassenheit, intact in the life of many Old Order communities today, is reflected by the verse on the front cover of the September, 1993, Old Order Mennonite publication, Home Messenger.

> *Every sorrow,*
> *Every smart,*
> *That the Eternal*
> *Father's heart*
> *Hath appointed*
> *me of yore,*
> *Or hath yet for*
> *me in store,*
> *As my life flows on*
> *I'll take*
> *calmly, gladly,*
> *for His sake,*
> *No more faithless*
> *murmurs make.*

[1] Donald F. Durnbaugh, ed. *The Brethren Encyclopedia*, 3 vols. (Philadelphia: Brethren Encyclopedia, Inc., 1984); and *The Mennonite Encyclopedia: A Comprehensive Reference Work on the Anabaptist-Mennonite Movement*, 5 vols. (Hillsboro, Kan.: Mennonite Publishing House, 1955, 1990).

[2] Harold S. Bender, ed., *Hutterite Studies: Essays by Robert Friedmann* (Goshen, Ind.: Mennonite Historical Society; *The Chronicle of the Hutterian Brethren* (Rifton, N.Y.: Plough Publishing House, 1987), vol. I; and Peter Rideman, *Confession of Faith* (Rifton, N.Y.: Plough Publishing House, 1970).

[3] Walter Klaassen, "Gelassenheit and Creation," *The Conrad Grebel Review* 7 (1991): 23-35.

[4] Chronicle of the Hutterian Brethren, 416.

[5] Sandra Cronk, "Gelassenheit: The Rites of the Redemptive Process in Old Order Amish and Old Order Mennonite Communities," *Mennonite Quarterly Review*, 55 (1981): 544.

[6] J. Cornelius Dyck, "The Suffering Church in Anabaptism," *Mennonite Quarterly Review* 59 (1985): 523.

[7] John H. Yoder, ed., and trans., *The Legacy of Michael Sattler* (Scottdale, Pa.: Herald Press, 1973), 23.

[8] Noah Good, "The Yielded Life," *Pastoral Messenger* (January 1943): 34.

[9] Beulah Stauffer Hostetler, "The Formation of the Old Orders," *Mennonite Quarterly Review* 66 (1992): 525.

[10] John M. Brenneman, *Pride and Humility* (Elkhart, Ind.: J.F. Funk and Bro., 1873).

[11] Theron F. Schlabach, "Reveille for Die Stillen im Lande: A Stir among Mennonites in the Late Nineteenth Century," *Mennonite Quarterly Review* 51 (1977): 213-26; idem, *Peace, Faith, Nation* (Scottdale, Pa.: Herald Press, 1988); and Joseph C. Liechty, "Humility: The Foundation of Mennonite Religious Outlook in the 1860s," *Mennonite Quarterly Review* 53 (1980): 531.

[12] Daniel Kauffman, *Bible Doctrine* (Scottdale, Pa.: Mennonite Publishing House, 1914), 470-85, 604-15.

[13] John A. Hostetler, *Amish Society* (Baltimore: The Johns Hopkins University Press, 1993, fourth ed.).

[14] Leo Driedger and Donald B. Kraybill, *Mennonite Peacemaking* (Scottdale, Pa.: Herald Press, 1994).

[15] *The Chronicle of the Hutterian Brethren*, I, 274.

[16] *Revised Minutes of the Annual Meetings of the German Baptist Brethren* (Elgin, Ill.: Brethren Publishing House, 1908), 129.

[17] Donald B. Kraybill, *The Riddle of Amish Culture* (Baltimore: The Johns Hopkins University Press, 1989).

[18] James C. Juhnke, *Vision, Doctrine, War: Mennonite Identity and Organization in America, 1890-1930* (Scottdale, Pa.: Herald Press, 1989).

2

Yieldedness and Accountability: Contemporary Applications and Prospects

by Fred W. Benedict

Brethren historian, Floyd Mallott, declared in his "Apologia" that "the biblical party of the Anabaptist wing of the Reformation represents in our century the clearest line of God's speaking."[1]

This essay on Anabaptism underscores the above quotation by an author and long-time teacher of church history.

First, it is imperative to define "yieldedness and accountability." Recently, I was much impressed by Paul Johnson's book, *Modern Times,* which describes a condition of yieldedness and accountability. In describing the rise of despotic Russian communism, he lays before the reader the character of Lenin and later those of Stalin and Hitler and the rule of terror they felt was indispensable for the success of their regimes. Indeed, they achieved yieldedness with terror and accountability with a system of informers and secret police.[2] Lately we have read of the Branch Davidian episode in Waco, Texas, which recalls to mind earlier events at Jonestown. Surely there seems to have been remarkable yieldedness and accountability manifest in the lives of these cult members.

None of the above examples satisfy. We want to concern ourselves with the Anabaptists—especially the "biblical party" of the Anabaptists. I believe one of the finest definitions has been expressed by Donald Kraybill. Speaking of the Amish he says,

> The value of structure of Amish life rests on *Gelassenheit*—the cornerstone of Amish values. Roughly translated, the German word means submission—yielding to a higher authority. It entails self-surrender, resignation to God's will, yielding to others, self-denial, contentment, and a quiet spirit. For early Anabaptists, Gelassenheit meant forsaking all ambition and yielding fully to God's will—even unto death. Christ called them to abandon self and follow his example of humility, service, and suffering.[3]

In the same work Kraybill says "talk of humility flies in the face of our cherished individualism, which seeks self-fulfillment and personal achievement at every turn."[4]

Harold Bender has said, "the original goal sought by Luther and Zwingli was an earnest Christian life."[5] In this they were sorely disappointed, and Luther occasionally lamented that his own people were worse than the unconverted.

Bender gives three major points of emphasis among the biblical Anabaptists: discipleship, brotherhood, and love and nonresistance.[6] Out of the Anabaptists' understanding of an intense personal discipleship flowed the rest of their Christian commitment, including the principle of Gelassenheit. J. Denny Weaver has well pointed out that a distinctive theological norm for first-generation Anabaptism seems to be a principle of "solidarity in Christ." Weaver says the "principle assumes not only that believers will follow the model of Jesus' teaching and acts, but also that believers participate in his work and he in theirs, if they are to be counted as members of Christ's body."[7] We may see that such an all-encompassing and thorough-going vision of discipleship would lead to obedience to Jesus' words and a church discipline.

It would seem that for the Anabaptists, yieldedness and accountability were not ultimate goals but attitudes of faith resulting from their total commitment. The attitudes were gifts of the Spirit that led from faith to faith. The goal was godliness. The gifts made the goal more precious, were means to the goal, and participated in the goal.

For the Anabaptists yieldedness and accountability were enablements of the Spirit of God to meet the severe crises of their time. These enablements were part and parcel of Gelassenheit.

Nonresistance was a prominent doctrine in the lives of many early Anabaptists. According to Murray Wagner, before 1460 Petr Chelcicky maintained that "Christians are collectively and individually members of an order set apart, distinct and withdrawn, and forbidden by apostolic injunction to serve the world's coercive institutions,"[8] and in 1524 Conrad Grebel wrote that

> true Christian believers are sheep among wolves, sheep for the slaughter; they must be baptized in anguish and affliction, tribulation, persecution, suffering, and death; they must be tried with fire and must reap the fatherland of eternal rest not by killing their body, but by mortifying their spiritual enemies.[9]

Many Christians of modern times have suffered no less gloriously than the Anabaptists. In our day many could give testimony that their victory was complete when the spirit of Gelassenheit settled over the soul. Ashish Chrispal of India says it so well:

> Jesus is saying that when we act from the standpoint of power and dominance, from control and violence, God cannot become present in the world. God becomes visible through those who put on the character of God, embodying God's sacrificial love, compassion and forgiveness. This is a costly endeavor in the presence of sin and evil. Yet it is the only hope of radically undermining the destructive power of evil."[10]

Another model for the Anabaptists was the early Christian church. According to Cornelius Krahn,

> the restitution of the true apostolic church or the Pauline 'body of Christ' in which there is a genuine practice of discipleship of Christ and separation from the world was the objective of Anabaptism. All Anabaptists in Switzerland, Germany, and the Low Countries pursued this as their goal.[11]

Murray Wagner speaks of Chelcicky's defense of a visible church over against the invisible or a politically defined church,

> Discipleship can never be measured by political requirements. It is made visible solely through its loyalty to the precepts of the primitive church. The belief and practice of the apostolic community stood as the one true guide to all Christian generations, claimed Chelcicky. Conformity to the separatist example of early Christianity was the only way a Christian could at least know that his conduct was not in contradiction to Christ's commandments. Chelcicky measured the behavior of Christians by the single apostolic standard which he found in the separatist ideal of the primitive church. Only faithful obedience to that example could be taken as a visible sign of election.[12]

Johann Loserth said, "More radically than any other party for church reformation the Anabaptists strove to follow the footsteps of the church of the first century and to renew original Christianity."[13]

If, then, Anabaptists generally accept the words of the apostles as being equally authoritative to those of Christ, they also subjected themselves to the will of the church. How can we account for this? The answer is simple: the cost of discipleship is high. Each person gives himself completely to Christ and the brethren, who, having given themselves to Christ, are indeed the body of Christ. To despise a member of the body, or the will of the body, is to despise the head of the body, Christ. For the head and the body are one. I think that as long as this certainty of solidarity with Christ persisted, individuals yielded themselves to Christ and the church and were willing to be held accountable to the church, to call false brethren to account, and to die for their faith. Let us again hear from Floyd Mallott: "I wish to record my judgment that the only path of return is to return to the ideal of a New Testament church, with the apostolic writings as authoritative law, norm, and guide."[14]

The Anabaptists had a high conception of Jesus Christ. The gospel of Christ was primarily the quest for godliness taught by and performed in the midst of the brotherhood, the body of Christ. With Christ and the church forming one body, there need be no distinction made between the authority of the word of Christ and that of the fellowship of believers; both are the will of God. The word of Christ was the word of Scripture. When members of the faith community personalized their discipleship with claims to unique private illumination of the Spirit, problems developed. When members agreed upon the word of Scripture, being brought into unity by the Spirit, we find a resulting yieldedness and accountability that is admirable.

How shall Anabaptists revive such gifts in the lives of church members today? If by this we mean recapturing today the zeal and power of the Anabaptists—we can't! In this age of modernity with constantly shifting scientific concepts of the cosmos; with Darwinian and Freudian revelations of nature and human behavior; with our gods of the sports and entertainment world; with our aping the opinion and trend setters, the liberal cultural elites of the media, of the arts and entertainment industries; and with our craven sensitivity to those who raise the eyebrow and smirk at traditional Judeo-Christian values—where are the certainties that formed the basis for Anabaptist yieldedness and accountability? Attempts to revive the spirit of yieldedness and accountability without an essential spiritual foundation will be short lived and may qualify as a fad. As Mallott looked back across his life, he confessed that he was "astonished at how many moods, whims, fancies, and tangents" he had participated in.[15]

Too often we look for dramatic examples of yieldedness and accountability, counting them as models, and overlook the quiet examples of faithfulness in the lives of the "little people." In America the struggle today is not with flesh and blood but is psychological, and the temptations to slide by our duty are perhaps more insidious than the clear choices facing early Anabaptists and overtly persecuted Christian.

In my own reading of the teachings of Jesus Christ, I conclude that the more faithful we are to those teachings, the more uncomfortable we often find ourselves in our surroundings. The stronger our faithfulness, the more we find in common with the "odd balls" of this world—the little people, the oppressed, the poor, the persecuted, the weak, the powerless. How complete, then, becomes identification with these when they are such because of the cause of Christ! And how strange when we find ourselves out of step with those of our own communions!

Robert Friedmann, speaking of the genuine discipleship and total submission to God's will of the first generation of Hutterites, said that "such prophetic conditions hardly persist in the long run; and among the second, third, and fourth generations of Anabaptists this principle of obedience becomes more and more formalized and external."[16] I think Friedmann's observation is true for all movements. How may we account for the fire in the first generation of Anabaptists? Besides the principles we have already outlined, the Anabaptists chose to deliberately circumscribe their focus. What the Anabaptists, Brethren, Methodists, Quakers, and others gave up in their formative periods made them a scandal to their contemporaries. With singleness of eye they eliminated what did not pertain to salvation. Let me say it this way: they deliberately gave up much of what we today hold in high esteem. Maybe much of what we are involved in today is religion, but it is not Christianity. (Here I speak to the Old Orders as well). If you were told that what counts with God is what you have not already been praised for; what has not already been counted to your credit by men; and what you have not already received a reward for, how much of your work will stand? Anabaptist teaching focused on the words of Jesus, his righteousness, participation in his righteousness, and complete obedience to the words of the Scripture.

We too easily compromise with the world's spirit. Denny Weaver correctly condemns unscriptural diversity when he speaks of being tired of those who appeal to Anabaptist pluralism to justify modern departures from biblical foundations and the spirit of Christ.[17]

Revival of the Anabaptist spirit will depend upon the conscious adoption of a pre-modern mindset. I am not speaking of unscientific viewpoints or of slavishly adopting the forms of contemporary conservative Anabaptist groups. I mean a singleness and simplicity, a rigid honesty, consistency, boldness or fearlessness, and much plainness of speech. Popular thoughtful uncertainties must be traded for some basic things most surely believed.

When believers become weary of seeking new syntheses in theology to grasp the world and shake it to enhance their reputations, or shape the world to conform to their own concepts of the kingdom of God, it is well to take the advice of the prophet, "Thus saith the Lord, 'Stand ye in the ways and see, and ask for the old paths, where is the good way, and walk therein, and ye shall find rest for your souls.'"[18]

In conclusion I will say, "it is the leaders." What if Simons, Blaurock, Grebel, Hutter, Ridemann, Marpeck, Hoffman, Hubmaier, and the rest, immediately after their calling, had suddenly become silent? There would have resulted no clear message from God from the Reformation to us today. The entire Western world would have been somewhat impoverished.

What would happen if two or three persons today were to unite their efforts upon the word of God, the Scriptures, and seek with their whole heart the spiritual foundations of the Anabaptists? I would say, borrowing from the words of Conrad Grebel, "they must be baptized in anguish and affliction and must reap the fatherland of eternal rest by mortifying their spiritual enemies."

Roland Bainton says,

> Let it now be said that the worth of [the Anabaptist] endeavor is not to be judged in the light of their contributions to history. They took their stand in the light of eternity regardless of what might or might not happen in history.[19]

Let us go and do likewise.

Postscript

While at the conference that gave rise to this book, a new topic emerged for me: what impact has the Anabaptist example had upon denominations today? In what ways has the Anabaptist example provoked action today in the Church of the Brethren, the Mennonites, and the Old Order groups? What concrete acts of renewal owe their existence largely to the Anabaptist experience?

You say, "Why, this meeting is an example." I ask, "Is it only so much hot air? We want the praise of men—not Gelassenheit!" (No, really I think we've made a good beginning!)

I'll add this much: When persecution comes to the Christian in America, you'll see the Anabaptist spirit arise in surprising ways and in unexpected places!

[1] Floyd E. Mallott, "Apologia," *Brethren Life and Thought* 1 (Spring 1965): 5.

[2] Paul Johnson, *Modern Times: The World from the Twenties to the Nineties* (New York: Harper Collins, 1991, revised edition).

[3] Donald B. Kraybill and Lucian Niemeyer, *Old Order Amish* (Baltimore and London: Johns Hopkins Press, 1993), 3. Also see Donald B. Kraybill, ed., *The Amish and the State*, (Baltimore and London: The Johns Hopkins Press, 1993), 12-4.

[4] Kraybill, *Old Order Amish*, 177.

[5] Harold S. Bender, "The Anabaptist Vision," ed. Guy F. Hershberger, *The Recovery of the Anabaptist Vision* (Scottdale: Herald Press, 1957), 40.

[6] Bender, "The Anabaptist Vision," 41, 42.

[7] J. Denny Weaver, "Discipleship Redefined: Four Sixteenth-Century Anabaptists," *Mennonite Quarterly Review* LIV (October 1980): 256.

[8] Murray L. Wagner, *Petr Chelcicky, A Radical Separatist in Hussite Bohemia* (Scottdale: Herald Press, 1983), 91.

[9] Bender, "The Anabaptist Vision," 49.

[10] Ashish Chrispal, dean and professor at Union Biblical Seminary, Pune, India, and pastor of St. Peter's Church, Panchgani, Maharashtra. From guest editorial in *Mennonite Weekly Review* (August 26, 1993): 4.

[11] Cornelius Krahn, *Dutch Anabaptism* (Scottdale: Herald Press, 1981), 258.

[12] Wagner, *Petr Chelcicky*, 92-4.

[13] Bender, "The Anabaptist Vision," 37, 38.

[14] Mallott, "Apologia," 4.

[15] Ibid., 6.

[16] Robert Friedmann, "The Hutterian Brethren," *Recovery of the Anabaptist Vision*, 90.

[17] J. Denny Weaver, "Is the Anabaptist Vision Still Relevant?" *Pennsylvania Mennonite Heritage* 14 (January 1991): 1-12.

[18] Jeremiah 6:16.

[19] Timothy George, *Theology of the Reformers* (Nashville: Broadman Press, 1988), 252.

Conversation
৯৯ XI ৩৩

Missions
& Outreach

Wilbert R. Shenk and Lois Barrett search for a distinctive concept of mission within a tradition not particularly known for evangelism. With the exception of the founders (sixteenth-century Anabaptists and eighteenth-century Brethren), Shenk finds little mission emphasis. In contrast, early Anabaptists relied heavily on the Great Commission and assumed that membership included a responsibility to witness, which they did enthusiastically to relatives, friends, neighbors, and co-workers while their preachers traveled widely to spread the faith. Shenk also identifies a "golden age" of mission from 1945-70, heavily laden with service.

Lois Barrett asserts that much in the tradition, particularly nineteenth-century Mennonite missions, mirrored developments in the Protestant mainstream and contained little Anabaptist distinctiveness. She argues, however, that Brethren and Mennonite mission could become distinctive if it embraced the two-kingdom approach of a "city on a hill," an alternate community in mission. This contrasts with traditional Protestant mission, a "Constantinian" viewpoint that reflected the interests of the larger nation and co-mingled racial, ethnic, and nationalist interests with those of the gospel. But when the church sees itself as outside the state—as a minority within the nation—it embraces a sense of mission that "not only demonstrates the life of the reign of God but invites others to become citizens of heaven."

1

Missions and Outreach:
The Anabaptist Heritage

by Wilbert R. Shenk

It was long taken for granted that mainstream scholars were either ignorant of the Anabaptist tradition or chose to ignore it in historical and theological studies.[1] This omission has been substantially redressed, of course, in the twentieth century insofar as the Radical Reformation belongs to the larger Reformation of the sixteenth century. Given the non-missionary ecclesiology characteristic of the Reformation, it is perhaps not surprising that most scholars have turned a blind eye to the missionary character of the Anabaptist movement. Less understandable is that after more than fifty years of research and writing on the missionary dimension of sixteenth-century Anabaptism—arguably, one of its greatest contributions—the theme remains marginal to Anabaptist studies.[2]

In his *History of Christian Missions* C. H. Robinson dates modern missions from the period 1580-1750.[3] After reviewing the attitudes of Luther, Zwingli, and Calvin with regard to missions, Robinson asserts that "the first theologian connected with the Reformation movements to maintain that 'the command to preach the gospel to all nations binds the Church' for all time was Adrianus Saravia."[4] In a 1590 treatise Saravia called the church to follow in the train of the apostles by embracing the task of evangelizing the world.

Kenneth Scott Latourette, always scrupulous in his use of the data and inclusive in scope, mentions the Anabaptists several times in his *History of the Expansion of Christianity*.[5] These references have to do with the Anabaptist contribution to separation of church and state and gaining recognition of the rights of individual conscience rather than its missionary character.

The interpretation by Gustav Warneck, father of modern missiology, of the attitude of the Reformers toward mission is particularly telling.[6] He identifies a number of reasons why the Reformers did not advocate missionary work. He candidly acknowledges that "we miss in the Reformers not only missionary action, but even the idea of missions, in the sense in which we understand them to-day."[7] Warneck brought to his study a strong commitment to the mainte-nance of the *corpus christianum*.[8] For him mission was tied to territory. Mission could never be directed toward Christian lands. Christendom was obligated to send missions to heathendom, and the term "mission" was reserved for this function alone, never as a way of describing the church's relation to its own environment. Warneck spoke of "Christianization" as the process of "filling the Volksatmosphere with Christian air," that is to say, this is the means by which conditions are created for "Volksconversion," which is the basis for the Volkskirche. Once this stage has been reached, the task of the church is continually to evangelize the people to awaken them to their latent faith.[9]

In spite of the flowering of Anabaptist studies in the twentieth century and the increasing appreciation shown for the sixteenth-century Anabaptists as a legitimate part of the Reformation, mission histories continued to pass over this chapter of history. This is especially odd in view of the substantial role played by the Free Churches in the modern mission movement.[10]

Eight decades after Warneck's death, David J. Bosch, a leading figure in mission studies for the past thirty years, in his magnum opus, *Transforming Mission* (1991), has recognized the sixteenth-century Anabaptists as pioneers in the recovery of mission in the life of the non-Roman Catholic church precisely because of their alternative view of the church and rejection of territoriality.[11]

The Scope of Anabaptist Missionary Activity[12]

The most comprehensive study of Anabaptist missionary outreach to date is that by Wolfgang Schaeufele, *Das missionarische Bewusstein und Wirken der Taeufer* (1966). Other studies have concentrated on particular aspects of Anabaptist mission: mission impulse, the use of scripture, and the view of church. In addition, numerous scattered references to individual Anabaptists engaged in outreach provide further clues to the scope of their witness.

Zollikon. The final step in the rupture between the Zurich Reformer Huldreich Zwingli and the nascent Anabaptist group was the baptism of Conrad Grebel, Felix Manz, George Blaurock, and others on the evening of January 21, 1525. The authorities lost no time in trying to suppress this new movement by banishing or imprisoning those involved. The locus of activity quickly shifted to nearby Zollikon. It was here in the following days that the premier Anabaptist congregation was formed among farmers and artisans.[13]

In addition to challenging the regnant meaning of baptism and the Lord's Supper, the Anabaptists redefined the church to mean those who had repented and experienced conversion and voluntarily accepted baptism. This crisis experience issued in a deepened sense of personal responsibility.

Although the Zollikon Anabaptist congregation itself would not last long under efficient official repression, its evangelizing initiatives spread rapidly to the surrounding areas. Much of this witness was given by inconspicuous personal contact. Since the movement remained largely a cell-group or house church, many people were brought to faith in these fellowships. Thus, each "congregation" was a center for evangelization, and every member was directly related to the action.[14]

Zollikon also began dispatching missioners. Marx Bosshard, a young Zollikon farmer, baptized in the early days of the Anabaptist movement, later served as an itinerant Anabaptist preacher in the highlands of Zurich.[15] For this he had several role models, including George Blaurock, known for his fiery preaching and wide itineration.

Essentially, the Anabaptist movement spread through two complementary actions, both characteristic of the New Testament church. On the one hand, leaders with apostolic gifts traveled far and wide preaching, baptizing, and organizing new congregations. On the other hand, members of each congregation were actively engaged in witness in their community and region in the course of daily living. What we have already observed of the Zollikon congregation became a widespread paradigm among Anabaptist congregations.

Apostolic leaders. Hans Hut has been called the apostle of the Anabaptists in Upper Austria. Herbert Klassen concluded:

> If the contribution of Hans Hut's life lies in the fact that he baptized more converts, founded more new congregations, and commissioned more Anabaptist apostles than any other early leader in South Germany, then the contribution of his teaching lies in his clear delineation of the crucial role of suffering discipleship and the corporate nature and missionary character of the church-brotherhood.[16]

Hut's ministry lasted only sixteen months. Following his baptism, May 26, 1526, at Augsburg, Hut went to Haina, where he won a number of converts; then he went to Erlangen. Next, he went to Swabia and then to Austria and Moravia. He returned to Augsburg and from there went to Nicolsburg at the end of 1526. In 1527 Hut traveled to Vienna, Melk, and Steyr. Escaping arrest there, Hut fled to Freistadt, Upper Austria. He next visited Gallneukirchen and Linz, "preaching and baptizing everywhere."[17] He had also worked at Passau, Schaeding, Braunau, Laufen, and Salzburg. By August, 1527, Hut was back in Augsburg for the special conference. In September he was arrested and died, awaiting trial, on December 6, 1527. Wherever he went he evangelized, baptized, admonished, and assisted the local congregations. It is apparent that Anabaptist believers were already present in many of the places he visited. This means that the movement had spread rapidly in the fifteen months after January, 1525.

The outstanding Anabaptist apostle of the second generation was the Dutch elder Leenaert Bouwens (1515-1582). For the last thirty years of his life, Bouwens ranged as far north as Holstein, North Germany, south to France, and east to Poland. He kept records of his journeys and of the number of people he baptized. His ministry fell into five discrete periods: 1551-54 (869 baptisms); 1554-56 (693 baptisms); 1557-61 (808 baptisms); 1563-65 (4,499 baptisms); and 1568-82 (3,509 baptisms) for a reported total of 10,378 people baptized.[18] Hut and Bouwens are representative of Anabaptist apostles who itinerated widely and did much both to spread the message as well as to stabilize and build up the local congregations throughout northern and central Europe.

Anabaptist "laity." Even though we have already made the point that the rank and file played a full role in the spread of the Anabaptist movement, it is worthwhile to examine this further.[19] People who decided to become

Anabaptists knew from the outset that this meant, in spite of the likelihood of persecution, the responsibility to witness to their faith in the world. This was accepted positively as a privilege rather than legal requirement. It was understood that these lay members were called to evangelize and invite people to repent, but baptism was administered by ordained leaders.

Based on testimony preserved in court records, one gets a clear impression of the sincerity, conviction, and zeal that motivated these lay members. In 1535 a peasant, Hans von Rueblingen, at his trial in Passau insisted that he and his cohorts compelled no one to join them, but wherever "they traveled or lived they spoke the word of the Lord."[20]

Anabaptist lay members used natural lines of relationship as channels of witness: family members, neighbors, friends, occupational colleagues, and employers. A Tyrolean master shoemaker, Valtein Luckner, had as apprentice, Matheis, an Anabaptist, who engaged his master in conversation about the Bible and matters of faith. In 1530 Jacob Hutter baptized Luckner, and later at his trial, Luckner relied on the statement of Matheis in summarizing his convictions: "One must live according to the will of God and be baptized according to faith."[21]

Based on his extensive study of Anabaptist missionary activity in South Germany, Wolfgang Schaeufele concludes that "the woman in Anabaptism emerges as a fully emancipated person in religious matters and as the independent bearer of Christian convictions."[22] Many accounts show them to have been vigorous evangelists among their families, friends, and communities. Late in the sixteenth century the Wuerttemberg government still considered Anabaptist women to be a serious threat because they "spread their faith through word of mouth or through booklets."[23] The government ordered single women to be expelled from the province and married women to be chained at home.

It was widely acknowledged that what gave particular power to the testimony of these Anabaptists was their exemplary lifestyle. In a period noted for low morals, the Anabaptists sought to put the ethical principles of the gospel into practice in daily discipleship. This did not save them from continuous persecution; rather, they tried to maintain a clear conscience in a hostile world.

Mission strategy. From what has been said thus far, it might be inferred that Anabaptist missions were largely unorganized and uncoordinated. In one respect this is undoubtedly true. Certainly, the local lay witness through hundreds of congregations proceeded essentially on this basis. But this is not the whole story.

In August, 1527, a group of more than sixty Anabaptist leaders met in Augsburg.[24] In contrast to the Schleitheim meeting held earlier the same year, the Augsburg conclave produced no written documents. From other contemporary accounts, however, it appears that several actions were taken. Most significant, the conference gave attention to the need for a comprehensive strategy for evangelizing Europe. The conference named missionary teams that went out from the meeting in small groups to visit existing Anabaptist congregations to strengthen these groups and to establish new congregations.

This concerted witness caused a further expansion of the movement with the inevitable result that civil and ecclesiastical authorities quickly took action against them. Within a year nearly all of these missioners had been martyred. This meeting has come to be known as the "Martyrs' Synod." This was only the first stage in formal planning for missionary action by Anabaptists.

Hutterian missions. Of all Anabaptists, the Hutterites had the most developed mission approach and continued this work longer than any other group.[25] Without this continuous missionary action they would never have won thousands of new members to their communitarian way of life. The Hutterites sent out missioners each spring and autumn. Over the years they covered the whole of Germany and Austria as well as visiting Switzerland, Italy, Belgium, the Netherlands, Poland, Bohemia, Slovakia, and Denmark. Such an effort could only be sustained by careful planning, preparation, and implementation. They kept records of their journeys and reported results.

The Hutterites developed a formal training program. Whether the school trained only those going out on mission assignments or was intended as a kind of basic formation in Christian discipleship for all new members is unclear.[26] The curriculum was organized under three rubrics: 1) Biblical history as warning; 2) penitential preaching (*Busspredigt*), i.e., the badness of the world; and 3) teaching concerning the church. Under the last head seventeen topics were covered: the need for forgiveness from sin, growing in faith and becoming mature in Christ, life in the Spirit, the meaning of the gospel, the mission task, relationship to the world, an extended section on Christian community, baptism and the Lord's supper, and Christian character (including Gelassenheit and *Gehorsam*). This training was practical and foundational.

Other resources were also provided to Hutterite missioners. A tract, "Valuable Directions and Instructions on How to Turn Unbelievers from Their Error,"[27] assumed to have been written by Leonhard Dax in the 1560s, was composed especially for missionary use. The tract discusses the human condition and need for God, the nature of the Christian community, and the relationship to the world, which does not recognize God. The tract urges people, in view of these facts, to come to faith in Jesus Christ and join the Body of Christ.

A Missionary Ecclesiology

The Great Commission. The Reformation of the sixteenth century had to do with the nature of the church. The Anabaptists envisioned a restored New Testament church. A variety of formulations have been put forward as to what this meant in the sixteenth century and how it was to be achieved. One such interpretive framework regards Anabaptism as a missionary movement for which the charter is the Great Commission.

In 1946 Franklin H. Littell wrote a pioneering essay, "The Anabaptist Theology of Mission," which makes the following statement: "No words of the Master were given more serious attention by his Anabaptist followers than his final command."[28] This observation has been echoed by others in the years since. Heinold Fast says

> "A glance at the *Taeuferakte*, which have an index of Scripture references, shows that this was the most quoted Scripture passage among the Anabaptists. With this passage infant baptism could be renounced easily and clearly, and the legitimacy of baptism by faith demonstrated."[29]

This established the irrefutable basis for evangelization in the world.

But, this interpretation has been challenged. Ray C. Gingerich insists, "We must reject, on the basis of the historical evidence, Littell's thesis regarding the centrality of the Great Commission in the mission consciousness of the Swiss and the South German-Austrian Anabaptists."[30] According to Gingerich, the Great Commission did not figure in the 1527 Augsburg conference and is not "the key to an understanding of the Anabaptist mission" generally. Critics believe the source of Anabaptist mission to lie deep in the nature of the church as the community which incarnates the life of Jesus as expressed in the socio-religious reality of the Anabaptist movement itself.

At issue here is not whether the Anabaptists acted in missionary ways by seeking to evangelize widely in Europe. Rather, the question centers on the source of motivation and the Anabaptists' conceptualization of what they were doing.

It is beyond the scope of this essay to explore this debate thoroughly. Several summary comments must serve as bridge to the next section. First, even a cursory reading of the sources shows that the Anabaptists—from as early as Manz's 1524 "Protestation"—consistently used particularly the Matthean and Markan versions of the Great Commission as the basis for their attack on paedobaptism and advocacy of believers baptism. Sometimes, but not always, they linked this to the preaching of the Gospel. Second, Littell and others who have emphasized the central role of the Great Commission have also recognized the way it was used as the basis for teaching believers baptism. Third, we need to ask how the Great Commission was used by the second generation leaders like Menno Simons and the Hutterians? Did they continue to find both believers baptism and mission in the Great Commission? In his "Reply to Gellius Faber," Menno said:

> Yet through no other command nor ordinance than to preach the Gospel, make disciples by means of the doctrine, baptize these same disciples, and so gather unto the Lord a peculiar people, who should walk in Christ Jesus in righteousness, truth, and obedience, as the regenerate children of God.[31]

This statement points to continuity between Manz and others of the first generation and Menno of the second.

The Great Commission in recent scholarship. One of the criticisms made both by those who believe the Great Commission played a role in defining the missionary dimension of Anabaptism and those who reject this interpretation is that we are reading twentieth-century assumptions and questions into the sixteenth century. In other words, the Great Commission has become stereotyped as the so-called charter of the modern missionary movement, and we misuse it when we try to understand a sixteenth-century movement through this frame.

Thus, at one point, Gingerich dismisses Littell's argument, saying "our study so far indicates that the passage was given ecclesiological significance, not mission except by implication."[32] Here the debate is made to turn on whether the Great Commission has ecclesiological or missiological meaning.

In recent years New Testament exegetes have done fresh work on the interpretation of the Great Commission that points to an alternative interpretation. The main lines of argument are as follows.

First, it is a mistake to treat the Great Commission as separable from the Gospels.[33] Essentially, this was what the Reformers did when they argued that these words, having been fulfilled by the first apostles, were no longer binding on the church. On the contrary, the Great Commission brings the development within each of the Gospels to a climax. One cannot fully grasp what has preceded if the climax is detached.

This leads to the second point. The Great Commission is the key ecclesiological statement in the Gospels, thereby requiring that ecclesiology always be interpreted missionally and mission always be interpreted ecclesially.[34] Thus, the Great Commission, freed from historical accretions and captivity to a slogan status, has the potential to challenge the ever-present centripetal tendency of the institutional church to focus on itself.

Third, viewed in this light, the Great Commission ought to be the basis for structuring or institutionalizing the church's relation to the world. The Great Commission calls us to understand the nature and work of the church in terms of its mission to be the body of Jesus the Messiah in the world, thereby continuing and extending his reconciling work in this eschatological age.

The Church-World Nexus. This brings us to the heart of the matter. We cannot turn to the sixteenth-century Anabaptists for an exposition of a theology of mission as has been done in the twentieth century. (One should bear in mind that such systematic theological writing on mission has made its appearance only in the present century, and much of it suffers from bondage to the Christendom view of mission.) But we may argue with confidence that the early Anabaptists, relying on their Biblicist approach to scripture and reading their socio-political times in light of the eschaton, were on firm ground in their interpretation of the church's relationship to the world. Intuitively they found in the Great Commission the power both to challenge the *corpus christianum*—in their rejection of paedobaptism and all that this symbolized—and to form themselves into local communities of faith that assumed responsibility for evangelizing the world, thus negating territoriality, and for living out the reality of the Messiah's eschatological reign. The sense of being called into service by the Messiah on behalf of the new order of salvation unavoidably placed them at odds with the old order in which the majority churches were deeply implicated. Withdrawal from society was not an option for the Anabaptists. The only faithful response was that of missionary witness regardless of the cost. The inevitable and logical consequence was that the Anabaptists should be a church of martyrs.[35]

Emergence of The Brethren

The foregoing survey leads us to ask what relevance the Anabaptist witness of the sixteenth century has to the church in the twenty-first century. The Anabaptist movement underwent fundamental redefinition as the sixteenth century wore on. The heirs to the Radical Reformation sought to preserve important features of the Anabaptist legacy, but by the seventeenth century reports of evangelistic efforts are rare. Three distinct patterns of adaptation can be identified: Dutch, North German/Prussian, and South German/Swiss. None of these put vigorous witness in the wider society, in the style of the Anabaptists, at the center of their life.

And yet eventually all who count themselves heirs of the Anabaptists—Mennonite and Brethren—would become involved in formally organized efforts of mission and service. That this would happen can be attributed to the continuing messianic resurgence by which the faith of the people of God is revitalized from time to time.

The birth of the Brethren in 1708 was accompanied by a sense of the imperative to call people to the primitive faith of the first Christians. As was true in the sixteenth century, the church of the eighteenth as a whole was deemed moribund. In Alexander Mack's earliest writing, *Basic Questions* (1713), the thirty-third question is: "Do you regard your church as superior to those of all other Baptist-minded [*Taufgesinnte*] of these or previous times, and if so, in which way and why?" Mack replies:

> It is true that we consider our church fellowship superior to these now-deteriorated Baptists [Mennonites], with whom we are acquainted, and whom we know. The reason is that they have deteriorated in doctrine and life, and have strayed far from the doctrine and life of the old Baptists [Anabaptists]. Many of them notice this and realize it themselves.[36]

As was true for the sixteenth-century Anabaptists, Mack bases his call for vital faith and believers baptism on the Matthean-Markan versions of the Great Commission.

This quest for renewal necessarily entailed "going to" one's neighbors and witnessing to the gospel.[37] The emergence of the Brethren, therefore, represents a new surge of messianic dynamic which brought reform of the church and restored New Testament faith. Mennonites were among those to whom these Brethren witnessed.

As may be inferred from what has just been reported, Mennonite and Brethren histories run along different paths in the eighteenth century with the Brethren pursuing renewal of the church. Mennonites were in a different mood.

Richard K. MacMaster has characterized the preoccupation of Mennonites in colonial North America as follows:

> In new and more tolerant American circumstances the central concern of eighteenth-century American Mennonite religious life was how to preserve the fervor and commitment of that suffering church of martyrs and refugees. To some extent Mennonites worked at the task by emphasizing responsibility toward one another through mutual aid.[38]

This disposition continued to shape Mennonite attitudes well into the twentieth century. Indeed, one may suggest that two notions have remained defining concepts for the heirs of the Anabaptists: community and peace. Following the lead of the modern mission movement, missionary activity began to be adopted in the nineteenth century, both at home and abroad, but mission was grafted in.

The Future of a Legacy

If one were to speak of a "golden age" of mission and service activity for the heirs of the Anabaptists, it would undoubtedly be the period 1945-1970 when these activities became truly global.[39] World War II was a watershed in geo-political terms, and the post-war period was a time of unprecedented economic prosperity in the industrialized nations. This convergence of large-scale relief and rehabilitation for war-devastated countries, the rapid dismantling of the European colonial empires after 1947, and economic prosperity enabled steady expansion of programs for a period of twenty years.

In view of this flowering, we may ask: was there anything that distinguished the mission and service of these heirs of the Anabaptists from Protestants generally? In other words, did the Anabaptist legacy inform twentieth-century Mennonite and Brethren missions and service programs? This is an important question that deserves a more considered answer than can be given here.[40] Several summary comments may be made.

1. The modern mission and service programs of Mennonites and Brethren—themselves the fruit of messianic renewal of which the modern mission movement is one important manifestation[41]—are based on the model and rationale of the modern missionary movement. Evangelical activism helped stimulate the heirs of the Anabaptists to renewed responsibility in evangelism and service. But this indebtedness extends well beyond becoming activist. Mennonites and Brethren depended on the missiology of Protestantism. Although the first generation of missionaries trained within the ambiance of the "Anabaptist Vision" were appointed to missionary service in the late 1940s, missiological reflection from an Anabaptist viewpoint does not come into its own until after 1970.

2. The great innovation in the twentieth century has been the discovery of "service" as a consequence of the Historic Peace Churches' opposition to military service. World War I provided a testing ground for the Historic Peace Churches. As World War II approached, the churches worked out a large-scale

program for their members who refused to bear arms but were ready to engage in an alternative through the Civilian Public Service (CPS) program. As has been widely noted, CPS was seminal, spawning a range of service ministries legitimated by a theology of peace-making.

3. Mennonite and Brethren theologies of peace and mission have been developed along separate tracks. Work on a theology of peace began considerably earlier and has been the main focus for the most creative and distinctive contribution of Mennonites and Brethren to Christian theology and ethics. In contrast, Brethren and Mennonite contributions to theology of mission are confined largely to the period since 1970.[42]

4. By 1970 it was apparent the "golden age" had ended and the first indicators of the new trend were beginning to show: support for mission was declining and support for service continued to be strong until about 1990 when signs of erosion on this front appeared. Undoubtedly, the changing fortunes of the international economy played a significant role in this change in outlook for all international programs.

5. Although the meaning of "community" is increasingly unclear in the local congregation, the dynamics of a church with a strong ethnic heritage presents a contrast to one that is oriented to a particular social class drawn from North American culture. The Anabaptists correctly focused on the nature of the church as the critical question of the sixteenth century. Evidence suggests this is the critical question for the twenty-first as well. Mennonites and Brethren are tempted to confuse the ethnic-based community for the community that arises in response to the reign of God. Treating the former as the *sine qua non* of ecclesia is a betrayal of the Gospel and the Anabaptist heritage; in the latter lies the promise of God's salvation (Acts 15). The former is merely self-serving; the latter is God's instrument of the *missio Dei*.

¹ Appreciation is expressed to C. J. Dyck, H. Wayne Pipkin, and David A. Shank for reading and commenting on a first draft of this paper.

² The two widely-used works by Walter Klaassen, *Anabaptism: Neither Catholic nor Protestant* (Waterloo: Grebel Press, 1973) and *Anabaptism in Outline: Selected Primary Sources* (Scottdale, Pa.: Herald Press, 1981), contain no mention of the missionary dimension. John S. Oyer, "Historiography, Anabaptist," *Mennonite Encyclopedia*, (Scottdale, Pa.: Herald Press, 1990), V, 378-82, though citing in his extensive bibliography several of the dissertations dealing with Anabaptist mission, omits reference to mission in his survey of the flowering of Anabaptist studies in the past forty years. J. Denny Weaver, *Becoming Anabaptist: The Origin and Signficance of Sixteenth-Century Anabaptism* (Scottdale, Pa.: Herald Press, 1987), uses the term "mission/missionary" several times to describe the activity of certain sixteenth-century figures but never suggests that an important dimension of the Anabaptist movement was its view of the church as a missionary presence in society. Weaver's work is valuable as a mirror of contemporary Mennonite self-understanding and the selective hanging on to the Anabaptist legacy. He suggests four "regulative principles" by which Anabaptist-Mennonites stake out their course in the modern world: separation, community, discipleship, nonresistance. This traditional Mennonite formulation is devoid of any compelling sense of mission to the world by which these "regulative principles" can be activated.

³ Charles Henry Robinson, *History of Christian Missions* (Edinburgh: T. and T. Clark, 1915).

⁴ Ibid., 43.

⁵ Kenneth Scott Latourette, *A History of the Expansion of Christianity: Three Centuries of Advance, 1500 A. D. to 1800 A. D.* (Grand Rapids: Zondervan, 1970; reprint of the 1939 edition).

⁶ For a thorough survey of the modern debate concerning the Reformers' attitudes toward mission, see the trenchant essay by John H. Yoder, "Reformation and Missions: A Literature Survey," ed. Wilbert R. Shenk, *Anabaptism and Mission* (Scottdale, Pa.: Herald Press, 1984), 40-50. Cf. David J. Bosch, *Transforming Mission: Paradigm Shifts in Theology of Mission* (Maryknoll: Orbis Books, 1991), 243ff.

⁷ Gustav Warneck, *Outline of a History of Protestant Missions from the Reformation to the Present Time*, trans. George Robson (Edinburgh and London: Oliphant, Anderson and Ferrier, 1901; trans. from the seventh German edition), 9.

⁸ In an address to the Centenary Missions Conference held in London in 1888, Warneck chided his Anglo-American colleagues: "Dear brethren in England and America, I believe that I speak in the name of all my German fellow-believers, if I urge upon you to cease from looking upon Germany, the land of Luther and Melanchthon, Arndt and Spener, Francke and Zinzendorf, Tholuck, Fliedner and Wichern, as a half heathen and rationalistic country," in James Johnston, ed., *Report of the Missionary Conference on Protestant Missions of the World* (London: James Nisbet and Co., 1888), II, 435. Warneck took umbrage at the fact that British Methodists were doing missionary work in Berlin.

⁹ See Hans Kasdorf, *Gustav Warneck's Missiologisches Erbe: Eine biographisch-historische Untersuchung* (Giessen/Basel: Brunnen Verlag, 1990) for a thorough study of Warneck's mission theory and theology.

¹⁰ See my essay, "The 'Great Century' Reconsidered," in *Anabaptism and Mission*, 158-77; and the rather cursory treatment by Kenneth Scott Latourette, "A People in the World: Historical Background," ed. James Leo Garrett, Jr., *The Concept of the Believers' Church* (Scottdale, Pa.: Herald Press, 1969), 242-9.

¹¹ David J. Bosch, p. 245ff.

¹² Throughout this essay all references to "Anabaptist" and "Anabaptist mission" have to do with the period 1525-c. 1590. Two generations of relentless persecution and official censure exacted a decisive toll. The remnant thereafter is identified as Mennonites, Hutterites and Brethren. By the end of the sixteenth century these erstwhile Anabaptists had deeply sublimated the missionary dynamic and a new ethos had emerged.

¹³ Fritz Blanke, *Brothers in Christ*, trans. Joseph Nordenhaug (Scottdale: Herald Press, 1961), traces and analyzes these developments.

¹⁴ The "discovery" in the twentieth century of the importance of the laity for the mission of the church is noteworthy. This has taken two forms. a) The theological reformulation is represented by a spate of books starting in the 1950s, with the French Catholic theologian Yves Congar's *Lay People in the Church*, trans. Donald Attwater (Westminster, Maryland: Newman Press 1957; Fr. orig. 1953) and Hendrik Kraemer's *A Theology of the Laity* (Philadelphia: Westminister, 1958). b) In terms of mission theory, the best known experiment has been Evangelism-in-Depth pioneered by R. Kenneth Strachan, leader of the Latin America Mission, who around 1960 propounded the theorem: "The expansion of any

movement is in direct proportion to its success in mobilizing its total membership in continuous propagation of its beliefs" (found in Strachan's book, *The Inescapable Calling* [Grand Rapids: Eerdmans, 1968], p. 108). Strachan's starting point was his concern for renewal of the church in Latin America and formulated his theorem in response. Later he recognized its rootage in the reality of the primitive church.

[15] Blanke, *Brothers in Christ*, 28.

[16] Herbert Klassen, "The Life and Teaching of Hans Hut," *Mennonite Quarterly Review* 33 (July 1959): 205. The more recent scholarly debate over the Hut legacy is not of immediate concern. Our interest is only descriptive with reference to the role he played as leader of the Anabaptist movement in Austria and South Germany in its formative stage. See Ray C. Gingerich, "The Mission Impulse of Early Swiss and South German-Austrian Anabaptists," (Ph.D. diss: Vanderbilt Univerwsity, 1980), for a sorting out of the issues around Hut's theology and relationships.

[17] "Hut, Hans," *Mennonite Encyclopedia: A Comprehensive Reference Work on the Mennonite-Anabaptist Movement*, 4 vols. (Scottdale: Mennonite Publishing House, 1956), II, 848.

[18] "Leenaert Bouwens," *Mennonite Encyclopedia*, III, 305; and N. van Der Zijpp, "From Anabaptist Congregation to Mennonite Seclusion," ed. Shenk, *Anabaptism and Mission*, 121.

[19] This section follows Wolfgang Schaeufele, "The Missionary Vision and Activity of the Anabaptist Laity," ed. Shank, *Anabaptism and Mission*, 70-87. (This essay summarizes Schaeufele's dissertation, "Das missionarische Bewusstein und Wirken der Taeufer," [Neukirchener Verlag des Erziehungsvereins, 1966]). Schaeufele shows that this early emphasis on lay responsibility and participation soon began to be damped by the growing role of ordained leaders in baptizing and organizing congregations. A practical reason for this was that (re)baptizing was a crime. If it was done by an itinerant evangelist—most of whom were ordained—there was less likelihood of arrest than if carried out by local residents.

[20] Ibid., 73.

[21] Ibid., 77.

[22] Ibid., 79. Over time, the role of women, as for the laity in general, was increasingly circumscribed. Further research is needed to clarify this and related questions.

[23] Ibid., 80.

[24] "Martyrs' Synod," *Mennonite Encyclopedia*, III, 529-31. Scholars are not agreed as to the nature of the Augsburg meeting, i.e., was it to deal with Hans Hut's apocalyptic teachings or developing an evangelistic strategy. Schaeufele, *Die missionarische Bewusstsein*, pp. 148-53, gives a convincing account from the latter viewpoint. For a reconstruction of the event and evaluation of its significance, see Gingerich, "The Mission Impulse of Early Swiss and South German-Austrian Anabaptists," 305-21. Gingerich summarizes the Augsburg "program" which undergirds the "mission impulse" as including: active engagement, covenantal community, eschatological expectation, persecution, collaboration of religio-political establishment against the Anabaptists, and eschatological "pull from beyond."

[25] These paragraphs follow Leonard Gross, *The Golden Years of the Hutterites* (Scottdale, Pa.: Herald Press, 1980), chapter 3; and Leonard Gross, "Sixteenth-Century Hutterian Mission," ed. Shenk, *Anabaptism and Mission*, 97-118.

[26] Wilhelm Wiswedel, "Die alten Taeufergemeinden und ihr missionarisches Wirken," *Archiv fuer Reformationsgeschichte* 41 (1948): 115. Wiswedel bases his description on the Codex Ritualis of 1590.

[27] Gross, *Golden Years*, 46.

[28] Shenk, *Anabaptism and Mission*, 18; and Littell's, chapter 4, "The Great Commission," *The Origins of Sectarian Protestantism* (New York: Macmillan, 1964), which contains various parallel statements.

[29] Heinold Fast, "The Anabaptist Understanding of Jesus' Great Commission," *Mission Focus*, XI, 1 (March 1983): 4.

[30] Gingerich, "The Mission Impulse of Early Swiss and South German-Austrian Anabaptists," 335. It must be kept in mind that Gingerich bases his analysis on the model from the sociological theory of Peter L. Berger and Thomas Luckmann. This model has its own inherent limitations. For Gingerich's analysis, (p. 36ff.) the key scripture is Matthew 18:15-20.

[31] J. C. Wenger, ed., *The Complete Writings of Menno Simons*, trans. Leonard Verduin (Scottdale, Pa.: Herald Press, 1956), 701. See also, 120, 303, 394, 633, 676, 681ff, 739. Menno moves easily between the baptism and evangelizing/discipling themes but generally keeps them integrally related.

[32] Gingerich, "The Mission Impulse of Early Swiss and South German-Austrian Anabaptists," 83, 224.

[33] See Bosch, *Transforming Mission*, 56f; Lucien Legrand, "The Missionary Command of the Risen Christ," *Indian Theological Studies* 23 (September 1986): 302ff.; and Otto Michel, "The Conclusion of Matthew's Gospel: A Contribution to the History of the Easter Message," ed. Graham Stanton, *The Interpretation of Matthew* (Philadelphia: Fortress Press, 1983; repr. from the German edition, 1950), 35.

[34] Gingerich, "The Mission Impulse of Early Swiss and South German-Austrian Anabaptists," 349, speaks movingly of the importance of mission to the ongoing vitality of the church: "Ultimately the movement turned back upon its own participants, ever anew infusing them with the power that impelled them as missioners. Those who sought to be redeeming were the recipients of the redemption they proclaimed. The saving missioners, as they perceived it, became the saved ones. This dialectic between the Movement and the individual participants was reflected in the motif of eschatological participatory solidarity with Christ." (See also ibid., 29). It is quite inadequate to take Matt. 18:15-20, with its inward focus on church order, as the basis for a doctrine of the church. Matt. 18:15-20 must be seen within the overall development of the messianic movement which Jesus instigates.

[35] The remarkable essay by Ethelbert Stauffer, "The Anabaptist Theology of Martyrdom," *Mennonite Quarterly Review* 19 (1945): 179-214, focuses the issue sharply.

[36] Donald F. Durnbaugh, ed., *European Origins of the Brethren* (Elgin, Ill.: Brethren Press, 1958), 340. Cf. Albert T. Ronk, *History of Brethren Missionary Movement* (Ashland, Ohio: Brethren Publishing Co., 1971), 9-11: "The same Mackian principle appears in the fact that an answer to another question about true obedience, shows in full acceptance of the Commission of Matthew 28:19, 20, to disciple and teach all nations full observance of the commands of Jesus. The command to teach is as strong as the command to baptize, and teaching the nations is mission of the highest order. . . . The consciousness of mission occupying the mind of the founding fathers was not purposefully expressed in their meager writings, but it is amply clear in what they did."

[37] For a fine overview see B. Merle Crouse, "Missions," ed. Donald F. Durnbaugh, *The Church of the Brethren Past and Present* (Elgin, Ill.: Brethren Press, 1971), 109-28. See also, "Missions," *The Brethren Encyclopedia*, 3 vols. (Philadelphia: Brethren Press, Inc., 1984), II, 857-63.

[38] Richard K. MacMaster, *Land, Piety, Peoplehood* (Scottdale, Pa.: Herald Press, 1985), 162.

[39] For the Mennonite/Brethren in Christ constituency, see my synoptic study, "Growth Through Mission," ed. Paul N. Kraybill, *Mennonite World Handbook: A Survey of Mennonite and Brethren in Christ Churches* (Lombard, Ill.: Mennonite World Conference, 1978), 20-31. For the Church of the Brethren see, Edward K. Ziegler, "Celebrating A Hundred Years of Missions," *Brethren Life and Thought* 21, (Autumn, 1976): 197-207.

[40] I have dealt with aspects of this in an unpublished essay, "Mennonites Within Evangelicalism: Beyond North America," which focuses on the interaction between Mennonites and Evangelicals in the development of the church outside Europe and North America since 1850.

[41] Cf., Wilbert R. Shenk, "Reflections on the Modern Missionary Movement: 1792-1992," *Mission Studies* 9 (1992): 62-78.

[42] During the period 1972-1992 the quarterly journal, *Mission Focus*, was a forum for discussion and development of an Anabaptist missiology among Mennonites. A generation of reflection and theological development has been gathered together in the recent volume edited by Wilbert R. Shenk, *The Transfiguration of Mission* (Scottdale, Pa.: Herald Press, 1993). A check of *Brethren Life and Thought*, starting with volume 1 (1955), turned up few articles on mission experience until the 1980s when an entire issue was devoted to Church of the Brethren missions. A similar perusal of *Mennonite Quarterly Review* indicates that the first mission-article was published in 1930 and dealt with a sociological theme. Franklin H. Littell's "The Anabaptist Theology of Mission" XXI, 1 (January 1947) was the only treatment on theology of mission until the 1960s. The number of mission-related articles has remained small and most treat the historical development of Mennonite missions.

2

The Anabaptist Vision
and Modern Mission

by Lois Barrett

In the Anabaptist tradition, it has often been assumed that the church's separation from the evil of the world and the church's mission were in tension with each other. That assumption came about, in part, because the modern missionary movement impacted the churches of Anabaptist heritage at a time when their separation from the world did not look very missionary. Years of being the "quiet in the land" had sometimes protected them from persecution. Trying not to keep up with all the fads of the day had sometimes protected them from assimilation. But, in the process, it seemed that a missionary vision had been lost. Was the faith understanding of the Anabaptists relevant to anyone else? Did they have any saving message for those outside of faith? Did they have a message to proclaim to the structures of government and society? The Anabaptists of the sixteenth century were considered dangerous; their spiritual heirs in the nineteenth century were considered curiosities.

In such a context, the modern missionary movement seemed to offer a corrective. If Brethren and Mennonites had lost their missionary zeal, perhaps the new missionary movement could help them reach out beyond themselves. Some of our forebears decided that the old ways would never die and left the Mennonite and Brethren churches for other groups that seemed more missionary in outlook. Others clung even more tightly to the old ways.

Still others tried to combine an Anabaptist identity and mission. Christian Krehbiel, a nineteenth-century leader in the General Conference Mennonite Church, thought there was a core of Mennonitism which Mennonites could retain while adopting the best of the new awakening. In his autobiography he wrote of a visit to the Mennonite church in Berne, Indiana, in the last third of the nineteenth century:

> Because the Mennonites were considered a dissolving sect the other churches felt free to proselyte among them. My visit was very welcome, and my first sermon was essentially one of encouragement with special emphasis on Mennonite tradition and the new awakening. Since the doors and windows were open to the summer weather, I gave my voice full rein and was heard by those standing far away. . . . My bold declarations stirred among Mennonites a consciousness of brotherhood and of their own worth, and among their neighbors a respect for Mennonites.[1]

Participation in the Great Awakenings of North American Christianity brought new life to Anabaptist groups. Yet this history has left them with a kind of schizophrenia. When it comes to discipleship and ethics, Anabaptists may take their cues from H. S. Bender, H. A. Fast, or Rufus Bowman, but when it comes to mission, they may take their cues from Donald McGavran. Peace people and evangelism people sometimes do not have the same theology or even speak the same language.

I know of no district conference within the General Conference Mennonite Church in which the peace and service committee is not separate from the evangelism committee or the mission committee. A few years ago when the Western District Conference was restructuring its committees, I and some others suggested that perhaps the peace and service committee could be combined with the evangelism committee as a testimony to the unity of the gospel message. The members of the evangelism committee responded, "Oh, no. Our concerns would just get lost." And the members of the peace and service committee responded, "Oh, no. Our concerns would get lost." So the separate committees remained.

In the earlier part of this century, when it was popular to talk in Mennonite circles about the "Mennonite distinctives," the list included things like conscientious objection to military service, not swearing oaths, or particular modes of dress—some of the practices that kept us separate from the world. But never was there a mention that the Mennonite understanding of mission was a "distinctive." It was usually assumed that their way of living out the Great Commission should be no different from any other denomination, and in fact, that Mennonites had a lot to learn from other churches. My thesis, on the other hand, is that there is a "distinctive" Anabaptist understanding of mission and that this understanding of mission, far from being in tension with the church's separation from the evil of the world, is vitally connected with it.

The Church Is in Mission by Being Different from the Evil of the World

Sometimes we have read the Schleitheim Confession of 1527 as if "separation from the world" meant isolation from the world. This early Anabaptist statement of faith, written in response to the issues of the sixteenth century, understands this separation as an ethical separation, not a geographical separation. It is explained as "separation from the evil and the wickedness which the devil has planted in the world" or "separation from the evil one." The document then lists some of the specific evils of that day and what activities pious Christians should avoid, including idolatry, attendance at state church functions, attendance at winehouses, and the use of weapons of violence. But nowhere does the Schleitheim Confession pit this separation from evil against witness to the world. The purpose of the document, in fact, is to turn people to the true faith.[2]

Separation from evil is really a definition of holiness. To be holy is to be separate or set apart, to be different, to be an alternative. That is what the Letter of 1 Peter (2:9-10) means when it says that the church is "a chosen race, a royal priesthood, a holy nation, God's own people." And the reason for being holy or separate or different is a missionary reason: "in order that you may proclaim the mighty acts of the One who called you out of darkness into God's marvelous light."

The church in mission separates itself from the evil of the world so that it can be and proclaim a living alternative to the evil ways of the world. The church is an alternative people, an alternative nation, an alternative culture to the dominant cultures around us.

Many Mennonites and Brethren spend much effort trying to hide how they are different. They want to make visitors to worship services feel at home by singing songs familiar in other denominations. Sometimes evangelistic ads assure readers that they are not Old Order and that they would have no idea how to hitch up a horse and buggy. It is true that for many modern Anabaptists separation does not necessarily mean unusual clothing, although it may be simple clothing. It does not necessarily mean a different language, although we may use some different vocabulary. It does not mean a rejection of higher education but a different kind of education. It does not mean a rejection of mission but a different kind of mission in the world.

If we are faithful to the gospel, the church will be a different social and political entity. It will be a different culture. As the second-century *Letter to Diognetus* described early Christians:

> They follow local customs in clothing, food, and the other aspects of life. But at the same time, they demonstrate to us the wonderful and certainly unusual form of their own citizenship. They live in their own native lands, but as aliens; as citizens, they share all things with others; but like aliens, suffer all things. Every foreign country is to them as their native country, and every native land as a foreign country.[3]

Conversion and learning discipleship involve naturalization into a new society, a new culture. In reality, all evangelism is cross-cultural. It involves the intersection of two cultures. It involves bringing people from one culture to another. It is a naturalization process. Conversion is not only salvation from past sins but a choosing of loyalties. Whom will we serve? To which community do we belong?

The Church Is the Only Christian Nation

If the church is God's holy nation, how do believers understand their relationship to the nation-states in which they live? Although Anabaptism has sometimes been credited with initiating the modern idea of separation of church and state, that is not very descriptive. Sixteenth-century Anabaptists did not advocate separation of church and state in the sense that the church should carry on certain privatized functions within a society, while a secular government should carry on other public functions.

What made the Anabaptists so threatening to society that many of them were executed was their understanding that the church was God's nation. Christ was the supreme ruler. Christians were citizens of heaven. The insistence on believers' baptism as entrance into the church was a political statement. Not to baptize infants meant a rejection of the idea that everyone who was born or who lived in a particular territory was a citizen of that territory. By their witness to believers' baptism, the Anabaptists were destroying Constantinian assumptions about the unity of church and state. Their witness, to which thousands in Europe responded, was a call to change political loyalties, to give allegiance to Christ as ruler.

This witness was given urgency by their conviction that the reign of God was at hand. Many in the sixteenth century, including the Anabaptists and even Luther, believed that they were living in the last days of the present age. The new heaven and the new earth would involve radically new political and social structures under the rule of God the righteous judge. The Anabaptists saw the church as a living witness in the present age to the shape of the age to come.

Although by the nineteenth century the official meshing of church and state was no longer a reality in most of North America, the mission of most of the church—Protestant and Catholic, conservative and liberal—still had a Constantinian flavor. "Real" mission was beyond the boundaries of the American empire or to darker-skinned immigrants to North American cities, those outside of northern or western European culture. Most Mennonite mission boards assumed the Constantinian definitions of mission. Mission was directed from those with more political power to those with less. In 1880 General Conference Mennonite missionaries to Indian Territory, for example, had as their aim to "Christianize and civilize" the Southern Arapaho.[4] Behind the "Christian nation" language, especially in the United States, was the assumption that the aims of the church and the aims of the state were one, and that each was called to reinforce the other.

But when the church recovers its understanding of itself as the "Christian nation," a minority people in the midst of the nations of the world, it rediscovers a new way of being in mission. I suggest that authentically Anabaptist—authentically biblical—mission comes from a minority, "separated" stance. It does not need the support of the nation-state nor of the dominant culture. In fact, the church gives its most authentic witness when it sees itself as God's holy nation in witness to the other peoples of the world.

The Church's Mission Is Nonviolent

This style of mission implies being a minority people, not depending on the backing of the state or political power or on military force to carry out the church's mission. The Constantinian mindset made it easy for North American missionaries to work in countries where there had been recent military victories. Such connection of mission with violent force or with more subtle forms of political coercion has left many North Americans with a bad taste regarding mission. Some would say that to be missionary is to be intolerant; to claim uniqueness for Jesus Christ is seen as coercive.

Such distaste is not a new phenomenon. In 1931, Edmund G. Kaufman in his history of Mennonite missions wrote:

> Proselyting by means of force, to which they were subjected in the past as it was conducted by state churches, has helped to make anything of that nature extremely distasteful to Mennonites. In some quarters even today any attempt at mission-work among people of non-Mennonite faith in America is considered somewhat as "casting pearls before swine."[5]

For an Anabaptist style of mission, putting peace and evangelism together has often meant including love of enemies by teaching "all things that [Jesus] commanded." It has meant putting peace at the center of the gospel by understanding that through the cross Christ reconciles us to God and to each other. But peace also speaks to the method of mission.

Being a minority people provides an opportunity for being in mission noncoercively. Peaceful mission is in dialogue with those who do not believe or who believe differently. It does not proceed from a position of violent power but from the power of the Holy Spirit. It is *gelassen* in its willingness to let people turn away from Christ rather than coerce them into compliant statements and actions. Yet peaceful mission is bold in its claims to represent the Ruler of the universe and to claim that Jesus Christ is the only Lord and Savior. Such a claim is neither intolerant nor disrespectful of any other faith or culture as long as this claim is made in the context of the gospel of peace, proclaimed by a holy, separated nation that wants to share its good news with others in a peaceful manner.

Evil Is Real, and Mission Is Dangerous

The last of the Beatitudes in Matthew 5 is "Blessed are those who are persecuted for righteousness' sake, for theirs is the kingdom of heaven." This blessing on the persecuted comes just three verses ahead of the missionary passage about being salt and light and the city on a hill. Jesus expected that people in the city on a hill, who are doing these things that go counter to the culture around them, will be persecuted. That is, in fact, what happened to Jesus, and he did not expect anything different for his followers.

Much of what passes for mission, especially in North America, takes no account of persecution, other than someone simply saying no to the message. Most of western civilization, including Christendom, is still locked into the Greek philosophy of Plato, which denies the reality of evil. According to Platonic thought, evil does not have a reality of its own; it is simply the absence of good, just as dark is the absence of light. The Hebrew world view, which Jesus shared, was that although God was the creator of a good world, the creatures of the physical world and the forces of the spiritual world could choose to do evil. God would win the final victory, but until then the forces of good and evil struggled. Salvation involved rescue from the powers of evil as well as empowerment by Christ's Spirit. A significant part of Jesus' ministry was the exorcism of demons, and the Apostle Paul understood that by Jesus' death and resurrection he had disarmed the powers and triumphed over them (Col. 2:15). This means that the church's mission is not so much a matter of "selling" the gospel to people who just haven't heard about a good thing yet, but a matter of rescue of people from the forces that are holding them captive.

Evangelism is a dangerous vocation, then, because those evil forces fight back. People discover inner and outer resistance to the gospel. People caught up in evil sometimes strike out at those who would upset their old ways of doing things. So evangelism sometimes means persecution.

Evangelism is also a dangerous vocation because evangelists live on the boundaries where cultures intersect. Evangelists need to know the culture of the church and the culture of the people whom they are trying to reach. Sometimes the boundaries are unclear. What is simply translating the gospel for a new setting, and what is a denial of the foundations of the gospel? Evangelists need a strong inner center, and they need to belong to a strong community that can keep them centered. In general, the more evangelists, peacemakers, and "ambassadors of reconciliation" on the boundaries, the more people required to hold down the center, and the stronger must be the center.

The witness of the Anabaptist martyrs is not irrelevant to our time, unless we have ignored the reality of evil. *Martyrs Mirror* saw the martyrs as nonviolent soldiers in God's war against evil.[6] We will find no reason for mission—and no urgency for mission—until we, like the martyrs, recognize the presence of evil in the world and engage in letting God rescue us and others from the grip of evil. That is not easy. It means getting in touch with the pain of others. It means getting in touch with our own pain. But only when we have done so can we rejoice not only in salvation from our own sin but also in salvation from our enemies.

To be in mission is to acknowledge the reality of evil. As God's nation we have seceded from the destructive systems of the world. We are in process of unhooking ourselves from the principalities and powers that hold us captive. And we are bringing the good news to others still caught in the grip of evil that God can rescue them. Salvation makes sense when we know from what we are being saved.

City on a Hill as an Image for Mission

I suggest that an appropriate image for the church in mission in our time is the city on a hill. In Matthew 5:14-16, Jesus tells his disciples,

You are the light of the world. A city built on a hill cannot be hid. No one after lighting a lamp puts it under the bushel basket, but on the lampstand, and it gives light to all in the house. Let your light shine before others, so that they may see your good works and give glory to your Father in heaven.

This image reminds us of the vision of Isaiah 2:2-4, in which the nations are streaming to Jerusalem, the mountain of the house of Yahweh, to learn to walk in God's paths.

This city on a hill is the alternative community in mission. It is a city, a political entity, an identifiable people who know who they are and whose they are, who claim Christ, not the Caesars of the world, as their Lord. Inheritors of the Anabaptist vision have sometimes known that city as simply a place of refuge from the storms of life. And it is important to have a place of refuge and healing when the evil of the world is affecting us. But this city of God is on a hill; it is visible. The city on a hill lets God's light shine through it so that it can be a demonstration of life under the reign of God. The city's light that is to shine so brightly is a beacon that not only demonstrates the life of the reign of God but invites others to immigrate to the city of God, to share that life, and to become citizens of heaven. It is the embassy of reconciliation, making the appeal for reconciliation with God, sharing in the witness to the gospel of peace not only to individuals but to structures and powers. It is the preview of the age to come, the sample of that heavenly city where God reigns over all.

The call to be God's holy nation, God's different people, God's alternative community, is a call to mission. It is our reason for proclaiming the mighty acts of the One who has called us from darkness to light. It is a call to others to come into the light, that they too may give glory to God.

1   Christian Krehbiel, "Autobiography," (unpublished manuscript, Mennonite Library and Archives, North Newton, Kan.), 51.

2   *The Legacy of Michael Sattler*, ed. and trans. John H. Yoder, *Classics of the Radical Reformation*, (Scottdale, Pa.: Herald Press, 1973), I, 27-43.

3   Quoted in Tim Dowley, et al., eds., *Eerdman's Handbook to the History of Christianity* (Grand Rapids: Eerdmans, 1977), 69.

4   Samuel S. Haury, letter to the editor, *The Mennonite* 1 (January 1886): 59; see also Columbus Delano, Secretary of the Interior Annual Report, in Executive Documents, 1873-74, Washington, D.C. Quoted in Lois Barrett, *The Vision and the Reality: The Story of Home Missions in the General Conference Mennonite Church* (Newton, Kan.: Faith and Life Press, 1983), 15, 20-2.

5   Edmund G. Kaufman, *The Development of the Missionary and Philanthropic Interest among the Mennonites of North America* (Berne, Ind.: Mennonite Book Concern, 1931), 51.

6   For example, see Jerome Segers' letter to his wife Lijsken Dircks, in Joseph F. Sohn, *The Bloody Theater or Martyrs Mirror of the Defenseless Christians* (Scottdale, Pa.: Herald Press, 1982, trans. from the Dutch edition of 1660, 13th English ed.). 504-7.

SELECTED REFERENCES

A Bibliography of Anabaptist-Related Books

Augsburger, Myron S. *Principles of Biblical Interpretation in Mennonite Theology.* Scottdale, PA: Herald Press, 1967.

Bauman, Clarence. *The Spiritual Legacy of Hans Denck: Interpretation and Translation of Key Texts.* Leiden: E. J. Brill, 1991.

Beachy, Alvin J. *The Concept of Grace in the Radical Reformation.* Nieuwkoop: DeGraaf, 1977.

Beahm, William M. *Studies in Christian Belief.* Elgin, Ill.: Brethren Press, 1958.

Bender, Harold S. *Two Centuries of American Mennonite Literature, 1727-1928.* Goshen, Ind.: Mennonite Historical Society, 1929.

Bender, Harold S., ed. *Hutterite Studies: Essays by Robert Friedmann.* Goshen, Ind.: Mennonite Historical Society, 1961.

Bender, Harold S., et al. *The Mennonite Encyclopedia.* 5 vols. 1955, 1959, 1990.

Bittinger, Emmert F. *Heritage and Promise: Perspectives on the Church of the Brethren.* Elgin, Ill.: Brethren Press, 1970.

Bittinger, Emmert F., ed. *Brethren in Transition: 20th Century Directions & Dilemmas.* Camden, Maine: Penobscot Press, 1992.

Bowman, Carl F. *A Profile of the Church of the Brethren.* Elgin, IL: Brethren Press, 1987.

Bowman, Carl F. "Beyond Plainness: Cultural Transformation in the Church of the Brethren from 1850 to the Present." Ph.D. Dissertation: University of Virginia, 1989.

Bowman, Carl F. *Brethren Society: The Cultural Transformation of a "Peculiar People".* Baltimore: Johns Hopkins University Press, 1995.

Bowman, Rufus D. *The Church of the Brethren and War: 1708-1941.* Elgin, Ill.: Brethren Publishing House, 1944.

Brethren Encyclopedia. *The Brethren Encyclopedia.* Three Vols. Philadelphia and Oak Brook, Ill.: The Brethren Encyclopedia, Inc., 1983.

Brethren Publishing. *The Brethren's Tracts and Pamphlets, Setting Forth the Claims of Primitive Christianity.* Vol. I. Gish Fund Edition. Elgin, Ill.: Brethren Publishing House.

Brethren Publishing. *Full Report of Proceedings of the Brethren's Annual Meeting.* Elgin, Ill: Brethren Publishing House, 1876-1930.

Brethren Publishing. *Minutes of the Annual Meetings of the Church of the Brethren.* Elgin, Ill: Brethren Publishing House, 1909.

Brown, Dale. *Brethren and Pacifism.* Elgin, Ill.: Brethren Press, 1970.

Brown, Dale. *Understanding Pietism.* Elgin, Ill.: Brethren Press, 1978.

Brubaker, Pamela. *She Hath Done What She Could: A History of Women's Participation in the Church of the Brethren.* Elgin, Ill: Brethren Press, 1985.

Brumbaugh, M. G. *A History of the German Baptist Brethren in Europe and America.* Elgin, Ill.: Brethren Publishing House, 1899.

Brunk, Gerald R., ed. *Menno Simons: A Reappraisal.* Harrisonburg, Va.: Eastern Mennonite College, 1992.

Burkholder, Christian. *Christian Spiritual Conversation on Saving Faith, for the Young in Questions and Answers,* English Translation of the 1803 German edition. Lancaster, Pa.: John Baer and Sons, 1857.

Burkholder, J. Lawrence. *The Problem of Social Responsibility from the Perspective of the Mennonite Church.* Elkhart, Ind.: Institute of Mennonite Studies, 1989.

Burkholder, John R. and Calvin Redekop, eds. *Kingdom, Cross, and Community.* Scottdale, Pa.: Herald Press, 1976.

Clasen, Claus-Peter. *Anabaptism: A Social History, 1525-1648.* Ithaca, NY: Cornell University Press, 1972.

Cronk, Sandra L. "*Gelassenheit*: The Rites of the Redemptive Process in Old Order Amish and Old Order Mennonite Communities." Ph.D. dissertation: University of Chicago, 1977.

Dove, Frederick D. *Cultural Changes in the Church of the Brethren.* Elgin, Va.: Brethren Publishing House, 1932.

Driedger, Leo and Donald B. Kraybill. *Mennonite Peacemaking: From Quietism to Activism.* Scottdale, Pa.: Herald Press, 1994.

Driedger, Leo and Leland Harder, eds. *Anabaptist-Mennonite Identities in Ferment.* Elkhart, Ind.: Institute of Mennonite Studies, 1990.

Durnbaugh, Donald F. *Brethren Beginnings: The Origin of the Church of the Brethren in Early Eighteenth-Century Europe.* Philadelphia: Brethren Encyclopedia, Inc., 1992.

Durnbaugh, Donald F. *The Believers' Church: The History and Character of Radical Protestantism.* Scottdale, Pa.: Herald Press, 1968.

Durnbaugh, Donald F., ed. *The Brethren in Colonial America.* Elgin, Ill.: Brethren Press, 1967.

Durnbaugh, Donald F., ed. *The Brethren Encyclopedia.* 3 vols. 1983/84.

Durnbaugh, Donald F., ed. *The Church of the Brethren: Yesterday and Today.* Elgin, Ill.: Brethren Press, 1986.

Durnbaugh, Donald F., ed. *European Origins of the Brethren.* Elgin, Ill.: Brethren Press, 1958.

Durnbaugh, Donald F., ed. *On Earth Peace.* Elgin, Ill.: Brethren Press, 1978.

Durnbaugh, Donald F., ed. *To Serve the Present Age: The Brethren Service Story.* Elgin, Ill.: Brethren Press, 1975.

Durnbaugh, Hedwig T. *The German Hymnody of the Brethren, 1720-1903.* Philadelphia: Brethren Encyclopedia, Inc., 1986.

Dyck, Cornelius J. *An Introduction to Mennonite History.* Third Edition. Scottdale, Pa.: Herald Press, 1993.

Eberly, William R., ed. *The Complete Writings of Alexander Mack.* Winona Lake, Ind.: BMH Books / Brethren Encyclopedia, Inc., 1991.

Eller, Vernard. *Towering Babble: God's People Without God's Word.* Elgin, Ill.: Brethren Press, 1983.

Eller, Vernard. *The Simple Life: The Christian Stance Toward Possession.* Grand Rapids, Mich.: Eerdmans, 1973.

Epp, Frank H. *Mennonites in Canada, 1902-1940.* Scottdale, Pa.: Herald Press, 1982.

Eshelman, Matthew M. *Nonconformity to the World, or a Vindication of True Vital Piety.* Dayton, Ohio: Christian Publishing Association, 1874.

Eshleman, Robert F. "A Study of Changes in the Value Patterns in the Church of the Brethren." Ph.D. Dissertation: Cornell University, 1948.

Finger, Thomas N. *Christian Theology: An Eschatological Approach.* Scottdale, Pa.: Herald Press, 1987-89.

Fitzkee, Donald R. *Moving Toward the Mainstream: 20th Century Change Among the Brethren of Eastern Pennsylvania.* Intercourse, Pa.: Good Books, 1995.

Flory, John S. *Literary Activity of the German Baptist Brethren in the Eighteenth Century.* Elgin, Ill.: Brethren Publishing House, 1908.

Friedmann, Robert. *Mennonite Piety Through the Centuries: Its Genius and Its Literature.* Goshen, IN: Mennonite Historical Society, 1949.

Friedmann, Robert. *The Theology of Anabaptism.* Scottdale, PA: Herald Press, 1973.

Friesen, Duane K. *Christian Peacemaking and International Conflict: A Realist Pacifist Perspective.* Scottdale, Pa.: Herald Press, 1986.

Friesen, Duane K., ed. *Weathering the Storm: Christian Pacifist Responses to War.* Newton, Kan.: Faith & Life Press, 1991.

Funk, Benjamin. *Life and Labors of Elder John Kline, the Martyr Missionary.* Elgin, Ill.: Brethren Publishing House, 1900.

Furcha, E. J. *Selected Writings of Hans Denck: 1500-1527.* Lewiston, NY: The Edwin Mellen Press, 1989.

Gillin, John L. *The Dunkers: A Sociological Interpretation.* New York: author, 1906.

Gish, Arthur G. *The New Left and Christian Radicalism.* Grand Rapids, Mich.: Eerdmans, 1970.

Gish, Arthur G. *Beyond the Rat Race.* Scottdale, Pa.: Herald Press, 1979.

Goertz, Hans-Jürgen. *Die Täufer: Geschichte und Deutung.* München: Beck, 1980.

Gross, Leonard. *The Golden Years of the Hutterites.* Scottdale, Pa.: Herald Press, 1980.

Harder, Leland, ed. *The Sources of Swiss Anabaptism: The Grebel Letters and Related Documents.* Scottdale, PA: Herald Press, 1985.

Hark, Ann. *Hex Marks the Spot.* New York: J. B. Lippincott Co., 1938.

Hark, Ann. *The Story of the Pennsylvania Dutch.* New York: Harper and Brothers, 1943.

Hark, J. Max, trans. *Chronicon Ephratense: A History of the Community of Seventh Day Baptists at Ephrata, Lancaster County, Penn'a.* Lancaster, PA: S. H. Zahm & Co, 1889.

Hartzler, J. S. *Mennonites in the World War.* Scottdale, Pa.: Herald Press, 1921.

Hershberger, Guy F. *The Way of the Cross in Human Relations.* Scottdale, Pa.: Herald Press, 1958.

Hershberger, Guy F., ed. *The Recovery of the Anabaptist Vision: A Sixtieth Anniversary Tribute to Harold S. Bender.* Scottdale, PA: Herald Press, 1957.

Holsinger, Henry R. *History of the Tunkers and The Brethren Church.* Oakland, CA: Pacific Press Publishing, 1901.

Horst, Irvin B. *The Radical Brethren: Anabaptism and the English Reformation to 1558.* Nieuwkoop: B. de Graaf, 1972.

Hostetler, Beulah Stauffer. *American Mennonites and Protestant Movements.* Scottdale, Pa.: Herald Press, 1987.

Hostetler, John A. *Amish Roots: A Treasury of History, Wisdom, and Lore.* Baltimore: Johns Hopkins University Press, 1989.

Hostetler, John A. *Amish Society.* 4th edition. Baltimore: Johns Hopkins University Press, 1993.

Hostetler, John A. *Hutterite Society.* Baltimore: Johns Hopkins University Press, 1974.

Hostetler, John A. and Gertrude E. Huntington. *Amish Children: Education in the Family, School, and Community.* 2d ed. New York, Harcourt Brace Jovanovich, 1992.

Hostetler, John A. and Gertrude E. Huntington. *The Hutterites in North America.* New York: Holt, Rinehart, and Winston, 1967.

Hutterian Brethren. *The Chronicle of the Hutterian Brethren.* Rifton, NY: Plough Publishing House, 1987.

Janzen, William. *Limits on Liberty: The Experience of Mennonite, Hutterite and Doukhobor Communities in Canada.* Toronto: University of Toronto Press, 1990.

Juhnke, James C. *Vision, Doctrine, War: Mennonite Identity and Organization in America, 1890-1930.* Scottdale, Pa.: Herald Press, 1989.

Kauffman, Daniel. *Bible Doctrine.* Scottdale, Pa.: Mennonite Publishing House, 1914.

Kauffman, J. Howard and Leland Harder. *Anabaptism Four Centuries Later.* Scottdale, Pa.: Herald Press, 1975.

Kauffman, J. Howard and Leo Driedger. *The Mennonite Mosaic: Identity and Modernization.* Scottdale, Pa.: Herald Press, 1991.

Keim, Albert N. *The CPS Story: An Illustrated History of Civilian Public Service.* Intercourse, Pa.: Good Books, 1990.

Keim, Albert N., ed. *Compulsory Education and the Amish: The Right Not to be Modern.* Boston: Beacon Press, 1975.

Klaassen, Walter. *Anabaptism: Neither Catholic Nor Protestant.* Waterloo, Ont.: Conrad Press, 1973.

Klaassen, Walter, ed. *Anabaptism Revisited: Essays on Anabaptist/Mennonite Studies in Honor of C. J. Dyck.* Scottdale, PA: Herald Press, 1992.

Klaassen, Walter, et al, eds. *Anabaptism in Outline: Selected Primary Sources.* Scottdale, Pa.: Herald Press, 1981.

Klassen, William. *Covenant and Community: The Life, Writings and Hermeneutics of Pilgram Marpeck.* Grand Rapids, MI: Eerdmans, 1968.

Klassen, William and Walter Klaassen, trans. and eds. *The Writings of Pilgram Marpeck.* Scottdale, Pa.: Herald Press, 1978.

Kniss, Fred L. "Disquiet in the Land: Conflict Over Ideas and Symbols Among American Mennonites, 1870-1985." Ph.D. diss.:University of Chicago, 1992.

Krahn, Cornelius. *Dutch Anabaptism.* Scottdale, Pa.: Herald Press, 1981.

Kraybill, Donald B. *The Riddle of Amish Culture.* Baltimore: Johns Hopkins University Press, 1989.

Kraybill, Donald B., ed. *The Amish and the State.* Baltimore: Johns Hopkins University Press, 1993.

Kraybill, Donald B. and Marc A. Olshan. *The Amish Struggle with Modernity.* Hanover, N.H.: University Press of America, 1994

Kraus, C. Norman. *Christians and the State.* Scottdale, Pa.: Herald Press, 1956.

Kreider, Robert S. and Rachel Waltner Goossen. *Hungry, Thirsty, A Stranger: The MCC Experience.* Scottdale, Pa.: Herald Press, 1988.

Kurtz, Henry. *The Brethren's Encyclopedia.* Columbiana, Ohio: author, 1867.

Lehman, James H. *The Old Brethren.* Elgin, Ill.: Brethren Press.

Longenecker, Stephen L. *The Christopher Sauers: Courageous Printers Who Defended Religious Freedom in Early America.* Elgin, Ill: Brethren Press.

Longenecker, Stephen L. *Piety and Tolerance; Pennsylvania German Religion, 1700-1850.* Metuchen, N. J.: Scarecrow Press, 1994.

Mallott, Floyd E. *Studies in Brethren History*. Elgin, Ill.: Brethren Publishing House, 1954.

MacMaster, Richard K. *Land, Piety, Peoplehood: The Establishment of Mennonite Communities in America, 1683-1790*. Scottdale, Pa.: Herald Press, 1985.

Mennonite Encyclopedia, The. Five Vols. Scottdale, Pa.: Mennonite Publishing House, 1956-1990.

Miller, Marcus. *Roots By the River: The History, Doctrine, and Practice of the Old German Baptist Brethren in Miami County, Ohio*. Covington, Ohio: Hammer Graphics, Inc., 1973

Miller, Robert H., Sr. *The Doctrines of the Brethren Defended*. . . . Indianapolis: Printing and Publishing House, 1876. Reprinted 1899, 1907.

Moyer, Elgin S. *Missions in the Church of the Brethren: Their Development and Effect Upon the Denomination*. Elgin, IL: Brethren Publishing House, 1931.

Murray, Stuart Wood. "Spirit, Discipleship, Community: The Contemporary Significance of Anabaptist Hermeneutics." Ph.D. dissertation: Oxford, The Whitefield Institute, 1992.

Nead, Peter. *Theological Writings on Various Subjects: or a Vindication of Primitive Christianity as Recorded in the Book of God*. New Edition. Dayton, Ohio: New Edition, 1866.

Nolt, Steven M. *A History of the Amish*. Intercourse, Pa.: Good Books, 1992.

Old German Baptist Brethren. *Minutes of the Annual Meetings of the Old German Baptist Brethren from 1778-1955*. Winona Lake, Ind.: BMH Publishing, 1981.

Olshan, Marc A. "The Old Order Amish as a Model for Development." Ph.D. dissertation: Cornell University, 1980.

Oyer, John S. and Robert S. Kreider. *Mirror of the Martyrs*. Intercourse, Pa.: Good Books, 1990.

Packull, Werner O. *Rereading Anabaptist Beginnings*. Winnipeg: CMBC, 1991.

Packull, Werner O. *Mysticism and the Early South German-Austrian Anabaptist Movement*. Scottdale, Pa.: Herald Press, 1977.

Peachey, Urbane, ed. *Mennonite Statements on Peace and Social Concerns, 1900-1978*. Akron, Pa.: Mennonite Central Committee, 1980.

Pipkin, H. Wayne and John H. Yoder. *Balthasar Hubmaier: Theologian of Anabaptism*. Scottdale, PA: Herald Press, 1989.

Redekop, Calvin W. *Mennonite Society*. Baltimore: Johns Hopkins University Press, 1989.

Redekop, Calvin W. and Samuel Steiner, Eds. *Mennonite Identity: Historical and Contemporary Perspectives*. Lanham, Md.: University Press of America, 1988.

Redekop, John H. *A People Apart: Ethnicity and the Mennonite Brethren*. Winnipeg: Kindred Press, 1987.

Rempel, John D. *The Lord's Supper in Anabaptism: A Study of the Christology of Balthasar Hubmaier, Pilgram Marpeck, and Dirk Philips.* Scottdale, Pa.: Herald Press, 1993.

Renkewitz, Heinz. *Hochmann von Hochenau (1670-1721).* Trans. William G. Willoughby. Philadelphia, Pa.: Brethren Encyclopedia, Inc., 1993.

Riedemann, Peter. *Account of Our Religion, Doctrine and Faith.* Trans. by the Hutterian Society of Brothers. Rifton, New York: Plough Publishing House, 1972.

Ronk, Albert. T. *History of the Brethren Church: Its Life, Thought, Mission.* Ashland, Ohio: Brethren Publishing Co., 1968.

Rupel, Esther Fern. "An Investigation of the Origin, Significance, and Demise of the Prescribed Dress Worn by Members of the Church of the Brethren." Ph.D. dissertation: University of Minnesota, 1971.

Ruth, John L. *Maintaining the Right Fellowship.* Scottdale, Pa.: Herald Press, 1984.

Sanger, S. F. and D. Hays. *The Olive Branch of Peace and Good Will to Men: Anti-war History of the Brethren and Mennonites, the Peace People of the South, During the Civil War, 1861-1865.* Elgin, IL: Brethren Publishing House, 1907.

Sappington, Roger E. *The Brethren in Industrial America.* Elgin, Ill: Brethren Press, 1986.

Sappington, Roger E. *The Brethren in the New Nation: A Sourcebook on the Development of the Church of the Brethren.* Elgin, Ill.: Brethren Press, 1976.

Sappington, Roger E. *Brethren Social Policy.* Elgin, Ill.: Brethren Press, 1961.

Schipani, Daniel, ed. *Freedom and Discipleship: Liberation Theology in an Anabaptist Perspective.* Maryknoll, NY: Orbis Books, 1989.

Schlabach, Theron F. *Gospel Versus Gospel: Mission and the Mennonite Church, 1863-1944.* Scottdale, Pa.: Herald Press, 1980.

Schlabach, Theron F. *Peace, Faith, Nation: Mennonites and Amish in Nineteenth-Century America.* Scottdale, Pa.: Herald Press, 1988.

Schmidt, Henry Jake. *Continuity and Change in an Ethical Tradition: A Case Study of North American Mennonite BrethrenChurch-State Rhetoric and Practice, 1917-1979.* Ph.D. dissertation: University of Southern California, 1981.

Schreiber, William I. *Our Amish Neighbors.* Chicago: University of Chicago Press, 1962.

Scott, Stephen. *The Amish Wedding and Other Special Occasions of the Old Order Communities.* Intercourse, Pa.: Good Books, 1988.

Scott, Stephen. *Plain Buggies: Amish, Mennonite, and Brethren Horse-drawn Transportation.* Intercourse, Pa.: Good Books, 1981.

Scott, Stephen. *Why Do They Dress That Way?* Intercourse, Pa.: Good Books, 1986.

Stauffer, Beulah. *American Mennonites and Protestant Movements: A Community Paradigm*. Scottdale, Pa.: Herald Press, 1990.

Stayer, James M. *The German Peasants' War and Anabaptist Community of Goods*. Montreal: McGill-Queens University Press, 1991.

Stayer, James M. *Anabaptists and the Sword*. Lawrence, Kan.: Coronado Press, 1976.

Stoeffler, F. Ernest, ed. *Continental Pietism and Early American Christianity*. Grand Rapids: Eerdmans, 1976.

Stoffer, Dale R. *Background and Development of Brethren Doctrines, 1650-1987*. Philadelphia: Brethren Encyclopedia, Inc., 1989.

Stoffer, Dale R. *The Background and Development of Thought and Practice in The German Baptist Brethren (Dunker) and the Brethren (Progressive) Churches (c. 1650-1979)*. Ph.D. thesis: Fuller Theological Seminary, 1980.

Swartley, Willard. *Slavery, Sabbath, War and Women: Case Issues in Biblical Interpretation*. Scottdale, PA: Herald Press, 1983.

Swartley, Willard, ed. *Essays on Biblical Interpretation: Anabaptist-Mennonite Perspectives*. Elkhart, Ind.: Institute of Mennonite Studies, 1984.

Swartley, Willard, ed. *Essays on Peace Theology and Witness*. Elkhart, Ind.: Institute of Mennonite Studies, Occasional Papers No. 12, 1988.

Toews, John B. *Czars, Soviets and Mennonites*. Newton, Kan.: Faith & Life Press, 1982.

Weaver, J. Denny. *Becoming Anabaptist: The Origin and Significance of Sixteenth-Century Anabaptism*. Scottdale, Pa.: Herald Press: 1987.

Wenger, John C. *The Doctrines of the Mennonites*. Scottdale, Pa.: Herald Press, 1950

Wenger, John C. *Pacifism and Biblical Nonresistance*. Scottdale, Pa.: Herald Press, 1968.

Wenger, John C, trans. and ed. *The Complete Works of Menno Simons*. Scottdale, Pa.: Herald Press, 1956.

Williams, G. *The Radical Reformation*. Philadelphia: Westminster, 1962.

Willoughby, William G. *Counting the Cost: The Life of Alexander Mack*. Elgin, Ill.: Brethren Press, 1979.

Winger, Otho. *History and Doctrines of the Church of the Brethren*. Elgin, Ill.: Brethren Publishing House, 1919.

Wiles, Virginia. "From Apostolic Presence to Self-Government in Christ: Paul's Preparing of the Philippian Church for Life in His Absence." Ph. D. dissertation: University of Chicago, 1993.

Wittlinger, C. *Quest for Piety and Obedience: The Story of the Brethren in Christ*. Nappanee: Evangel Press, 1978.

Yoder, John Howard, ed. *The Legacy of Michael Sattler*. Scottdale, Pa.: Herald Press, 1973.

Yoder, John Howard. *Nevertheless: The Varieties and Shortcomings of Religious Pacifism*. Revised edition. Scottdale, Pa.: Herald Press, 1992.

Yoder, John Howard. *The Politics of Jesus*. Grand Rapids, Mich.: Eerdmans Publishing, 1972.

Yoder, John Howard. *The Priestly Kingdom: Social Ethics as Gospel*. South Bend: Notre Dame University Press, 1984.

Ziegler, Jesse H. *The Broken Cup*. Elgin, Ill.: Brethren Publishing House, 1942.

THE CONTRIBUTORS

Stephen C. Ainlay is Professor of Sociology and Anthropology at College of the Holy Cross in Worcester, Massachusetts.

Ronald C. Arnett is Professor and Chair of the Department of Communications at Duquesne University in Pittsburgh, Pennsylvania.

Jeff Bach is Assistant Professor of Brethren Studies and Director of Peace Studies at Bethany Theological Seminary in Richmond, Indiana.

Lois Barrett is Executive Secretary of Home Missions for the General Conference Mennonite Church, based at their offices in Newton, Kansas.

Fred W. Benedict, President of Brethren Encyclopedia, Inc. and editor of *Old Order Notes*, resides in Union City, Ohio.

John David Bowman is Director of Satellite Studies at Bethany Theological Seminary's Susquehanna Valley Satellite and Pastor Of Christian Education at the the Lancaster, Pennsylvania Church of the Brethren.

Dale W. Brown, Professor Emeritus at Bethany Theological Seminary, resides in Elizabethtown, Pennsylvania, where he teaches at Bethany's Susquehanna Valley Satellite

Donald F. Durnbaugh, Professor Emeritus at Bethany Theological Seminary, is Archivist at Juniata College in Huntingdon, Pennsylvania.

Nadine Pence Frantz is Associate Professor of Theology at Bethany Theological Seminary in Richmond, Indiana.

Donald B. Kraybill is Professor of Sociology and Director of the Young Center for the Study of Anabaptist and Pietist Groups at Elizabethtown College in Elizabethtown, Pennsylvania.

Robert R. Miller is Instructor in Religion and Campus Chaplain at Bridgewater College in Bridgewater, Virginia.

Steven M. Nolt is a Ph.D. student at the University of Notre Dame in South Bend, Indiana.

Dawn Ottoni-Wilhelm is pastor at the Stone Church of the Brethren in Huntingdon, Pennsylvania.

John D. Roth is Associate Professor of History at Goshen College in Goshen, Indiana and editor of *Mennonite Quarterly Review*.

John L. Ruth, a Mennonite church historian and retired pastor, resides in Harleysville, Pennsylvania.

Gerald Shenk is Associate Professor of Church and Society at Eastern Mennonite Seminary in Harrisonburg, Virginia.

Wilbert R. Shenk is Associate Professor of Missions and Director of the Missions Training Center at Associated Mennonite Biblical Seminaries in Elkhart, Indiana.

Morris E. Sider is Professor of History and English Literature at Messiah College in Grantham, Pennsylvania.

Dale R. Stoffer is Assistant Professor of Historical Theology at Ashland Theological Seminary in Ashland, Ohio.

Willard Swartley is Professor of New Testament at Associated Mennonite Biblical Seminaries in Elkhart, Indiana.

J. Denny Weaver is Professor of Religion at Bluffton College in Bluffton, Ohio.

Virginia Wiles is Assistant Professor of Religion at Muhlenberg College in Allentown, Pennsylvania.